SADDAM ON TRIAL

Saddam on Trial

Understanding and Debating the Iraqi High Tribunal

Michael P. Scharf
Case Western Reserve University
School of Law

Gregory S. McNeal
Case Western Reserve University
School of Law

Carolina Academic Press
Durham, North Carolina

10 Digit ISBN 1-59460-304-9
13 Digit ISBN 978-1-59460-304-4

LCCN 2006933161

CAROLINA ACADEMIC PRESS
700 Kent Street
Durham, North Carolina 27701
Telephone (919) 489-7486
Fax (919) 493-5668
www.cap-press.com

Printed in the United States of America

Dedicated to the memory of award winning Boston Globe journalist Elizabeth Neuffer, a dear friend who gave her life covering the story of justice in Iraq and U.S. Army soldiers Captain Christopher Seifert and Specialist Armer Burkhart who gave their lives so others could be free.

It is not the critic who counts; not the man who points out how the strong man stumbles, or where the doer of deeds could have done them better. The credit belongs to the man who is actually in the arena, whose face is marred by dust and sweat and blood; who strives valiantly; who err, who comes short again and again because there is no effort without error and shortcoming; but who does actually strive to do the deeds; who knows great enthusiasms, the great devotions; who spends himself in a worthy cause; who at the best knows in the end the triumph of high achievement, and who at the worst, if he fails, at least fails while daring greatly, so that his place shall never be with those cold and timid souls who neither know victory nor defeat.

President Theodore Roosevelt[1]

Contents

PREFACE

Saddam Hussein. Derided as "the Butcher of Baghdad," the Iraqi leader was toppled from power by a U.S. military invasion in 2003, charged with the most serious crimes known to mankind, and then brought to justice before a novel war crimes court known as the Iraqi High Tribunal (IHT).

From October 2005 through July 2006, Saddam and seven of his henchmen engaged in a legal battle of epic proportions, with their lives literally in the balance. The first of several planned trials before the Iraqi High Tribunal, this proceeding focused on the destruction of the town of Dujail and the torture and murder of its inhabitants in retaliation for a 1982 failed assassination attempt. Billed by the international media as "the real trial of the century," the televised proceedings were punctuated by gripping testimony of atrocities, controversial judicial rulings, assassination of defense counsel, the resignation of judges, scathing outburst by the defendants, allegations of mistreatment, hunger strikes, and even underwear appearances.

Was it a mistake to try Saddam in Baghdad before a panel of Iraqi judges rather than before an international tribunal? Was the Iraqi High Tribunal a legitimate judicial institution? Were the proceedings fundamentally fair? Did the judges react properly to the defendants' attempts to derail the proceedings? Did the Prosecution prove its case? Did Saddam have any valid defenses? What precedents did this extraordinary trial set?

We wanted to answer these questions. At the outset of the IHT's first trial, we sought to do something unique—bring together a select group of the world's leading experts on international criminal law, engage them in an ongoing scholarly debate regarding these issues and the unfolding developments in the trial of Saddam Hussein, and publicize that debate in real time for the world to view over the world-wide web. Our hope was that by posting such expert commentary on the internet, we could entice the public to tune in to the trial, and to think about the bigger issues, not just the sound bites and headlines. And it worked!

During the trial, our website, "Grotian Moment: The Saddam Hussein Trial Blog" logged over 100,000 visits. Named for Hugo Grotius, the father of the field of international law, a "Grotian moment" is a legal development that is so significant that it radically transforms the content of customary international law or the interpretation of treaty-based law. The website was linked to by the Library of Congress, the Department of Defense, and most major newspapers, radio, and television news outlets. The work of our experts earned a "Web Winner" award from The Philadelphia Inquirer newspaper, the "Blog of the Month" award by Catholic University of America, the "Website of the Month" award by New York Law School, and the "Blog of the Week" award by University of Washington Law School. In addition, the IHT, itself, began to post its trial exhibits, indictments, and other documents on our Website, which soon established itself as the number one site on the internet for information about the trial of Saddam Hussein.

The content on the website quickly grew to thousands of pages—far too much for the casual reader to digest. And since websites are inherently temporary, we realized that there was a need to publish the material in a more digestible and permanent form. This book thus reproduces the best of the expert essays, and includes English translations of the most important documents related to the trial. It also includes a psychological profile of Saddam Hussein written by a former CIA profiler, a glossary of key legal terms, a timeline of the trial, a summary of the evidence and testimony, and recommendations for future trials.

This book is written in a style intended to appeal to the general reader, as well as to law students, undergraduates, academics and journalists. At the same time, we hope policy makers and jurists will benefit from our critiques and recommendations related to the future of international war crimes trials.

As with any endeavor of this nature, we owe a debt of appreciation to those who assisted us. In particular we recognize the outstanding efforts of Brianne Draffin and Carl Roloff, without whom this book would not be possible. We also thank our expert contributors, whose bios appear at the back of the book.

Michael P. Scharf & Gregory S. McNeal
Cleveland, Ohio, July 2006

SADDAM ON TRIAL

PART I

Background

Introduction

By Michael P. Scharf

On December 10, 2003, the Iraqi Governing Council established the Iraqi High Tribunal (IHT), a unique judicial body created to prosecute Saddam Hussein and other former Iraqi leaders for war crimes, crimes against humanity, genocide, and the crime of aggression. Shortly thereafter, I wrote an essay for the International Bar News (the newsletter distributed to the 20,000 members of the International Bar Association across the globe) which concluded that the IHT would likely suffer from the perception that it was a "puppet court of the occupying power" since its statute had been drafted during the occupation by the United States, its funding was coming from the United States, its judges were selected by a U.S.-appointed provisional government, and the judges and prosecutors were to be assisted by U.S. advisors.

Seven months later, I received a phone call from Greg Kehoe, the Director of the Regime Crimes Liaison Office in Baghdad (RCLO), the U.S. government agency established to assist the IHT. "Professor Scharf, would you be willing to help us train and provide legal advice to the judges who will be presiding over the trial of Saddam Hussein?"—the surprisingly clear voice on the other end of the line asked. "I'm not sure you have the right guy," I replied. "Are you aware that I've taken strong public stands against the U.S. invasion of Iraq, and I have been highly critical of the IHT?"—I added. "Yes, we've done our homework," the voice from Baghdad answered. "We also know that you helped create the Yugoslavia Tribunal when you worked for the Department of State Office of Legal Adviser, that you've trained judges from all over the world in international humanitarian law, and that the War Crimes Research Office you run at Case School of Law currently provides research assistance to the Yugoslavia Tribunal, the Rwanda Tribunal, the Special Court for Sierra Leone, and the International Criminal Court." He then told me that the content of my training sessions would be completely up to me to design, and that I could publicly say anything I wanted about the IHT when I returned from the training sessions. "Listen, Professor Scharf," he continued, "Do you want to stay on the sidelines and hurl criticisms at the Tribunal, or do you want to get involved in an effort to make it a more fair and effective judicial process?"

During the next several months, I traveled numerous times to the United Kingdom, where I led a series of training sessions for the IHT judges and the IHT prosecutors that culminated in a mock trial. What I learned from this experience convinced me that I had been largely wrong about the Iraqi High Tribunal. As an introduction to this book, it seems appropriate to begin by describing the five revelations that altered my view about the IHT.

First, I learned that Iraqis had played a much greater role in drafting the IHT Statute than had been reported in the press. Exhibit A would be the fact that the Iraqis had insisted, over initial U.S. objections, on the inclusion of a provision in the Statute (Article 14) that would enable the IHT to prosecute Hussein for the crime of aggression, in addition to war crimes, crimes against humanity, and genocide. This is paramount because no one has been charged with the crime of aggression since the Nuremberg trial in 1945. The United States, which itself has been accused of waging aggressive wars, had successfully blocked the inclusion of this crime from the Statutes of the Yugoslavia Tribunal, the Rwanda Tribunal, the Special Court for Sierra Leone, and the permanent International Criminal Court. But the Iraqis, who viewed the unprovoked attacks by Hussein against Iran in 1980 and Kuwait in 1990 as tragic follies, would not back down to U.S. pressure. Thus, the inclusion of the crime of aggression was the first signal that the IHT would be an Iraqi-led, rather than an American-controlled project.

Second, I became convinced that the IHT judges would not be under the influence of the United States since the United States did not have any direct control over the selection process. The IHT judges were selected by the Iraqi provisional government with the assistance of the Iraqi Bar Association, an association of 21,000 lawyers throughout Iraq. During the regime of Hussein, Iraq was a surprisingly litigious society with a thriving legal system presided over by 1,000 judges. From those judges, 150 were excluded from consideration as potential IHT judges because they had been affiliated with Hussein's special security courts or were active members of the Ba'ath party. The vetting process was not infallible, however, and in the middle of the Dujail trial, one of the IHT judges was forced to step down when the De-Ba'athification Commission charged that he had been a member of the Ba'ath party who had slipped through the vetting process. Similarly, a number of jurists in exile and those who had belonged to anti-Ba'ath groups were excluded from consideration because they were perceived as being potentially biased against the members of the former regime. Consequently, the Iraqi provisional government could ultimately select its IHT judges from a pool of about 750 judges.

Third, I learned that the Department of Justice's Regime Crimes Liaison Office in Baghdad, which was established to assist the IHT in training its judges, drafting the IHT Rules of Procedure and Evidence, and preparing case files for prosecution, would not be the puppet master of the IHT. The RCLO is made up of a half-dozen Assistant U.S. Attorneys and Judge Advocate General (JAG) lawyers from across the United States who have volunteered for temporary assignment to Baghdad. The Director of the RCLO, Greg Kehoe, told me that his office had been given an extraordinary amount of autonomy from Washington, which had decided to remain at arms-length in order to counter the appearance of undue influence over the IHT. Moreover, the RCLO had decided to partner with the internationally respected International Bar Association, the International Association of Penal Law, and other NGOs, which would take the lead in conducting training sessions for the IHT judges and IHT prosecutors. And in contrast to what I initially understood, the RCLO staff would not themselves be filling the advisor slots identified in the Statute. Instead, those positions went to independent experts from around the world selected with the help of the International Bar Association.

Fourth, I came away with a good sense of the general character of several of the IHT judges from the training sessions, including the two judges who presided over the Saddam trial—Rizgar Amin and Ra'uf Abdul Rahman. On the whole, they were an incredibly committed and brave group, who agreed to risk their lives by accepting their commission. Most impressive in this regard was Ra'id Johui al-Saadi, the 35-year-old Chief Investigating Judge who presided over the initial appearance of Hussein before the IHT on July 1, 2004, and later became the public spokesman for the Tribunal. As a result of extensive media coverage of that event, Judge Ra'id has become nearly as recognizable a figure in Iraq as Hussein. Judge Ra'id told me that he was given the option to hide his face from the cameras during the proceedings, but he declined to do so because he did not want the IHT to be subject to the same criticism that has been levied against hooded judges in Peru and Chile. He was willing to put his personal safety at risk as the price to show the face of Iraqi justice and the IHT's commitment to fairness. His example was subsequently followed by the IHT judges who presided over the Dujail trial, who decided to authorize gavel-to-gavel television coverage of the proceedings—the first time court proceedings were ever broadcast on television in a Middle Eastern nation. Furthermore, the IHT judges stressed their commitment to acquit defendants if the prosecution does not meet its burden and prove its case "to a moral certainty"—the Iraqi equivalent of the American beyond reasonable doubt standard. Citing the example of Nuremberg, where three of the twenty-two Nazi defendants were found not guilty, several of the IHT judges remarked that they felt that acquittals in the IHT trials, when warranted, would confirm the fairness and impartiality of the Iraqi High Tribunal. I felt that this kind of commitment to transparency and fairness would bode well for the IHT process.

However, for this Tribunal to be viewed as a truly legitimate court, it must be independent not only of the United States but of the Iraqi executive and legislative branches, as well as the ordinary Iraqi court system. The IHT Statute attempts to accomplish this goal through various measures such as prohibiting prosecutors from seeking or receiving "instructions from any Governmental Department or any source." However, the strongest evidence of the IHT's independence has come from the IHT judges themselves. For example, during the January 30, 2005 elections in Iraq, interim Iraqi Prime Minister Ayad Allawi repeatedly promised that the trial of Saddam Hussein and Chemical Ali would begin imminently, a statement that elicited cheers at every campaign stop. But, the IHT judges resisted this pressure to rush the trials, making it clear that trials of this magnitude could not begin for many months, at least not until the judges had been fully trained, the investigating judges and prosecutors had completed their investigations, and the defense counsel had been given adequate time to prepare their case. On the other hand, in January 2006, when the first presiding judge, Rizgar Amin, resigned from the IHT under criticism in the press and reportedly from the Iraqi government that he was not maintaining enough control of the courtroom in the face of Saddam Hussein's disruptive tactics, critics of the IHT quickly asserted that this confirmed that the Tribunal was under the undue influence of the Iraqi government.

Fifth, I became familiar with the Statute and the Rules of Procedure (reproduced in the back of this book), which were designed to fully comply with international human rights standards. Much has been made in the press of U.N. Secretary-General Kofi Annan's opposition to the IHT. News articles have cited Mr. Annan's concerns about the fairness of the IHT procedures and his opposition to the death penalty and these articles have reported his forbiddance of Yugoslavia Tribunal judges from participating in the IHT training sessions. The evidence suggests, however, that Mr. Annan's actions were more a reflection of his desire to make a statement opposing the U.S. invasion of Iraq than any material substantive and procedural concerns about the IHT and its due process. The Rules of Procedure, which detail the due process rights of the defendants, were still in the development stage when Mr. Annan voiced his opinion against the IHT. Hence, it was premature of Mr. Annan to declare that the IHT procedures were inconsistent with international norms and standards. The Rules of Procedure, promulgated by the IHT and approved by the Iraqi National Assembly, address many of the concerns voiced by critics of the IHT, especially the potential use of so-called "torture evidence" against the defendants. Indeed, the Rules of Procedure contain a sweeping exclusionary rule, under which the IHT is to deem inadmissible any evidence that was not given voluntarily or that was obtained by means that cast substantial doubt on its reliability and veracity. In fact, the Rules of Procedure actually afford more protection of the rights of the defendant than U.S. law by providing that all interrogations, following a waiver of the right to remain silent, must be video-taped in order to ensure that no coercive tactics were employed.

As for the issue of the death penalty, I learned after discussing the matter with the IHT judges that it was not something that the United States had insisted on, but was something that the Iraqi people strongly felt was a necessary option, at least with respect to defendants who were convicted of crimes against humanity and genocide, the worst crimes known to humankind. In fact, the U.S. negotiators had warned the Iraqis that the insistence on the death penalty would make it difficult to obtain cooperation from the United Nations and European States, which have long opposed this practice. But Iraq has always had the death penalty, going back to the Code of Hammurabi (1750 BC), history's earliest comprehensive legal text. And, citing the Napoleonic precedent, the Iraqis were extremely concerned that without the death penalty, convicted leaders could one day return to power, as Hussein had done after being released from prison in 1968. Though I am not a supporter of the death penalty, especially in the United States where it has a record of discriminatory application, I could see how the Iraqis could conclude that it was right for them. As a sovereign country with a new democratically elected government it seemed to me that the world should respect the Iraqis' decision.

Thus, I became convinced that the IHT was designed to be a more fair and independent institution than had been generally portrayed in the press. While it is not a true international tribunal as many of us would have preferred, the IHT can be characterized as an "internationalized domestic tribunal." It has jurisdiction over international offenses, borrowing definitions from the Statutes of the Yugoslavia and Rwanda Tribunals, and its Statute provides that the IHT should "resort to the relevant decisions of international courts or tribunals as persuasive authority" in interpreting those crimes. Its Rules of Procedure, which supplement the existing Iraqi Code of Criminal Procedure, are modeled upon those rules and procedures used by the modern international war crimes tribunals. And while no international judges have been appointed to its bench, its statute and its rules require that international experts be assigned to advise and to assist investigative judges, trial judges, appeals chamber judges, the Prosecutions Department, and the Defense Office. I was privileged to have been included among those advisers, and to have been subsequently asked to head an academic consortium of law schools, whose students have provided dozens of research memoranda to the IHT judges on the most difficult issues that they face.

On the other hand, I am keenly aware that fairness on paper does not necessary translate into fairness in practice, and I have been critical of several of the IHT's rulings during the Dujail trial. At the same time, one must recognize that maintaining order in a court when faced with defendants and defense counsel that have made it their strategy to disrupt or hijack the proceedings, while simultaneously maintaining fairness and strictly adhering to due process, is a supremely difficult challenge that few jurists in the world have had to face. As the Dujail trial unfolded, the IHT presiding judges wrestled with these challenges with varying degrees of success. The judges faced intense criticism from some quarters that they were not heavy handed enough while others suggested that they were too heavy handed. With scathing outbursts, boycotts, hunger strikes, and even underwear appearances—all broadcast on television throughout the world—the trial turned out to be an extremely messy affair. But this was to be expected; indeed it was what we prepared the judges for during the training sessions. And despite these difficulties, the Tribunal soldiered on. In between the disruptions and frequent recesses, dozens of documents, photos, and videos were authenticated and admitted into evidence, and hundreds of witnesses gave eye-witness accounts and faced cross examination.

Was the first trial before the IHT a success? That is a question that has perhaps as many possible answers as there are expert essays in this book. It certainly held the interest of both Iraqis and the world-wide public. I, myself, appeared over two hundred times on national television and radio news to provide commentary on trial developments. In answering that question, I am reminded of a remark one of the IHT judges made during the final training session in England. At the end of a discussion of the application of Yugoslavia Tribunal case law to the IHT, one of the judges turned to me and asked: "Professor, do you think in ten years you might be sitting here with a group of judges from another country talking about the application of the case law of the IHT to their war crimes tribunal?" The very existence of this book suggests that the answer is yes, the IHT, too, has made a significant contribution to the development of international humanitarian law.

Events Leading to the Creation of the IHT[2]

By M. Cherif Bassiouni

Introduction

Iraq consists of several civilizations, and its history dates back several millennia.[3] Its legal tradition goes back to one of the world's oldest codifications, the Code of Hammurabi, promulgated some 3750 years ago.[4]

Iraq, as it is known today, was unified in 1918 by the British Empire after the defeat of the Turkish Ottoman Empire in World War I.[5] Britain administered Iraq as a League of Nations mandate from 1922 to 1932, when Iraq became an independent state and was admitted to the League of Nations.[6] The Hashemite monarchy, established by the British government in 1922,[7] was toppled by a bloody military coup in 1958.[8] This coup was followed by two Ba'athist military coups, in 1963 and in 1968.[9] During the latter coup, Saddam Hussein was head of the security forces, and he was later elevated to Vice President.[10] In 1979, he took over the presidency after Ahmed Hassan Al-Bakr resigned.[11] (Al-Bakr later died under mysterious circumstances.)[12] Saddam's repressive Ba'athist regime was marked by consistent brutality and violence against the Iraqi people,[13] by a bloody war of aggression against Iran in 1980, which lasted until August 1988,[14] and by the occupation of Kuwait from August 1990 until February 1991, when a coalition led by the United States[15] drove Iraqi forces from Kuwait pursuant to UN Security Council Resolution 678.[16] Thereafter, the Shi'a in the South, at the urging of the United States, rebelled against the Saddam regime and were ruthlessly crushed.[17] The Kurds in Iraqi Kurdistan (in the northern part of the country) engaged in a struggle against Saddam's regime and were also the object of ruthless repression between 1988 and 1991.[18] A unilateral U.S.-UK-imposed no-fly zone over Iraqi Kurdistan brought that region relief from attacks by Saddam's forces and de facto autonomy from the Baghdad-based Ba'ath government.[19]

The Ba'ath regime is estimated to have killed more than 500,000 Iraqi citizens from 1968 to 2003.[20] No one knows what the actual numbers are, as no international or national investigation has ever documented summary executions and disappearances at the hands of the regime.

At first, these crimes consisted of assassinations of Ba'ath party members who were not supportive of the then-strongman General Bakr and who were skeptical of Saddam, then deemed an overly ambitious upstart even among Ba'athists.[21] Then, in the early 1970s, there were highly publicized executions of prominent religious leaders who opposed the regime.[22] Their killings were done in a manner designed to send a terror-inspiring message to the rest of the population.[23] By the mid- to late 1970s, widespread and systematic disappearances, extrajudicial executions, torture, arbitrary arrests, and detentions took place in blatant ways.[24]

These practices remained the regime's hallmark for almost thirty-five years. Many of the disappeared and executed were subsequently discovered in unmarked mass graves.[25] Among the better-known facts are the killing of some 8000 Kurds of the Barzani clan in 1983;[26] the brutal repressive campaign carried out against the Kurds in 1987 to 1988, known as the Anfal Campaign, which resulted in an estimated 182,000 deaths;[27] the gassing-to-death of some 4000 to 5000 Kurds in Halabja; the forceful displacement of Kurds in the Kirkuk region; and the forceful removal of an estimated 140,000 She's from the Marshland region, on the Iranian border.[28] Notwithstanding the dreadful catalogue of crimes committed by this repressive regime and countless brazen abuses of power by Saddam, his sons, and his relatives, the international community tolerated the situation, and major powers maintained economic and financial ties to the regime.

Another aspect of the regime's malfeasance is the squandering of the country's assets on the development of weapons of mass destruction ("WMDs") and the embezzlement of public funds by Saddam and his sons and relatives.[29]

It is also noteworthy that the regime's two aggressive wars, the Iraq-Iran War (1980 to 1988) and the Gulf War (1990 to 1991), led to the death of what is estimated to be more than one million Iraqis.[30] Further, the UN sanctions are estimated to have caused the deaths of 500,000 children and older and gravely ill persons.[31] Admittedly, the international community deserves blame for maintaining sanctions that had such a negative impact on the civilian population, but it was also the Saddam regime that made decisions on allocating resources that produced these results....

The Evolution of Thought on Post-Conflict Justice: 1991 to 2004

What follows is a brief chronology of events concerning post-conflict justice proposals and ideas that took place over more than a decade.[32]

Post-Gulf War: 1991 to 2001

After Iraq's invasion of Kuwait in 1990, its exiled government in Saudi Arabia, some other governments, and some nongovernmental organizations ("NGOs") called for the prosecution of war crimes arising out of the occupation of Kuwait. Some NGOs also called for the prosecution of the Ba'ath regime leadership for crimes committed in Iraq and for war crimes prosecution for violations of international humanitarian law during the Iraq-Iran War of 1980 to 1988.[33] In January 1991, a Saudi law firm in Riyadh floated an idea whose origin was assumed to be a U.S. government source.[34] The proposal was for an Arab League initiative to establish an Arab war crimes tribunal for Iraq. However, the idea never percolated to the Arab League's political echelons because it met with lack of interest in Arab governments.[35] This was followed by a suggestion, also believed to be U.S.-inspired, that the Gulf Cooperation Council (which includes Saudi Arabia, Kuwait, Bahrain, the United Arab Emirates, Qatar, and Oman) sponsor a war crimes tribunal, but it is believed Saudi Arabia did not welcome the idea.[36] At that time, the George H. Bush Administration was not willing to involve the UN in the process and was not desirous of pursuing it unilaterally. The United States, however, started to amass a large volume of documents and engaged in large-scale interrogation of Iraqi prisoners of war in Saudi Arabia for use in future prosecutions. This data was scanned and computerized by the Department of Defense ("DOD"), and it was reportedly stored in Boulder, Colorado.[37]

No progress was made for the next three years until the Clinton Administration in 1994 undertook preliminary informal consultations with Security Council members with a view to establishing a commission to investigate the Iraqi regime's domestic crimes and war crimes against Iran and Kuwait. The commission was to be modeled on the Security Council's 1992 Commission of Experts to Investigate Violations of International Humanitarian Law in the Former Yugoslavia.[38] Certain NGOs informally proposed broadening the mandate of this proposed commission to include the investigation of other crimes in the context of internal conflicts and political violence committed by the Ba'ath regime since it took power in 1968, including the use of chemical weapons by the Iraqi armed forces against Iraqi Kurds, as well as an array of violations committed against the Kurds, the She's, and other Iraqi citizens. Between 1995 and 1997, the Clinton Administration continued its informal consultations at the UN with Security Council members, but it met with opposition from other permanent members of the Security Council.[39] In the face of this opposition, the Clinton Administration abandoned its efforts to establish such a commission.[40]

The Bush Administration Period: 2001 to 2004

Shortly after 2001, the idea of a Security Council commission to investigate the Saddam regime's violations of international humanitarian law and human rights law was floated within the George W. Bush Administration but was soon discarded. This may have been due to ideologically based opposition to a UN-led effort, as well as the fact that it originally was a Clinton Administration idea. However, in 2002, the Department of State ("DOS") included post-conflict justice issues, particularly the establishment of an ad hoc tribunal, as a component of its "Future of Iraq" Project.[41] This year-long effort involved over one hundred Iraqi expatriates from different parts of the world, including Iraqi-Americans and non-Iraqi experts.[42] It had several working groups, one of which was a "Working Group on Transitional Justice" consisting of forty-one Iraqi expatriate jurists and a number of U.S. experts,[43] including this writer, who prepared several options for a post-conflict justice plan.[44]

In March 2003, before the U.S.-led coalition forces attacked Baghdad and amidst concerns that the Ba'ath regime would use WMDs,[45] the idea of establishing an ad hoc international criminal tribunal by the Security Council was again briefly considered.[46] This idea was abandoned within days, however, when concerns relating to the Iraqi forces' use of WMDs did not materialize, and Baghdad fell with few U.S. casualties.[47]

After the U.S.-led coalition forces took control of Iraq, it became increasingly clear that some form of tribunal would have to be established to address the Ba'ath regime's violations of international humanitarian law, international human rights law, and Iraqi law. The following three alternatives were considered by the Bush Administration, the UN, and the NGO community, which are incidentally the same as those proposed by this writer in the context of the Future of Iraq Project mentioned above: (1) an international tribunal established by the Security Council similar to the ad hoc international criminal tribunals for the former Yugoslavia and Rwanda;[48] (2) a mixed international and national tribunal similar to the one established in Sierra Leone,[49] and (3) a national Iraqi tribunal with some international support. The last option was favored by the Bush Administration and this writer, while the NGO community favored one of the first two.[50] However, efforts within the U.S. government relating to the establishment of the tribunal were put on the back burner in April after the DOD began apprehending a number of important leaders of the Ba'ath regime. At that time, it was believed that the DOD was more interested in obtaining intelligence from these individuals regarding a number of key issues, including WMDs and the whereabouts of Saddam Hussein and his two sons, Uday and Qusay,[51] than in establishing a tribunal.[52] However, the Administration always intended to prosecute Saddam Hussein and the leaders of his regime.

During April and June 2003, several NGOs, led by Human Rights Watch and the Open Society Institute with informal participation by UN representatives, met in New York to discuss the above-mentioned three options.[53] The preference of most of the experts who participated in these meetings was for an ad hoc international criminal tribunal established by the Security Council with jurisdiction over crimes committed during the Iraq-Iran War of 1980 to 1988 and during the invasion and occupation of Kuwait from 1990 to 1991 and over crimes committed against the Kurds, the She's, and other Iraqi citizens. The next option was for a mixed national and international tribunal as was used in Sierra Leone.[54]

The NGO community felt that the scope and severity of the crimes committed by the Ba'ath regime required the creation of a specialized international tribunal and that the Iraqi judiciary did not have the capacity to undertake complex prosecutions. In addition, it expressed concerns for the ability of Iraqi judges to be fair and impartial. On the other hand, the Bush Administration was opposed to the idea of an international tribunal established by the Security Council, preferring instead a national Iraqi tribunal that it could help fashion and influence.[55] This writer, who was present at most of these meetings, favored the option of an Iraqi tribunal based on Iraqi law with international support.[56]

Between April and September 2003, the Bush Administration, while still favoring an Iraqi tribunal, remained unsure of what specific course of action to follow regarding post-conflict justice in Iraq and ignored the recommendations of the Department of State ("DOS") Future of Iraq Project's "Working Group on Transitional Justice."[57] Though it was apparent that an international tribunal would enjoy the greatest amount of international legitimacy, the ability to establish such a tribunal through the Security Council was doubtful, given the limited role the UN was afforded by the United States in Iraq. Additionally, even if it were possible for the Security Council to establish a tribunal, the experiences of the International Criminal Tribunal for the Former Yugoslavia ("ICTY") and International Criminal Tribunal for Rwanda ("ICTR") suggest that it would be costly and time-consuming.[58] Moreover, a tribunal under UN auspices would not impose the death penalty for any of the convicted perpetrators, and the Iraqi people would most likely oppose the elimination of this penalty, which has always existed in its criminal laws.[59]

The Administration's views were that (1) an Iraqi tribunal would allow the people of Iraq to assume responsibility for trying high-ranking Iraqi Ba'ath officials for past political violence committed against them; (2) such a tribunal would provide a strong foundation for a system of government based on the rule of law; and (3) while any tribunal is likely to deliver a message regarding impunity, an Iraqi tribunal would send a particularly powerful message to Arab and Muslim leaders and their people that individuals responsible for systematic repression are no longer guaranteed impunity. These views were in harmony with the international community's expectations of post-conflict justice,[60] the difference being in the nature of the process.[61]

In September 2003, the idea of an Iraqi national tribunal bolstered by international support was being actively pursued by the DOD, the DOS, and the Department of Justice ("DOJ"), and it was coordinated by the National Security Council ("NSC"), but there was no comprehensive plan for post-conflict justice in Iraq. Nor was there someone with high enough authority to establish policy and coordinate justice issues—a problem which still exists.[62] The conclusion was to have the initiative come from the Governing Counsel ("GC"), subject to the approval of the Coalition Provisional Authority ("CPA").[63]

Administering the IHT

Between September and December 2003, the Statute of such a tribunal was drafted and approved by the GC and the CPA. In accordance with the established process, the GC approved a decree on December 9, 2003, establishing the IHT, and on the same day, the CPA issued Order 48 (in Arabic, "decree"), containing the Statute. On December 10, after CPA Administrator Paul Bremer signed the order, it was published in the CPA's Official Gazette.[64] Thus, it became an official institution of the occupying power.[65]

Shortly after the IHT was established, CPA Administrator Paul Bremer announced that the United States would make $75 million available to it,[66] and the DOJ dispatched a team of prosecutors and investigators to Iraq in early March 2004 to gather the evidence to be used in prosecutions, to organize the Tribunal, and to give on-the-job training to its judges and prosecutors.[67] While these U.S. prosecutors and investigators had a great deal of experience and expertise to share with their Iraqi counterparts, they knew little about the Iraqi legal system and the Iraqi legal culture. Further, what the DOJ specialists had to offer in terms of experience with large-scale criminal prosecutions did not fit well with a completely different legal system and a substantially different legal culture. This led to their assumption of a more directive, and necessarily more visible role. To some extent, this was obvious in the choreographed arraignment of Saddam Hussein on July 1, 2004. The Iraqi criminal justice sys-

tem does not have that type of arraignment procedure. Though the investigative judge acted with poise and dignity, Saddam all but stole the show, adding
to the perception that this was an American-run operation.[68] Since Iraqi judges,
investigative judges, and prosecutors lack the experience to conduct these types
of complex criminal prosecutions, the vacuum drew U.S. specialists more into
the process, thus increasing the visibility of U.S. involvement.[69]

However, the judges, investigative judges, and prosecutors of the IHT have
gradually taken ownership of the process, and have courageously assumed
their responsibilities.[70] As the judges, investigative judges, prosecutors, investigators, and staff of the IHT gained more confidence, the process gradually
became more Iraqi, and the role of the Regime Crimes Liaison Office
("RCLO") became more supportive. Thus, as time goes on, it is inappropriate to refer to the IHT as an American creature dominated by the U.S. government. In fact, since June 28, 2004, and the passage of sovereignty to the
interim government, the U.S. mission in Iraq has assumed the characteristics
of a diplomatic mission that is very mindful of Iraq's sovereignty.

Legal Authorities for the Creation of the Iraqi High Tribunal

By Michael A. Newton

History is replete with individuals certain of their own superiority and
moral impunity. Charles I demanded to know "by what authority—legal, I
mean—do you sit as a court to judge me?"[71] When given a copy of his indictment before the International Military Tribunal at Nuremberg, Herman
Göring stroked the phrase '[t]he victor will always be the judge and the van-
quished the accused' across its cover.[72] Slobodan Milosevic has demonstrated
utter contempt for a tribunal that in his words represents 'a lawless act of political expediency' that has perpetrated a "terrible fabrication" in order to 'destroy and demonize' him.[73] Likewise, Saddam Hussein demonstrates a patho-
logical narcissism that shows his contempt for the rule of law. Even as the
American soldier from the Fourth Infantry Division pulled him from his spider-hole, Hussein defiantly stated "I am Saddam Hussein, the president of
Iraq."[74]

During his first appearance before an Iraqi Special Tribunal (IST) (later re-
named Iraqi High Tribunal) investigative judge, Hussein was notified of his
rights and acknowledged receipt of those rights in writing with the accompanying signature of the investigative judge as required by Iraqi Criminal Pro-

cedure law. Hussein challenged the legal authority of the IHT and demanded to know "how can you charge me with anything without protecting my rights under the constitution."[75] He argued with the investigative judge and denied any jurisdiction over him by saying "I'm elected by the people of Iraq. The occupation cannot take that right away from me."[76]

The Legal Backdrop of Occupation

All of the procedural and substantive components of the IHT function in the shadow cast by its inception during the period of coalition occupation. The circumstances surrounding the Tribunal's formulation are at once the most potent legal and political hurdle to its long-term reputation. On an analytical level, the revalidation of the IHT by Iraqi authorities following the return of full sovereignty makes an analysis of its formation under the umbrella authority of the CPA a moot point. However, the development of the IHT has served to clarify the normative content of occupation law as it relates to the principles of transitional justice. The relationship of a subjugated civilian population to the foreign power temporarily exercising de facto sovereignty is regulated by the extensive development of the law of occupation.[77] As a matter of legal rights and duties, Iraq was considered as occupied territory when it was 'actually placed under the authority of the hostile army.'[78] This legal test is met when the following circumstances prevail on the ground: first, that the existing governmental structures have been rendered incapable of exercising their normal authority; and second that the occupying power is in a position to carry out the normal functions of government over the affected area.[79] For the purposes of United States policy, occupation is the legal state occasioned by 'invasion plus taking firm possession of enemy territory for the purpose of holding it.'[80] Although a state of occupation does not 'affect the legal status of the territory in question,'[81] the assumption of authority over the occupied territory implicitly means that the existing institutions of society have been swept aside.

Because the foreign power has displaced the normal domestic offices, the cornerstone of the law of occupation is the broad obligation that the foreign power 'take *all* the measures in his power to restore, and ensure, as far as possible, public order and safety.'(emphasis added)[82] In the authoritative French, the occupier must preserve 'l'ordre et la vie publics' (*ie* public order and life').[83] On that legal reasoning alone, the establishment of the IHT could have been warranted under the inherent occupation authority of the Coalition as an integral part of the strategic plan for restoring public calm and peaceful stability to the civilian population across Iraq. From that perspective, the IHT is the intellectual twin to the International Criminal Tribunal for the Former Yugoslavia (ICTY) because the United Nations Security Council established the ICTY with a groundbreaking 1993 Resolution[84] that was premised on the legal authority of the Security Council to 'maintain or restore international peace and security.'[85]

As criminal forums conceived and created pursuant to the broader responsibility of the authorities empowered to maintain or restore peace and security, both the ICTY and IHT were appropriate non-military mechanisms (though each was creative in its own time and in different ways). The IHT and ICTY were both founded on the assessment by the officials charged with preserving stability and the rule of law that prosecution of selected persons responsible for serious violations of international humanitarian law would facilitate the restoration of peace and stability ('l'ordre et la vie publics' in the language of the 1907 Hague Regulations). After the first defendant, a Serb named Dusko Tadic, challenged the legality of the ICTY, the Trial Chamber ruled that the authority of the Security Council to create the tribunal was dispositive.[86]

Just as the Security Council has the 'primary responsibility' for maintaining international peace and security,[87] the CPA had a concrete legal duty to facilitate the return of stability and order to Iraq after the fall of the regime. Indeed, the CPA Mission Statement read as follows:

The Coalition Provisional Authority (CPA) is the name of the temporary governing body which has been designated by the United Nations as the lawful government of Iraq until such time as Iraq is politically and socially stable enough to assume its sovereignty. The CPA has been the government of Iraq since the overthrow of the brutal dictatorship of Saddam Hussein and his deeply corrupt Ba'ath Regime in April of 2003.

The Minimalist Principle

The legal framework of occupation rests on a delicate balance that has been particularly challenged by the events on the ground in Iraq. On the one hand, the civilian population has no lawful right to conduct activities that are harmful to persons or property of the occupying force, and may be convicted or interned based on such unlawful activities.[88] Article 42 of the 1949 Geneva Convention Relative to the Protection of Civilian Persons in Time of War (hereinafter referred to by its more common appellation 'the IVth Geneva Convention') specifically permits the deprivation of liberty for civilians if 'the security of the Detaining Power makes it absolutely necessary.'[89] Even large-scale internment may be permissible in situations where there are 'serious and legitimate reasons' to believe that the detained persons threaten the safety and security of the occupying power.[90] At the same time, the coercive authority of the occupying power is limited by a specific prohibition against making any changes to the governmental structure or institutions that would undermine the benefits guaranteed to civilians under the Geneva Conventions.[91]

Thus, the baseline principle of occupation law is that the civilian population should continue to live their lives as normally as possible. This concept may be termed the minimalist principle, though some observers have termed it the principle of normality.[92] As a policy priority flowing from the mandates of the IVth Geneva Convention, domestic law should be enforced by domestic officials insofar as possible, and crimes not of a military nature that do not affect the occupant's security will normally be delegated to the jurisdiction of local courts.[93] The IHT Statute fits this legal/policy model precisely as it was created and subsequently ratified by Iraqi authorities as an Iraqi domestic statute.

However, occupation law does not doggedly elevate the provisions of domestic law and the structure of domestic institutions above the pursuit of justice. Despite the minimalist principle, international law allows reasonable latitude for an occupying power to modify, suspend or replace the existing penal structure in the interests of ensuring justice and the restoration of the rule of law. In its temporary exercise of functional sovereignty over the occupied territory, and as a pragmatic necessity, the occupation authority must ensure the proper functioning, *inter alia*, of domestic criminal processes and cannot abdicate that responsibility to domestic officials of the civilian population who may or may not be willing or able to carry out their normal functions in pursuit of public order.[94] Pursuant to the baseline principle of normality, Article 43 of the 1907 Hague Regulations mandates that the occupying power must respect, 'unless absolutely prevented, the laws in force in the country.'[95]

The Legitimacy of the IHT under Occupation Law

The duty found in Article 43 of the Hague Regulations to respect local laws unless 'absolutely prevented' (in French 'empêchement absolu') imposes a seemingly categorical imperative. However, rather than being understood literally, *empêchement absolu* has been interpreted as the equivalent of 'nécessite.'[96] Under the obligations of modern human rights law, the occupier may amend local law to 'remove from the penal code any punishments that are 'unreasonable, cruel, or inhumane' together with any discriminatory racial legislation.'[97] For example, the Israeli decision to confer the vote in mayoral elections on women who had not formerly enjoyed this right would probably comport with the Article 43 obligation of an occupier.[98] In the post World War II context, this meant that the Allies could set the feet of the defeated Axis powers 'on a more wholesome path'[99] rather than blindly enforcing the institutional and legal constraints that had been the main bulwarks of tyranny.[100]

Article 64 of the IVth Geneva Convention explained the implications of older 1907 Hague Article 43 language by explaining the exception to the minimalist principle in more concrete terms. In ascertaining the implications of Article 64 with regard to the occupation in Iraq, it is important to realize its drafters did not extend the 'traditional scope of occupation legislation.'[101] Hence, the law of the Geneva Convention amplified the concept of necessity understood at the time to be embedded in the old Hague Article 43. Article 64 incorporates the baseline of normality within the confines of protecting the legal rights of the civilian population. Article 64[102] accordingly reads as follows:

The penal laws of the occupied territory shall remain in force, with the exception that they may be repealed or suspended by the Occupying Power in cases where they constitute a threat to its security or an obstacle to the application of the present Convention. Subject to the latter consideration and to the necessity for ensuring the effective administration of justice, the tribunals of the occupied territory shall continue to function in respect of all s covered by the said laws.

The Occupying Power may, however, subject the population of the occupied territory to provisions which are essential to enable the Occupying Power to fulfill its obligations under the present Convention, to maintain the orderly government of the territory, and to ensure the security of the Occupying Power, of the members and property of the occupying forces or administration, and likewise of the establishments and lines of communication used by them.

The plain language of Article 64 must be interpreted in good faith in light of the object and purpose of the IVth Convention,[103] which seeks to alleviate the suffering of the civilian population and ameliorate the potentially adverse consequences of occupation subsequent to military defeat. The first paragraph balances both the minimalist intent of the framers with the overriding purpose of balancing the concurrent rights of both the civilian population and the right of the occupier to maintain the security of its forces and property. The second paragraph of Article 64 morphed the implicit meaning of 'necessary' drawn from the old Hague Article 43 into an explicit authority to amend the domestic laws in order to achieve the core purposes of the Convention. Article 64 has thus been accepted in light of the common sense reading and the underlying legal duties of the occupier to permit modification of domestic law under limited circumstances.[104]

Legal Authority for the Formation of the IHT

The IHT as it exists today is cloaked in a seamless garment of legality both in terms of its origination and in its ongoing existence as a distinct branch of Iraqi bureaucracy. The touchstone of analysis for the promulgation of the IHT is to recognize that the CPA mission statement gave it affirmative authority as the 'temporary governing body designated by the United Nations as the lawful government of Iraq until such a time as Iraq is politically and socially stable enough to assume its sovereignty.'[105] The CPA posited its power as the occupation authority in Iraq in declarative terms: 'The CPA is vested with all executive, legislative, and judicial authority necessary to achieve its objectives, to be exercised under relevant UN Security Council resolutions, including Resolution 1483 (2003), and the laws and usages of war.'[106]

The appellation 'Coalition Provisional Authority' was a literal title in every aspect: 1) It represented the two states legally occupying Iraq (the United States and the United Kingdom) as well as the coalition of more than twenty other states referred to in Resolution 1483 as working 'under the Authority' 2) it was intended to be a temporary power to bridge the gap to a full restoration of Iraqi sovereign authority, and 3) (perhaps most importantly) it exercised the obligations incumbent on those states occupying Iraq in the legal sense, and conversely enjoyed the legal authority flowing from the laws and customs of war. This understanding of CPA status comports with the diplomatic representations made at the time of its formation.[107] The United Nations Security Council unanimously recognized 'the specific authorities, responsibilities, and obligations under applicable international law of these states [the members of the coalition] as occupying powers under unified command (the Authority).'[108]

Though strikingly similar to the declaration of allied power in occupied Germany after World War II,[109] CPA Regulation 1 was founded on bedrock legal authority flowing from the Chapter VII power of the Security Council as supplemented by the preexisting power granted to the CPA under the law of occupation.[110] Security Council Resolution 1483 passed unanimously on 22 May 2003, and called upon the members of the CPA to 'comply fully with their obligations under international law including in particular the Geneva Conventions of 1949 and the Hague Regulations of 1907.'[111] Resolution 1483 is particularly noteworthy for the formation of the IHT because the Security Council specifically highlighted the need for an accountability mechanism 'for crimes and atrocities committed by the previous Iraqi regime.'[112] The Security Council further required the CPA to exercise its temporary power over Iraq in a manner 'consistent with the Charter of the United Nations and other relevant international law, to promote the welfare of the Iraqi people through the effective administration of the territory.'[113]

Resolution 1483 operated in conjunction with the residual laws and customs of war to establish positive legal authority for the formation of the IHT by the CPA and Governing Council. The subtle linkage between Article 43 of the Hague Regulations and Article 64 gave the CPA broad discretion to delegate the authority for promulgation of the IHT to the Governing Council as a matter of necessity. At its core, Article 64 protects the rights of citizens in the occupied territory to a fair and effective system of justice. As a first step, and citing its obligation to ensure the 'effective administration of justice,' the CPA issued an order suspending the imposition of capital punishment in the criminal courts of Iraq and prohibiting torture as well as cruel, inhumane, and degrading treatment in occupied Iraq.[114] Exercising his power as the temporary occupation authority, Ambassador Bremer signed CPA Order No 7, which amended the Iraqi Criminal Code in other important ways seeking to suspend or modify laws that 'the former regime used … as a tool of repression in violation of internationally recognized human rights.'[115]

Furthermore, the subsequent promulgation of CPA Policy Memorandum No. 3 on June 18, 2003 was based on the treaty obligation to eliminate obstacles to the application of the Geneva Conventions because it amended key provisions of the Iraqi Criminal Code in order to protect the rights of the civilians in Iraq.[116] The IVth Geneva Convention prescribed a range of procedural due process rights for the civilian population in occupied territories that presaged the evolution of human rights norms following World War II.[117] The implementation of these goals in Iraq accorded with the established body of occupation law and simultaneously fulfilled the requirements of Security Council Resolution 1483 pursuant to the duty of all states to 'accept and carry out the decisions of the Security Council.'[118] Though Policy Memorandum No. 3 effectively aligned Iraqi domestic procedure and law with the requirements of international law, it was at best a stopgap measure that was neither designed nor intended to bear the full weight of prosecuting the range of crimes committed by the regime. Indeed, Section 1 of the original June 18, 2003 Policy Memorandum No. 3 expressly focused on the 'need to transition' to an effective administration of domestic justice weaned from a 'dependency on military support.'[119]

The second paragraph of Article 64 of the IVth Convention is the key to understanding the promulgation of the IHT. Juxtaposed against the Article 64 authority to 'subject the population of the occupied territory to provisions which are essential to enable the Occupying Power to fulfill its obligation under the present Convention,'[120] Article 47 of the IVth Convention makes clear that such 'provisions' may include sweeping changes to the domestic legal and governmental structures. Article 47 implicitly concedes power to the occupying force to 'change the institutions or government' of the occupied territory, so long as those changes do not deprive the population of the benefits of the Civilians Convention.[121] Of particular note to the negotiation of the IHT, Article 47 also prevented the CPA from effectuating changes that would undermine the rights enjoyed by the civilian population 'by any agreement concluded between the authorities of the occupied territories and the Occupying Power.'[122]

Thus, the CPA could not hide behind the fig leaf of domestic decision-making to simply stand by as domestic authorities in occupied Iraq created a process that would have undermined the human rights of those Iraqi citizens accused of even the most severe human rights abuses during the period of the 'entombed regime.' United States Army doctrine reflects this understanding of the normative relationship with the reminder that 'restrictions placed upon the authority of a belligerent government cannot be avoided by a system of using a puppet government, central or local, to carry out acts which would have been unlawful if performed directly by the occupant.'[123]

The Commentary to the Civilians Convention also makes clear that the occupying power may modify domestic institutions (which would include the judicial system and the laws applicable thereto) when the existing institutions or government of the occupied territory operate to deprive human beings of 'the rights and safeguards provided for them' under the Civilians Convention.[124] These provisions of occupation law are consistent with the allied experiences during the post-World War II occupations, and were intended to permit future occupation forces to achieve the salutary effects inherent in rebuilding or restructuring domestic legal systems when the demands of justice require such reconstruction. Against that legal backdrop, direct CPA promulgation of the IHT Statute and the accompanying reforms to the existing Iraqi court system could have been justified based on any of the three permissible purposes specified in Article 64 of the Civilians Convention (ie fulfilling its treaty obligation to protect civilians, maintaining orderly government over a restless population demanding accountability for the crimes suffered under Saddam, or enhancing the security of coalition forces).

In other words, both Articles 47 and 64 provided a positive right to the CPA to impose a structure on the Iraqis for the prosecution of the gravest crimes of the Ba'athist regime. Given the state of occupation law, the reality of the matter is that the delegation of authority to the Governing Council to establish the IHT meant that it was grounded in the soil of sovereignty rather than being susceptible to a portrayal of the Tribunal as a vehicle for foreign domination. If the CPA had the power to unilaterally create a structure for the prosecution of leading Ba'athists, the decision to delegate responsibility for developing and promulgating the IHT to the Iraqi officials follows as a logical extension. Closer examination shows that the formation of the IHT under the authority of the Iraqi Governing Council actually mirrored the practice in World War II occupations in which the British and Americans created guidelines to direct Germany towards democracy, but ultimately gave the Germans great latitude in rebuilding their country.[125]

Saddam Hussein: A Political Psychology Profile[126]

By Jerrold M. Post, MD

Introduction

Identified as a member of the "axis of evil" by President George W. Bush, Saddam Hussein's Iraq continues to pose a major threat to the region and to Western society. Saddam has doggedly pursued the development of weapons of mass destruction, despite UN sanctions imposed at the conclusion of the Gulf crisis. To deal effectively with Saddam Hussein requires a clear understanding of his motivations, perceptions, and decision-making. To provide a framework for this complex political leader, a comprehensive political psychology profile has been developed, and his actions since the crisis analyzed in the context of this political psychology assessment.

Political Personality Profile

Saddam Hussein, president of Iraq, has been characterized as "the madman of the Middle East." This pejorative diagnosis is not only inaccurate but also dangerous. Consigning Saddam to the realm of madness can mislead decision makers into believing he is unpredictable when in fact he is not. An examination of the record of Saddam Hussein's leadership of Iraq for the past 34 years reveals a judicious political calculator, who is by no means irrational, but is dangerous to the extreme.

Saddam Hussein, "the great struggler," has explained the extremity of his actions as president of Iraq as necessary to achieve "subjective immunity" against foreign plots and influences. All actions of the revolution are justified by the "exceptionalism of revolutionary needs." In fact, an examination of Saddam Hussein's life and career reveals this is but the ideological rationalization for a lifelong pattern in which all actions are justified if they are in the service of furthering Saddam Hussein's needs and messianic ambitions.

Painful Beginnings — The "Wounded Self"

Saddam Hussein was born in 1937 to a poor peasant family near Tikrit, some 100 miles north of Baghdad, in central-north Iraq. But the central lines of the development of Saddam Hussein's political personality were etched before he was born, for his father died of an "internal disease" (probably cancer) during his mother's pregnancy with Saddam, and his 12-year-old brother died (of childhood cancer) a few months later, when Saddam's mother, Sabha, was in her eighth month of pregnancy. Destitute, Saddam's mother attempted suicide. A Jewish family saved her. Then she tried to abort herself of Saddam, but was again prevented from doing this by her Jewish benefactors. After Saddam was born, on April 28, 1937, his mother did not wish to see him, strongly suggesting that she was suffering from a major depression. His care was relegated to Sabha's brother (his maternal uncle) Khayrallah Talfah Msallat in Tikrit, in whose home Saddam spent much of his early childhood. At age three Saddam was re-united with his mother, who in the interim had married a distant relative, Hajj Ibrahim Hasan. Hajj Ibrahim, his step-father, reportedly was abusive psychologically and physically to young Saddam.

The first several years of life are crucial to the development of healthy self-esteem. The failure of the mother to nurture and bond with her infant son and the subsequent abuse at the hands of his step-father would have profoundly wounded Saddam's emerging self-esteem, impairing his capacity for empathy with others, producing what has been identified as "the wounded self." One course in the face of such traumatizing experiences is to sink into despair, passivity and hopelessness. But another is to etch a psychological template of compensatory grandiosity, as if to vow, "Never again, never again shall I submit to superior force." This was the developmental psychological path Saddam followed.

From early years on, Saddam, whose name means "the One who Confronts," charted his own course and would not accept limits. According to his semi-official biography, when Saddam was only ten, he was impressed by a visit from his cousin who knew how to read and write. He confronted his family with his wish to become educated, and when they turned him down, since there was no school in his parents' village, he left his home in the middle of the night, making his way to the home of his maternal uncle Khayrallah in Tikrit in order to study there. It is quite possible that in the approved biography Saddam somewhat embellished his story, but there is no mistaking his resentment against his mother and step-father that emerges from it.

Khayrallah Inspires Dreams of Glory

Khayrallah was to become not only Saddam's father figure but also his political mentor. Khayrallah had fought against Great Britain in the Iraqi uprising of 1941 and had spent five years in prison for his nationalist agitation. He filled the impressionable young boy's head with tales of his heroic relatives—his great grandfather and two great uncles—who gave their lives for the cause of Iraqi nationalism, fighting foreign invaders. He conveyed to his young charge that he was destined for greatness, following the path of his heroic relatives and of heroes of the radical Arab world. Khayrallah, who was later to become governor of Baghdad, shaped young Hussein's worldview, imbuing him with a hatred of foreigners. In 1981, Saddam republished a pamphlet written by his uncle entitled "Three Whom God Should Not Have Created: Persians, Jews, and Flies."

Khayrallah tutored his young charge in his view of Arab history and the ideology of nationalism and the Ba'th party. Founded in 1940, the Ba'th party envisaged the creation of a new Arab nation defeating the colonialist and imperialist powers, and achieving Arab independence, unity, and socialism. Ba'th ideology, as conceptualized by its intellectual founding father, Michel Aflaq, focuses on the history of oppression and division of the Arab world, first at the hands of the Ottomans, then the Western mandates, then the monarchies ruled by Western interests, and finally by the establishment of the "Zionist entity." Thus inspired by his uncle's tales of heroism in the service of the Arab nation, Saddam has been consumed by dreams of glory since his earliest days, identifying himself with Nebuchadnezzar, the King of Babylonia who conquered Jerusalem in 586 B.C., and Saladin, who regained Jerusalem in 1187 by defeating the Crusaders. But these dreams of glory, formed so young, were compensatory, for they sat astride a wounded self and profound self-doubt.

Saddam was steeped in Arab history and Ba'thist ideology by the time he traveled with his uncle to Baghdad to pursue his secondary education. The school, a hotbed of Arab nationalism, confirmed his political leanings. In 1952, when Saddam was 15, Nasser led the Free Officer's revolution in Egypt and became a hero to young Saddam and his peers. As the activist leader of Pan Arabism, Nasser became an idealized model for Saddam. Only by courageously confronting imperialist powers could Arab nationalism be freed from Western shackles.

At age 20, inspired by Nasser, Saddam joined the Arab Ba'th Socialist Party in Iraq and quickly impressed party officials with his dedication. Known as a "street thug," he willingly used violence in the service of the party, and was rewarded with rapid promotion. Two years later, in 1958, apparently emulating Nasser, Army General Qassem led a coup which ousted the monarchy. But unlike Nasser, Qassem did not pursue the path of socialism and turned against the Ba'th party. The 22-year-old Saddam was called to Ba'th Party headquarters and given the mission to lead a five-man team to assassinate Qassem. The mission failed, reportedly because of a crucial error in judgment by Saddam. But Saddam's escape to Syria, first by horseback across the desert and then by swimming a river, has achieved mythic status in Iraqi history. During his exile, Saddam went to Egypt to study law, rising to the leadership ranks of the Egyptian Ba'th Party. He returned to Iraq after 1963, when Qassem was ousted by the Ba'ths, and was elected to the National Command. Aflaq, the ideological father of the Ba'th party, admired young Hussein, declaring the Iraqi Ba'th party the finest in the world and designating Saddam Hussein as his successor.

Rivalry with Assad to Be Supreme Arab Nationalist Leader

Despite—or rather because of—fellow Ba'thist Hafez al-Assad's success in taking control of Syria, Saddam confronted the new Syrian Ba'th leadership in a party meeting in Iraq in 1966. The split and rivalry persist to this day, for there can be only one supreme Arab nationalist leader, and destiny has inscribed his name as Saddam Hussein.

With the crucial secret assistance of military intelligence chief Abdul Razzaz al Nayef, Saddam mounted a successful coup in 1968. In "gratitude" for services rendered, within two weeks of the coup, Saddam arranged for the capture and exile of Nayef, and subsequently ordered his assassination.

This act was a paradigm for the manner in which Saddam has rewarded loyalty and adhered to commitments throughout his career. He has a flexible conscience: commitments and loyalty are matters of circumstance, and circumstances change. If an individual, or a nation, is perceived as an impediment or a threat, no matter how loyal in the past, that individual or nation will be eliminated violently without a backward glance, and the action will be justified by "the exceptionalism of revolutionary needs." Nothing must be permitted to stand in "the great struggler's" messianic path as he pursues his (and Iraq's) revolutionary destiny, as exemplified by this extract from Saddam Hussein's remarkable "Victory Day" message of August 8, 1990

This is the only way to deal with these despicable Croesuses who relished possession to destroy devotion ... who were guided by the foreigner instead of being guided by virtuous standards, principals of Pan-Ara-bism, and the creed of humanitarianism … The second of August … is the legitimate newborn child of the struggle, patience and perseverance of the Kuwaiti people, which was crowned by revolutionary action on that immortal day. The newborn child was born of a legitimate father and an immaculate mother. Greetings to the makers of the second of August, whose efforts God has blessed. They have achieved one of the brightest, most promising and most principled national and Pan-Arab acts.

Two August has come as a very violent response to the harm that the foreigner had wanted to perpetrate against Iraq and the nation. The Croesus of Kuwait and his aides become the obedient, humiliated and treacherous dependents of that foreigner … What took place on 2 August was inevitable so that death might not prevail over life, so that those who were capable of ascending to the peak would not be brought down to the abysmal precipice, so that corruption and remoteness from God would not spread to the majority … Honor will be kept in Mesopotamia so that Iraq will be the pride of the Arabs, their protector, and their model of noble values.

Capable of Reversing His Course

Saddam's practice of revolutionary opportunism has another important characteristic. Just as previous commitments must not be permitted to stand in the way of Saddam's messianic path, neither should he persist in a particular course of action if it proves to be counterproductive for him and his nation. When he pursues a course of action, he pursues it fully; if he meets initial resistance, he will struggle all the harder, convinced of the correctness of his judgments. But should circumstances demonstrate that he has miscalculated, he is capable of reversing his course. In these circumstances, he does not acknowledge he has erred, but rather that he is adapting to a dynamic situation. The three most dramatic examples of his revolutionary pragmatism and ideological flexibility are in his ongoing struggle with his Persian enemies.

Yields on Shatt al Arab to Quell the Kurdish Rebellion

Saddam had forced a mass relocation of the Kurdish population in 1970. In 1973, he declared that the Ba'th party represented all Iraqis, that the Kurds could not be neutral, and that the Kurds were either fully with the people or against them. Indeed, this is one of Saddam's basic principles, "He who is not totally with me is my enemy." The Kurds were therefore seen as insidious enemies supported by foreign powers, in particular the Iranians. In 1973, the Kurdish minority, supported by the Shah of Iran, rebelled. By 1975, the war against the Kurds had become extremely costly, having cost 60,000 lives in one year alone. Demonstrating his revolutionary pragmatism, despite his lifelong hatred of the Persians, Saddam's urgent need to put down the Kurdish rebellion took (temporary) precedence. In March 1975, Saddam signed an agreement with the Shah of Iran, stipulating Iranian sovereignty over the disputed Shatt al Arab waterway in return for Iran's ceasing to supply the Kurdish rebellion.

The loss of the Shatt al Arab waterway continued to rankle, and in September 1980, sensing weakness and confusion in the Iranian leadership, Saddam invaded Khuzistan province, at first meeting little resistance. One of his first acts was to cancel the 1975 treaty dividing the Shatt al Arab waterway. After Iraq's initial success, Iran stiffened and began to inflict serious damage not only on Iraqi forces but also on Iraqi cities. It became clear to Saddam that the war was counterproductive.

Attempts to End the Iran-Iraq War

In June 1982, Saddam reversed his earlier militant aggression and attempted to terminate hostilities, offering a unilateral ceasefire. Khomeini, who by now was obsessed with Saddam, would have none of it, indicating that there would be no peace with Iraq until Saddam no longer ruled Iraq, and the Iran-Iraq War continued for another bloody six years, taking a dreadful toll, estimated at more than a million. In 1988, an indecisive ceasefire was agreed upon, with Iraq sustaining an advantage, retaining control of some 700 square miles of Iranian territory and retaining control over the strategic Shatt al Arab waterway. Saddam, who maintained 500,000 troops in the disputed border, vowed he would "never" allow Iran sovereignty over any part of the waterway until Iran agreed to forgo its claim to the disputed waterway. Saddam declared he would not agree to an exchange of prisoners, nor would he withdraw from Iranian territory. But revolutionary pragmatism was to supersede this vow, for he desperately needed the 500,000 troops that were tied up in the dispute.

Reverses Policy on Disputed Waterway

On August 15, 1990, Hussein agreed to meet Iranian conditions, promising to withdraw from Iranian territory, agreeing to an exchange of prisoners and, most importantly, agreeing to share the disputed Shatt al Arab waterway. Never is a short time when revolutionary pragmatism dictates, which was important to remember in evaluating Saddam's vow of 1990 to never relinquish Kuwait, and his continued intransigence to Western demands.

Reversal of Hostage Policy

The decision to release all foreign hostages fits this pattern. As with other misdirected policies in the past, Saddam initially pursued his hostage policy with full vigor, despite mounting evidence that it was counterproductive. When it became clear to him that it was not protecting him from the likelihood of military conflict, as initially conceived, but was actually unifying the international opposition, he reversed his policy. His announcement followed an especially strong statement by Secretary Baker concerning the use of "decisive force," but the anger of his former ally, the Soviet Union, was undoubtedly important as well. Moreover, the timing was designed not only to play on perceived internal divisions within the United States, but also to magnify perceived differences in the international coalition, a demonstration of his shrewdly manipulative sense of timing.

A Rational Calculator Who Often Miscalculates

The labels "madman of the Middle East" and "megalomaniac" are often affixed to Saddam, but in fact there is no evidence that he is suffering from a psychotic disorder. He is not impulsive, acts only after judicious consideration, and can be extremely patient; indeed he uses time as a weapon. While he is psychologically in touch with reality, he is often politically out of touch with reality. Saddam's worldview is narrow and distorted, and he has scant experience outside of the Arab world. His only sustained experience with non-Arabs was with his Soviet military advisors, and he reportedly has only traveled outside of the Middle East on two occasions—a brief trip to Paris in 1976 and another trip to Moscow. Moreover, he is surrounded by sycophants, who are cowed by Saddam's well-founded reputation for brutality and who are afraid to contradict him. He has ruthlessly eliminated perceived threats to his power and equates criticism with disloyalty.

In 1979, when he fully assumed the reins of Iraqi leadership, one of his first acts was to meet with his senior officials, some 200 in number, of which there were 21 officials whose loyalty he questioned. The dramatic meeting of his senior officials in which the 21 "traitors" were identified while Saddam watched, luxuriantly smoking a Cuban cigar, has been captured on film. After the "forced confessions by a "plotter" whose family had been arrested, the remaining senior officials were complimented for their loyalty by Saddam and were rewarded by being directed to form the execution squads.

In 1982, when the war with Iran was going very badly for Iraq and Saddam wished to terminate hostilities, Khomeini, who was personally fixated on Saddam, insisted there could be no peace until Saddam was removed from power. At a cabinet meeting, Saddam asked his ministers to candidly give their advice, and the Minister of Health suggested Saddam temporarily step down, to resume the presidency after peace had been established. Saddam reportedly thanked him for his candor and ordered his arrest. His wife pleaded for her husband's return, indicating that her husband had always been loyal to Saddam. Saddam promised her that her husband would be returned. The next day, Saddam returned her husband's body to her in a black canvas bag, chopped into pieces. This powerfully concentrated the attention of the other ministers who were unanimous in their insistence that Saddam remain in power, for it emphasized that to be seen as disloyal to Saddam is not only to risk losing one's job, but could forfeit one's life. Thus Saddam is deprived of the check of wise counsel from his leadership circle. This combination of limited international perspective and a sycophantic leadership circle has in the past led him to miscalculate.

Saddam's Psychological Characteristics: Malignant Narcissism

Exalted Self Concept: Saddam Is Iraq, Iraq Is Saddam

Saddam's pursuit of power for himself and Iraq is boundless. In fact, in his mind, the destiny of Saddam and Iraq are one and indistinguishable. His exalted self-concept is fused with his Ba'thist political ideology. Ba'thist dreams will be realized when the Arab nation is unified under one strong leader. In Saddam's mind, he is destined for that role.

No Constraint of Conscience

In pursuit of his messianic dreams, there is no evidence he is constrained by conscience; his only loyalty is to Saddam Hussein. When there is an obstacle in his revolutionary path, Saddam eliminates it, whether it is a previously loyal subordinate or a previously supportive country.

Unconstrained Aggression in Pursuit of His Goals

In pursuing his goals, Saddam uses aggression instrumentally. He uses whatever force is necessary, and will, if he deems it expedient, go to extremes of violence, including the use of weapons of mass destruction. His unconstrained aggression is instrumental in pursuing his goals, but it is at the same time defensive aggression, for his grandiose facade masks underlying insecurity.

Paranoid Orientation

While Hussein is not psychotic, he has a strong paranoid orientation. He is ready for retaliation, and, not without reason, sees himself as surrounded by enemies. But he ignores his role in creating those enemies, and righteously threatens his targets. The conspiracy theories he spins are not merely for popular consumption in the Arab world, but genuinely reflect his paranoid mindset. He is convinced that the United States, Israel, and Iran have been in league for the purpose of eliminating him, and finds a persuasive chain of evidence for this conclusion. His minister of information, Latif Jassim, who was responsible for propaganda and public statements, probably helped reinforce Saddam's paranoid disposition and, in a sense, is the implementer of his paranoia.

It is this political personality constellation—messianic ambition for unlimited power, absence of conscience, unconstrained aggression, and a paranoid outlook—which makes Saddam so dangerous. Conceptualized as malignant narcissism, this is the personality configuration of the destructive charismatic, who unifies and rallies his downtrodden supporters by blaming outside enemies. While Saddam is not charismatic, this psychological stance is the basis of Saddam's particular appeal to the Palestinians who see him as a strongman who shares their intense anti-Zionism and will champion their cause.

Views Self As One of History's Great Leaders

Saddam Hussein genuinely sees himself as one of the great leaders of history, ranking himself with his heroes: Nasser, Castro, Tito, Ho Chi Minh, and Mao Zedong, each of whom he admires for adapting socialism to his environment, free of foreign domination. Saddam sees himself as transforming his society. He believes youth must be "fashioned" to "safeguard the future" and that Iraqi children must be transformed into a "radiating light that will expel" traditional family backwardness. Like Mao, Saddam has encouraged youth to inform on their parents' antirevolutionary activity. As God-like status was ascribed to Mao, and giant pictures and statues of him were placed throughout China, so too giant pictures and statues of Saddam abound in Iraq. Asked about this cult of personality, Saddam shrugs and says he "cannot help it if that is what they want to do."

Probably Over-Reads Degree of Support in Arab World

Saddam Hussein is so consumed with his messianic mission that he probably over-reads the degree of his support in the rest of the Arab world. He psychologically assumes that many in the Arab world, especially the downtrodden, share his views and see him as their hero. He was probably genuinely surprised at the nearly unanimous condemnation of his invasion of Kuwait.

Saddam at the Crossroads in 1990–91

It is not by accident that Saddam Hussein has survived for more than three decades as his nation's preeminent leader in this tumultuous part of the world. While he is driven by dreams of glory, and his political perspective is narrow and distorted, he is a shrewd tactician who has a sense of patience. Able to justify extremes of aggression on the basis of revolutionary needs, if the aggression is counterproductive, he has shown a pattern of reversing his course when he has miscalculated, waiting until a later day to achieve his revolutionary destiny. His drive for power is not diminished by these reversals, but only deflected.

Saddam Hussein is a ruthless political calculator who will go to whatever lengths are necessary to achieve his goals. But he is not a martyr and his survival in power—with his dignity intact—is his highest priority. Saddam has been characterized by Soviet Foreign Minister Primakov and others as suffering from a "Masada complex," preferring a martyr's death to yielding. This is assuredly not the case, for Saddam has no wish to be a martyr, and survival is his number one priority. A self-proclaimed revolutionary pragmatist, he does not wish a conflict in which Iraq will be grievously damaged and his stature as a leader destroyed.

While Saddam's advisors' reluctance to disagree with Saddam's policies contributes to the potential for miscalculation, nevertheless his advisors are able to make significant inputs to the accuracy of Saddam's evaluation of Iraq's political/military situation by providing information and assessments. Moreover, despite their reluctance to disagree with him, the situation facing the leadership after the invasion of Kuwait was so grave that several officials reportedly expressed their reservations about remaining in Kuwait.

As the crisis heightened in the fall of 1990, Saddam dismissed a number of senior officials, replacing them with family members and known loyalists. He replaced the Petroleum Minister Chalabi, a highly sophisticated technical expert, with his son-in-law, Hussein Kamal. Moreover, he replaced his Army

Chief of Staff General Nizar Khazraji, a professional military man, with General Hussein Rashid, commander of the Republican Guards and a Tikriti. Tough and extremely competent, Rashid is both intensely ideological and fiercely loyal. It was as if Saddam was drawing in the wagons. This was a measure of the stress on Saddam, suggesting that his siege mentality was intensifying. The fiercely defiant rhetoric was another indicator of the stress on Saddam, for the more threatened Saddam feels, the more threatening he becomes.

While Saddam appreciated the danger of the Gulf crisis, it did provide the opportunity to defy the hated outsiders, a strong value in his Ba'th ideology. He continued to cast the conflict as a struggle between Iraq and the United States, and even more personally as a struggle between the gladiators: Saddam Hussein versus George Bush. When the struggle became thus personalized, it enhanced Saddam's reputation as a courageous strongman willing to defy the imperialist United States.

When President George H.W. Bush depicted the conflict as the unified civilized world against Saddam Hussein, it hit a tender nerve for Saddam. Saddam has his eye on his role in history and places great stock in world opinion. If he were to conclude that his status as a world leader was threatened, it would have important constraining effects on him. Thus the prospect of being expelled from the United Nations and of Iraq being castigated as a rogue nation outside the community of nations would be very threatening to Saddam. The overwhelming majority supporting the Security Council resolution at the time of the conflict must have confronted Saddam with the damage he was inflicting on his stature as a leader, despite his defiant rhetoric dismissing the resolutions of the United Nations as reflecting the United States' control of the international organization.

Defiant rhetoric was a hallmark of the conflict and lent itself to misinterpretation across cultural boundaries. The Arab world places great stock on expressive language. The language of courage is a hallmark of leadership, and there is great value attached to the very act of expressing brave resolve against the enemy in and of itself. Even though the statement is made in response to the United States, when Saddam speaks it is to multiple audiences; much of his language is solipsistic and designed to demonstrate his courage and resolve to the Iraqi people and the Arab world. There is no necessary connection between courageous verbal expression and the act threatened. Nasser gained great stature from his fiery rhetoric threatening to make the sea red with Israeli blood. By the same token, Saddam probably heard the Western words of President Bush through a Middle Eastern filter. When a statement of resolve and intent was made by President George H.W. Bush in a public statement, Saddam may well have discounted the expressed intent to act. This underlines the importance of a private channel to communicate clearly and unambiguously. The mission by Secretary of State Baker afforded the opportunity to resolve any misunderstandings on Saddam's part concerning the strength of resolve and intentions of the United States and the international coalition.

Gulf Crisis Promotes Saddam to World Class Leader

Throughout his 22 years at the helm of Iraq, Saddam Hussein had languished in obscurity, overshadowed by the heroic stature of other Middle Eastern leaders such as Anwar Sadat and Ayatollah Khomeini. But with the Gulf crisis, for the first time in his entire career, Saddam was exactly where he believed he was destined to be—a world-class political actor on center stage commanding world events, with the entire world's attention focused upon him. When his rhetoric was threatening, the price of oil rose precipitously and the Dow Jones average plummeted. He was demonstrating to the Arab masses that he is an Arab strongman with the courage to defy the West and expel foreign influences.

Now that he was at the very center of international attention, his appetite for glory was stimulated all the more. The glory-seeking Saddam would not easily yield the spotlight of international attention. He wanted to remain on center stage, but not at the expense of his power and his prestige. Saddam would only withdraw if he calculated that he could do so with his power and his honor intact, and that the drama in which he was starring would continue.

Honor and reputation must be interpreted in an Arab context. Saddam had already achieved considerable honor in the eyes of the Arab masses for having the courage to stand up to the West. It should be remembered that, even though Egypt militarily lost the 1973 war with Israel, Sadat became a hero to the Arab world for his willingness to attack—and initially force back—the previously invincible forces of Israel. Qadhafi mounted an air attack when the United States crossed the so-called "line of death." Even though his jets were destroyed in the ensuing conflict, Qadhafi's status was raised in the Arab world. Indeed, he thanked the United States for making him a hero. Thus Saddam could find honor in the 1990 confrontation. His past history reveals a remarkable capacity to find face-saving justification when reversing his course in very difficult circumstances. Nevertheless, it would be important not to insist on total capitulation and humiliation, for this could drive Saddam into a corner and make it impossible for him to reverse his course. He would, in fact could, only withdraw from Kuwait if he believed he could survive with his power and his dignity intact.

By the same token, he would only reverse his course if his power and reputation were threatened. This would require a posture of strength, firmness and clarity of purpose by a unified civilized world, demonstrably willing to use force if necessary. The only language Saddam Hussein understands is the language of power. Without this demonstrable willingness to use force, even if the sanctions were biting deeply, Saddam is quite capable of putting his population through a sustained period of hardship.

It was crucial to demonstrate unequivocally to Saddam Hussein that unless he withdrew, his career as a world-class political actor would be ended. The announcement of a major escalation of the force level was presumably designed to drive that message home. The U.N. resolution authorizing the use of force unless Iraq withdrew by January 15 was a particularly powerful message because of the large majority supporting the resolution.

The message almost certainly was received. In the wake of the announcement of the increase in force level, Saddam intensified his request for "deep negotiations," seeking a way out in which he could preserve his power and his reputation. That President Bush sent Secretary of State Baker to meet one-on-one with Saddam was an extremely important step. In the interim leading up to the meeting, the shrewdly manipulative Saddam continued to attempt to divide the international coalition.

Considering himself a revolutionary pragmatist, Saddam is at heart a survivor. If in response to the unified demonstration of strength and resolve he did retreat and reverse his course, this would only be a temporary deflection of his unbounded drive for power. It was a certainty that he would return at a later date, stronger than ever, unless firm measures were taken to contain him. This underlines the importance of strategic planning beyond the immediate crisis, especially considering his progress toward acquiring a nuclear weapons capability. If blocked in his overt aggression, he could be expected to pursue his goals covertly through intensified support of terrorism.

Saddam will not go down in the last flaming bunker if he has a way out, but he can be extremely dangerous and will stop at nothing if he is backed into a corner. If he believes his very survival as a world-class political actor is threatened, Saddam can respond with unrestrained aggression, using whatever weapons and resources are at his disposal; in what would surely be a tragic and bloody final act.

Why Saddam Did Not Withdraw from Kuwait

In the political psychology profile prepared for the congressional hearings on the Gulf crisis in December 1990, recapitulated above, it was observed that

Saddam was by no means a martyr and was indeed the quintessential survivor. The key to his survival in power for 22 years was his capacity to reverse his course when events demonstrated that he had miscalculated. We believed he could again reverse himself if he concluded that unless he did so his power base and reputation would be destroyed, and if by so doing he could preserve his power base and reputation.

How can it be, then, that this self-described revolutionary pragmatist, faced by an overwhelming array of military power that would surely deal a mortal blow to his nation, entered into and persisted in a violent confrontational course? Cultural factors probably contributed to his calculation and miscalculation. Saddam may well have heard President Bush's Western words of intent through a Middle Eastern filter and calculated that he was bluffing. It is also possible he downgraded the magnitude of the threat, likening it to the characteristic Arab hyperbole. Even though he expected a massive air strike, he undoubtedly was surprised by the magnitude of the destruction wrought on his forces.

But more importantly, the dynamic of the crisis affected Saddam. What began as an act of naked aggression toward Kuwait was transformed into the culminating act of the drama of his life. Although he had previously shown little concern for the Palestinian people, the shrewdly manipulative Saddam had wrapped himself and his invasion of Kuwait in the Palestinian flag. The response of the Palestinians was overwhelming. They saw Saddam as their hope and their salvation, standing up defiantly and courageously to the United States to force a just settlement of their cause. This caught the imagination of the masses throughout the Arab world and their shouts of approval fed his already swollen ego as he went on a defiant roll.

Intoxicated by the elixir of power and the acclaim of the Palestinians and the radical Arab masses, Saddam may well have been on a euphoric high and optimistically overestimated his chances for success, for Saddam's heroic self-image was engaged as never before. He was fulfilling the messianic goal that had obsessed him—and eluded him throughout his life. He was actualizing his self-concept as leader of all the Arab peoples, the legitimate heir of Nebuchadnezzar, Saladin, and especially Nasser.

His psychology and his policy options became captives of his rhetoric. He became so absolutist in his commitment to the Palestinian cause and to not yielding Kuwait until there was justice for the Palestinian people and U.N. resolutions 242 and 338 had been complied with, that it would have been extremely difficult for him to reverse himself without being dishonored. To lose face in the Arab world is to be without authority. Unlike past reversals, these absolutist pronouncements were in the full spotlight of international attention. Saddam had, in effect, painted himself into a corner. The Bush administration's insistence on "no face-saving" only intensified this dilemma.

Not only, then, had Saddam concluded that to reverse himself would be to lose his honor, but he also probably doubted that his power base would be preserved if he left Kuwait. Saddam doubted that the aggressive intention of the United States would stop at the border of Iraq. For years he had been convinced that a U.S.-Iran-Israeli conspiracy was in place to destroy Iraq and remove Saddam from power.

Earlier, Foreign Minister Aziz had indicated "everything was on the table," but by late December the semblance of diplomatic flexibility had disappeared, and Saddam seemed intent on challenging the coalition's ultimatum. It is likely that Saddam had concluded that he could not reverse himself and withdraw without being dishonored, and that he needed to enter the conflict to demonstrate his courage and to affirm his claim to pan-Arab leadership.

Saddam expected a massive air campaign and planned to survive it. In the succeeding ground campaign, he hoped to engage the U.S. "Vietnam complex." As he had demonstrated in the Iran-Iraq War, he believed his battle-hardened troops could absorb massive casualties, whereas the weak-willed United States would not have the stomach for this, and a political-military stalemate would ensue. By demonstrating that he had the courage to stand up against the most powerful nation on earth, Saddam's credentials as pan-Arab leader would be consolidated and he would win great honor. In the Arab world, having the courage to fight a superior foe can bring political victory, even through a military defeat. Sadat, for example, won great honor in 1973 by leading the attack against previously invincible Israel, even though Egypt lost the military conflict. Indeed, his enhanced prestige permitted him to approach Israel as equal negotiating partner, and ultimately led to the Camp David Accords. Saddam's political hero and model, Nasser, gained great honor for attacking the imperialists in the 1956 Suez campaign, even though he lost.

Saddam hoped to consolidate his place in Arab history as Nasser's heir by bravely confronting the U.S.-led coalition. On the third day of the air campaign, his minister of information, Latif Jassim, declared victory. To the astounded press he explained that the coalition expected Iraq to crumble in two days. Having already survived the massive air strikes for three days, the Iraqis were accordingly victorious, and each further day would only magnify the scope of their victory.

It was revealed in January that under Saddam's opulent palace was a mammoth bunker, fortified with steel and pre-stressed concrete. The architecture of this complex is Saddam's psychological architecture: a defiant, grandiose facade resting on the well-fortified foundation of a siege mentality. Attacked on all sides, Saddam remains besieged and defiant, using whatever aggression is necessary to consolidate his control and ensure his survival.

Saddam after the Conflict

Iraqi domestic support for Saddam Hussein was drastically eroded after the Gulf War. By late 1996, a series of betrayals, failures and disappointments had left him in a more precarious domestic position than at any time since March 1991. There have been three main areas of change for Saddam since the conflict. Increased Security Vulnerabilities, Strengthening International Support, Increased Importance of WMD Program.

Increased Security Vulnerabilities

A principle of Saddam's leadership that has always been true—ensuring his domestic stability and eliminating internal threats to his regime—has intensified in the post-war period, and is Saddam's central concern. The three greatest threats to Saddam's domestic stability have come from a dramatically weakened military, fractures in tribal loyalties, and fault lines in his family.

Weakened Military

Immediately after the conflict was terminated in March 1991, Saddam's major source of support, the Iraqi army, was gravely weakened. Once the fourth largest army in the world, the Iraqi army, its proud reputation as the most powerful military force in the Gulf shattered, its ranks and materiel depleted, and its morale destroyed, represented now a grave threat to Saddam's survival.

- The Iraqi armed forces, including the Republican Guard, became disillusioned with Saddam's regime.
- The standard of living for soldiers had reached the lowest level ever.
- The No-Fly Zone over the north/south was seen as a humiliating affront to the once powerful military. Moreover, Kurdish control over the north was a painful reminder that Iraq was powerless and at the mercy of the United States.
- The U.N. sponsored weapons inspections were a continuing humiliation and demonstration of Saddam's lack of control over Iraq's sovereignty.
- A rising tide of disillusion, desertion and resentment led to repeated coup attempts by different military factions against Saddam.

- In March 1995, two regular army brigades suffered severe losses from clashes with the Kurds and Iraqi National Congress (INC), further humiliating Saddam and the military.

Fractures in Tribal Loyalty

Within the larger Sunni tribal system there were signs of weakening solidarity. Of the five most important Sunni tribes that had been the core of Saddam's support, and were in leadership roles throughout the military, three were involved in coup attempts against Saddam. A 1990 plot involved Jubbur members of the Republican Guards and regular army units. Officers of the 'Ubayd tribe were involved in coup plotting in 1993–1994. Al-Bu Nimr (of the Dulaym tribe) revolted against Saddam in 1995. Frictions within Saddam's al-Bu Nasir tribe also compounded problems—by late summer in 1996, five "houses" within the tribe had grievances with Saddam or his family. While Dulaymis and 'Ubaydis continue to serve in Republican Guard and key security positions, they have been removed from most sensitive positions and are closely watched. Overall, the threat of a large-scale tribal uprising remains remote, though Saddam is no longer able to trust his once loyal tribes.

Fault Lines in the Family

Uday

The temperament and unconstrained behavior of Saddam's oldest son Uday, 38, has been a continuing issue. He has a reputation as the "bad boy" of Iraq, and is greatly feared among the population of Baghdad. He has been involved in several widely publicized incidents, but Saddam had regularly either overlooked Uday's excesses or, if the event was too public to ignore, dealt with it in the mildest of manner. Prior to the conflict in the Gulf, there were reports of violent excesses involving Uday. In one incident in 1988, Uday, drunk at a party, used an electric carving knife to kill one of his father's aides. In a second dramatic public event that year, Uday, angry with Saddam's personal valet for his role in facilitating an affair Saddam was having with a married Iraqi woman (whose husband was rewarded for not objecting with the Presidency of Iraqi Airlines), crashed a party being held in honor of Suzanne Mubarak, the wife of the Egyptian president Hosni Mubarak. Uday beat the valet to death in full view of all the guests. As a result of this, Saddam put Uday on trial for murder but in response to the family members of the victim who "pleaded for leniency," Saddam exiled Uday to Switzerland. A year later, after having been declared persona non grata by Swiss authorities, Uday returned to Iraq where he began reintegrating himself into Iraqi society.

In 1995, Uday reportedly shot one of his uncles in the leg and killed six "dancing girls" at a party, not coincidentally the night before his brother-in-law, Hussein Kamal, defected. It is believed that Uday played a major role in causing the defection of Kamal, whom he saw as threatening his relationship with his father.

In 1996, an assassination attempt on Uday left him bedridden for at least six months with both his legs shattered. He was reportedly temporarily paralyzed following the assassination attempt. There have been some reports that he was left paraplegic from the injury and continues to be paralyzed from the waist down. There are rumors that he was left impotent, which, given the nature and location of the paralyzing spinal cord injury, may well be true. He remains in general poor health.

Hussein Kamal's Defection and Assassination: A Major Turning Point

Hussein Kamal, a cousin of Saddam, married Saddam's favorite daughter, Rghad. Kamal rose through the ranks of Saddam's inner circle with meteorlike speed, garnering him the resentment of the military core as well as other insiders. After having held several sensitive security positions, Kamal went on to found the Republican Guard and eventually became one of the few insiders who had access to Saddam Hussein, magnifying Uday's feelings of rivalry and jealousy. In August 1995, reportedly after having been threatened by Uday, Hussein Kamal and his brother Saddam Kamal, who also had married a daughter of Saddam's, fled to Jordan with their wives where they received asylum. Hussein Kamal provided copious information concerning Iraq's special weapons program, of which he had been in charge, greatly embarrassing Saddam and setting back his goals of ending the sanctions regime. Six months later, in February 1996, in what might be characterized as "assisted suicide, Iraqi style," both men and their wives returned to Iraq after Saddam provided assurances that they would be safe and forgiven. Within 48 hours of their arrival back in Iraq, both men had been murdered." Uday reportedly played a key role in orchestrating the murder of Kamal and his brother.

Demotion of Uday

Saddam demoted and publicly humiliated Uday after Kamal's flight, demonstrating that he believed Uday was responsible for the conflicts in the family that led to the defection. Saddam torched Uday's collection of vintage cars and stripped him of his leadership role restoring Iraq's military equipment. He forced Uday to abandon his command of Saddam's private army dedicated to Saddam's protection, the Fidaiyiin. And, most importantly, Saddam elevated his younger son Qussay to the regime's most powerful security position. This demonstrated to all that even being a member of the immediate family, indeed Saddam's favorite child, will not protect one from Saddam's wrath if one's actions threaten the regime.

Qusay

While Uday is part of Saddam's problem, Qusay is part of the solution. Since 1989, Saddam has been preparing Qusay for the duty of czar of internal security. Qusay has worked closely with the former head of internal security, General Abd Hamid Mahmud (or Ihmid Hmud). They are in charge of the SSO, the most formidable of all security bodies, and in charge of security inside all security bodies, including the Himaya and the Special Republican Guard (SRG). The president's security rests mainly on them, but they are also in charge of concealment and deployment of Iraq's non-conventional weapons.

Qusay is also the supreme authority when it comes to "prison cleansing," the execution of hundreds of political prisoners to make room for new ones in Iraq's crowded prisons. He is also the one who authorizes executions of military and security officers suspected of disloyalty. Starting in 2000, Qusay started receiving a great deal of coverage by the Ba'th party and is now referred to as "Warrior Qusay." Supplanting Uday in the succession, he has been named Saddam's deputy "in the event of an emergency." Since 2001, Qusay has also been a member of the Regional Leadership (RL) of the Ba'th party in Iraq, and Deputy Secretary of its important Military Bureau (al-Maktab al-'Askari). The promotion of Qusay to the RL is seen as the first step toward his inclusion in the RCC and, eventually, his promotion to the RCC Chairmanship and Presidency.

Strategic Shift

The family disarray culminating in the Hussayn Kamil defection and assassination, and the decline of Uday and his replacement as director of security forces by Qussay, signaled a major change of strategy. No longer could the loyalty of his family be unquestioningly relied upon. Rather it was necessary for Saddam to strengthen the Ba'ath party and rely more centrally on long standing party loyalists.

Redemption and Restoration of Morale Courtesy of the Kurds

In late August of 1996, Saddam Hussein authorized elements of the Republican Guard to attack the Kurdish city of Irbil following the Patriotic Union of Kurdistan (PUK)'s securing of military assistance from Iran. The Guard "smashed" the PUK and the U.S.-backed INC. The seizure of Irbil was a major success for Saddam. This triumph after a series of setbacks and reminders of their diminished status restored the morale of Republic Guard (and their faith in Saddam). It demonstrated the regime was still very much in control and was a major power throughout the country. It also showed the fractionation and impotence of the opposition movements in Iraq and was a powerful demonstration of the risk of rising against Saddam. This was a major turning point for the regime in terms of restoring its power position—had the Guard not taken Irbil, it is likely that Saddam's support would have been so undermined that his position would have been in grave jeopardy.

U.N. Resolution 986

Facing an imminent economic collapse in 1996, Saddam was forced to accept U.N. Resolution 986, the so-called Oil-For-Food deal. This represented a great humiliation because it glaringly infringed on the national sovereignty of Iraq, and indirectly on Saddam's personal honor. Saddam also feared it would undermine international pressure to lift the sanctions imposed on Iraq following the Gulf War: As long as the suffering of the Iraqi people could be alleviated through the Resolution, the embargo could stay on forever. But eventually Saddam had no choice but to accept the recommendations of his economic advisers. On November 25, Iraq announced its acceptance of the Resolution.

There were considerable advantages as a result of accepting Resolution 986. The sale of oil greatly improved Iraq's international and regional standing. That the food and medicines distributed to the population alleviated the people's suffering was less important than the fact that, from now on, Saddam could save the sums he had had to spend on food for his impoverished people. The disadvantages were minor by comparison, for credit for the increase in supplies went mainly to the regime, not to the U.N. It did diminish the regime's ability to trumpet as loudly as before the suffering of the Iraqi people; thus, it may well be that the crisis Saddam provoked with the U.N. in October–November 1997 over UNSCOM inspections was prompted by fear that the humanitarian issue would no longer be an issue, and that the embargo would remain. (In reality, the Iraqi regime still trumpeted the suffering with considerable success, with the help of Western humanitarian groups).

Strengthening International Support

In the events leading up to the 1990 invasion of Kuwait and the subsequent Gulf crisis, Saddam had been extremely isolated, misjudging the impact of his actions not only upon his Arab neighbors, the so-called "near abroad," but also on major international actors on whose support he had previously been able to count, especially Russia and France. He had regularly seriously miscalculated both the risks of his actions and the degree of his support. His foreign policy initiatives in the interim have demonstrated a much surer and more sophisticated hand. Having learned from experience, he has worked assiduously to strengthen identified vulnerabilities.

Near Abroad

In his diplomatic efforts towards the "Near Abroad," Saddam has been quite effective. Having been surprised by the lack of support for Iraq during the Gulf Crisis, Saddam has worked assiduously to rebuild relations with his regional neighbors. Relying heavily on his increased economic power generated as a result of increased oil sales, Iraq has become a crucial partner for these nations. While in the past Iraqi politics were driven primarily by internal politics and factors, it has been external factors that have begun to open up new opportunities for Iraqi policies and help to ameliorate Saddam's domestic problems. His immediate neighbors (the Near Abroad) have had the greatest impact:

Syria

The most telling example of Saddam's modus operandi when he feels weak and under great threat is provided by his tremendous resolve to mend his fence with his oldest Middle Eastern rival alive, President Hafiz al Asad and his regime. The years 1997–1998 saw the beginning of a new relationship between Iraq and Syria. Saddam extended an olive branch to Asad and the latter reciprocated in kind. Although ties were mainly limited to economic and diplomatic areas, this relationship was the beginning of Iraq's acceptance back into Middle Eastern politics.

The two countries signed a free-trade agreement. As a result of this agreement, mutual trade volume grew from $500 million in 2000 to around $1 billion in 2001. According to some reports, mutual trade in 2001 actually reached almost $2 billion. By the middle of 2002, it was estimated that the annual value of trade exchange between the two countries would exceed $3 billion.

Iran

After taking power in 1997, Iranian president Khatami sought to improve relations with the U.S. and Saudi Arabia, something that worried Saddam a great deal. However, hindered by internal politics those relationships have not had the expected impact, which left more room for an improvement of Iraqi-Iranian relations.

Turkey

Turkey's strong ties to the United States and insistence on working with the U.S. on Iraqi matters are a great source of frustration for Baghdad. Turkish military forays into autonomous Iraqi Kurdistan, too, elicit bitter condemnations from Baghdad; even though Saddam is no longer in control of Kurdistan, such forays are seen in Baghdad as infringing on its sovereignty. Turkish-Iraqi economic ties saw a quantum leap since December 1996. Just before the invasion of Kuwait, Turkey's annual exports to Iraq amounted to around $400 million. In 2000, it reached already almost the same annual rate as in 1990, $375 million, and in 2001, it almost doubled to $710 million. By the end of 2001, it was estimated that Turkey would be exporting $2 billion worth of products to Iraq in 2002.

Jordan

While it did not participate in the international anti-Iraqi war coalition and was unwilling to confront Iraq politically, Jordan has consistently distanced itself from Iraq since the early 1990s. Much like Turkey, Jordan is getting the best of both worlds: it maintains excellent relations with the U.S. and Israel, including receiving U.S. economic aid; it thwarts, as best it can, Iraqi attempts to smuggle weapons through its territory to the Palestinians; and continues to receive cheap oil from Saddam and to trade with Iraq. Saddam is fully aware of this practice, but he does not seem to care; for him, Jordan is an important avenue to the outside world. Even more importantly, securing Jordan's objection to an American attack against him is now his top priority. Jordanian complicity with a U.S. offensive will mean Saddam's immediate demise, as it will provide the U.S. with the most effective bridgehead from which to launch the attack and prevent him from launching his own missiles against Israel.

Saudi Arabia

Until March 2002, the Saudis remained opposed to the Iraqi regime and moved to improve relations with Iran as a counter to Iraq in the event that the United States could not live up to its commitments of security, or should the Saudi regime be compelled to ask the American forces to leave the country. The first deviation from this stance occurred in December 1997, when Prince Abd Allah called upon the Gulf Co-Operation Council (GCC) states to "overcome the past with its events and pains." This was interpreted as a call for rapprochement with Saddam's Iraq. Saudi Arabia, like other regional players, expected to boost exports to Iraq—from about $200 million in 2000 to about $600 million in 2001.

Other Gulf States

In the Spring of 2002, the U.A.E. ratified a free trade agreement with Iraq that had been signed in November 2001. The most significant feature of this deal is that the six members of the Gulf Cooperation Council (GCC) will merge their markets into a customs union in 2003. This will give Iraq open access to the entire GCC market. By mid-2002, the U.A.E. was already one of Iraq's biggest economic partners in the region.

The only Gulf state that, by mid-2002, was still hostile to Saddam's regime was Kuwait: Despite Iraq's alternating offers of "friendship" and undisguised threats, Kuwait has steadfastly refused to improve bilateral relations. Kuwaiti officials refused an Iraqi offer to visit Iraqi prisons to prove there are no Kuwaiti POWs being held, and continue to be highly critical of the Iraqi regime. It seems that Kuwait is also sympathetic to the idea of an American-inspired violent regime change in Baghdad. If so, Kuwait is the only Arab state to support such a military operation.

Egypt

Egypt was the main Arab participant in the anti-Iraqi coalition of 1990–91. And yet, Iraqi-Egyptian relations started to pick up significantly the moment Iraq's buying power surged. Trade became meaningful, and in January 2001, Iraq and Egypt signed a free trade zone agreement. According to Iraq's Trade Minister, Muhammad Mahdi Salih, upon his visit to Cairo, the mutual trade in 2000 reached $1.2 billion, triple the 1999 figure. The minister expressed the hope that in 2001 the volume would go beyond $2 billion. Egypt is the fourth largest trading partner for Iraq, after France, Russia and China.

Far Abroad

Saddam's patient diplomacy towards Russia and France, both of which have significant economic interests in an Iraq freed of economic shackles with Iraq owing them a combined $11 billion, have permitted him to challenge the UN-SCOM inspections regime with relative impunity, knowing these permanent Security Council members with veto power could be counted upon to weaken reprisals against Iraq. China too has supported his beleaguered regime international forums, as have Kenya and Egypt. These countries took up the fight that sanctions were hurting the Iraqi people more than the regime and that lifting sanctions was the only way to alleviate the suffering of the Iraqi people—creating a sense that Washington, not Iraq, was increasingly isolated.

Weapons of Mass Destruction

To Saddam, nuclear weapons, and weapons of mass destruction in general, are important—indeed critical. After all, world-class leaders have world-class weapons. Especially since the military was grievously wounded by the 1991 conflict, with a marked reduction in conventional strength, unconventional weapons have become all the more important. Moreover, defying the international community on this matter is a regular reminder to the military of his courage in defying the superior adversary and that he has not and will not capitulate.

Weapons Inspections

Despite tactical retreats in October–November of 1997, and January–February of 1998, Iraq succeeded in winning important concessions on the sanctions front relating to weapons inspections. This was crucial in continuing to build Saddam's support among the Iraqi people—it was seen as a victory. The embargo is dissipating slowly, and yet Saddam did not have to give up his WMDs. Today the Iraqi people have a better standard of living, many aspects of the embargo are gone, Saddam has his WMDs, and his power elite feels more empowered—resulting in solidifying Saddam's position in Iraq.

Indeed, when UNSCOM left Iraq in December 1998 and was not allowed back, this was a major victory for Saddam in the eyes of the Iraqi people. The United Nations had been forced out of Iraq, and Saddam was unscathed. The challenge of the UNSCOM inspections regime strengthened Saddam's internal support, diminishing the internal threat as he demonstrated his ability to weaken and challenge the international coalition while retaining the coveted

WMD program and weakening support for the sanctions regime. The divisions within the UN that Saddam helped promote were so deep that Saddam concluded that he was essentially immune to UN reprisals for pursuing unconventional weapons programs, which have become all the more important to him given the weakening of his military in terms of personnel, conventional weaponry and material. Since 1999, there have been no meaningful coup attempts; those who might have challenged a leader perceived to be a loser did not dare challenge a leader who had successfully challenged the United Nations and the United States.

Return to International Community/Change of Image

Saddam has continued to work to increase his standing in the international community, seizing on opportunities to change his image, including bolstering his image within the Arab community.

Starting in the early 1990s, Saddam began working to change his image as a secular leader. This "return to Islam" can be seen in the increased Islamic language used by Saddam, the introduction into Iraq of the Qur'anic punishment of severing the right hand for the crime of theft, forbidding the public consumption of alcohol, and decapitation with a sword for the "crimes" of prostitution, homosexuality and providing a shelter for prostitutes to pursue their occupation. On the cultural level, a few million Qur'an books were printed in Iraq and given free, and people are being forced to attend Qur'an courses in many walks of society, starting with schools. In the same vein, a law issued in the late 1990s made it possible to release Muslim prisoners who learned the Qur'an in jail. Another component of the "Islamization" campaign is the construction of extravagant mosques—The new Saddam Mosque, (construction began in 1999) is one of the largest in the Middle East after the one in Mecca.

Saddam has also fashioned himself as the patron of the Palestinian cause. He has increased the original "reward" that was paid to families of suicide bombers from $10,000 to $25,000. In addition, Iraq informed the Palestinian Authority and public that it had asked permission from the Security Council to dedicate one billion Euros (around $940 million) from its New York Escrow to the Intifadah. There are other forms of support that, while not substantial, are still serving Saddam's propaganda machine. For example, a few of the Palestinians wounded in the Intifadah have been hospitalized in Baghdad. Also, Iraq sent a number of lorries through Jordan and the Jordan River bridges to the West Bank full of humanitarian goods. Israel allowed these lorries to cross over.

Other Signs of Iraq's Growing Acceptance in the International Community

In August of 2000, Venezuelan President Hugo Chavez bucked international convention and traveled to Iraq to meet with Saddam Hussein. He was the first head of state to visit Iraq since the Gulf War, signaling Iraq's growing acceptance in the international community. Two months later, Iraq was invited to attend the Arab Summit for the first time since the start of the Gulf Crisis, indicating a thawing in Arab attitudes toward Iraq. In another sign of normalcy, Baghdad's international airport re-opened in the Fall of 2000. When a hijacked Saudi airliner landed in Baghdad in October of 2000 and all passengers were released unharmed, there was a great deal of international praise for Saddam Hussein.

In January of 2001, humanitarian flights began arriving daily from abroad, and Iraqi airlines began operating (even in the no-fly zones). As oil-production recovered to pre-war levels, food rations increased, power cuts became less severe, and drinking water and sewer services have been dramatically improving. In a calculated step to garner international favor, Saddam offered to allow Kuwaiti officials to inspect Iraqi prisons in January of 2002; this offer was rejected. Finally, in March of 2002, at the Beirut Arab Summit, Saudi Crown Prince Abd Allah hugged and kissed Izzat Ibrahim al-Duri, Saddam's Deputy Chairman of the RCC, in front of the world's TV cameras. This ended more than a decade of bitter hostility and was a visible symbol that Saddam's Iraq had been fully welcomed back into the community of Arab nations.

Saddam continues to strengthen his reputation both by his re-Islamization program, and by his ostentatious support for the Palestinian people, further endearing him to his Arab neighbors. Saddam has pledged $881 million (USD) from oil revenues for the Palestinian people.

The Use of International Crisis

Saddam has found that international crises are helpful to him in retaining power in his country, and his string of foreign policy successes have allowed him to stunt the growth of internal opposition. For Saddam, success is not limited to the elimination of domestic opposition; such elimination is only a pre-condition to achieve his continuing ambition to be recognized as the pre-eminent leader in the region and a worthy successor to Nasser. However, in order to be able to become a world class leader, he needs, in the first place, to control the domestic scene, and in his mind, control means absolute control, namely the complete elimination of any opposition. In order to achieve that,

Saddam has always been ready to confront anybody, including world powers. The most damaging outcome of any crisis is one that shows him as a failure as a leader. Thus Saddam regularly promotes international crises to shore up his internal position.

While assuredly Saddam's position today is much weaker than it was on the eve of the invasion of Kuwait in 1990, he has demonstrated a more sophisticated leadership both in terms of internal security vulnerabilities, and in terms of diplomacy both with his Arab neighbors and Turkey, the "near abroad," as well as with his "far abroad." He has patiently and assiduously worked to reduce his vulnerabilities and to strengthen his position, both internally and internationally.

Conclusion

Saddam's survival in power is his continuing goal. A rational calculator who can bob and weave and is astutely Machiavellian, he has shrewdly managed to sustain the loyalty of his military and to weaken international opposition. That he has been sophisticated and better attuned to the context of his leadership both internally and internationally does not however lessen a still persistent danger—that when Saddam is backed into a corner, his customary prudence and judgment are apt to falter. On these occasions he can be dangerous to the extreme—violently lashing out with all resources at his disposal. The persistent calls for regime change may well be moving him into that dangerous "back against the wall" posture. The setting afire of the Kuwaiti oil fields as he retreated in 1991 is an example that might well be repeated with his own Iraqi oil fields, as if to say, "If I can't have them no one will." Moreover, with his back to the wall it is probable that he would attempt to use chemical/biological weapons against Israel and against U.S. armed forces in the region. The question then will be the degree to which he can continue to sustain the loyalty of his senior military commanders or whether they can be induced to not obey Saddam in extremis in order to safeguard their own futures. Of one thing we can be sure, this is a man who "will not go gentle into that good night, but will rage, rage against the dying of the light."

Postscript

At the time this updated political personality profile of Saddam was developed, the tension was palpable as war with Iraq seemed inevitable. But the international community was badly divided. Significant opposition was present in the European community to the requirement advocated by the United

States, and its principal ally Great Britain to eliminate the threat posed by the Iraqi regime, with France and Germany in particular leading the opposition, indicating that the inspection regime required more time to carry out their mission. Russia too opposed military action against Iraq, as did China. Putting legitimate policy disagreements aside, and other factors of national interest, that France, Russia and China opposed military intervention can assuredly be credited in part to the patient and significant courting of the "far abroad" described in the profile.

In fact, prior to the initiation of conflict on March 19, 2003, there was a systematic campaign to soften Iraq's air defenses, with targeted attacks in response to violation of the no-fly zone. And an effort was underway on a number of fronts to weaken the ties between Saddam and his military leaders. In November, 2002, Secretary of Defense Rumsfeld stated publicly that the generals have an important role to play in the reconstruction of Iraq, but of course if they get involved in weapons of mass destruction, all bets are off. This was followed several weeks later by a statement by President Bush to the effect that Saddam may well order his generals to use weapons of mass destruction against alliance forces. If he does so, the generals would be well advised to disobey those orders. Contact was made with the Iraqi Defense Minister suggesting he preserve the lives of his soldiers in a war they were sure to lose and encourage his forces to not fight. In the immediate lead-up to the conflict, and during the early weeks of the conflict, the battlefield was leafleted with fliers advising that any regional commander who ordered the use of weapons of mass destruction would be help culpable under the war crimes act, and that claims of "just following orders" would not protect them from prosecution.

In the conflict, there was a surprising lack of resistance with a pace of advance not contemplated, perhaps a reflection of some of the preparatory efforts cited above. I had thought it was likely that Saddam would order the use of weapons of mass destruction in a terminal spasm, and could well order setting Iraqi oil fields afire as he had in his exodus from Kuwait.

In actuality, the feared chemical/biological weapons attack did not occur. Why not? The short answer is that we do not know. But let me suggest several possibilities. First, because of the split in the international community that led to the disarray in the United Nations and the U.S.-Great Britain decision to enter conflict outside of the U.N. umbrella, Saddam may have reflected that too early a use of these weapons would have dissolved the uncertainty he had fostered and promote international unity in the requirement to eliminate his regime. Then the extremely rapid advance of alliance troops and collapse of Iraqi military resistance may have made it too late to use these weapons. Moreover, Saddam may well have ordered their use, but the military responding to the effective information operations campaign may well have concluded it would be imprudent in terms of their own best interest to not follow those orders. Chemical/biological and nuclear weapons have not yet been found, leading many to doubt their existence in the first place. We should recall however that the failure of weapons inspectors to find these weapons had nearly led to the lifting of sanctions prior to the defection of Hussein Kamal who revealed the nature of the programs and where the weapons had been cached. There is no question that Saddam had been bent on pursing CBRN weapons programs. Saddam has had years to perfect concealment techniques, and the administration at this time has not located any weapons sites. Whether they were dismantled just prior to the onset of conflict or will be discovered has not yet been determined.

At the end of the first Gulf conflict (1991), Saddam's conventional military capabilities were gravely weakened. Saddam required at least the appearance of weapons of mass destruction to maintain his powerful, threatening image in the region, and to maintain the loyalty of his military. Is it possible that this was a giant bluff to maintain his image of strength? Perhaps, but if so, at what a large cost, an estimated $96 billion during the course of the sanctions regime, but nevertheless perhaps preferable to being the victim of a coup. Another intriguing possibility has been raised by David Kay, chief of the inspections team, who suggests that Saddam may well have not known that he did not have these weapons in his arsenal, for his scientific establishment may have been afraid to let him know the true state of their WMD programs.

How many of Saddam's military leaders were "loyal at the barrel of a gun" is unknown. After 1991, those who too early had raised their heads to signify their enthusiasm for the imminent overthrow of the Saddam Hussein regime were hunted down ruthlessly, and with their families were jailed, tortured and executed. One could not expect early defections. And as long as the inner leadership, especially Saddam and his two sons Qusay and Uday remained on the loose, the possibility of fear of reprisal remained. In the conduct of the war, the targeting of senior leadership conveyed that they were the principal target and paved the way for lower level military to defect. With the killing in a firefight of Qusay and Uday, it was, for Saddam, literally "the end of the line." This had to have had a profound impact upon Saddam, who had seen his leadership perpetuated through his sons. An increasingly organized resistance to U.S. occupation was mounted, with episodic audiotapes from Saddam Hussein encouraging "a holy war." Until Saddam was killed or captured, his shadow would continue to darken the political landscape.

It was predicted that Saddam would not take the path of Idi Amin, who recently died, waiting in exile. He remained concerned with his historical reputation and would not take any steps to diminish his stature as heroic pan-Arab leader. For the same reason, it was not anticipated that he would suicide as Hitler did in the last flaming bunker or permit himself to be taken alive, but would likely go out as his sons did, in a blaze of guns.

In fact, he was taken alive, and without a struggle. How ironic that it should have come to this: Saddam Hussein, who began life in a mud hut near Tikrit, ended his political career in a so-called "spider-hole" in the ground, beneath a mud hut near Tikrit. But considering Saddam's psychological makeup, his end was, if not inevitable, certainly fitting. From mud hut to mud hut, this represented the economic and psychological poverty at Saddam's core, his wounded self. Indeed, as the mud hut is the architectural motif for the inner layer of Saddam's psychology, in projecting the likely conduct of Saddam Hussein in the second trial of the (new) century, after that of Slobodan Milosevic, it is necessary to understand his complex psychology. In these regards, it is useful to consider the three principal layers of Saddam's psychology, layers for which the architecture of his three principal residences provide an apt metaphor. The mud hut represents the wounded self at his very core. He has devoted his life and career to overcompensating for this profound insecurity.

The magnificent palaces dotting the Iraqi landscape can be seen as the architectural model for his dreams of glory, his compensatory grandiose self, with their inlaid woods, fine marble and gold accouterments in the bathrooms. But what underlay the palaces? In January of 1991, German architectural plans revealed details of a massive bunker that had been constructed beneath the Presidential palace. Built with pre-stressed concrete and steel, it was designed to withstand all but a direct nuclear blast. Bristling with weapons, fitted with sophisticated communications equipment, with a helicopter and disguised exit, the bunker had enough food and water to last for a year and a half. This was the architectural motif for the default position in his political psychology, a siege state, ready to be attacked, ready to defend.

But the Saddam Hussein we saw initially during his capture was neither the man in the bunker, nor the palace occupant. After he was assisted out of the spider-hole, he meekly bowed his head to have a medic examine his scalp for lice, obediently opening his mouth for a dental exam. This was, briefly, the shattered self. The importance of the images of a meek, humiliated Saddam giving up without a fight to his American captors cannot be overstated. The pictures of his capture showed to the world a broken man emerging from the hole beneath the mud hut, submitting without a fight to the will of his captors.

This is not to say that the image of a broken man would persist. Indeed, within hours, he had regained his composure, was in his characteristic defiant grandiose mode, and, identifying himself as the President of Iraq, imperiously asked who was negotiating with him. It was anticipated that this psychological default position would be manifest in court, which was abundantly confirmed in the July 2004 appearance.

Defiant Defendant Saddam Hussein: Following in Milosevic's Footsteps

A clean-shaven, well dressed Saddam Hussein walked into the courtroom on July 1, 2004, a rather remarkable change from six months earlier. The shattered self-image of a broken man pulled from a spider-hole near Tikrit would only serve as a temporary break in Saddam's grandiose facade. His defiant behavior in front of the Iraqi judge demonstrated a return to his default position and revealed striking parallels with Milosevic's conduct in court. It was as if he carried with him a mental "textbook full of lessons" derived from years of testimony by Milosevic.

As the next trial of the century unfolds on the international stage, there exists a striking similarity, which we believe is not a coincidence, between the courtroom conduct of Saddam in his first court appearance and that of Milosevic during his trial. Like Slobodan, the grandiose Saddam very much enjoys and craves his role as a major actor in the international arena. However, in the case of Hussein, that desire has been apparent from the early years of his career, unlike Milosevic, who was a grey apparatchik until his transformation at age forty-six. In what was supposed to be a brief preliminary hearing, largely administrative in nature, the defiant dictator turned it into his own political platform. Within twenty-six minutes, Saddam managed to exchange combative words with the judge, question the legitimacy of the court system, play up his hero image to Arab supporters, and invoke history to his defense. At one point, he even turned the table on the presiding judge, aggressively interrogating the judge on his position and credentials, and fuming at the news of the judge's appointment by the Coalition Provisional Authority. The first court appearance demonstrates his narcissistic desires to turn the courtroom into his world stage and maintain control over the proceedings. These striking parallels with Milosevic are not merely a coincidence. There is reason to believe that Saddam was actively following the Milosevic trial up until his capture in December 2003, just as he has closely observed the downfall of other powerful leaders.

Unlike Milosevic, Saddam, whose attendance at Cairo University's law school was only nominal, is not well versed in jurisprudence and courtroom tactics. Nevertheless, he will almost certainly overestimate his own legal brilliance. Such behavior would mirror his controlling nature as commander-in-chief of the Iraqi armed forces, even though he had no requisite training in military leadership. Furthermore, even if he does identify a principle defense attorney, it is assuredly the case that he will be actively involved in his defense strategy.

Saddam's initial statement in the courtroom was a repetition of that same, now infamous, phrase that the captured dictator first uttered when he came out of the spider-hole: "I am Saddam Hussein, the president of Iraq." Convinced that he is still the ruler of the Iraqi people, Saddam outright denied the court's authority to strip him of his title, and rejected the legitimacy of the war in which he was captured. "I'm elected by the people of Iraq. The occupation cannot take that right away from me." His fixation with a proper title was apparent by his frequent interruptions to correct the judge, whom he cast as a shameful and disgraceful Iraqi. In one particular instance, as the judge rattled off the preliminary war crime indictments, Saddam's demands to be honored with the proper title led him to snap back: "I did all these things as president so don't strip me of that title." It is a striking reminder of the grandiose facade still at play and demonstrates his inability to cope with political reality. Moreover, it is an illustration of a narcissistic individual who is able to disregard and detach himself from the severity of the charges at hand, in order to make a basic point regarding the mere phrasing of his title.

He refused to acknowledge the accusations of the Halabja gassing attack, mocking casually that he had "heard about that on the television reports." But it was the charge detailing Iraq's 1990 invasion of Kuwait that ignited a fury within, provoking a chain of ill-mannered outbursts and body language. "In Kuwait I was protecting the Iraqi people from those Kuwaiti dogs who wanted to turn Iraqi women into 10-dinar prostitutes." Just as Milosevic presented Kosovo as "the cradle of Serbian civilization" and "an integral part of the 'sovereign state of Serbia,'" Saddam used a similar argument for Kuwait. "I am surprised you are charging me with this. You are Iraqi and everyone knows Kuwait is part of Iraq." He spoke rather defensively of the aggressive actions taken against Kuwait, asserting that it was an agent of the U.S. and Israel. However, there was more to this courtroom display of incitement and rage. Underlying the invasion of Kuwait were Saddam's self-serving interests to achieve his destined role as the heroic Arab leader, unifying the pan-Arab nation and defending against the aggression of the West. Saddam's courtroom conduct thus far reveals his refusal to accept his inevitable fate and determination to instead cling to past dreams of glory. For example, when asked by the judge where he lived, the former dictator quickly replied, "I live in each Iraqi's house," a true testament to his grandiose self-concept.

Saddam's remark that "this is all a theater by Bush, the criminal, to help him with his campaign" is one indication of the type of defense testimony to come. The courts must anticipate a shifting of blame to the Western powers for Saddam will likely employ political invectives to attack the West's double standards. This will require careful planning and consistent limit setting by the court or Saddam will again take over as he did during his brief court appearance in July 2004.

In the case of Saddam Hussein, an Iraqi style domestic tribunal has won out over the Milosevic-style, ad-hoc international criminal court. The Iraqi people feel strongly motivated to prove to the world, that as a nation of law, Iraq is capable of carrying out justice, against even its most brutal dictators. There is a strong desire to reestablish the pride of Iraq's glorious past, when the Hammurabi code played an important role in the development of the law—a tradition that was set aside during the Saddam Hussein years.

Saddam has come a long way from the days of his humiliating capture, when he surrendered instantly with no resistance. But, this was but a temporary break in his grandiose facades. Defiant and unrepentant, he saw the trial as a way of returning to the international stage, seeking to reinstate his heroic legacy. Brought to trial on alleged false charges, he portrayed himself as a nationalist hero, who in service to his country has courageously defended his people from outside aggression. Saddam feels that his entire nation has been put on trial, not just Saddam the individual.

While Saddam will play an active role with his defense team, there is no indication that he will be defending himself and accordingly, in terms of the structure of the proceedings, he will not have the freedom that Milosevic enjoyed.

As Saddam continues to dismiss the inevitable reality of his fate, he clings to his past, playing to his supporters and manipulating the trial proceedings. With the Milosevic model in place, Saddam will continue to use the ongoing trial principally to seize the spotlight as his final act on the world stage. As the trial continues, with now new charges of crimes against humanity, it remains to be seen which layer of his psychology—the shattered self seen during his capture from the spider-hole, the psychological siege state, or the grandiose facade—will determine his courtroom conduct. Based on our understanding of Saddam Hussein's political personality and the early indications from his preliminary appearance and his conduct in the courtroom thus far, we doubt that the meek and shattered self will again be seen, but believe a mien of grandiose defiance will be evident throughout the court proceedings, as he continues to plays to history and his radical Arab followers, demonstrating his courage in defying the West.

PART II

THE IRAQI HIGH TRIBUNAL

Basic Information about the Iraqi High Tribunal

What's in a Name?

The judicial body that prosecuted Saddam Hussein was originally called the "Iraqi Special Tribunal," a name selected in 2003 by Ambassador Paul Bremer, head of the Coalition Provisional Authority (the occupying authority in Iraq). The democratically elected Iraqi National Assembly objected to that appellation because the word "special" in their opinion evoked "special courts" which Saddam had used as a political weapon against his enemies and which are not permitted under the new constitution. The Court was re-named by the Iraqi National Assembly through August 2005 legislation approving the Court's Statute and Rules. There was some initial confusion about how to translate the new name of the Court. However, there was no dispute that the new statute uses the words "Iraq," and "High" or "Higher," but some people translated the last part as "Criminal Court" and others as "Tribunal." The translators of the Department of Justice Regime Crimes Liaison Office initially preferred "Iraqi Higher Criminal Court," but then the Tribunal itself issued an official statement in which it said that in English the court should be called the "Iraqi High Tribunal."

What Is the Iraqi High Tribunal?

The Iraqi High Tribunal (IHT) is a judicial body that was established by the U.S.-appointed Iraqi Governing Council on December 10, 2003, and later ratified by the Iraqi National Assembly, to prosecute high level members of the former Iraqi regime who are alleged to have committed war crimes, crimes against humanity, genocide, and aggression. It is composed of two, five-person Trial Chambers, and a nine-person Appeals Chamber. The IHT has been called an "internationalized domestic court" since its statute and rules of procedure are modeled upon the U.N. war crimes tribunals for the former Yugoslavia, Rwanda, and Sierra Leone, and its statute requires the IHT to follow the precedent of the U.N. tribunals. Its judges and prosecutors are to be assisted by international experts. But it is not fully international, since its seat is Baghdad, its Prosecutor is Iraqi, and its bench is composed exclusively of Iraqi judges.

Why Not an International Court?

Many critics of the IHT felt that it would be better to try Saddam Hussein before an international tribunal. But the Statute of the International Criminal Court (ICC) precludes that Court from trying cases that involved crimes committed prior to July 2002. Since most of Saddam Hussein's crimes were committed before that time, the ICC would not have been a good venue for the trial. Creating a new U.N. ad hoc war crimes tribunal, like the tribunals for the former Yugoslavia and Rwanda, requires the approval of the U.N. Security Council. In the aftermath of the controversial U.S. invasion of Iraq, several countries that wield a veto on the Council reportedly made it known that they would not vote for an ad hoc tribunal to try Saddam Hussein. Polls taken in Iraq indicated that the Iraqi people themselves overwhelmingly expressed the view that Saddam Hussein and the other former leaders of the Regime should to be tried in Iraq by Iraqi judges. Finally, officials in the Bush Administration favored an Iraqi domestic court, rather than an international tribunal, because they felt that they could exercise a greater degree of control over such an institution.

What Is the Status of Saddam Hussein's Trial?

Saddam Hussein was apprehended by U.S. forces near his hometown of Tikrit in December 2003. The first trial of Saddam Hussein, together with eight other former Iraqi officials, before the IHT began on October 19, 2005. The trial, which was designed to be completed within three months, dragged on for three times that long due to frequent recesses and interruptions.

What Are the Specific Charges against Saddam Hussein?

Rather than join the defendants and offenses and hold a single, comprehensive trial like the one held at Nuremberg, the IHT decided to proceed with a dozen mini-trials. The first case to be brought against Saddam Hussein involved his role in the 1982 execution of 148 Iraqi civilians in Dujail, a predominantly Shiite town north of Baghdad, in response to a failed assassination attempt on Saddam. Among other charges that will be prosecuted in subsequent trials, Saddam Hussein stands accused of ordering the slaughter of some 5,000 Kurds with chemical gas in Halabja in 1988, killing or deporting more than 200,000 Northern Iraqi Kurds during the Anfal campaign in the 1980s, invading Kuwait in 1990, and drying rivers, killing hundreds of thousands of Marsh Arabs in response to their 1991 uprising. In addition to Saddam, eleven high-ranking Iraqi officials are in custody awaiting indictments, including Abid Hamid al-Tikriti, a former presidential secretary, Ali Hassan al-Majid ("Chemical Ali"), Saddam's cousin and advisor, and Tariq Aziz, the former deputy prime minister.

What Body of Laws Does the IHT Employ?

The IHT has jurisdiction over crimes committed in Iraq or abroad (e.g., in Iran or Kuwait) between 1968 and 2003 by former regime members. The IHT's subject matter jurisdiction is comprised of a mix of international law crimes and domestic law crimes that existed prior to Saddam's ascension to power in 1968. The international law offenses are (1) war crimes, (2) the crime of aggression, and (3) the crime of genocide. The domestic law crimes are (1) manipulation of the judiciary; (2) wastage of national resources and squandering of public assets and funds; and (3) acts of aggression against an Arab country. The IHT's procedural law is comprised of a mix of international law procedures set forth in the IHT's Rules of Procedures, supplemented by the Rules of Procedure of the Iraqi Criminal Code. Traditional Islamic Law, "sharia," is not applied by the IHT. The IHT is empowered to imprison convicted persons for up to life or subject them to capital punishment.

What Is the Nationality of the Lawyers and Judges?

Saddam's legal team was led by Khalil Dulaimi, an Iraqi lawyer. It included a number of distinguished defense counsel from across the globe, including former U.S. Attorney General Ramsey Clark. The IHT is comprised of fifty investigative, trial, and appellate judges, all of whom are native Iraqis—mostly of Shiite or Sunni ethnic origin. The IHT Statute prohibits anyone from serving as a judge who was a member of the Ba'ath party. Each judge was nominated and vetted by the Iraqi Governing Council with the assistance of the 21,000 member Iraqi Bar Association. Five judges will preside over each trial, and nine different judges will preside over each appeal. The names of most of the judges have not been disclosed for security reasons.

Dramatis Personae

The trial of Saddam Hussein involved a colorful mosaic of personalities from Iraq and around the world. We briefly describe some of the key figures here.

The Judges

Although five judges made up the Trial Chamber in the Dujail Trial, for security reasons only the Presiding Judge's identity was disclosed during the proceedings.

The first Presiding Judge in the Dujail trial was **Rizgar Mohammed Amin** (1957–), a Kurd who grew up as the privileged son of a wealthy landlord in Sulaymaniya, the Kurdish city founded several hundred years ago by his tribal ancestors, the Jaffs. Amin excelled at his studies and was dispatched to Baghdad University to study law, graduating in 1980. As an ambitious lawyer in Baghdad, he refused to join Hussein's Ba'ath Party. Once back in his hometown in the early 1990s, he refused to join the Patriotic Union of Kurdistan, the party that runs the eastern half of the semiautonomous Kurdish enclave. Nonetheless, his legal abilities propelled him to the top of the judicial establishment in both Baghdad and Sulaymaniya. In Kurdistan, he is legendary as the judge who sentenced to death both a powerful Kurdish warlord convicted of double homicide in 2000 and a German woman found guilty of murdering her Kurdish husband in 2003. Amin acted despite domestic political pressure in the case of the warlord and pressure from Berlin in the woman's case.

Half-way through the trial Judge Rizgar Mohammed Amin resigned, and was replaced by **Ra'ouf Abdul Rahman** (1942–), a Kurd from the town of Halabja, where Saddam Hussein's security forces are accused of killing about 5,000 Kurdish Iraqis in a chemical gas attack in 1988. Judge Ra'ouf Rahman lost some of his relatives in the attack, although no immediate family members. The 64-year-old judge trained at Baghdad University's law school, from where he graduated in 1963. He worked as a lawyer in the capital Baghdad, then in the city of Sulaymaniyah. He was appointed as the chief judge of the Kurdistan Appeals Court in 1996. He has two sons and one daughter.

The Prosecutor

The Chief prosecutor in the Dujail trial was **Jaafar Mousawi** (1957–), a Shiite Muslim. Jaafar Mousawi is described as "a very humble, simple man" who rose from poverty as the oldest of nine children to become a judge. The son of a low-level Health Ministry employee in Baghdad, he worked at his uncle's spice shop from age six. Excelling in his studies, he got accepted at the University of Baghdad. After studying English for three years, he switched to law, and eventually became a judge under Saddam Hussein's rule. Neither his nor his wife's family suffered personally under the former government. Mousawi has two sons and two daughters, all in school. The entire family recently moved into a residence in the Green Zone, the fortified government enclave in Baghdad where the trial is taking place.

The Defense Counsel

Retained by Saddam Hussein's oldest daughter, Raghad Hussein, **Khalil al-Duleimi** (1966–) was the lead Counsel representing Saddam Hussein in the Dujail trial. The forty-year-old Sunni hails from the troubled Anbar province in Western Iraq. Before the American invasion, he was a member of the Ba'ath party and Legal Advisor in the Iraqi Ministry of Health. Assisting al-Duleimi were two-dozen of the world's most prominent defense attorneys, including Najib Nuaimi, the former Qatari Justice Minister and Mahathir Mohamad, the former Prime Minister of Mayaysia.

Saddam Hussein's most prominent foreign lawyer was **Ramsey Clark** (1927–), who had served as the U.S. Attorney General under President Lyndon B. Johnson. During his years at the Justice Department, he supervised the drafting and executive role in passage of the Voting Rights Act of 1965 and Civil Rights Act of 1968. More recently, Clark has become controversial for his political views and clients. He is affiliated with *Vote To Impeach*, an organization advocating the impeachment of President George W. Bush for the 2003 invasion of Iraq. Clark is the founder of the International Action Center, an organization claiming that North Korea is not a violator of human rights. Before taking on the case of Saddam Hussein, Clark represented Slobodan Milosevic before the International Criminal Tribunal for the Former Yugoslavia.

Clark was assisted by **Curtis F. Doebbler,** an international human rights lawyer who has represented individuals *pro bono* before international tribunals in Europe, Africa and the Americas during the last ten years. Doebbler's biography says his clients have included "an estimated 2 million internally displaced persons in Khartoum State, approximately 3,500 Ethiopian refugees in Sudan, dozens of political activists in Sudan, the Democratic Republic of Congo, Peru and Afghanistan, and dozens of human rights defenders in numerous countries around the world."

The Seven Co-Defendants

Next to Saddam Hussein, the highest ranking defendant was his half-brother, **Barzan Ibrahim Hassan al-Tikriti** (1951–). Barzan Ibrahim was eighteen when he took part in the 1968 coup that brought Saddam Hussein's Ba'ath Party to power. As Saddam Hussein came to power in 1979, Barzan Ibrahim was given a prominent role in the General Intelligence (Mukhabarat), while Sa'dun Shakir, Saddam Hussein's cousin, served as its head. In 1982 Barzan Ibrahim replaced Sa'dun as its director due to the latter's failure to prevent an assassination attempt on Saddam Hussein's life. While serving as head of Iraqi intelligence, Barzan Ibrahim was responsible for the repression of religious and ethnic minorities including forced deportation, disappearances and murder. Barzan Ibrahim reportedly participated in the deportation and mass murder of the inhabitants of the village of Dujail after an attempt on Saddam Hussein's life. By the end of 1983, Barzan Ibrahim was replaced as head of Mukhabarat by Fadil Barak al-Tikriti. Saddam Hussein sent Barzan Ibrahim to Switzerland in 1988 and made him Iraq's ambassador to the UN in Geneva until 1998. In Geneva, up until 1995, Barzan Ibrahim handled Saddam Hussein's personal fortune. A criminal complaint was filed against him in Switzerland in September 2001 by a member of the Barzani tribe, for the crimes committed in 1983. But Barzan Ibrahim was not arrested.

The man who sat next to Saddam Hussein in the Defense Dock during the trial was **Awad Hamed al-Bander** (1946–), former chief justice of the Iraqi Revolutionary Court. According to the indictment, he conducted show trials which often lead to summary death sentences.

The other defendants were: **Taha Yassin Ramadan**, former bank clerk and longtime Saddam Hussein aide who was Iraq's Vice President from 1991; and **Abdullah Kazim Ruwaid, Ali Dayih Ali, Mohammed Azzawi Ali**, and **Mizher Abdullah Ruwaid**, Ba'ath Party officials in Dujail region, believed responsible for Dujail arrests.

Key Witnesses

By far the most high profile witness to testify in the Dujail trial was **Tarek Aziz**, the former Foreign Minister of Iraq. Aziz was born near Mosul, in Tell Kaif, Iraq, in 1936. Originally named Mikhail Yahunna, he was born of a modest Chaldean Catholic family. In the late 1950's, he joined the Ba'th Party as one of its early members. He then changed his name to Tarek Aziz, meaning "Glorious Path". Tarek Aziz first met Saddam Hussein through their common involvement in then outlawed Ba'th Party. Following the Ba'th coup in

1963, he was hired as editor of the Ba'ath party newspaper. Over the years, he held a series of positions in the Ba'ath party, finally becoming Ba'th party leader on the in 1977. In 1979, he was appointed Deputy Prime Minister, where his primary role was to act as a diplomat of foreign policies. In April 1980, he was the target of an assassination attempt, but was not injured. In 1984, Iraq and the US officially restored diplomatic relations after a meeting at the White House between Tarek Aziz and President Ronald Reagan. Tarek Aziz managed American support for Iraq in its eight-year conflict with Iran, and helped forge strong economic ties with the Soviet Union and France. He became Iraq's top negotiator with the UN after Iraq's surrender to the US led Coalition forces.

Saddam Hussein and the Charges against Him

At the end of the prosecution's case, the IHT issued formal charging instruments against Saddam Hussein and his seven co-defendants. Saddam is charged with the deaths of nine people who were killed in the first days of the crackdown on the town of Dujail in 1982, the unlawful arrest of 399 townspeople, the torture of women and children, and ordering the razing of farmlands in retaliation for the assassination attempt against Hussein. Contrary to erroneous press reports, Hussein was in fact also charged with the deaths of the 148 who were sentenced to death by his Revolutionary Court. The indictments of Saddam's co-defendants are reproduced in the Appendix.

The Indictment of Saddam Hussein

English Translation of the Charges Against Saddam Hussein

Accusation Document
Scene of the Crime: Al-Dujayl, Town/Salah-al-Din
Governorate/Baghdad
Date of the Crime: July 8, 1982 until January 16, 1989

I, Judge (Ra'uf Rashid 'Abd-al-Rahman), the Presiding Judge of the First Criminal Court of the Iraqi High Tribunal accuse you (Saddam Hussein Al-Majid) of the following:

At the time you were the President of the Republic of Iraq, the General Commander of the Armed Forces, and the Chairman of the former Revolutionary Command Council, and on July 8, 1982 as you were visiting the town Al-Dujayl, which falls under the administrative jurisdiction of Salah-al-Din

Governorate, and under the claim that gun shots were fired against the cars escorting your motorcade, you issued orders to the military and security organizations, the Intelligence Service, the Popular Army, and the Ba'th Party organization in Al-Dujayl to launch a wide scale and systematic attack to shoot and use all kinds of weapons and helicopters to kill, arrest, detain, and torture large numbers of the residents of Al-Dujayl (men, women, and children).

Afterwards, you issued orders to remove the orchards and demolish their houses. Based upon these orders, the organizations and the troops killed nine people that day and the following day. Groups of families totaling to 399 individuals were arrested and detained at the Investigation and Interrogation Department (Al-Hakimiyyah) of the disbanded Office of the Head of the Intelligence Service and under the command of the accused (Barzan Ibrahim Al-Hasan), according to the documents attached to the case. The detainees were subject to torture by the intelligence officers; during the interrogation and due to torture by electricity, battering the head with metal rods, prevention from sleeping, and other torture methods, a group of the detainees died. The other detainees were transferred to Abi-Ghurayb Prison under the supervision of the disbanded Intelligence Service. At the mentioned prison, their torture continued and many of them were killed and died due to the usage of the aforesaid means of torture.

Many of the detainees (men, women, and children) were transferred to Liyyah Compound in the desert and which is designed to shelter Bedouin nomads and their livestock in the area of Al-Samawah. They were detained there for four years during which they were subject to torture and deliberate harsh health and living conditions in addition to deprivation from food and medication in the desert, where one detainee was killed. A number of the members of detained families also died.

Based on your direct orders, the National Security Affairs Department of the disbanded Presidential Diwan referred 148 people, including those who died in detention due to torture in the Investigation and Interrogation Department (Court of the Intelligence Service) and Abi-Ghurayb Prison, including juveniles whose ages are less than 18 years to the cancelled Revolutionary Court, headed by the accused 'Awwad Hamad Al-Bandar, who issued an irrevocable decision sentencing them all to death by hanging in a brief trial that only took one session. The sentence was in accordance with decision number 744/ (SATTS J)/1984 on June 14, 1984.

People who were not trialed were convicted knowing that they were killed during the interrogation at the intelligence court due to torture. In addition to that, some of those who were not sentenced to death and executed were juveniles who have not reached the age of 18, the fact that violates article (79) of the (amended) penal code number (111) of 1969 and the juvenile protection code number ( ) of 1983 and also violates the procedures stipulated in the amended Law of Criminal Procedure number (23) of 1971. The sentence also violates clause (6) of article (5) of the international declaration for civil and political rights, dated December 16,1966, effective March 23, 1975 and which is ratified by the Iraqi Republic on February 18, 1969 and that stipulates the (inadmissibility sentencing individuals below 18 years of age to death).

You promptly ratified the abovementioned mass execution sentence and in accordance with the presidential decree, numbered (778) on June 16, 1984, that you signed. Afterwards, you, issued a decision, numbered (1283) on October 24, 1982 from the disbanded Revolutionary Command Council in your capacity as its chairman, to confiscate the agricultural lands and orchards of the residents of Al-Dujayl and then sweeping these orchards. The bodies of the slain were concealed and were not handed over to their relatives. The fate of a number of detainees, including six juveniles, is still unknown.

Based on that, you have committed crimes to which the following apply: paragraphs A, D, W, H, U, I, of clause (First) of Article (12) of the Iraqi High Tribunal Law number 10 of 2005 and which stipulates the following:

First. For legal purposes, crimes against humanity mean any of the below mentioned actions when these actions are committed in a widespread or systematic attack against a civilian population, and knowledge of such an attack:

A: Murder
D: Relocation
H: Imprisonment and severe deprivation in any other way of physical freedom in contrast with basic regulations of the international law
W: Torture
U: Compulsory concealment of people
I: Other inhumane acts that are of similar characteristics and that deliberately cause severe suffering or serious damage to the body or mental or physical health ion of the population or its compulsory transportation

In reference to paragraphs (First, Second and Third) of the Article (15) of the Iraqi High Tribunal Code which stipulates the following:

First. The person who commits a crime which is within the jurisdiction of the court, is responsible for it in his personal character and will be subject to penalty according to the stipulations of this code

Second. The person is considered responsible according to the stipulations of this code and to the stipulations of the penal code if he commits the following:

> a. If the person commits the crime personally, in participation, or via another person regardless if this person is criminally responsible or not
> b. Ordering the committing of a crime that was in fact committed, initiated, or urged and perpetrated to be committed.
> c. Contributing with a group of people in a collaborative criminal intention to commit a crime or to start committing it, provided that this participation is deliberate

Third. The official title of the accused is not a reason to exempt him from penalty or to commutate the penalty whether the accused is the president of the state, a member in the Revolutionary Command Council, a prime minister or a member in the Cabinet or member in the Ba'th Party Command. It is inadmissible to use the immunity as a pretext to be relieved from the responsibility of the crimes mentioned in the articles (11), (12), (13), and (14).

Fourth. The Supreme President is not exempted from the criminal liability of the crimes committed by his subordinates, if the President is aware or has reasons to be aware that his subordinate has committed or is about to commit these acts and the President did not take the necessary and suitable measures to prevent these acts or submit the case to the competent authorities for interrogation and trial.

Can Saddam Hussein Get a Fair Trial?[127] — A Debate between Saddam's Lawyer and Michael P. Scharf

Professor Curtis Doebbler:

Thank you very much. I want to thank Case Western Reserve University for being willing to host such a debate like this. There have been many other places that have shied away from discussing this issue although I think it is a very vital issue for human rights and, as I will try to indicate, a very vital issue for the values that underlie our society here in the United States. So I want to thank them very much, and to thank particularly Professor Scharf for being willing to join me in this forum.

The first issue that has to be addressed is the fact that this whole situation, the trials, what is happening right now in Iraq, the military involvement, the soldiers that are being killed, the civilians that are being killed, the destruction of Fallujah, all this has taken place in violation of international law. I have been to more than sixty countries after the invasion of Iraq in March 2003, and I have not met one lawyer with whom I had to argue about the illegality of the invasion, except in the United States. In every other country I visited, and meeting with some of the heads of state of those countries and some of their most senior lawyers, they were unequivocally convinced that the United States' aggression against Iraq was a violation of international law, a violation of Article 2(4) of the Charter of the United Nations, which represents binding international law for the United States. So we have to look at it from that perspective.

In other words, think about it as if another country came to the United States, decided it didn't like President Bush and the Republicans in power because they thought that President Bush was a war criminal for having committed crimes of aggression against other countries, invaded the United States, and then put him on trial claiming that they would give him a fair trial. That is the situation right now that we face in Iraq. And I think it is important for us not to lose sight of that, the crucial starting point is the illegal use of force against the territorial integrity and political independence of another sovereign country in violation of international law.

Furthermore, even today, some would say that there is still an ongoing use of force against the people of Iraq and there is certainly an occupation of large parts of Iraq. This occupation is an illegal occupation, in part, because it was based on an illegal use of force, in part, because it is an occupation by a foreign power that has acted oppressively in the areas that it occupies.

So the second important aspect to understand is that Iraq, at least large parts of the country, are in a state of occupation. Legally, that means that there is law that applies to an occupier and how an occupier can treat the people of a country, how it can treat the institutions of a country, and in Iraq, the United States, I suggest, has not abided by this law.

In fact, part of that law, the Fourth Geneva Convention, states that an occupying power may not dissolve the judicial bodies of a country and institute its own judicial bodies. The United States has dissolved the judicial institutions of Iraq, and it has instated its own judges.

Yes, many of these judges were taken from among Iraqi judges, but only after Iraqi judges were politically vetted to decide which ones should stay. And they did not vet them for their legal competence; no, they vetted them in a process they called de-Ba'athification, a process to which every single one of the judges was subjected because ever single judge in Iraq, with maybe an insignificant number of exceptions, were members of the Ba'ath Party.

In fact, the most senior judges in Iraq were senior members of the Ba'ath Party. These judges were excluded from the judiciary. It is not a huge number, 180 of maybe 900 judges, but they are the most senior judges. The judges that are left are some of the most junior judges. Some of them were not even judges before, and now they have been made, by essentially decree, judges. These are the individuals who will be part of the court.

Now, I'd like to go through each judge's background and say this is the judge who is going to be in the court, and these are his qualifications or lack of qualifications. But I cannot do that. I cannot do that because I don't know who the judges are of that court. I know one person who is an investigating judge only because a television tape of the initial appearance in July leaked out, but that should not have even been made public according to the American authorities, and that person is a very junior judge, not a very senior judge.

So we have a situation where the occupying power has created a tribunal of, in our opinion, less than competent judges that will be trying one of the most complex and possibly one of the most important cases in recent history. Certainly, I think that is inappropriate, but more importantly, I think that is a breach of international law guarantees of a fair, competent, independent, and impartial tribunal.

The court is not independent because it is created by an occupying power through a process by which the judges are chosen based not on their legal qualifications but on a political vetting. The court is not impartial prima facie in the words of the State Department, commenting on South American countries, because faceless judges are prima facie, an illegitimate form of judiciary. And they violate the provisions of due process in a variety of ways.

If there is to be a court in Iraq that tries individuals for international crimes, such a court must have the authority to try every individual who has committed a crime against international law in Iraq. That includes crimes of aggression, which are not included in the statute right now, despite what you heard about some of the allegations—and I will come to that in a second— that includes being able to try the nationals of other countries that may have committed these crimes.

Probably not many of you are old enough to remember, but one of the greatest criticisms leveled at the Nuremberg and Tokyo processes after World War II by one of the judges who participated in that process, Judge Rollings, a Dutch judge of the Tokyo tribunal, was that that process was not legitimate because it was only "victor's justice" and in his words, that is, "not justice at all."

If we are going to have a system of the rule of law applied to Iraq if the occupying power and, hopefully, eventually, a sovereign Iraqi Government that represents the people of Iraq is going to deal with issues in their country that require a judiciary to deal with them, we need to have a fair judiciary established in that country. We do not have that right now.

I want to go through some of the due process rights that are being violated and that need to be respected in this instance. I mentioned some of them already, and because many of you are law students, I will point out, although not with the jurisprudence, we don't have time for that here, at least some of the provisions of international law, which are relevant.

For example, many of you know that Article 14 of the International Covenant of Civil and Political Rights provides for a competent, independent, and impartial tribunal. This right is also provided for in the American Declaration on the Rights and Duties of Man, which although not a binding treaty on the United States, has been accepted many times by the Inter-American Commission as reflecting customary international law that the United States must abide by, and those of you who studied constitutional law are certainly aware that the United States courts have said that customary international law is part of United States law.

Also, the Geneva Conventions, Article 84, subparagraph 2 of the Third Geneva Convention specifically, contains the right to be judged by an independent and impartial tribunal.

One also has a right to be informed of the charges against him in a timely manner. That is in both the Third Geneva Convention, Article 104, and the International Covenant of Civil and Political Rights Article 14, sub-paragraph 3(a). The right to be informed of charges against you is not the right to stand before somebody who points at you and says "We think you have done many bad things," or to even come before one who rails against you based on his perception of what might be public values.

It is the right to come before a court where you are presented with a prima facie case of facts against you and where you are able to reply to those facts, and most importantly, it is a chance to understand what provisions of law you have violated.

I don't know if any of you have seen—I have watched it numerous times as you can imagine—the process which took place apparently in Baghdad at the beginning of July 2004. Not one provision of law was mentioned in relation to any charges. In fact, at one point, the judge held up the law, and said that this is the basis of the establishment of the tribunal and the President replied that he was holding up the criminal law that was signed into law by the President.

The judge didn't even have the sense to open the book he was holding, and look at that criminal law and cite some of its provisions. That in my view— and I think the view of any criminal lawyer—is a travesty of justice. If you are brought before a criminal tribunal in this country, I hope that they will cite a provision of law that you have violated in any indictment or allegations against you.

I will not go through all of the due process rights. There are more than 20 rights that have been violated, but because of time, I just want to point out one or two important ones, particularly one that is important to myself as one of the counsel for the individual concerned, and that is the right to be able to have contact with a lawyer and not just any lawyer, not like in Guantanamo, where the state decides who your lawyers are.

I represent some individuals in Guantanamo Bay as well, and do you know what the Government told me? If I wanted to see those individuals, I have to sign an agreement stating that I would essentially tell the Government anything that was mentioned in my communications between them. That is an inappropriate manner for the government to respect somebody's right to legal counsel. This right requires a defendant be able to consult with legal counsel of his own choosing and to be able to consult in confidence, and to be able to facilitate a defense.

Seeing that the time is running out, let me just end here because as you can see, it takes quite a long time just to get through the basic principles being violated in this case—but let me just conclude by mentioning that it is not only Iraqis from whom we are setting a bad example by disrespecting or ignoring the rule of law, but it is important to all of you in this room, or at least those of you who are lawyers, because the law is based on respect for the law and respect for the rule of law for everybody equally. Thank you.

Professor Michael Scharf:

Let me begin by thanking Mr. Curtis Doebbler for coming to Cleveland this morning, braving the winds of the Chicago Airport to make it here for this nationally televised debate. We actually met on line after I had written a piece entitled "Can this Man Get a Fair Trial," which appeared in the Washington Post Outlook Section a few weeks ago. There was a Washington Post online discussion, in which Mr. Doebbler wrote, "Dear Michael: I have followed your online chat with interest, even encouraging some of my volunteers to participate. Rather than debate your many wrong or misleading statements on-line, I would like to invite you to debate me in person. Maybe the Washing Post would sponsor such a debate or maybe even your law school. As you undoubtedly are aware, I am one of the lawyers for Mr. Saddam Hussein, and I am intimately familiar with the proceedings in the case. Best regards, Curtis Doebbler."

I wrote back "Dear Curtis: I would enjoy very much a public debate with you. Would you have any interest in coming to Case Western Reserve University for such an event?" And here we are now.

The other thing I want to do is provide a disclaimer. Although I was one of five experts from around the world selected by the Department of Justice Regime Crimes Liaison Office in Baghdad to help train the IHT judges, I must stress I do not speak for the Iraqi High Tribunal or the Department of Justice, and I have not received any financial compensation for my assistance. I am assisting the IHT because I feel very strongly that this will be one of the most important trials of our lifetime, and I want to make sure that this trial complies fully with international human rights standards.

Now, let me begin by responding to Mr. Doebbler's attempt to link the issue of the validity of the invasion in 2003 with the question of the legitimacy of the Iraqi High Tribunal process.

First of all, the Security Council of the United Nations, representing all the countries in the world, recognized in Resolution 1546 that the occupation ended and the Iraqi Interim Government was sovereign as of June 30, 2004. It has recognized the legitimacy of the Iraqi Interim Government, as well as the process for democratic elections to be held at the end of this month. Further, in calling for accountability for violations of international humanitarian law, the Security Council made a distinction between what many countries feel was an unauthorized invasion and the issue of what to do next.

Secondly, if the democratically elected Government of Iraq approves the statute and the judges of this tribunal, there would be no issue of a violation of the Geneva Conventions because that would severe any argument that this was a statute and a court that was set up solely by an occupying Government. The new Iraqi Government could do this indirectly by approving the funding for the IHT and continuing its operations, including the construction of its facilities, the issuance of indictments, the conduct of investigations, and the commencement of trials.

And third, Mr. Doebbler's argument smacks of what is known in international law as the *tu quoque* defense. This is Latin for "you also." And it is a defense that the Nuremberg defendants raised sixty years ago; it is a defense Milosevic has raised at his trial before the Yugoslavia Tribunal in The Hague, and it is almost always raised by former leaders accused of war crimes. International courts have always dismissed this defense as invalid.

In doing so, they say it is true that in wars and in foreign affairs many countries violate international law, but when a tribunal is set up to prosecute defendants, the only question is: were these defendants guilty of the crimes charged? And the fact that opposing leaders may have also violated international law or committed war crimes does not excuse the guilt of these defendants. Therefore, the *tu quoque* defense is not a valid defense. It may resonate as a television sound bite, but legally, it doesn't hold water.

Now, with respect to judging the legitimacy of the Iraqi High Tribunal, there is international precedent that gives us a guide for making this determination and that comes out of the Yugoslavia Tribunal set up by the U.N. Security Council in 1993. In its first judgment, known as the *Tadic* case, the Tribunal ruled on whether it was validly established and what it means to be a legitimate tribunal. The Yugoslavia Tribunal focused on three criteria:

First of all, international law requires that a war crimes tribunal be established by a statute, not just executive fiat. There has to be some controlling document. Well, the Iraqi High Tribunal does have a statute. It is interesting to most people who have read that statute that it looks an awful lot like the statute of the Yugoslavia Tribunal and the Rwanda Tribunal.

Secondly, the Yugoslavia Tribunal said that to be legitimate a war crimes tribunal has to be independent from the executive and legislative branches. Now, according to the Iraqi High Tribunal, it is independent. The judges are specifically prohibited from taking direction from the Iraqi Government or U.S. Government. The president and the legislature of Iraq cannot control the Iraqi High Tribunal much like our legislature and president can't control our own courts.

For evidence that the IHT is independent in fact as well as on paper, I point out that Provisional Prime Minister Ayad Allawi, who is running for election, has been saying on the campaign trail that the trial of Saddam Hussein and Chemical Ali must start imminently. And there is quite a bit of pressure from him and others who would like to see these trials commence as soon as possible. But the Iraqi High Tribunal said "no, the trials cannot start because we do not yet have our rules of procedure; the defense counsel has not had time to prepare their case; and we will not and shall not be bullied by the executive branch because we are independent," proving, in fact, that the IHT meets the second criterion.

And third, the Yugoslavia Tribunal said that war crimes tribunals have to comply with fundamental norms of due process, which are enumerated in the Covenant on Civil and Political Rights, as Mr. Doebbler mentioned.

Next, Mr. Doebbler attacked the fairness of the Iraqi High Tribunal process, and I believe in assessing the fairness of any tribunal we have to ask three questions: First, are there fair procedures? Second, are there impartial judges? And third, is there equality of arms between the defense counsel and the prosecution?

With respect to the first of these factors, fair procedures, those are set out in Article 20 of the Iraqi High Tribunal statute, which is modeled on the Yugoslavia Tribunal statute and the Rwanda Tribunal statute. The due process protections include the presumption of innocence; the right to be informed promptly and in detail of the charges and to have adequate time and facilities to prepare a defense and to communicate freely with counsel of choice; the right to be tried without undue delay; the right to be present during trial and to appointment of counsel; the right to have counsel present during questioning; the right to examine and confront witnesses; the right against self-incrimination and not to have silence taken into account in determining guilt; and the right to disclosure by the Prosecution of exculpatory evidence, and witness statements; and the right to appeal. These rights will be further elaborated upon in the rules of procedure of the Iraqi High Tribunal, which should be coming out after the elections and very soon.

Next, with respect to impartial judges, Mr. Doebbler stressed that their identities have been kept secret. He mentioned that the only judge the world has seen is the one young judge, thirty-five year old Judge Ra'id, who presided over Saddam Hussein's televised hearing last July, and Mr. Doebbler alleged that Judge Ra'id's face was only shown because the footage leaked out.

Judge Ra'id is one of the judges I got to know best in London because he spoke fluent English. Judge Ra'id told me the story of how his image was released to the world during the July 1st hearing. He told me that he was given the option of having his face electronically blocked out and his voice distorted, but he and his colleagues were so committed to the perception of fairness, that they didn't want the IHT to be seen as the kind of hooded judges used in Chile and in Peru in the past that have been so criticized by human rights organizations.

So Judge Ra'id said he was willing to take the risk to his security to have his face shown to the world, and that the other judges throughout the trial will do the same, notwithstanding the fact that there are threats against them because they want to show the world how committed they are to fairness.

The judges who were selected by the Iraqi government and bar association range in age from thirty-five for Judge Ra'id, who despite his youth is extremely competent; all the way up to the mid-sixties. And most have between fifteen and twenty years experience on the bench.

Now, in London, we spent a lot of time going over the specific crimes of genocide, crimes against humanity, war crimes, and the crime of aggression because these are crimes that no national judges have experience with. Even the distinguished jurists selected by the U.N. to serve on the Yugoslavia Tribunal and the Rwanda Tribunal needed to attend training sessions to learn this unique area of the law.

And I learned through these training sessions and simulations that the IHT judges really grasped the nuances of this area of law. I also learned that they were very committed to the possibility of acquittal. They were very interested to learn that the Nuremberg Tribunal had acquitted three of the twenty-two major Nazi defendants tried after World War II, and several of the IHT judges said "if the prosecution doesn't prove its case, we will acquit because we think that will prove to the world how fair this tribunal is."

There is actually an advantage to having Iraqi judges as opposed to international judges preside in this case. There is a myth of Nuremberg and the other international tribunals that the target population will think international judges are more fair and an international tribunal's judgment more credible. In fact, the U.S. Government conducted opinion polls in Germany after Nuremberg that showed that most of the German people, 85 to 90 percent of them, thought that the Nuremberg trials were not legitimate, that the judges were not fair, and that the Nazi defendants, Goering et al., were not guilty.

One might be tempted to dismiss these numbers because Nuremberg represented a kind of victor's justice, since the judges were from the four allied nations: the U.S., the U.K., Russia, and France. What about the modern international war crimes tribunals? Well, the Yugoslavia Tribunal has experienced the same thing. During the trial of Slobodan Milsosevic, the Serb people have been polled, and they say overwhelmingly that Milosevic is not getting a fair trial, that these international judges are not fair, and they don't believe that Milosevic is guilty.

Now, if you ask the German people today if they believe in Nuremberg and the guilt of the Nazi leaders, they say, "yes," and there is some empirical data that suggests that these views changed in the 1960s at a point when the German people started having their own trials of the Nazis who had not been prosecuted at Nuremberg.

And this strongly suggests that Iraqi trials by Iraqi judges are most likely to convince the Iraqi people of the crimes of the Ba'athist regime—provided they are proven by credible evidence in an open and fair trial.

Another advantage of domestic trials is that they enable defendants to effectively subpoena witnesses, whereas Milosevic has not been able to compel witnesses to testify at his trial since the international tribunal lacks any type of constabulary.

Finally, let me turn to the question of equality of arms. The fact that distinguished lawyers like Mr. Doebbler and Ramsey Clark are on the defense team suggests that Saddam Hussein, if anything, has the stronger side representing him against the Iraqi prosecutors. I have no doubt that every single procedural issue that possibly can be raised will be raised by this superb defense team which consists of over twenty of the world's most prominent criminal lawyers.

Defense counsel will raise these issues in front of the five trial judges. They will raise them again in front of the nine appeals chamber judges, and Saddam Hussein will get his fair day in court. At the end of the day, if there is a mountain of evidence proved against him and a record is created like the twenty-two volumes appended to the Nuremberg judgment, I think history will look back and say that Saddam Hussein was fairly tried, although it was a tough case to try. I mean, obviously, when you are dealing with an Adolf Hitler, a Slobodan Milosevic, or a Saddam Hussein, these are especially tough cases to try fairly in the face of world public opinion. But the IHT, I believe, is capable of bending over backwards to maintain fairness, and the real challenge is going to be for it to convince the rest of the world that the trial of Saddam Hussein was fair. Thank you.

Professor Doebbler:

Thank you very much. There are so many things to reply to I don't know where to start because I think Mike has a very different understanding of the facts.

But I must congratulate you because some of these judges I and my colleagues have known for decades, and we are not able to evaluate their competence. After one week, you are able to determine that they will provide a fair trial. So I congratulate you sincerely on that foresight and ability to look into their minds.

I must say, though, I would rather have my little sister representing me if she was able to have access to me, to talk with me, to bring me law books, to be able to facilitate some sort of defense, then even a lawyer as prestigious as yourself, if they tied you up and shipped you off to Siberia and didn't give you any contact to me but merely said you are my lawyer, that doesn't help. It is not a matter of who represents the individual; it is a matter of being able to prepare a defense, and the first criteria for that is that you have access to the individual you represent.

And don't take my word for it that this is an unfair trial situation. Take the word of a High Commissioner for Human Rights of the United Nations, the word of the head of the tribunal right now, the chief prosecutor of the tribunal in The Hague, the word of Amnesty International, they have all said that.

I find somewhat whimsical this restatement, which constantly resurfaces from journalists and others, of this *tu quoque* defense. It only seems to be the other side that mentions it. Perhaps you want to raise that defense for us, but it is not something right now that is even being considered by the defense except to listen to it from the other side.

You may well have access to the judges. You may know who the judges are, but the point of due process is that—and the point of equality of arms, as you pointed out—is that the defense team and the defendant know these people and have access to them and have access to the evidence.

It is very possible that there are, as the U.S. has claimed, 35,000 tons of evidence available. But we have not seen one ounce of that evidence, and I wish that one of you are sometimes put in a position—or I should say—I wish you never to be put in a position of having to defend an individual when you have no access to that individual and no access to any of the evidence that is being used to allegedly prosecute—or maybe in this case the better word is persecute—that individual.

And finally, Michael raises the issue of polls. You know, before the Iraqi war, a poll that was done I believe by CNN—but you might correct me on that—said that most people in the world in the United States and outside, believed that American President George W. Bush was a greater threat to peace and security than Iraqi President Saddam Hussein. Maybe we have the wrong guy in the dock? Thank you.

A Timeline of the Dujail Trial

- March 20, 2003: US and coalition forces begin invasion of Iraq.
- April 2003: United States lists 55 most-wanted members of the former regime in the form of a deck of playing cards. Former Deputy Prime Minister/Foreign Minister Tarik Aziz is taken into custody.
- May 1, 2006: US announces the end of major combat operations in Iraq.
- July 13, 2003: US-led Occupational Authority known as the Coalition Provisional Authority (CPA) appoints a 25-member Governing Council of Iraqi leaders as a first step toward the reestablishment of sovereignty.
- December 10, 2003: With advice from the Coalition Provisional Authority, the Iraqi Governing Council promulgates the Statute for the Iraqi Special Tribunal.
- December 13, 2003: Saddam captured in a "spider hole" in Adwar, 10 miles south of his hometown of Tikrit.
- March 8, 2004: Iraqi Governing Council signs interim constitution known as the Law of Administration for the State of Iraq for the Transitional Period (TAL). Article 48(A) of the TAL provides that the Statute establishing the Iraqi Special Tribunal issued on 10 December 2003 is confirmed.
- May 28, 2004: The Iraqi Governing Council chooses Ayad Allawi as prime minister of the interim government.

- June 28, 2004: The Occupation Authority turns formal power over to Allawi's interim government. UN Security Council Resolution 1546 is adopted, recognizing that the interim government possesses full power and sovereignty of the State of Iraq. The record of debate on the resolution made it clear that the Security Council saw the transfer of power from the CPA to the Interim Government as the end of occupation.
- July 1, 2004: Saddam is arraigned before Judge Ra'id Juhi; he rejects charges of war crimes and genocide.
- Jan 30, 2005: Iraqis elect 275-seat National Assembly; Shiite Muslim-dominated party wins 48 percent of votes, Kurdish alliance 26 percent.
- March 29, 2005: The Iraqi National Assembly convenes.
- April 6, 2005: Lawmakers elect Kurdish leader Jalal Talabani as president, and Adel Abdul-Mahdi, a Shiite, and interim President Ghazi al-Yawer, a Sunni Arab, to serve as vice presidents. The next day, the President's council selects Shiite Arab Ibrahim al-Jaafari as prime minister.
- April 28, 2005: The new Iraqi government is approved by the Iraqi National Assembly.
- July 17, 2005: First criminal case is filed against Saddam Hussein, stemming from the 1982 massacre of dozens of Shiite villagers.
- August 10, 2005: The Iraqi National Assembly approves the Statute, Rules, and list of judges for the Iraqi High Tribunal (changing the name from Iraqi Special Tribunal).
- August 28, 2005: Constitutional committee signs draft charter, after long negotiations and over objections of many Sunni Arab leaders.
- October 15, 2005: Referendum on proposed constitution is held.
- October 19, 2005: Start of the Dujail trial. Saddam Hussein defiantly questioned the validity of the court before he and his seven co-defendants pleaded not guilty to charges of ordering the killing of 148 Shias from the village of Dujail. After just over three hours, the trial was adjourned until 28 November, to give the Defense time to prepare its case and to give the Prosecution time to ensure security for its witnesses.
- October 20, 2005: Saadoun Janabi, lawyer for co-defendant former judge Awad al-Bander, is seized from office and killed.
- November 8, 2005: Gunmen fire on car carrying Adil al-Zubeidi, who is killed, and Thamer Hamoud al-Khuzaie, who is wounded. Both are on team defending Saddam's half-brother Barzan al-Tikriti and former Vice-President Taha Yassin Ramadan.
- November 28, 2005: The trial reconvenes for a day, during which Saddam calls Americans "occupiers and invaders" and complains about treatment by his U.S. captors. The trial heard its first witness testimony, from a for-

mer Iraqi intelligence officer named Waddah al-Sheikh, who investigated the 1982 assassination attempt which triggered the alleged massacre in Dujail. In his testimony, taped before his recent death from cancer, Waddah al-Sheikh said hundreds of people were detained after the ambush in Dujail, which was estimated to have been carried out by between seven and 12 assailants. "They rounded up 400 people from the town—women, children and old men. Saddam's personal bodyguards took part in killing people," he said. "I don't know why so many people were arrested. [Barzan Ibrahim al-Tikriti] was the one directly giving the orders." Mr Sheikh noted that Saddam Hussein had decorated intelligence officers who had taken part in the operation. At least four defense lawyers failed to turn up and the trial was adjourned until 5 December so the defense team could replace two murdered lawyers.

• December 5, 2005: The trial resumes, but defense lawyers walk out when denied right to challenge court's legitimacy; chief judge Rizgar Amin then reverses itself and allows former U.S. Attorney General Ramsey Clark to speak.

• December 6, 2005: Five witnesses testify, including a woman identified as "Witness A," who was 16 at the time of the Dujail crackdown and tells of beatings and electric shocks by the former president's agents.

• December 7, 2005: Trial adjourns after a truncated session that Saddam refuses to attend, a day after yelling: "I will not come to an unjust court! Go to hell!"

• December 21, 2005: Saddam claims Americans beat and "tortured" him and other defendants and prays openly in court despite judge's order for trial to proceed. Two witnesses gave accounts of torture at the hands of the Iraqi security services and said Dujail had been attacked by helicopter gunships following the attempt to assassinate Saddam. One, referred to as Witness G, who gave evidence anonymously from behind a curtain, told the court that Saddam Hussein's half-brother Barzan al-Tikriti, had been present at the detention centre. "When I was being tortured, Barzan was sitting and eating grapes," he said. Defendant Barzan al-Tikriti interjected, "My hand is clean," he said, holding it up.

• December 22, 2005: Investigating Judge Ra'id Juhi reports that he saw no evidence to verify Saddam's claims that he was beaten while in U.S. custody. Three witnesses testified at a brief closed session, speaking from behind a curtain to conceal their identities. One, referred to as Witness H, said he was eight years old during the killings in Dujail. He said his grandmother, father and uncles had been arrested and tortured, and that he had never seen his male relatives again. Saddam Hussein addressed the Court to argue that the witness was too young at the time of the incident for his testimony to be reliable.

- January 15, 2006: Chief Judge Rizgar Amin submits his resignation after complaints by politicians and fficials that he failed to control court proceedings.
- January 23, 2006: Court officials name Ra'ouf Abdel-Rahman, another Kurd, to replace Amin. Amin's deputy, Saeed al-Hammash, is also replaced amid accusations he belonged to Saddam's former ruling Baath Party. Al-Hammash denies claims.
- January 24, 2006: Trial's scheduled resumption abruptly postponed for five days amid confusion over new judges and absence of witnesses.
- January 29, 2006: Trial resumes with a new no-nonsense judge, Raouf Abdel-Rahman, presiding. Defendant Barzan is ejected after refusing to keep quiet and calling the court "a daughter of a whore" Saddam Hussein is ejected from the courtroom after shouting "down with traitors" and "down with America." The defense walks out after a stormy exchange. The judge appointed four new defense lawyers to act as stand-by counsel.
- February 1, 2006: The trial resumed in the absence of the defendants and retained counsel, who were boycotting the trial. The Court said that the court-appointed stand-in defense counsel would serve as lawyers for the defense. The court heard from five prosecution witnesses, including a women who testified that she was arrested by Saddam Hussein's security forces and tortured in prison. She said she was stripped naked, hung by her feet and kicked repeatedly in the chest by the then intelligence chief Barzan al-Tikriti.
- February 2, 2006: The trial continued in the absence of the defendants and retained counsel, who were boycotting the trial. Two witnesses testified of acts of torture they endured
- February 13, 2006: Saddam Hussein caused uproar as he was forcibly returned to the court after having boycotted sessions with his seven co-defendants. He shouted slogans against the US and the new chief judge, Raouf Abdul Rahman, who he continued to insist must be removed on the grounds he was biased. Judge Rahman pressed on with the case. "The law states that if the defendants refuse to appear before the court, he will be forced to appear," he said. Two key former Saddam Hussein aides appeared as witnesses—the former head of Saddam Hussein's office, Ahmed Khudayir, and the former chief of foreign intelligence, Hassan al-Obeidi. Khudayir was shown a document, purported to contain his signature, which apparently showed Saddam Hussein had ratified killings at Dujail in 1982. Khudayir said: "I don't remember. I don't remember anything at all."
- February 14, 2006: Saddam Hussein announced he and his seven co-accused had been on hunger strike for three days in protest at the way the court was treating them. Saddam Hussein's half-brother Barzan Ibrahim

al-Tikriti appeared dressed in long underwear for the second day running to signal his rejection of the court. Two former intelligence officials appeared—one hidden behind a curtain, the other, Fadil Mohammed al-Azzawi speaking in open court. A former culture minister and personal aide to Saddam Hussein, Hamed Youssef Hamadi, also appeared. He was shown a piece of paper recommending rewards for six officials for their part in the Dujail arrests, bearing the hand-written word "agreed". Defendant Barzan al-Tikriti addressed the court, insisting that he had ordered the release of Dujail prisoners and had nothing to do with the massacre.

- February 28, 2006: Saddam Hussein's defense team makes its first appearance in a month after boycotting the trial on the grounds that the chief judge is biased. The team immediately calls for the chief judge and chief prosecutor to be removed and for the trial to be postponed. The chief judge refuses and two top defense lawyers walk out. Chief prosecutor Jaafar al-Moussawi presents a memo dated 16 June 1984. He says it contains the signature of Saddam Hussein approving the death sentences of 148 Iraqi Shias from the village of Dujail, where the ex-president survived an assassination attempt in 1982. Another document, dated two days earlier and announcing the death sentences, is signed by co-defendant Awad al-Bandar, Mr Moussawi alleges.

- March 1, 2006: The chief prosecutor presents more documents and letters that he claims implicate those on trial, including death certificates of nearly 100 Dujail villagers, as well as transfer orders showing how their families were sent into the desert and their properties seized. One letter reveals that four of the accused were executed by mistake, while two were released by mistake. Another shows that nearly 50 died during interrogation, rather than by hanging. In a dramatic turn, Saddam Hussein acknowledges he ordered trials that led to execution of dozens of Shi'ites in the 1980s but says he acted within the law. "Where is the crime?" he asks.

- March 12, 2006: Former Baath party official Mizhir Abdullah Ruwayyid appears in court to deny testimony by witnesses accusing him of helping round-up Dujail residents and demolish their property.

- March 13, 2006: Co-defendant Awad Hamad al-Bandar testifies on his own behalf. He acknowledges he sentenced 148 Shias from Dujail to death, but says this was done "in accordance with the law".

- March 15, 2006: The prosecution showed a letter, apparently signed by Defendant Barzon Tikriti, asking for several intelligence officials to be commended for their work in Dujail. In an address to the Court, Saddam Hussein praises the ongoing insurgency as "the resistance to the American invasion". After Saddam Hussein rejects the judge's warnings against using the trial as a political platform, the press is barred from the rest of the hearing.

- April 4, 2006: The Iraqi High Tribunal announces that Saddam will stand trial on new charges of genocide in the case called the Anfal campaign in which thousands of Kurds were killed in the late 1980s.
- April 5, 2006: The prosecution produces identification cards suggesting that 28 people whose executions the former Iraqi leader approved had been under 18—the minimum legal age for the death sentence under his rule. Meanwhile, a defense lawyer is ordered from the court by the judge when she tried to display photos of Iraqis tortured in US-run prisons.
- April 17, 2006: Handwriting experts say Saddam Hussein signed the death warrants for 148 Shias in Dujail in 1984, prosecutors claim. The prosecution reads out a report by experts who say the signature on the orders matches the writing of the former Iraqi leader, at the resumption of his trial. Defense lawyers claim the experts cannot be independent because they have links to Iraq's interior ministry, and call for a fresh set from abroad.
- April 19, 2006: Judge Ra'ouf Rahman announces that handwriting experts have concluded that signatures on documents—including the death warrants of Dujail villagers—did belong to Saddam Hussein.
- April 24, 2006: The prosecution plays a recording it says is of a telephone conversation between Saddam Hussein and former Iraqi Vice-President Taha Yassin Ramadan, discussing the destruction of farmland in Dujail. It also hears a report by more handwriting experts confirming the signatures of Saddam Hussein and six of his co-defendants on documents linking them to the crackdown on Shia villagers.
- May 15, 2006: At the conclusion of the Prosecution's case, the judges issue a formal charging document.
- May 16, 2006: All defendants appear in court, as witnesses testify in defense of four of the lesser-known defendants. Witnesses screened by a curtain testify that the defendants are good men and low-ranking officials with no responsibility or involvement in the killings in Dujail.
- May 24, 2006: Tariq Aziz, former Foreign Minister testifies on behalf of Saddam Hussein, saying the defendants cannot be guilty for the deaths of 148 men following a 1982 assassination attempt on Saddam Hussein because the state had a right to punish such an action. Saddam Hussein's director of personal security, Abed Hamid Mahmud, gives details of how the assassination attempt was made.
- May 29, 2006: Two defense witnesses testify on the fairness of the trial in which 148 Shia men from Dujail were sentenced to death over their alleged involvement in an assassination attempt against Saddam Hussein.

- May 30, 2006: A witness for the defense tells the court that 23 of the 148 Shia villagers said to have been executed over their alleged involvement in an assassination attempt against Saddam Hussein are in fact alive.
- May 31, 2006: One defense witness accuses the chief prosecutor of bribing him to give false testimony. The defense shows DVD footage to discredit a key prosecution witness.
- June 5, 2006: Saddam's defense team says 10 people out of 148 said to have been killed after the attempt on his life are still alive. The defense team also contests the authenticity of the documents presented in the case, demanding the trial to be halted to investigate its claims.
- June 12, 2006: Judge Ra'ouf Rahman announces that action has been taken against four witnesses who were arrested for falsely testifying that the prosecutor of trying to bribe them to give false evidence.
- June 19, 2006: In closing statements, prosecutors ask the judges to sentence Saddam Hussein, Barzan Tikriti, and Awad al-Bandar to death. The Prosecutor says that there is not enough evidence to convict one of the lesser defendants.
- June 21, 2006: Gunmen kidnap and kill Khamis al-Obaidi, the number two lawyer on Saddam's defense team. His body is found in the northern Ur area of Baghdad.
- July 10, 2006: Saddam and his defense counsel boycott the closing arguments to protest the security situation. Braking ranks with the other defense attorneys, lawyers for Abdullah Kazim Ruwayyid and his son Mizhar give their closing statements.
- July 11, 2006: Saddam and his defense counsel continue their boycott, forcing a two-week adjournment to give court-appointed lawyers time to prepare final arguments. The judge tells the lawyers the court is prepared to appoint its own lawyers to take their place, adding that they will harm their clients if they continue their boycott.
- July 24, 2006: Stand-by defense lawyers make closing arguments, and trial concludes.
- October 16, 2006: Judges announce their verdict.

PART III

EXPERT ANALYSIS OF DISCRETE ISSUES

Section 1: Issues Related to Establishment and Approach of the Tribunal

Does It Make Good Sense to Start with the Dujail Case, Rather Than a Greater Atrocity Like the Anfal Campaign?

By Michael P. Scharf

The Iraqi High Tribunal has decided to try Saddam Hussein and other former Ba'ath regime leaders in a series of cases, focusing on specific incidents, rather than in one mega trial like the Slobodan Milosevic case before the Yugoslavia Tribunal in The Hague. There are those who question the wisdom of trying Saddam Hussein for the incident at Dujail as the first case before the Iraqi High Tribunal. After all, only a few hundred people were killed there, and Saddam Hussein stands accused of murdering hundreds of thousands elsewhere. But I believe the decision to start with Dujail was brilliant for three reasons.

First, the evidence for the Dujail prosecution is extremely strong. Eye witnesses (both victims and members of the armed forces) are reportedly available to testify; forensic evidence has reportedly been collected and preserved; and video and documents reportedly exist which prove the atrocity, as well as who ordered it and how it was carried out. And it is far easier to prove the elements of a crime against humanity (the charge in the Dujail case), than the elements of genocide (the charge in the Anfal case).

Second, the Dujail case does not lend itself to as many defenses as the other charges do. If Saddam Hussein's lawyers argue that his subordinates acted without authority in Dujail, he can still be held responsible under the principle of command responsibility for failing to punish those subordinates for the atrocity. If the defense team argues that Saddam Hussein's actions were justified as self-defense in response to acts of terrorism, the prosecution can easily prove that his response (razing the town, executing the townspeople, and destroying the surrounding date palm groves) was disproportionate and therefore unjustifiable.

Finally, it makes a lot of sense to begin with a less important and less complex case because it will enable the Tribunal to focus on the broad legal challenges to the process which are brought by the defense. Once these are disposed of in the Dujail case, the principle of res judicata will prevent the Defense from re-litigating them in subsequent trials, enabling the Tribunal to focus entirely on the factual and legal complexities of those more difficult cases.

Does Saddam Hussein Have a Right to Represent Himself?

By Michael P. Scharf

Saddam does not have the right to represent himself. At the start of the Slobodan Milosevic trial before the International Criminal Tribunal for the Former Yugoslavia in February 2002, the presiding judge, Britain's Richard May, ruled that "under international law, the defendant has a right to counsel, but he also has a right not to have counsel." Judge May's ruling gave Milosevic the chance to make unfettered speeches throughout the trial. In contrast, a defendant is ordinarily able to address the court only when he takes the stand to give testimony during the defense's case-in-chief, and in the usual case, the defendant is limited to giving evidence that is relevant to the charges, and he is subject to cross examination by the prosecution. The decision to permit Milosevic to represent himself in court also affected the ability of the judges to control the dignity of the proceedings. As his own defense counsel, Milosevic has been able to treat the witnesses, prosecutors and judges in a manner that would earn ordinary defense counsel a citation or incarceration for contempt of court. In addition to regularly making disparaging remarks about the court and browbeating witnesses, Milosevic digresses at length during cross-examination of every witness, despite repeated warnings from the bench. Milosevic, who spends his nights at the tribunal's detention center, has no incentive to heed the judge's admonitions.

To the extent that he is playing not to the court of law in The Hague, but to the court of public opinion back home in Serbia, Milosevic's tactics are proving quite effective. The daily broadcasts of his trial (paid for by the U.S. Agency for International Development) have consistently ranked among the most popular television shows in Serbia. His approval rating in Serbia doubled during the first weeks of his trial. A poll taken half way through the trial found that thirty-nine percent of the Serb population rated Milosevic's trial performance as "superior," while less than twenty-five percent felt that he was getting a fair trial, and only thirty-three percent thought that he was actually responsible for war crimes. Milosevic has gone from the most reviled individual in Serbia to number four on the list of most admired Serbs, and in December 2003, Milosevic easily won a seat in the Serb parliament in a nation-wide election. The decision to permit Milosevic to represent himself has thus undermined one of the most important aims the Security Council sought to achieve in creating the Yugoslavia Tribunal: to educate the Serb people, who were long misled by Milosevic's propaganda, about the acts of genocide, crimes against humanity, and war crimes committed by his regime.

Like Milosevic, Saddam Hussein is also an attorney by training, with his law degree from the prestigious Cairo University. Taking a page out of Milosevic's play book, Saddam Hussein's legal staff is likely to file a pre-trial motion, asserting that Saddam Hussein has a right to represent himself before the IHT. Must the IHT grant Hussein's motion, thereby enabling Hussein to appear on the nightly news throughout the Middle East, riling against the illegal U.S. invasion of Iraq, insisting that the United States was complicit in Iraqi war crimes against Iran, and encouraging his followers to step up the acts of violence against the United States and new Iraqi government? The answer is no.

When the Iraqi Transitional National Assembly re-promulgated the IHT Statute on August 11, 2005, it replaced the clause from the December 10, 2003 version of the IHT Statute (Article 20(d)(4)) that had provided that the accused has a right "to defend himself in person or through legal assistance of his own choosing" with a new provision (Article 19(4)(d)) that states only that the accused has a right "to procure legal counsel of his choosing." Based on the Milosevic precedent, Saddam Hussein's lawyers are likely to argue that fundamental human rights law, enshrined in the Covenant on Civil and Political Rights, an international treaty to which Iraq is a party, requires that Hussein be allowed to represent himself, notwithstanding this change to the IHT Statute. Like the original wording of the IHT Statute, Article 14(3)(d) of the Covenant provides that a defendant has the right "to defend himself in person or through legal assistance of his own choosing." But the negotiating record of the Covenant indicates that the drafters' concern was with effective representation, not self-representation. Based on the negotiating record, distinguished commentators such as Cherif Bassiouni have concluded that "whenever it is in the best interest of justice and in the interest of adequate and effective representation of the accused, the court should disallow self-representation and appoint professional counsel." It is also significant that most civil law countries including France, Germany, Denmark, and Belgium, among others, require that defendants be represented by counsel in serious criminal cases. Interpreting the clause in the European Convention on Human Rights with the same language as Article 14(d)(3) of the Covenant, the European Court of Human Rights has affirmed the right of States to assign a defense against the will of the accused in the administration of justice.

Even if there is an international right to self-representation, it would be at most a qualified right. In its 1975 ruling in *Feratta v. California*, the U.S. Supreme Court held that there is a right to self-representation in U.S. courts, but that the "a right of self-representation is not a license to abuse the dignity of the courtroom." U.S. appellate courts have subsequently held that the right of self-representation is subject to exceptions—such as when the defendant acts in a disruptive manner or when self-representation interferes with the dignity or integrity of the proceedings (as would be the case with Saddam Hussein). Drawing on this precedent, in September 2004, the Yugoslavia Tribunal reversed Judge May's earlier ruling, and held instead that Milosevic had to have trial counsel for the remainder of his trial. In the Yugoslavia Tribunal's view: "If at any stage of a trial there is a real prospect that it will be disrupted and the integrity of the trial undermined with the risk that it will not be conducted fairly, then the Trial Chamber has a duty to put in place a regime which will avoid that. Should self-representation have that impact, we conclude that it is open to the Trial Chamber to assign counsel to conduct the defense case, if the Accused will not appoint his own counsel." This decision was affirmed by the Appeals Chamber of the Yugoslavia Tribunal in November 2004. Other international tribunals, including the Rwanda Tribunal in the *Barayagwiza* case and the Special Court for Sierra Leone in the Norman case have also assigned counsel over the objections of a defendant who wished to represent himself.

International Law requires that Saddam Hussein be afforded a fair trial, which can best be achieved by ensuring that he is vigilantly represented by distinguished legal counsel, not by permitting him to represent himself.[128]

Does Saddam Hussein Have a Right to Represent Himself?

By William Schabas

Inspired by the example of Slobodan Milosevic, Saddam Hussein may choose to represent himself in court. He seems to have no shortage of lawyers. One report says that as many as 2,000 attorneys claim to be retained. But Saddam is surely an intelligent and articulate advocate, and can probably do a competent job.

Article 14 of the International Covenant on Civil and Political Rights, the principal human rights treaty governing Iraq, a person accused of a criminal 'to defend himself in person or through legal assistance of his own choosing'. There can be no ambiguity about the text of this provision. However, in its rulings on the Milosevic case, the International Criminal Tribunal for the former Yugoslavia has held that this is not an unlimited right, and that there are implicit exceptions.

One exception, of course, is the defendant who disrupts the proceedings. This should not be confused with an accused who undertakes an aggressive and vigorous defense. But where a defendant does not comport in an appropriate manner, he or she may be removed from the courtroom. Really, the rule is no different whether the defendant is represented by counsel or not. Nor is it any different with respect to any other individual in the courtroom.

Assuming, for the sake of argument, that Saddam is mature enough to behave appropriately, are there any other grounds allowing the court to deny him the right of self-representation?

The ICTY seems to have endorsed the idea that an accused person's ill health, at a level rendering him or her unable to put in a full day's work, might be a good reason. However, in the Milosevic case the Appeals Chamber did not seem to think that the medical problems of the accused, which had reduced the pace of the trial significantly, were so important as to justify counsel being imposed. It seems unfair, indeed discriminatory, to deny the right of self-defense because of poor health, which is, in effect, a form of disability. Would a blind man be denied the right of self-defense? The ICTY Appeals Chamber found one isolated decision in the United States that denied the right of self-defense to a stuttering defendant.

The Special Court for Sierra Leone has also ruled that the right of self-defense can be denied in the interests of a speedy trial. This is only one of several questionable decisions by that body. The ICTY Appeals Chamber passed in silence over the Special Court's ruling; if it had anything positive to say about it, surely the judgment would have been mentioned.

There is no support in the case law for the proposition that an important accused, like Saddam Hussein or Slobodan Milosevic, forfeits the right of self-defense because of his or her position, although this idea seems to have been entertained by some academic writers. Their logic is hard to follow. If they are right, why doesn't it apply to the right to defense generally? After all, the accused is certainly required to instruct defense counsel. How does denying an important accused the right of self-defense differ from denying such a person the right of defense altogether?

The right of self-defense is set out unambiguously in article 14 of the International Covenant, and any limitations have been applied very strictly by the ICTY Appeals Chamber. So while Saddam Hussein might forfeit this right by behaving inappropriately, as long as he follows the rules the right can't be taken away from him.

I have never believed the tired old saw about a man who defends himself having a fool for a client. Saddam Hussein knows the facts and the issues. No person can be more familiar with the case and the charges. He may well prove to be his best lawyer. Good luck to him!

Should the Saddam Hussein Trial Be Televised?

By Christopher M. Rassi

My first thought was that Saddam Hussein's trial should not be televised for fear of taking away from the seriousness of the trial and making it seem like entertainment, especially at a time when Iraqis are concerned about survival and building their country. However, if it is not televised, the Iraqi High Tribunal ("IHT") could be taking away from the importance of his trial as it can serve several important functions in the transition to democracy and the rule of law in Iraq. The strongest arguments not to televise the trial have led me to believe that it should in fact be transmitted across the country and the Middle East. If the IHT is to have a positive effect on the new Iraq, the trial of Saddam Hussein must be perceived by the Iraqi people and those around the Middle East as legitimate and fair. Only time will tell if this will happen, but assuming that it can be portrayed as such by Iraqis from the outset is unrealistic unless Iraqis are involved in the whole process, and aware of all developments surrounding the trial. As such, the IHT Trial Chamber should permit the broadcasting of the trial under Rule 50 of the Rules of Procedure and Evidence.

At first glance, one would think that the IHT should take a page from the Milosevic trial in deciding whether to televise the Saddam Hussein trial. On the surface, a lesson from the televised trial of the former Yugoslav president is that a televised trial in a country that is still recovering from massive destruction can make viewers believe that the trial is not going as planned, and shift the blame from those being tried to those that caused much of the current destruction and plight. Milosevic's antics in court and his accusations played on Serbs back home watching the trial.

However, it should be noted that the Saddam Hussein trial does not have the same inherent shortcoming of the Milosevic trial. The Judges can continue to maintain decorum in the courtroom. Unlike the televised trial of Milosevic at the International Criminal Tribunal for the former Yugoslavia in The Hague, the trial of Saddam Hussein has the potential to be civilized from the outset. With attorneys present, the Judges at the IHT will not have to deal with Saddam Hussein personally making a mockery of the court room in his treatment of the witnesses, prosecutors, and themselves in a manner that would earn ordinary defense counsel expulsion from the courtroom. Also due to the presence of attorneys, the Judges will be able to keep Saddam Hussein from making disparaging remarks about the IHT.

When it comes down to it, broadcasting the trial appears the honest and most reliable method for legitimizing the IHT with Iraqis. The media will be flooding the trial and will portray the proceedings in their own way, with their own bias. Limiting the video clips chosen by the IHT media office to snippets of the trial on the news can be seen by Iraqis and those in the Middle East as attempts to portray propaganda—after all, how could everyone know what is really taking place when only televised portions and highlights are released. Rules 48 ("the arrangements of protecting the victims and the witnesses) and 51 ("closed sessions") offer safeguards to protect against the presence of broadcast media, as well as any other type of media, in the most sensitive and secret of proceedings.

Much depends on whether the IHT is seen as legitimate by the Iraqis, and the rest of the world. There is too much at stake not to have it televised around the country, and around the Middle East, this early in the process. Let us not forget that although prosecutors will pin prime responsibility on Saddam Hussein and other top Ba'ath figures, and disclose the way the Iraqi armed forces and security services were compelled to commit war crimes and crimes against humanity against foreign nationals and Iraqi citizens alike, Iraqis faced much devastation as a result of the occupation, even up until today. The IHT will not address these plights. The IHT will not address the legality of the occupation. But what the trial will do is broadcast in the region what the people of Iraq suffered through the regime of Saddam Hussein. As such, even though the trial might not vindicate the occupation and the tragedy that resulted from the war, it might nonetheless facilitate national reconciliation in the short term. There is a need to document the mass scale of these atrocities and share it with the rest of the country. This might not, in the eyes of Iraqis, justify the American invasion and diminish support for opposition groups which continue to wage a guerilla war against U.S. and other foreign troops and officials stationed in Iraq, but every Iraqi should be informed about the trial. It is vital that the Iraqi people be convinced that the IHT is fair and impartial.

Should the Saddam Hussein Trial Be Televised?

By Michael P. Scharf

When I met with the IHT judges in London in October 2004 as one of the expert trainers enlisted by the Regime Crimes Liaison Office, we discussed the issue of televising the Saddam Hussein trial. I cautioned the judges that there were many risks associated with televising a major criminal trial, as can be seen in the cases of Slobodan Milosevic and O.J. Simpson, but the judges seemed generally to favor televising their proceedings.

The judges felt that public support for the IHT would be enhanced through television cameras in the courtroom by showing the Iraqi people a fair judicial process and exposing them to the evidence submitted to the Court. Rule 50 of the Revised IHT Rules of Evidence and Procedure (August 2005), provides that broadcasting the IHT's proceedings is prohibited unless the IHT Trial Chamber specifically rules that it is permitted. The decision whether to televise the Saddam Hussein trial will thus not be made until the beginning of the trial.

The use of television cameras in U.S. courtrooms has also been the subject of much debate and controversy. In the 1965 case of Estes v. Texas, the U.S. Supreme Court ruled that the Sixth Amendment right to a public trial does not mean that a trial should be televised. While U.S. Federal Courts to this day do not permit the televising of criminal trials, several state courts have experimented with televised trials with mixed results. For example, the presence of broadcast media can inhibit witnesses from testifying, thereby, impairing the ability of the prosecution and defense from obtaining evidence; cameras encourage some judges and lawyers to play to the cameras, creating a celebrity status for them and thus depriving defendants of effective counsel and fair and impartial decisions by judges; and heightened public clamor resulting from television coverage will inevitably result in prejudice.

The record of televising international war crimes trials has also been mixed. Slobodan Milosevic played to the cameras throughout his trial and his dramatic courtroom antics have garnered him admiration in Serbia. In the Media Trial before the Rwanda Tribunal, the presiding judge had to go to extraordinary lengths to suppress the dramatic antics of defense counsel who was playing to the broadcast media.

To avoid these problems, rather than televise the Saddam Hussein trial gavel to gavel, the IHT Press Office should release daily televised highlights of the trial to the media pool. And at the end of the trial, a documentary should be produced by the IHT with extensive footage from the trial, so that a video record of the case can be made available to the Iraqi public in an easily accessible form.

The IHT Should Consider Appointing Foreign Judges to Enhance the Legitimacy and Capacity of the Court

By Laura A. Dickinson

The Iraqi High Tribunal is poised to begin some of the most important war crimes trials of this century, both for Iraq and the world at large. Whatever one may think about the legality and morality of the Iraq war, it is difficult to dispute that Saddam Hussein and his associates should be brought to trial for the widespread atrocities they are accused of having committed. Criminal prosecutions have the potential not only to adjudicate individual responsibility, but also to create a historical record, to send a message that Iraq is committed to the rule of law, and to pave the way for broader societal healing. Yet these worthy goals are imperiled by the ongoing conflict in the country, by the real risks such conflict poses to the courageous judges who have stepped forward to serve on the tribunal, and by concerns that the tribunal will not be independent or impartial. It is my view, therefore, that the Iraqi government should seriously consider exercising its authority under the IHT statute to appoint foreign judges in order to enhance the legitimacy and capacity of the court, and thereby fulfill its promise as a "hybrid" domestic-international court.

Iraq chose to create a "hybrid" domestic-international court to address the atrocities committed during the regime of Saddam Hussein. Some policy-makers and scholars had argued that only a purely international tribunal—composed entirely of foreign judges trying cases under international law in a courtroom safely outside the territory of Iraq—could mete out fair justice in the Iraqi cases. Others had suggested that a domestic court was more appropriate, in order to enable Iraqi participation in the process and to prevent any overtones of imperialism. Yet in the end Iraq chose create a hybrid of the two, a court that has some international and some domestic components (although to be sure, in its current structure it more closely resembles a domestic court). For example, the court has the authority to apply both domestic and international law. In addition, the IHT Statute requires the appointment of international advisors, who will advise the judges and prosecutors on international law and will "monitor" the Tribunal's observance of due process principles. The Statute includes no formal role for the United Nations, but the judge who serves as President of the Tribunal may request assistance from the U.N. in appointing the non-Iraqi experts. And while the judges of the court are currently all Iraqi nationals, the Statute provides that the government can appoint non-Iraqi judges if such a move is deemed "necessary." The court thus resembles, and has the capacity to resemble even more closely, a growing number of hybrid domestic-international courts around the world—from East Timor, to Sierra Leone, to Kosovo, to Cambodia—that hold special promise in the adjudication of war crimes.

Scholars and policy-makers have paid less attention to hybrid domestic-international courts than to purely international or purely domestic tribunals, but such courts offer distinct advantages. Such courts are "hybrid" because both the institutional apparatus and the applicable law consist of a blend of the international and the domestic. Foreign judges sit alongside their domestic counterparts to try cases prosecuted and defended by teams of local lawyers working with those from other countries. This hybrid model has developed in a range of settings, generally post-conflict situations where no politically viable full-fledged international tribunal exists, as in East Timor or Sierra Leone, or where an international tribunal exists but cannot cope with the sheer number of cases, as in Kosovo. Most recently, an agreement to create a hybrid court in Cambodia has been reached. Because of their hybrid character, such courts have special advantages in gaining legitimacy among multiple populations, as well as in promoting capacity-building and the rule of law.

With respect to legitimacy—which I am here defining quite broadly to mean those factors that tend to make the decisions of a juridical body acceptable to various populations observing its procedures "on the ground"— hybrid courts have advantages over purely domestic tribunals on the one hand, and purely international tribunals on the other. Not surprisingly, the perceived legitimacy of domestic judicial institutions in post-conflict situations is often in question. To the extent that such institutions exist at all, they typically will have suffered severely during the conflict. The physical infrastructure often will have sustained extensive, crippling damage, and the personnel is likely to be severely compromised or lacking in essential skills. Judges and prosecutors may remain in place from the prior regime, which may have backed the commission of widespread atrocities. Thus, the state may continue to employ the very people who failed to prosecute or convict murderers or torturers or ethnic cleansers. Alternatively, the new regime may replace the old personnel almost completely, resulting in an enormous skill and experience deficit, as well as the danger of show trials and overly zealous prosecution for past crimes. At the same time, broad acceptance of purely international processes may be difficult to establish as well. For example, in light of the continuing ethnic tensions within the region, the ICTY was established at the Hague, far removed from the scene of the atrocities, and the court was staffed by international judges and staff. However, the lack of connection to local populations has been problematic.

Hybrid courts can solve some of these legitimacy problems. In Kosovo and East Timor, the addition of international judges and prosecutors to cases involving serious human rights abuses may have enhanced the perceived legitimacy of the process, at least to some degree. In both contexts, the initial failure of U.N. authorities to consult with the local population in making governance decisions generally, and decisions about the judiciary specifically, sparked public outcry. Thus, in both Kosovo and East Timor the appointment of foreign judges to domestic courts to sit alongside local judges and the appointment of foreign prosecutors to team up with local prosecutors helped to create a framework for consultation.

The appointment of international judges to the local courts in these highly sensitive cases may also have helped to enhance the perception of the independence of the judiciary. In Kosovo this was most apparent, as the previous attempts at domestic justice had failed to win any support among Serbs. Indeed, Serbian judges refused to cooperate in the administration of justice, and the verdicts in the cases tried by ethnic Albanians were regarded by the ethnic Serbian population as tainted. In contrast, the verdicts of the hybrid tribunals garnered considerable support, even among Serbs.

As compared to purely domestic and purely international institutions, hybrid courts may also better promote local capacity-building, which is often an urgent priority in post-conflict situations. The conflicts in Kosovo and East Timor virtually eliminated the physical infrastructure of the judiciary, including court buildings, equipment, and legal texts. But even more devastating than the physical loss was the loss in human resources. In Kosovo, only Serbs had the experience and training to work as judges and prosecutors; yet these Serbs often refused to work in the new system because doing so would constitute a betrayal of their ethnic heritage. There were some Albanians with legal training, but they had been almost completely excluded from the system for many years and therefore had little experience. In East Timor, the capacity deficit was even more severe because the Indonesians, who had staffed the judiciary had evacuated, and few Timorese possessed any legal training or experience. Yet a purely international process that largely bypasses the local population does little to help support local capacity.

The hybrid process thus offers advantages in the arena of capacity-building as well. The side-by-side working arrangements allow for on-the-job training that is likely to be more effective than abstract classroom discussions of formal legal rules and principles. And the teamwork can allow for sharing of experiences and knowledge in both directions. Foreign actors have the opportunity to gain greater sensitivity to local issues, local culture, and local approaches to justice at the same time that local actors can learn from foreign actors. In addition, hybrid courts can serve as a locus for international funding efforts, thereby pumping needed funds into the rebuilding of local infrastructure.

In view of the potential threats to the IHT's legitimacy, both inside and outside Iraq, the Iraqi government should seriously consider drawing from the lessons of the other hybrid courts and further develop the IHT's hybrid character. Specifically, by appointing foreign judges, the Iraqi government might enhance perceptions, both within Iraq and in the broader international community, of the court's independence. Specifically, the addition of foreign judges might serve as a shield for the domestic judges, as was the case in Kosovo, and help to create a sense of each panel's neutrality as to all ethnic groups within Iraq. At the same time, the appointment of foreign judges with experience in international human rights or humanitarian law might provide a welcome infusion of expertise in these areas, while at the same time offer opportunities for these experts to develop knowledge of Iraqi law and Iraqi approaches to these issues.

Thus, by taking advantage of the potentially hybrid nature of the court, the IHT could both lend greater legitimacy to its process and help build the expertise and capacity of the local Iraqi justice sector. And, to combat any potential nationalist fears about the imposition of "western" justice on Iraqis, the foreign judges might be drawn from Arab or Muslim countries. For example, judges or lawyers involved in recent human rights trials in Indonesia might be willing to serve. And while making the court a true hybrid is obviously not a panacea, I believe it would place the IHT and the emerging Iraqi justice system on firmer footing than it is today.

Sex Matters: The Invisibility of Women at the Iraqi Tribunal[129]

By Simone Monasebian

> *"This is a man's world*
> *This is a man's world*
> *But it wouldn't be nothing*
> *Nothing without a woman or a girl."*

"It's A Man's Man's World", James Brown, 1964

Shortly after the fall of Saddam Hussein, United Nations Security Council Resolution 1483,[130] affirmed "the need for accountability for crimes and atrocities committed by the previous Iraqi regime." The same Resolution pledged to affirm gender equality in the rule of law. I suppose it sounded like a good idea at the time.

Hopes that Iraq's recovery and reconstruction would create new opportunities for women, were at first only minimally realized. While coalition officials did meet with women's groups to hear their demands for a postwar Iraq, not enough was done in the early days of the occupation to address the needs of Iraqi women or include them in discussions about Iraq's future.[131] The legal team appointed by the coalition to excise Hussein's anti-human rights amendments to Iraq's 1969 legal code was made up exclusively of male lawyers and judges.[132] The United States Department of State noted that the participation of women in the postwar reconstruction process had been inadequate.[133] In July 2003, hundreds of women demonstrated in Baghdad, demanding inclusion in shaping the political future of their country.

Today, some 100 days after the opening of what has been characterized as the "trial of the century", little, if anything, is said or written about the invisibility of women in a Y chromosome courtroom—devoid of women judges, prosecutors, and defense attorneys.[134] And so I feel constrained to ask: Is this a man's world?

In a tribunal funded to the tune of over $138 million dollars, and represented as an example of the best a New Iraq has to offer its people, it seems the only acceptable role for women in the courtroom has been that of victim. This, despite Iraq's long tradition of women in public life, dating back to the monarchy, and continuing into the Saddam years.

Although women have played important roles in Saddam's Iraq, his regime is alleged to have systematically used rape for political purposes.[135] Like its predecessors in The Hague, and Africa, the Iraqi tribunal is empowered to try such crimes of sexual and gender violence.[136] And as the first woman to appear in the Iraqi court recounted having been forced to take off her clothes by a security agent, beaten and then tortured with electric shocks,[137] I wondered about the message a male only war crimes tribunal sends.

Holding perpetrators of mass violations against women accountable for their acts has been a slow and tortuous process. It remains to be seen whether the Iraqi tribunal will seriously prosecute these types of widespread and systematic crimes against women in the post-Dujail cases. Experience has shown that including women judges in war crimes tribunals makes a difference. Elizabeth Odio-Benito, one of the first female judges at the International Criminal Tribunal for the former Yugoslavia (ICTY) recounted her experience there as follows:

"About one year after the tribunal was set up, we faced the first public appearance of the Court. I was one of the three judges in this trial. I noticed that rape and sexual violence were absent in the indictment. This being my first experience as a judge, I did not always behave in the traditional way. I pointed out the necessity to examine crimes of rape and sexual violence. Everybody was very shocked by this. But soon they learned that this would be very successful. Sexual violence started to appear among the charges."[138]

Navanethem Pillay, the first female judge at the International Criminal Tribunal for Rwanda (ICTR), who went on to become the first woman President of that Court, has argued that:

"Who interprets the law is at least as important as who makes the law, if not more so … I cannot stress how critical I consider it to be that women are represented and a gender perspective integrated at all levels of the investigation, prosecution, defense, witness protection and judiciary."[139]

And what of Judge Pillay's statement that sex matters? We know that rape and sexual violence in Rwanda was first prosecuted in the ICTR because of her. In the now landmark case of Prosecutor v. Akayesu, Pillay, the only woman judge at the ICTR at the time, pursued an inquiry into rape with two women called by the prosecutor to testify to other crimes. It was only because of her intervention that the prosecution eventually amended their charges to include sexual violence counts. The Akayesu case became "[t]he first judgment to recognize rape and sexual violence as constitutive acts of genocide, and the first to advance a broad definition of rape as a physical invasion of a sexual nature, freeing it from mechanical descriptions and required penetration of the vagina by the penis. The judgment also held that forced nudity is a form of inhumane treatment, [footnote omitted] and it recognized that rape is a form of torture and noted the failure to charge it as such under the rubric of war crimes. [footnote omitted]."[140]

Learning a great deal from the successes and failures of the ICTR and ICTY, the Statute of the International Criminal Court requires fair representation of women judges, and, that, in the selection of judges, prosecutors and other staff, the need for legal expertise on violence against women or children must be taken into account.[141] Such requirements recognize "the significance of crimes against women, and the need for expertise at every level to ensure these crimes are effectively investigated and prosecuted. To achieve this it is imperative that individuals with expertise in the investigations and prosecutions of gender crimes are recruited by the Court."[142]

While including women in positions of power does not guarantee sensitivity to issues of gender justice, the experience of women in this respect should not be discounted. Nor should we underestimate the positive impact that women in the courtroom would have on Iraqis and their neighbors. As Shirin Ibadi, the first woman from a Muslim country to be awarded the Nobel Peace Prize, noted in her 2003 acceptance speech:

"Undoubtedly, my selection will be an inspiration to the masses of women who are striving to realize their rights, not only in Iran but throughout the region—rights taken away from them through the passage of history. This selection will make women in Iran, and much further a field, believe in themselves. Women constitute half of the population of every country. To disregard women and bar them from active participation in political, social, economic and cultural life would in fact be tantamount to depriving the entire population of every society of half its capability."

Including women in positions of power at the various war crimes tribunals set up through the UN made a difference on daily basis. I have no doubt that my experience as a prosecutor at the ICTR was shaped for the better by the presence of powerful women leading that tribunal. I also saw firsthand the effect this had on the women who testified. Insuring that Iraqi women play a prominent role in their own tribunal could go a long way towards their acceptance and inclusion in other sectors of the New Iraq. Today, Rwanda leads the world as having more women parliamentarians than any other country. I wish the same for my Iraqi sisters.

We say it is important for the "Iraqi people" to be seen meting out justice to their own, in a court of their own, but the term "Iraqi people" has become a euphemism for "Iraqi men." In a Court where the cast of male characters is ever changing due to death, injury, boycotts, firing, resignation and the like, consideration should be given to finally bringing a woman into the fold. For those who may say "Iraq is not ready for this", my Iraqi sisters ask, "if not now then when." Must it always be "women and children last?" Gender parity and justice is never convenient.

A February 2005 Amnesty International report titled "Iraq: Decades of Suffering, Now Women Deserve Better" explains "the many ways in which women and girls in Iraq have suffered from government repression and armed conflict in disproportionate or different ways from men, and also how they have been targeted as women. It also shows how discrimination is closely linked to violence against women, and the particular ways in which women have suffered from the breakdown in law and order in many parts of the country since the overthrow of Hussein." Now more than ever, it is important that we include women in powerful roles. After decades of suffering, the women of Iraq deserved a prominent place in bringing the Hussein regime to justice. We often justify the controversial hundreds of millions we spend on war crimes courts by arguing that they are not just about punishment; but also about creating a reliable historical record; facilitating reconciliation; and, inspiring the population with exemplary justice—a model of a fair court to which others may aspire and replicate. A womanless court falls short of that mark.[143]

What if a Different U.S. Strategy Had Built a Different Court for Iraq?

By David Scheffer

The trials of former Iraqi President Saddam Hussein and many of his regime's top officials will demonstrate whether the Bush administration's judicial strategy for post-war Iraq is likely to work. Will it compensate for an intervention and occupation that so boldly challenged fundamental principles of international law? I need not make the case for how serious the situation is in Iraq today or how the U.S. performance there might fare with any reasonable cost-benefit analysis or scrutiny under the law of war (particularly with respect to detainees). But it is fair to ask whether in the realm of rule of law challenges a different judicial and Security Council strategy could have been pursued prior to Operation Iraqi Freedom in March 2003. After all, an alternative U.S. strategy, particularly with respect to accountability for atrocity crimes (genocide, crimes against humanity, serious war crimes, aggression), had developed steadily during the Clinton Administration, from 1993 through 2000. So I will indulge in a "what if" exercise on accountability. The Iraqi experience of recent years desperately needs such an alternative perspective—a Plan B, if you will—so that we might better understand the merits and flaws of current policies.

Imagine where we would be today if, in September 2002 when President George W. Bush challenged the United Nations General Assembly to be "relevant" and confront Iraq's alleged non-compliance with Security Council resolutions, particularly those pertaining to weapons of mass destruction (WMDs), he had coupled that challenge with a far more persuasive evidentiary case: the quarter century record of the Iraqi regime's alleged atrocity crimes against its own people and other countries. Bush had the standing and leverage at that moment in history to achieve what had been a critical goal of the Clinton Administration and should have been pursued (despite all of Bush's "anything but Clinton" policies) with the changing of the guard in January 2001.

The critical moment in history had arrived when President Bush stepped up to the podium of the UN General Assembly on September 12, 2002, to seek Security Council action on Iraq. I contended then and I would maintain today that the stars were aligned on that day to achieve the objective we, with strong bipartisan support, had spent almost eight years of the Clinton Administration striving to build support for among key governments. President Bush, who made reference to the alleged atrocities of the Iraqi regime but focused his call for action on Iraq's disarmament obligations under Security Council resolutions, could have called on the Security Council to create immediately a powerful international criminal tribunal to investigate, indict, and when possible apprehend and bring to trial those officials of the Iraqi regime responsible for atrocity crimes. Branding properly investigated Iraqi officials as indicted fugitives of an international criminal tribunal would have done far more to isolate and discredit them (both internally and abroad) than any political condemnation from western capitals or the United Nations on what has proven to be a false reading of any WMD threat from Iraq.

There likely would have been support for such an initiative during the fall of 2002 when Security Council members were prepared to get tough with Baghdad, but wanted the basis for their action to be both credible and lawful and to be viewed as such by the public. With American and British military intervention looming, France and Germany could have pointed to the judicial cases unfolding against Iraqi officials as the stronger basis to support ultimate action to replace the regime, particularly after a further phase of WMD inspections. The legal memoranda prepared by lawyers in the British Government in 2002 and early 2003, reported in recent months, might have read somewhat differently if there had been a basis in law to apprehend Iraqi officials indicted by an international criminal tribunal established under UN Charter Chapter VII authority. The U.S. Congress, which had long sought the indictment of Saddam Hussein, might have strengthened the use of force authorization in the much-debated language of the Authorization for Use of Military Force Against Iraq Resolution of 2002 by including a law enforcement component to it, drawing, in fact, on prior Congressional resolutions seeking to bring Saddam Hussein to justice. The preparation for judicial investigations and prosecutions would have been much further advanced and strengthened with international participation and support by the time of an intervention than proved to be the case once the largely American cast of investigators finally began their work in earnest during the occupation.

By September 2002 the evidence of atrocities was significant and far more convincing than all the so-called intelligence about suspected WMD capabilities. It was remarkable following the March 2003 intervention when journalists, the Coalition Provisional Authority, the White House, and the Pentagon reported the discovery of mass graves and torture chambers as if these had never been anticipated and the allegedly criminal actions of the Iraqi regime were being exposed thanks to the Anglo-American intervention. Anyone who worked the Iraq account during the 1990's had reason to believe that torture chambers existed and that mass graves had to dot the landscape of Iraq to account for the reported hundreds of thousands of victims of the regime during the 1980's and 1990's. The real question was where the torture chambers and mass graves would be located and how many bodies of what identity would be found within the graves. The discovery of such sites is important as evidence for trials and for the historical record in Iraq, but the discoveries themselves should have nothing to do with ex post facto justifications for the intervention.

Whatever evidence of atrocity crimes might have justified—at least to some—a humanitarian intervention or law enforcement intervention into Iraq in 2003 already existed on the public record at the time. The critical issue would have been, if raised, whether there was sufficient political will to rely, to a significant degree, on that kind of evidence backed up by the investigations of an international criminal tribunal rather than only WMD suspicions to authorize military action. The political will to act based on the extensive record of atrocity crimes as the target of an international criminal tribunal and some of which reportedly were continuing in Iraq, may not have emerged by March 2003. However, the international tribunal's mandate and initial investigations might have provided the additional justification to garner enough Security Council support (or acquiescence) for an alternative path, proposed by (non-permanent Security Council member) Chile in early March 2003, to give the UN weapons inspectors a final though limited opportunity to complete their work within a deadline set by the Council, failing which coalition action would have been authorized.

Perhaps that is too much of a "what if" stretch. But in my view the alternative U.S. strategy should have been to seize the day in September 2002 to build the court that would have created a law enforcement context for the Security Council's further deliberations on Iraq and its WMD capabilities. The debate in the Council and the final Anglo-American decision to intervene relied instead on a fundamentally flawed WMD assessment of Iraq. It was only in the aftermath when, several months later and lacking any WMD discoveries, the alleged criminal character of the Iraqi regime emerged in Bush Administration briefings as a growing and perhaps primary rationale for the intervention, as if such news was a discovery we should all credit to the intervention and occupation, and then somehow deduce that it was the rationale all along for Operation Iraqi Freedom.

So "what if" an international criminal tribunal on Iraq had been established by the Security Council? It could have been structured to include significant participation by Iraqi judges, prosecutors, investigators, and defense counsel following the intervention. It could have authorized that trials ultimately to be held or continued in Iraq when the security situation permitted. It could have attracted technical and financial support from Europe, Latin America, and the United Nations rather than be dependent on the support of one of the occupation powers, the United States. It would have been independent of any meddling domestic political influence or perceptions of victor's justice.

But "what if" is a strictly historical perspective. The Iraqi High Tribunal is here to stay and it deserves the best efforts of all who are invested in its pursuit of justice.

Legitimacy of the August 11, 2005 Revised Iraqi High Tribunal Statute

By Christopher M. Rassi

The Iraqi Governing Council promulgated the Statute of the Iraqi High Tribunal (the "IHT") on December 10, 2003 (the "2003 Statute"). On March 8, 2004 the Iraqi Governing Council promulgated the Law of Administration for the State of Iraq for the Transitional Period (the "TAL"). The TAL, established by the Iraqi Governing Council before the restoration of Iraqi sovereignty, is Iraq's Interim Constitution and preserves and continues the 2003 Statute in force and effect. Article 48 of the TAL confirms the 2003 Statute as "issued on 10 December 2003." It also declares that the 2003 Statute "exclusively defines the [IHT's] jurisdiction and procedures, notwithstanding the provisions of [the TAL.]"

On August 11, 2005, the Transitional National Assembly instituted a revised Statute for the IHT (the "2005 Statute") which abrogated in full the 2003

Statute. Despite the TAL's Article 48, the Iraqi Transitional Government has the power to replace the 2003 Statute with a revised Statute without amending the TAL itself. The TAL only confirmed the 2003 Statute, and refers back to the 2003 Statute itself for exclusive interpretive authority, which gives power to the new elected Government of Iraq. Article 37 of the 2003 Statute states that "[t]he Governing Council or the Successor Government has the powers to establish other rules and procedures in order to implement this [2003] Statute." Article 32 of the 2003 Statute further states that "[t]he powers conferred on the Governing Council in this Statute shall be transferred to the executive authority in any future government (the "Successor Government") established following the disbanding of the Governing Council." Not only did the Transitional National Authority have the Constitutional power to replace the Statute, but this act lends legitimacy to the very institution of the IHT. Commentators have questioned the legitimacy of the IHT, which was initially created and designed by occupiers and an unelected government. The 2005 Statute, established by the Transitional National Assembly, should alleviate the fears of those that believe that the IHT is not the work and will of the elected Iraqi Government. Further, such an act ensures that the IHT will continue to operate even though its founding Government has been replaced.

Should Saddam Hussein Be Exposed to the Death Penalty?

By Michael Newton

The people of Iraq have a legal and moral right to build a structure for the prosecution of the leading figures in the Ba'athist regime, and the sovereign government representing those people has every right under international law to preserve preexisting Iraqi laws that permit the imposition of the death penalty. Both international human rights law and occupation law explicitly permit the imposition of capital punishment provided that the judicial process comports with recognized standards of justice. The Statute of the Iraqi High Tribunal will be implemented against the backdrop of Rules of Procedure that have been carefully calibrated to mesh with the provisions of Iraqi procedural law to produce such a fair process. The people of Iraq suffered through the years in which the regime spearheaded by Saddam systematically perpetrated some of the most inhuman and large scale crimes in world history. The best estimates indicate that 50,000 to 100,000 Kurds were murdered under Ba'athist rule, while some 2,000 Kurdish villages were destroyed. 900,000 Iraqi civilians were driven from their homes, while an estimated 10,000 political opponents were summarily executed. The mass graves of Iraq are filled with the loved ones of average citizens who simply disappeared. The one common experience shared by all Iraqis, whatever their religion or class, was an osmosis of fear and uncertainty that is the very antithesis of the rule of law. Under these circumstances, it would be the worst form of legal colonialism and international paternalism to dictate appropriate punishments from outside Iraq.

Just four days after the Iraqi Governing Council promulgated the Statute of the Iraqi High Tribunal, I was in Baghdad as a member of the team of international experts presenting a seminar on investigating and prosecuting international crimes in accordance with international norms. The diverse group of 96 Iraqi judges, prosecutors, and lawyers who gathered in Baghdad were among the first Iraqis outside the Governing Council to review the Statute. I was in the room with those Iraqi judges and prosecutors when they learned of the successful capture of President Hussein. As the celebratory AK-47 fire began outside, the normally dignified audience responded to the electric news with a frenzy of joy and palpable relief. One of the judges hugged me and exclaimed "Today is day one!" His spontaneous vision captured the sense of many Iraqis that the definitive end of the Hussein regime was a watershed event for those dedicated to leading Iraq towards stability and sovereignty founded on respect for human rights and the rule of law.

Ambassador Bremer's temporary abrogation of the Iraqi law permitting the imposition of the death penalty had nothing to do with any extraterritorial application of the European Convention of Human Rights, and everything to do with his obligations as the temporary occupation authority in Iraq. In Resolution 1483 passed on May 22, 2003, the Security Council unanimously exercised its Chapter VII authority to call upon the members of the Coalition Provisional Authority (CPA) to "comply fully with their obligations under international law including in particular the Geneva Conventions of 1949 and the Hague Regulations of 1907." All members of the United Nations have specifically accepted the principle that their obligations under the United Nations Charter prevail over "any other international agreement." Thus, the CPA exercise of Chapter VII authority superseded the obligations of any of those individual states that are parties to any treaty limiting the imposition of capital punishment.

Resolution 1483 affirmatively required the CPA to exercise its temporary power over Iraq in a manner "consistent with the Charter of the United Nations and other relevant international law, to promote the welfare of the Iraqi people through the effective administration of the territory." The law of occupation found in the IVth Geneva Convention presaged the subsequent development of human rights norms by protecting the basic right of citizens in the occupied territory to a fair and effective system of justice. Pursuant to these principles of occupation law and the binding Chapter VII mandate of the Security Council, the CPA cited its duty to ensure the "effective administration of justice," when it issued CPA Order Number 7 on June 9, 2003 that suspended the imposition of capital punishment in the criminal courts of Iraq and prohibited torture as well as cruel, inhumane, and degrading treatment in occupied Iraq. The suspension of capital punishment was only one aspect of the larger effort to suspend or modify laws that "the former regime used … as a tool of repression in violation of internationally recognized human rights." It had nothing to do with an external treaty obligations related to capital punishment that some members of the coalition had accepted as a matter of their sovereign prerogative outside Iraq.

Though CPA policy directives effectively aligned Iraqi domestic procedure and law with the requirements of international law, it was at best a stopgap measure that was neither designed nor intended to bear the full weight of prosecuting the range of crimes committed by the regime. The original CPA mission statement pointed to its purpose as the "the temporary governing body which has been designated by the United Nations as the lawful government of Iraq until such time as Iraq is politically and socially stable enough to assume its sovereignty." After the return of full sovereignty, the decisions about guilt or innocence of any particular defendant charged in the IHT and the subsequent punishment should appropriately be determined by the judges applying the laws of a sovereign Iraq. If the judges of the Iraqi High Tribunal believe that the evidence has established the guilt of a particular official, they should be free to impose any punishment permitted by law which they deem to be the most beneficial to restoring an Iraq in which people are free to live their lives and love their families secure in the knowledge that the rule of law protects them.

Should Saddam Hussein Be Exposed to the Death Penalty?

By William Schabas

The Statute of the Iraqi High Tribunal does not make any express reference to the possibility that convicted persons be subjected to capital punishment. The reference is indirect, a concession to the British lawyers involved in drafting the instrument. But there seems little doubt that Saddam Hussein is on trial for his life.

As a sovereign country, Iraq is of course free to choose the penalties it wishes to impose on convicted persons, subject to international human rights norms. Iraq is a party to the International Covenant on Civil and Political Rights, which allows States which have not abolished the death penalty to impose it 'for the most serious crimes in accordance with the law in force at the time of the commission of the crime […] pursuant to a final judgment rendered by a competent court'.

In October 2003, the U.S. viceroy for Iraq, Paul Bremer suspended the death penalty in Iraq. He was not required to do this under the Geneva Conventions, which allow prisoners of war and even civilians to be executed by the occupying power under certain conditions. Rather, he was responding to concerns by his partners in the occupation, the United Kingdom. As a State party to the European Convention on Human Rights, and its two protocols concerning abolition of the death penalty, Britain cannot participate in executions of persons 'within its jurisdiction'. Recent case law of the European Court of Human Rights indicates that occupied territories are protected by the European Convention and its protocols, even if they are outside Europe.

The Bremer order suspending capital punishment proves that Britain understood it was bound by the European Convention and its protocols with respect to criminal justice in Iraq. It also confirms that the United Kingdom was not a silent and ineffective partner in the occupation, but rather one capable of insisting that its own human rights obligations be honored.

But the European Convention not only prohibits actual execution, it also forbids European States from handing over suspects to jurisdictions that might impose capital punishment. Otherwise, they would be able to do indirectly what they cannot do directly.

As a partner in the occupation, Britain should not have allowed Saddam Hussein to be handed over to Iraqi civilian authorities without obtaining assurances that the death penalty would not be imposed. The United Kingdom must ensure that Saddam is not executed. While the Iraqi justice system is not bound by European law, it surely owes some respect to the British and should ensure that London does not transgress its international obligations.

Such an approach was followed in 2001 by U.S. Courts, in a case involving one of the El Qaeda terrorists who bombed the embassies in East Africa. The suspect has been apprehended in South Africa and handed over to FBI agents without obtaining assurances that the death penalty would not be imposed. The South African Constitutional Court later determined that this violated the suspect's rights. A New York court honored the South African position and refused to impose the death penalty.

Under international human rights obligations, the United Kingdom should not have allowed Saddam Hussein to be turned over to Iraqi justice without obtaining assurances concerning the death penalty. Yet under article 77 of the fourth Geneva Convention, States are required, at the end of occupation, to turn over all detained persons. This conflict of legal norms raises problems about the relationship between human rights law and international humanitarian law. According to recent pronouncements of the International Court of Justice, humanitarian law is *lex specialis*, and this suggests that the Geneva Convention obligation takes precedence over the human rights provisions. But General Comment 29 of the Human Rights Committee takes the position that the norm more favorable to the individual is the one that takes precedence. This difficulty shows that human rights law and international humanitarian law are not always compatible. Depending upon the interpretative approach that is followed—that of the International Court of Justice or that of the Human Rights Committee—the answer to this question may be different.

Should Saddam Hussein Be Exposed to the Death Penalty?

By Michael P. Scharf

When I was training the IHT judges, I learned that the United States had tried to dissuade the Iraqi negotiators from including the death penalty in the IHT Statute because it would make it difficult for the United Kingdom and United Nations to support the IHT, but that the Iraqis insisted on it. I asked them why the death penalty was important. They gave me four answers.

First, Iraqis are fiercely proud of their legal tradition, as the country that created the first criminal code (the Code of Hammurabi) some 3,700 years ago. Since then, Iraq has always had a death penalty, and Iraqis consider its continued existence an important part of their cultural heritage.

Second, they wanted to avoid the "paradox of inversion" that marked the experience of the International Criminal Tribunal for Rwanda. The most culpable perpetrators of the Rwandan genocide are prosecuted by the International Tribunal, where they can get at most a life sentence, while lower level offenders are prosecuted by Rwandan domestic courts, where they are often subject to capital punishment for their crimes.

Third, they were worried that persons convicted of the most heinous crimes known to humankind (genocide, crimes against humanity, and grave breaches of the Geneva Conventions) might later be granted amnesty by a subsequent

Iraqi regime. Citing the Napoleonic precedent, the Iraqis were extremely concerned that without the death penalty, convicted leaders could one day return to power, as Hussein himself had done after being released from prison in 1968.

Finally, they pointed out that international law does not outlaw the death penalty. The International Covenant on Civil and Political Rights permits capital punishment "for the most serious crimes in accordance with the law in force at the time of the commission of the crime." Twelve of the defendants tried by the Nuremberg Tribunal after WWII were sentenced to death. Today, more than half the countries of the world still impose capital punishment, and many States that have abolished the death penalty in recent years still maintain an exception for serious violations of international humanitarian law.

I am personally not a proponent of the death penalty, especially in the United States where studies show that it is often carried out in a discriminatory manner. But in the context of an Iraqi trial for Iraqi leaders accused of the worst crimes known to humankind, I can understand the Iraqi insistence on the availability of capital punishment. When the democratically elected Iraqi Transitional National Assembly re-promulgated the IHT Statute on August 11, 2005, it reconfirmed the Iraqi people's desire that capital punishment be available to the Iraqi High Tribunal. As a sovereign country and fledgling democracy, Iraq's decision should be accorded deference from the international community.

This does not mean that Saddam Hussein, if convicted, will be executed forthwith. The IHT Statute does not allow trials in absentia. Thus, if Saddam Hussein is convicted and sentenced to death in the first trial, the IHT may issue a stay of execution to enable Saddam Hussein to be tried for other incidents so that a historic record of the abuses of his regime can be developed.

Does the IHT Protect the Basic Right to the Assistance of Counsel?

By Michael Newton

International law emphatically protects the right to the assistance of counsel in presenting a fair and full defense against criminal charges, and this right is embedded in domestic procedures around the world, to include Iraq. This basic right to counsel operates against the backdrop of two principles that are part of the legal framework for fair trials (and explicitly included in the IHT): 1) the right to be presumed innocent until proven guilty in accordance with the law, and 2) the right not to be forced to testify or to admit the guilt of the charged offenses. In an internationally televised appearance of Saddam Hussein on television on July 1, 2004, an investigating judge informed him of a list of seven preliminary charges pursuant to the basic right of all suspects under Article 19 of the IHT Statute, "[t]o be informed promptly of the detail, nature, cause and content of the charge against him" At that time, there was no indictment issued against Saddam Hussein or any other defendant.

The work of the investigating judge at that early stage of the proceedings was centered on establishing whether a prima facie case existed against Saddam Hussein sufficient to warrant holding him under Iraqi legal control and custody. Under Iraqi criminal procedure law, as reflected in Article 18 of the IHT Statute, an Investigative Judge may initiate investigations on the basis of information obtained from any source, particularly from the police, and any governmental and nongovernmental organizations. The Investigative Judge evaluates the information to decide whether there is sufficient basis to commence the investigation, and once an investigation has commenced, is empowered to question suspects, victims, or other witnesses as well as to issue sub poenas for documentary evidence related to the offenses under investigation. It is a crime under Iraqi law for any official or agent to extract evidence from an accused, witness, or informant "in order to compel him to confess to the commission of an or to make a statement or provide information about such or to withhold information or to give a particular opinion," and this provision applies to the work of the IHT.

During the first appearance before the investigative judge, the IHT Rules stipulate that the investigating judge must notify all suspects of the following rights "in a language he speaks and understands:"

> 1. The right to legal assistance of his own choosing, including the right to have legal assistance provided by the Defense Office if he does not have sufficient means to pay for it;
> 2. The right to have the free assistance of an interpreter if he cannot understand or speak the language to be used for questioning;
> 3. The right to remain silent. In this regard, the suspect or accused shall be cautioned that any statement he makes may be recorded and may be used in evidence.

Article 23 of the Iraqi Law on Criminal Proceedings requires that any statement of the accused to the investigating judge is recorded in the written record and "signed by the accused and the magistrate or investigator." Thus, every suspect (to include Saddam Hussein) who has appeared before the IHT investigative judges to date has been notified of their rights to counsel and has acknowledged their comprehension of those rights in writing.

Apart from the specific admonition noted above to the suspect or accused that any statement may be recorded and used as evidence (which is acknowledged and signed by both the accused and the investigative judge), the IHT requirements exceed many domestic statutes in other nations by requiring:

Whenever an Investigative Judge questions an accused, the questioning shall be recorded by audio, video, court reporter or by other means. The accused shall be informed that the questioning is being recorded. At the conclusion of the questioning the accused shall be offered the opportunity to clarify anything he has said, and to add anything he may wish, and the time of conclusion shall be recorded. The content of the recording shall then be transcribed (if done by audio or video) as soon as practicable after the conclusion of questioning and a copy of the transcript supplied to the suspect.

Of course, as would be expected, an accused may voluntarily waive his right to have legal assistance during questioning, but only if the Investigative Judge determines that the waiver is voluntarily and intelligently made. The Investigative Judge "shall not proceed without the presence of counsel" when questioning a suspect who has invoked the right to assistance. Furthermore, if a suspect has waived his right to counsel but then invokes that right, "the questioning should be stopped and never resume again until the defense (sic) be present." These provisions comport fully with the relevant human rights provisions and are in complete accordance with the practices of other international tribunals.

Should the IHT Engage in Plea Bargaining?

By Michael P. Scharf

"Plea bargaining"—While no single definition of the term is universally accepted, the practice may encompass negotiation over reduction of sentence, dropping some or all of the charges, or reducing the charges in return for admitting guilt, conceding certain facts, foregoing an appeal, or providing cooperation in another criminal case. It is widely used in common law countries that employ the adversarial system; though far less common, there is a trend toward its increasing use (for less serious crimes) in a number of civil law countries that employ the inquisitorial system; and in 2001, the ad hoc international tribunals, based on a hybrid of the common law and civil law systems, began to experiment with the practice.

At its inception, the Yugoslavia Tribunal (ICTY), the first international criminal Tribunal since World War II, declared that plea bargaining was inconsistent with its unique purpose and functions. The crimes within the Tribunal's jurisdiction were simply seen as too reprehensible to be bargained over. Its sister ad hoc, the Rwanda Tribunal (ICTR) followed suit, sentencing Jean Kambanda, former prime minister of Rwanda, to life imprisonment despite the fact that he pled guilty to genocide, enabling the Tribunal to forego a lengthy and uncertain trial.

But as the case loads of the ad hoc tribunals expanded exponentially, pressure mounted for them to begin to employ plea bargaining as a means of conserving judicial resources. One of the first international plea bargains occurred in the case of Biljana Plavsic, who had served as deputy to Bosnian Serb leader Radovan Karadzic, and later replaced him as President of the Republika Srpska. Known as the "Serbian Iron Lady," Mrs. Plavsic had been charged with committing genocide. In return for her guilty plea on the lesser charge of persecution (a crime against humanity), the Prosecution agreed to drop the genocide charge and to recommend a relatively light sentence. Though Mrs. Plavsic steadfastly refused to cooperate in any other way with the Tribunal (including turning down a request to testify against former Yugoslav President Slobodan Milosevic), the Trial Chamber sentenced her to all of eleven years imprisonment in a posh Swedish prison—with full credit for time already served and the possibility of early release for good behavior. The Plavsic plea bargain, which has been harshly criticized by expert commentators, presents several lessons for the Iraqi High Tribunal:

First, the IHT should not let any of the most high ranking and most culpable defendants enter into plea bargains. Leaders charged with genocide or heinous crimes against humanity, for example, should never be offered a plea agreement.

Second, plea bargaining should never be used by the IHT solely as a means to conserve judicial resources. Rather, plea agreements should only be offered in return for critical testimony or other significant cooperation.

Third, "charge bargaining" (where the prosecution agrees to drop the most significant charges) should never be used. "Sentence bargaining," in which the defendant pleads guilty to the initial charge in return for a promise of a lenient sentence is preferable because it does not distort the historic record that is being written through the IHT.

Finally, if and when a defendant enters into a plea agreement with the IHT, he should be required to append a signed document detailing the facts underlying the original charges. Similar to the full admissions that were required as a condition for receiving immunity from prosecution by the South Africa Truth and Reconciliation Commission, this would ensure that the full truth about the perpetrator's involvement in atrocities is revealed, while at the same time providing a benefit to the defendant in exchange for his admission and guilty plea.

Should the IHT Engage in Plea Bargaining?

By Paul Williams and Brianne McGonigle

Plea bargaining is when the defense and prosecution engage in discussions surrounding an agreement on the situation of the accused. Usually, the prosecution offers a reduction in a charge, a dismissal of pending charges, and/or a promise to request or recommend a particular sentence. Plea bargaining, a frequent practice in most Common Law traditions but rarely used in Civil Law traditions, has a number of benefits. Plea bargains save time, money and resources. In addition, plea bargains offer much more than simply aiding in the technical process. Some victims have stated that they received more comfort from a guilty plea than had the defendant been found guilty by the court. Remorse, recognition and reconciliation play a major role in the plea bargaining process.

Its benefits aside, a defendant has the right to plead guilty, to give up a public trial and to take responsibility for his or her actions. So long as the process is protected and safe-guarded, judges will still have the ultimate say in whether or not to accept a plea of guilty. In the event that plea bargains become an option at the Iraqi High Tribunal, they certainly can be useful to the prosecution, but they may also facilitate the process of reconciliation. Moreover, plea bargains have been largely successful at the ad hoc International Criminal Tribunal for the former Yugoslavia (ICTY) and the International Criminal Tribunal for Rwanda (ICTR), and will likely occur at the International Criminal Court (ICC).

Originally, the ICTY and ICTR Statutes did not provide for guilty pleas in the absence of a full trial. Only later, when the Rules for each Tribunal passed, did the Tribunals provide for guilty pleas. At the ICTY, Rule 62 governs guilty pleas; however, there are no formal rules or provisions governing the plea-bargaining process at the ICTY. This is similar for the ICTR. Nonetheless, the practice has emerged in the jurisprudence of the tribunals, resulting in a number of guilty pleas. The plea agreements reached between Prosecution and Defense are not binding on the Judges of the ICTY or ICTR, and in practice the Judges have chosen to both increase and decrease recommended and agreed upon sentences.

The average sentence for defendants pleading guilty before the ICTY is approximately 11 years. In contrast, defendants convicted after completion of a trial at the ICTY are given a sentence on average of 17 years. Thus far, neither Defense nor Prosecution are able to predict with any precision how many years the Judges will decide to give a defendant who has struck a plea agreement with the Prosecution. Instead, both sides can only try to weigh mitigating and aggravating factors. Based on the jurisprudence of the ICTY and ICTR, mitigating factors include at what stage of the process the defendant chose to plead guilty, what remorse was shown by the defendant, and to what extent is the defendant willing to cooperate with the Prosecution. Aggravating factors include the position of the accused when the crimes took place and the gravity of the s charged. A defendant's superior position, therefore, acts as an aggravating factor. Because the ICTY and ICTR are struggling to finish all trial chamber cases by 2008, plea bargains aid in the completion strategy.

The Rome Statute for the International Criminal Court provides both that a defendant may enter a guilty plea and that the judges may still order that a trial take place regardless of the plea. Should the Trial Chamber at the ICC decide that the interests of justice or the interests of the victims require a full trial of the accused, regardless of the plea entered, the court may order that that trial continue under the ordinary trial procedures. This could be an option for the Iraqi High Tribunal.

We do not fully agree that none of the major offenders from Saddam's regime should be offered a plea bargain. Instead, plea bargains have many benefits, one of which is having those who plead guilty to testify against other high-ranking officials. Often, it is the high-ranking officials who best understand the chains-of-command and the orders given. Prosecutors often have little evidence to work with and the testimony of a colleague who admitted guilt would be significant. Moreover, those who plead guilty will likely still serve large sentences.

Although many argue that the Iraqi justice system is alien to plea bargain, the entire Iraqi High Tribunal is an alien process to Iraqis. Plea bargains offer many noteworthy benefits to the victims, the court system, and to the defendants that should not be ignored.

Whose Justice Anyway?

By David M. Crane

Is the justice in Iraq, we, as the international community, seek, the justice the victims want? I am not so sure. As international criminal justice evolves into a discipline within our profession, it is imperative that we consider the cultural aspects of the justice we seek on behalf of victims of atrocity. It may not be the outcome they want whether it is in Iraq or elsewhere.

Justice comes in many forms in our own societies. It does likewise in others, as well. We've seen attempts in Rwanda, in an overwhelmed justice system, to try thousands upon thousands of perpetrators of the genocide in the early 1990's. Additionally, while in Sierra Leone, I saw the Truth and Reconciliation Commission seek to reconcile truth and justice for the victims of that ten-year long civil war, along with the international tribunal there, where I was its' Chief Prosecutor, along with customary reinsertion of child soldiers back into society through cleansing ceremonies. This was justice.

In Iraq we should not ignore, but respect, how the judges, as well as the staff of the IHT, are overlaying their law and custom over the proceedings. Despite my disdain for the way the IHT was created outside of international norms by the United States, I must say I am impressed by the way the judges are carefully taking Iraqi law, along with various principles of international law, and shaping it for their use to ensure that justice is done from an Iraqi point of view. It has become their tribunal, despite the public perception that it is a U.S. manipulated aberration. It is the Iraqi's who are going to have to live with the result and I think that the judges know this as well. In my mind, the IHT has only one chance to get it right, as we did in West Africa. One slip and the entire process could unravel. The fragile respect for the rule of law shattered.

How did we take culture and custom into consideration in West Africa? First, we went out and listened to the people, asking them what was justice to them and what result they would want to see happen. Secondly, we took that input and factored it in to our discussions on who we indicted, why, and under what charges. Third, we listened to the victims as they made their statements and ensured that each team had the appropriate Sierra Leonean presence during the interviews. Gender and child victims were especially cared for culturally. This allowed us to understand the witness' perspective and to take care that this perspective was given its due. Factoring in culture, also, allowed for us to plan for that perspective in preparing our case in chief. Fourth, we continued to monitor our witnesses and victims throughout the entire process by creating a witness management program within my office, a first-ever unit in a tribunal. It was run by Sierra Leoneans. Fifth, we ensured that all personnel within my office were culturally aware of their surrounding and that they respected where they were. It was one of my key briefing points during my welcome of newcomers. I would encourage my office to embrace the culture and learn from it. I believe it was helpful as we prepared for and examined our witnesses in court. To be able to watch Sierra Leoneans come in and give testimony in their language, with their perspectives to the crime(s) given respected, and to see them walk out with their heads held high; knowing this, and that true justice had been done, both internationally and locally, was an important signal to the people and West Africa that the rule of law, regardless of how it is applied, is more powerful than the rule of the gun.

Though we cannot, nor would I even suggest otherwise, substitute customary approaches to our international criminal procedures, practitioners should still seek ways to ensure that the victims, the citizenry and populace, have a sense that what is being done is just, and to the extent it will mesh with custom and culture so much the better. In West Africa we did not want this to be seen as white man's justice, a charge the indictees leveled at us from time to time. With care and respect for the local culture and custom, we avoided that charge. Tribunals are created for and about the victims. We should never forget that.

Section 2: Issues Related to the Conduct and Administration of the Trial

What Will Ramsey Clark's Participation Mean for the Saddam Hussein Trial?

By Michael P. Scharf

When the Saddam Hussein trial resumed on November 28, former U.S. Attorney General Ramsey Clarke was seen seated at the Defense table next to lead defense counsel Khalil Dulaimi. Under the IHT (formerly IST) Statute, non-Iraqi lawyers are permitted to assist in the defense, but this was the first time a member of Saddam's army of high powered foreign lawyers was allowed into the courtroom, signifying Clark's special status. This essay explores what Ramsey Clark's presence will mean for the Saddam Hussein trial.

There are three reasons why a distinguished defense lawyer might take on a case like Saddam Hussein's. First, a highly successful defense attorney might be attracted by the ultimate challenge of a nearly impossible case, involving a defendant who is widely considered to be guilty of the charges. A prominent example of this would be Harvard law professor Alan Dershowitz, who defended Claus von Bulow in 1984 on a charge of attempting to murder his wife with an injection of insulin, a case later dramatized in the 1990 film "Reversal of Fortune" staring Glenn Close, Jeremy Irons, and Ron Silver as Dershowitz. Second, the lawyer might seek the international media attention and fame such a high-profile case may bring. The OJ Simpson case, for example, transformed little-known defense attorney Johny Cochrane into a household name around the world. Finally, the lawyer might want to use the case as a means to promote the lawyer's own political agenda.

Ramsey Clark falls largely into the third category. Clark is founder and current Chairman of the International Action Center, the largest antiwar movement in the United States. A vocal critic of U.S. military actions around the globe, in Op Eds and newspaper interviews, he calls U.S. government officials "international outlaws," accusing them of "killing innocent people because we don't like their leader." Clark has said that rather than Saddam Hussein, it is the U.S. that should go on trial, pointing to the unlawful invasion, the subsequent destructive siege of Falluja, torture in prisons and the military's role in the deaths of thousands of Iraqis.

Clark is known for turning international trials into political stages from which to launch attacks against U.S. foreign policy. He has represented Liberian political figure Charles Taylor during his 1985 fight against extradition from the United States to Liberia; Elizaphan Ntakirutimana, a Hutu leader implicated in the Rwandan genocide; PLO leaders in a lawsuit brought by the family of Leon Klinghoffer, the wheelchair bound elderly American who was shot and tossed overboard from the hijacked Achille Lauro cruise ship by Palestinian terrorists in 1986; and most recently Slobodan Milosevic, the former leader of Serbia who is on trial for genocide before the International Criminal Tribunal for the Former Yugoslavia in The Hague.

Much as Clark objected to the 2003 U.S. invasion of Iraq, Clark joined the defense for the former Serb leader in 2001 because he objected to the 1999 NATO bombing of Serbia, which also had not been authorized by the U.N. Security Council. For a preview of Clark's Saddam Hussein trial strategy, one can examine Clark's tactics in the Milosevic trial. On the eve of the Milosevic trial in September 2001, the Coalition for International Justice faxed me a draft brief prepared by Ramsey Clarke, which he had distributed to the press and NGOs. This document—which contained bombastic argument headings such as "Creation of the International Criminal Tribunal for the Former Yugoslavia Was a Lawless Act of Political Expediency by the United States Designed to Demonize and Destroy an Enemy," "Powers that Create Ad Hoc International Criminal Tribunals Divert Attention from their Own Offenses," "The Violence and Division Within Yugoslavia Since the Collapse of the Soviet Economy Was Caused by U.S.-Led Acts Designed to Balkanize the Federal Republic of Yugoslavia with the International Tribunal as Principal Weapon"—was never filed in court. Rather, it was designed for the court of public opinion.

Building on the theme of Clark's brief, the Milosevic defense began with Hollywood-quality video and slide show presentations showing the destruction wrought by the 1999 NATO bombing campaign. Though the acts of NATO were not relevant to any of the charges or defenses, and therefore not likely to help Milosevic obtain an acquittal, the presentation had an immediate impact on Milosevic's popularity back home in Serbia. The tactic transformed Milosevic from the most reviled individual in Serbia to number four on the list of most admired Serbs, and soon thereafter Milosevic (campaigning from the courtroom) easily won a seat in the Serb parliament in a nationwide election.

For the Saddam Hussein Trial to be fair and credible, there must be equality of arms between the prosecution and defense. Thus, the active involvement of high-powered defense lawyers like Ramsey Clark on the defense team is an important ingredient to the success of the endeavor. Like Clark, I published articles in opposition to the 2003 invasion of Iraq. But I don't think Clark's strategy of putting the United States on trial will be constructive. Since the "Tu Quoque" (you also) defense is not legitimate, it won't help his client's case. In an editorial that Ramsey Clark published in the LA Times last January, entitled, "Why I'm Willing to Defend Saddam," he wrote "This trial will write history, affect the course of violence around the world and have an impact on hopes for reconciliation within Iraq." But as the Milosevic case has demonstrated, Clark's strategy of putting the United States on trial is likely to incite greater opposition to and violence against the new Iraqi government and the U.S. troops stationed in Iraq. Ironically, Clark's trial strategy will result in lengthening the amount of time U.S. troops must remain in Iraq, rather than hastening their withdrawal as Clark has advocated.

What Will Ramsey Clark's Participation Mean for the Saddam Hussein Trial?

By Paul Williams and Brianne McGonigle

I agree with Michael Scharf in that for the Iraqi High Tribunal "to be fair and credible, there must be equality of arms between the prosecution and defense." The involvement of high-powered, experienced, and passionate defense attorneys is not only an important ingredient to ensure a fair and credible trial, it is essential. It was also essential that the court offered all participants of the court, judges, prosecution and defense attorneys, equal protection from the start of the trial process—which, unfortunately, it failed to do. Ramsey Clark's participation may or may not aid in the functioning of the IHT, but it does raise the question: to whom does a defense attorney at the IHT owe the greatest duty—the court or their client?

If defense attorneys at the IHT owe their duty to the court, then their obligations are to justice, not their clients, essentially making them officers of the court. They should refrain from raising issues on the legitimacy of the court because they know that the arguments will not aid in mounting a credible defense for the Accused. Although the defense attorney could still "act in the best interests of the Accused," the defense attorney would make the determination of what those interests are rather than having the Accused make those decisions for himself.

In contrast, almost all national professional codes and the codes of international criminal tribunals, acknowledge that attorneys, particularly criminal defense attorneys, owe, first and foremost, a fundamental duty to their clients, but also a duty to the interests of justice. I would argue that defense attorneys, whether retained by the defendant or appointed by the court, owe the greatest duty to their client while acting in the interests of justice. It is their duty to raise issues, so long as permitted by the court, that the Accused finds of fundamental importance, such as the legitimacy of the tribunal.

If Saddam Hussein requests or sanctions Ramsey Clark to address grievances concerning the legitimacy of the court and the defense team's safety, it is Ramsey Clark's duty, as his attorney, to do so. His boundaries are governed by the Judge, the Rules of the Tribunal, and his home bar association—not by public opinion. In addition, the issues defense attorneys addressed are valid concerns. Whether they are addressed at the appropriate time is for the Judge to decide. Defense attorneys at Nuremberg, the ICTY, and the ICTR have all addressed the issue over their respective court's legitimacy. Although the argument continually fails, many would agree it needs to be stated for the historical record.

Part 5, Section 3, Rule 29 (Third) of the August 2005 revised IHT Rules of Procedure and Evidence states, "In the performance of his [Defense Counsel] duties, a counsel must adhere by the relevant provisions whether they are of the Tribunal Statute, these Rules or any other rules or regulations adopted by the Special Tribunal. In addition, he must adhere by any code of practice and ethics governing his profession." As of now, there is no specific Code of Conduct for Defense Counsel before the IHT; therefore, it is, in part, the responsibility of the judge, not Defense Counsel, to control the courtroom and set the boundaries for attorneys in order to ensure decorum in the courtroom. According to Rule 31 of the August 2005 revised IHT Rules of Procedure and Evidence, a judge has the authority to impose legal proceedings against counsel if counsel's conduct becomes offensive or abusive or demeans to dignity and decorum of the Tribunal or obstructs the proceedings. In addition, a judge may, with the approval of the President of the Court, communicate any misconduct of counsel to the professional body in his state of admission. It is for the judge to decide whether Ramsey Clark's assertions at the IHT disrupt the court proceedings.

All defendants deserve a high-powered, experienced, and passionate defense attorney—for Saddam Hussein, Ramsey Clark embodies these traits. The general public may not agree with his methods, but it is up to the Judge, the rules of the court, the ethical code of his profession and his client to set his boundaries. Until that time when he is cautioned, his duty to his client is in the interest of justice.

Was the First Day of the Trial a Success?

By Michael P. Scharf

I spent the day on October 19, 2005, viewing the proceedings and commenting on the Saddam Trial for a variety of U.S. and Foreign news media, including CNN, Fox News, ABC News, MSNBC, and the BBC (London). I was struck by the near consensus among American journalists that the first day of the trial was quite a success, and the near consensus among foreign journalists that it was a train wreck. While people of different countries are prone to see in a war crimes trial what they want to see, I think there are some objective indicators by which to measure the success of the first day of the Saddam Trial, which I discuss in this essay.

First, the judge selected to preside over the trial, Rizgar Mohammed Amin, was an inspired choice. Judge Amin proved himself to be among the very best and the brightest of the IHT judges that I worked with in training sessions in London last fall and spring. The gray-haired Judge Amin is Kurdish, which is less objectionable in a trial involving mainly Shi'ite victims. But what I remembered most about him was his calm temperament, infectious smile, and patient demeanor. The man is a rock. Unlike Judge Richard May, who tried to shout down Slobodan Milosevic when he acted in a disrespectful or disruptive manner at the Yugoslavia Tribunal, Judge Amin deftly handled Saddam Hussein's outbursts and refusal to answer his questions in a calm but firm manner. By the end of the hearing, Saddam Hussein went from defiant to cooperative, entering a plea of "not guilty" (rather than refuse to do so as Slobodan Milosevic had done in The Hague). Moreover, Judge Amin's first decision in the trial was to grant the some of the defendants' request to allow them to wear their head coverings in court, demonstrating that he was committed to being respectful of their fundamental rights.

Second, the judges decided to televise the proceedings gavel to gavel (with a twenty minute delay to handle witness protection and security concerns). Moreover, Judge Amin decided not to have his visage electronically obscured even though televising his identity would put him at great risk of assassination by Saddam Hussein's supporters. During the training sessions, the judges talked about the importance of "transparency," and showing the "face of justice," so that the IHT would not be subject to the kind of criticism leveled at some Latin American courts which have employed hooded judges. While there are risks that Saddam Hussein and his lawyers will try to use the televised trial as a political stage, the judges felt that on balance the importance of transparency outweighed this risk.

Third, despite some glitches with the video equipment which temporarily delayed the proceedings, the first day of the trial was very well choreographed, with a great deal of symbolism that was apparent to the Iraqi people if not the press. For example, by asking Saddam Hussein to identify himself and state his former profession, Judge Amin was demonstrating that in his courtroom Saddam Hussein was an ordinary criminal defendant, entitled to no better or worse treatment than any other criminal defendant. When the defendant refused to answer the question and began to attack the legitimacy of the proceedings, Judge Amin said quietly but resolutely, "Sit down. We'll note that you are Saddam Hussein, former President."

The Defendants were seated in a traditional Iraqi dock, which looks like a pen with four-foot high sides, as opposed to the "cage" that some media had reported would be used. It was particularly significant that the person seated next to Saddam Hussein in the first row of the defendant's pen was Awad Hamed al-Bandar, who had been the Chief Judge of Saddam Hussein's Revolutionary Court. In a previous essay, I address why the Dujail case was a good one to start with, but until I saw the assigned seating positions of the defendants on the first day of the trial, I had not focused on the fact that this is likely to be the ONE case in which the Revolutionary Court itself will be on trial. Under Saddam Hussein, the Revolutionary Court was used as a weapon against Saddam's political opponents, and Judge Abandar himself allegedly signed the warrant to execute the victims of Dujail. In this way, the Dujail case will be similar to the Altstoetter ("Justice") trial at Nuremberg, which was later portrayed in the Academy Award winning movie, "Judgment at Nuremberg," staring Spencer Tracy, Judy Garland, Marlena Deitrich, Maximilian Shell, and William Shatner. This was said to be one of the most important of all of the Nuremberg trials, since it established the precedent that judges who participate in a court system which perverts the law can be held responsible as accomplices to crimes against humanity—a precedent that has not been employed in sixty years until the Dujail case.

After Judge Amin had the defendants identify themselves, he established that each was represented by counsel, and then took thirty minutes to explain to them their rights before the IHT. Judge Amin used this opportunity to demonstrate to the defendants and the world that the IHT was governed by the highest standards of due process and defense rights, imported from the Rules of Procedure of the Yugoslavia and Rwanda Tribunals.

This was followed by the Prosecutor's recitation of the charges and the main facts that the Prosecution intended to prove at trial. The most significant revelation was that the Prosecutor intended to enter into evidence a written order, signed by Saddam Hussein himself, for the retaliatory actions against the town of Dujail and its citizens. In this way, the world learned that Saddam Hussein might be convicted on the strength of his own records, much like the Nazis were at Nuremberg.

As the three hours of proceedings drew to a close, Judge Amin announced that the Tribunal had decided to grant the defense motion for a temporary adjournment of the trial to give the defense team forty more days to further prepare its case, to give the Prosecution time to guarantee the safety of reluctant witnesses, and to give the Iraq government a chance to publish the new (August 11, 2005) revised version of the IHT Statute in the Official Gazette (similar to the U.S. Congressional Record)—which is necessary for it to come into force.

The proceedings didn't all go like clockwork (there were some equipment glitches and Saddam Hussein got into a tussle with a security guard when he tried to escort the defendant by the arm on the way out of the courtroom). And like any war crimes trial, the rest of the trial is likely to see its share of errors and missteps. But I believe the first day will be remembered as a showdown between the defiant Saddam Hussein and the patient, avuncular Judge Amin. It will be remembered as a day in which the tribunal treated the defendants with respect and dedicated itself to ensuring their rights. It was a good day for the IHT!

The Significance of the Kidnapping/Murder of Defense Counsel

By Michael P. Scharf

I'm writing this essay just a few minutes after learning that a second member of the Saddam Trial defense team, Abdel al-Zubeidi, was killed in a drive-by shooting. It is awful that the life of another brave lawyer was cut short. And it will certainly raise questions about the capacity of the Iraqi High Tribunal to guarantee a fair trial and to stick to its schedule

But the public and the press needs to recognize that the defense attorneys in part brought this tragic situation upon themselves when they elected to have their faces and identities broadcast during the first day of the trial, and when they subsequently refused to accept the Iraqi Government and U.S. military's offers of security. Now they are seeking to exploit the tragic—but not unforeseeable—murders of their colleagues in an attempt to derail the proceedings.

This is not the first trial in the world in which there is a high risk to the safety of the trial participants. The same types of concerns have been successfully dealt with in the trials of major drug lords in Central America and major terrorists in Europe and Latin America. In those trials, the defense counsel, prosecutors, judges and witnesses accept protection by the military or police. The difference here is that defense attorneys wanted their faces and identities to be broadcast, and then refused to accept protection.

Four of the five judges and three of the four prosecutors chose not to have their faces shown or their names identified in the TV broadcast for their protection. The defense counsel chose not to follow their lead because they want to be able to try the case in the court of public opinion. In fact, the day before he was killed, al-Zubeidi, gave an extensive interview to the New York Times.

After the murder of Sadoun Nasouaf al-Janavi, counsel to defendant Awad al-Bander, two weeks earlier, the Iraqi Government and the U.S. military each independently offered to provide security for the defense counsel. The U.S. government said it would relocate the defense counsel and their families to the Green Zone, provide around the clock protection of their homes and offices, and provide armed escort to them for the remainder of the trial. The defense lawyers declined, saying that they did not trust the Iraqi Government or U.S. military. This was a ploy; a deadly gambit to justify their boycott of the trial and attempt to delay or derail the proceedings.

The defense counsel did not have any legitimate reason to reject the offer of security, since it would not have interfered with their work. In the civil law system, which governs the proceedings of the IHT and is employed in a majority of countries around the world, defense counsel are not expected to go out into the field to conduct independent investigations and take witness statements. That work has already been done by the neutral Investigative Judge, who undertook a thorough investigation, and has transferred the copious case file, including thousands of pages of witness statements, to both the prosecution and defense. In the civil law system, the lawyers for both sides work almost entirely from the case file—something the defense counsel can do from the safety of their own offices. Having U.S. troops guard their homes and offices, and provide armed escort to and from the Courthouse is certainly an inconvenience, but it would not prevent them from doing their job of vigilantly defending their client.

The Defense argument that the trial should be moved in light of the killings is also unfounded. Moving the trial won't protect the members of their families back in Iraq; only acceptance of security can do that. And no venue is absolutely safe from terrorist attacks, while the $100 million IHT courtroom was built to withstand even a rocket attack. Most importantly, moving the trial would undermine the defense attorneys' ability to effectively try their case, since a court sitting outside of Iraq would not have the power to effectively compel witnesses to testify at the request of the defense.

Judge Amin still has a card to play in an effort to persuade the defense counsel to accept U.S. military protection, or perhaps private security guards of their choice paid for by the United States. If the defense lawyers continue to refuse to do so and to boycott the trial, Judge Amin may remind them that as duly appointed defense counsel, they are officers of the court, and have a responsibility to accept the security and continue to participate in the trial, or they can face sanctions such as fines, imprisonment, and disbarment, and they can be replaced by court-appointed defense counsel who will not play these kinds of high-risk games in an effort to disrupt the proceedings.

Finally, there needs to be an independent investigation into who killed the defense attorneys, perhaps conducted by the United Nations, drawing on the recent precedent of the UN launched investigation of Syrian involvement in the murder of the Prime Minister of Lebanon.

The Significance of the Kidnapping/Murder of Defense Counsel

By Raymond M. Brown

The kidnapping and murder of Sadoun Nasouaf al-Janavi, counsel to Awad al-Bander is more than just a personal tragedy for his family and a blow to his client's defense. It raises a fundamental challenge to the legitimacy of this first IHT trial and conceivably to the functioning of the Tribunal itself. A court cannot claim legitimacy if it is attached to a regime which can not guarantee the physical safety of trial participants. Protected participants must include defense lawyers representing despised or controversial defendants.

This is not to suggest that any persons or groups associated with the establishment of the Court or the functioning of its processes are responsible for this criminal act. To the contrary, I assume that they regret this violent episode and have done everything that could be asked of them to prevent it.

Nonetheless, the purposeful slaughter of defense counsel shines a bright light on the emerging dark secret of the "system" of international justice (a system I still support.) That secret is the imbalance between the resources of prosecutors and the defense. Justice Jackson acknowledged this problem in his famous Nuremberg opening. (The inadequacy of his response to his own rhetorical "question" remains for me a flaw in his universally praised allocution.) Early in his statement Jackson noted:

Before I discuss particulars of evidence, some general considerations which may affect the credit of this trial in the eyes of the world should be candidly faced. There is a dramatic disparity between the circumstances of the accusers and of the accused that might discredit our work if we should falter, in even minor matters, in being fair and temperate.

There will be time enough in this book to examine more broadly potential resource "disparities" at the IHT and perhaps at the IMT. Right now we must focus on the resource which is the sine qua non for any fair trial. That essential ingredient is the service of zealous defense counsel who can investigate, confer, speak and work without fear. A regime which cannot guarantee the opportunity for defense counsel to perform this way cannot claim to dispense justice in its courts.

Although David Crane and I probably differ on "disparity" questions at the Special Court in Sierra Leone I can say that within the confines of the Special Court compound, or in Freetown, or on the complex journey to and from Sierra Leone's capital I never felt unsafe. I am not aware of any defense counsel expressing fear for his or her physical safety in a way that implicated the discharge of their functions.

Whether this feeling of safety was because, or in spite of the precautions taken by the UN I cannot say. However, it is important to remember that Sierra Leone had just emerged from a decade of civil war and that unrest continued in western Liberia as the SCSL trials commenced.

A Battalion of Nigerian (UNAMSIL) troops surrounded the Court and Detention facilities. The Court's Director of Security insisted that non-Sierra Leoneans not visit Eastern portions of the country adjacent to Liberia without Military escorts. Finally, the Special Defender arranged (for better or worse) for Defense counsel to fly on UNAMSIL's rickety fleet of ancient ex-Soviet helicopters. (Two of these craft crashed the day before we departed the U.S. for trial). Resource disparities existed at the Special Court but murder of defense counsel and the consequent chilling or inhibition of vigorous representation did not.

It may be that a lifetime spent as defense counsel dealing with permutations of fear and intimidation in municipal and international fora have biased me. It may also be that my strong opposition to the proffered legal, strategic and foreign policy bases for the war in Iraq have predisposed me to see the specter of illegitimacy leach from an occupation regime to the IHT whose coattails it has sought to ride to international legitimacy.

Biased or not, I cannot see how a single trial or a judicial system can survive assaults on the quality of its justice if it cannot provide an opportunity for defense counsel to function without fear of non-judicial execution. This is especially true if the accused are persons, like Saddam and his satraps who are already believed to be culpable by all the world except their most fervent followers.

The venue issue from which this problem flows is not new to international legal decision making. The disappearance of normal state functions in Yugoslavia and Rwanda presaged decisions to place the Ad Hoc Tribunals in the Hague and Arusha (the latter despite criticism from the RPF). Different circumstances on the ground influenced placement of arguably "mixed" courts in East Timor, Sierra Leone and prospectively in Cambodia.

The choice to hold IHT trials in Iraq while security remains a deep problem raises the unwelcome aroma of political decision making. Allowing trials to proceed in an environment where the process is tainted by violence and fear undermines legitimacy. Whether the choice is legal or political, it is a bad one.

Should the IHT Relocate Outside of Iraq?

By Laura A. Dickinson

The recent killing of two defense attorneys raises serious questions about whether the IHT can operate fairly and impartially inside Iraq under current conditions. Today, gunmen shot and killed Abdel al-Zubeidi, who was representing Hussein's co-defendant, the former Iraqi Vice President Taha Yassin Ramadan. Another defense attorney, Thamir al-Khuzaie was seriously wounded. Last week, Saadoun al-Janabi, the defense attorney for Hussein co-defendant Awad al-Bandar, was also brutally killed. The sustained targeting of defense counsel seriously compromises the legitimacy of the trials. Iraqi authorities should thus seriously consider moving the proceedings, at least temporarily, to a nearby location outside Iraq such as Dubai.

The decision to hold the proceedings within Iraq reflects a strong commitment of Iraqis to own the process domestically. The location of a war crimes tribunal outside the territory where crimes occurred, as in the case of the International Tribunal for the former Yugoslavia, may contribute to a disconnect between the work of the tribunal and the local populations affected by its work. Indeed, such a disconnect can threaten the legitimacy of a war crimes tribunal. Yet the security situation has so deteriorated within Iraq that any benefit of domestic proceedings is in danger of being completely overshadowed by the risk of violence.

Iraqi authorities should thus seriously consider moving the proceedings temporarily to a nearby location such as Dubai. A temporary move would preserve the essentially domestic character of the proceedings yet at the same time would also address the concern that proceedings in Iraq cannot take place fairly due to security concerns. Such a move would would both signal the tribunal's commitment to secure conditions for all participants as well as help improve actual security on the ground. Moreover, such a temporary move is not without precedent. For example, the agreement between the United Nations and the government of Sierra Leone to establish a hybrid domestic-international war crimes tribunal provides that the court "shall have its seat in Sierra Leone" but "may meet away from its seat if it considers it necessary for the efficient exercise of its functions, and may be relocated outside Sierra Leone, if circumstances so require." While the risk of attack on lawyers, judges, defendants, witnesses, and others involved in the proceedings could exist anywhere in the world, the greatest risks undoubtedly are posed within Iraq. Iraqi authorities should thus seriously consider holding proceedings outside the country until the security situation improves.

Should the IHT Relocate Outside of Iraq?

By Michael Newton

If Iraqi authorities decide to move the proceedings of the Iraqi High Tribunal out of Iraq, they would take a visible step towards subordinating civilized society to the forces of anarchy and lawlessness. The deaths of defense attorneys Abdel al-Zubeidi and Saadoun al-Janabi are a grave challenge to the work of the Tribunal, but their tragic deaths could have been prevented if they had been willing to accept the protection proffered by the authorities as well as other offers by the U.S. military. The killers have figuratively declared war on Iraqi society and they should not be allowed even the propaganda victory that would necessarily accompany a forced relocation of the trial proceedings. Moving the trials would result in extensive delays that, in the end, would not be guaranteed to ensure the safety of court officials any more than the protective measures already in place inside the Green Zone today. Moreover, relocation of the infrastructure and personnel of the court would endanger the security systems already in place to protect evidence. The symbolism of such a move would be an unmistakable indicator to the population, and to the watching wider regional audience, that the intentions of Iraqi officials to restore stability to civil society can be shaken and ultimately destroyed if only the criminals persist. The recent murders in Iraq are reminiscent of the wave of attacks against the courageous officials in Colombia who began to take on the drug cartels on behalf of their society. The systematic attacks in Colombia began with the 1984 murder of Rodrigo Lara Bonilla, who was the sitting Minister of Justice. In 1985, terrorists stormed the Palace of Justice and murdered eleven Supreme Court judges who supported the extradition of drug traffickers. In 1986 another Supreme Court Justice was murdered by drug traffickers, as were a well known police captain and a prominent Colombian journalist who had spoken out against the cartels. These narco-terrorists then commenced a lasting campaign of bombings in shopping malls, hotels and neighborhood parks killing scores of innocent people and terrorizing the general population. Much like the citizens of Colombia more than two decades ago, the people of Iraq are vigilant and hopeful that their nation has the strength of character and will to persist until the law abiding patriots succeed in returning stability and peace, not to mention the relative economic prosperity and educational opportunity of the pre-Baathist era.

It is indeed true that the sustained targeting of defense counsel has the potential to seriously undermine the ongoing trial and other investigative work of the tribunal as it prepares additional cases. The judges of the trial already in progress should convene a meeting of defense counsel in the near future to reiterate that those who committed these senseless acts of lawlessness should never be allowed the public triumph of derailing orderly and fair trial processes. The judges should discuss with defense counsel the additional support that they need in preparing their cases for the next phase of trial, and focus on the additional measures that can be implemented to ensure the personal safety of the lawyers and their families. Rather than permitting the targeted murderers of defense attorneys who had declined offers of protection from the Iraqi government, to create a gulf time and space between the victims who suffered under the regime and the trial process, the IHT judges should now mandate measures of protection on the remaining attorneys. One of the innovations of the IHT is the reality that the defense attorneys are governed by the Iraqi law on lawyers, and are therefore obligated under the full range of domestic ethical and legal obligations as officers of the court. They must obey the lawful orders of the judges in order to represent their clients. Finally, the judges should be mindful of the requirements of the Iraqi criminal procedure code of 1923 (which apply in full to these trials). Paragraph 212 of the procedural code states that the "court is not permitted to rely upon a piece of evidence which has not been brought up for discussion or referred to during the hearing, nor is it permitted to rely on a piece of paper given to it by a litigant without the rest of the litigants seeing it." This provision is, of course a necessary component of an integrated trial procedure that complies with international norms. The defense attorneys are already in possession of the investigative files provided by the investigating judge, and should now solicit the assistance of the trial judges in addressing evidentiary difficulties which may be caused by the continued insurgency in Iraq. The right to a full and fair defense that is incorporated in Article 19 of the tribunal statute necessarily includes the right to gather and present defense evidence. Moving the trials in the absence of any demonstrated effect on the ability of the defense teams to represent their clients would be an overreaction that would set of an inevitable ripple of other obstacles to timely and fair trial proceedings. Iraqi authorities and the officials charged with the implementation of the Higher Criminal Court Statute should stand firm in their determination to demonstrate a trial process that is dedicated to the highest principles of justice and fairness; the current location of the tribunal in Baghdad is the situs most likely to carry that message to the people of Iraq and hence most likely to create lasting societal soil in which the rule of law can flourish.

Who Won the Battle of Wills in the December Proceedings of the Saddam Trial?

By David Crane

The histrionics we have viewed this past few days is very typical of these tyrants who have been brought low by the law. Regardless of the circumstances, they tend to do this, e.g. Goering at Nuremberg, Milosevic at The Hague, Hinga Norman at Freetown. These are men who all believed they were above the law and used the law as a tool for their own gain. I suspect when the former President of Liberia, Charles Taylor, whom I indicted for 17 counts of war crimes and crimes against humanity while sitting as President (only the second time in history), is brought to the tribunal in Freetown, Sierra Leone that he too will rage against the system, so to speak.

All in all I think, despite the confusion, which invariably happens at the beginning of any new tribunal, from Nuremberg to the present, the judge did a credible job. Despite the perception (which can't be discounted), the judge won. Stop and think ... here we have the most powerful man in the middle east, a tyrant who ruled absolutely for over 30 years, humbled before the law and made to follow the rules. He even whined about having dirty underwear and a dirty shirt. This happened at the tribunal in Sierra Leone as well.

The tribunal in Sierra Leone is largely done with a year or so to go. Two thirds of the prosecution cases are done, eighty percent of the defendants chose not to go to court after the first few days or weeks. The rule is that as long as they choose to do so, and they are represented by counsel in court, it marches forward. In Sierra Leone, we had them sign a waiver each day and we gave them a television monitor to watch in the detention center should they choose to do so. Thus the commentary on CNN is erroneous.

Note, though I mention Nuremberg, and other international tribunals by way of illustration, as I have told you before, the IHT is a far cry from any of them, yet it will be, unfortunately, the only way we can seek justice for the victims and the people of Iraq. So be it.

Who Won the Battle of Wills in the December Proceedings of the Saddam Trial?

By David Scheffer

At the end of a long CNN interview I was asked whether any defendant had not shown up for a trial before an international criminal tribunal. My first point was to emphasize, because of the context of all we had just discussed in the interview about Saddam's tactics, that no defendant had shut down his criminal trial before an international tribunal in the past 15 years by simply refusing to show up in the courtroom (following arrest or surrender, obviously). I was just starting to explain the nuances to that by mentioning ICTR defendants who had balked at appearing, and was going then to proceed to the excellent Sierra Leone precedents cited by David Crane below and arrangements that can be made with counsel and with the defendant consenting (and I had been emphasizing earlier in the interview the important role Saddam's counsel was fulfilling in his absence today), and then I wanted to mention the unique Rule 61 proceedings of the ICTY, when my television journalism 10 seconds were up as the producer voiced into my left ear, "Please end your answer now!" Thus the point had to be concluded prematurely. I don't think I was erroneous; I just did not have the air time necessary to complete my explanation on this question.

Who Won the Battle of Wills in the December Proceedings of the Saddam Trial?

By Michael P. Scharf

As to "who won the battle of wills," let me begin by noting that this is a common defense tactic, not just in international trials, but also in highly politicized domestic trials even in the U.S. The most notable example was the Chicago Seven Trial (Abbey Hoffman, et. al), in which the leaders of the anti-war movement were prosecuted on the charge of conspiring to cause riots to disrupt the 1968 Democratic National Convention in Chicago. At one point in that trial, the judge had to gag and bound defendant Bobby Seales to constrain him from making frequent outbursts in an effort to disrupt the trial. This only led to a greater sense that the trial was unfair, which was the very point the defendants were seeking to establish. Interestingly, Ramsey Clark was involved in that trial too, as an adviser to the Defense team. In fact, when the defense tried to call Ramsey as a witness, the judge refused to allow him to testify, and the defense counsel shouted out that the decision was the greatest miscarriage of justice in the history of American jurisprudence, earning the lawyer a contempt citation from the judge. Ramsey Clark is clearly importing the disruptive trial strategies that were perfected in the Chicago Seven Trial for use in the trial of Saddam Hussein, seeking to achieve similar results.

Consistent with international standards of due process, Judge Amin could have Saddam Hussein brought to the courtroom by force, and he could have him placed in a glass booth like Adolf Eichmann was at his trial in Israel, to prevent him from disrupting the trial with outbursts. But that would only add to the appearance of injustice, which Judge Amin is desperately trying to avoid. So, instead, he is likely to arrange for Saddam to follow the trial by video link from the detention center, a strategy that other international trials have successfully employed. Most likely, Saddam will quickly choose to come back to court once he realizes that his absence has not derailed the trial, since he can score more points being in court than from the detention center.

It is also noteworthy that Saddam Hussein's outbursts and pledge to boycott the proceedings followed the testimony of witness A, a female victim of his atrocities. Saddam knew that her moving testimony could be extremely damaging to his standing within the Iraqi Sunni community unless he could find a way to quickly distract media and public attention from it. In this he succeeded, as the media has devoted far more attention to Saddam's outbursts and "battle of the wills with the judge" than to the substance of the compelling witness testimony. But with 40 witnesses still to go, I don't think he'll be able to successfully repeat that feat over and over. So while Saddam may have scored more points in the first three days of the trial, Judge Amin, with his patient but firm approach, is likely to prevail over the long haul.

Who Won the Battle of Wills in the December Proceedings of the Saddam Trial?

By Christopher Rassi

Like Saddam Hussein, in the famous Media Case (Judgment from December 2003) at the International Criminal Tribunal for Rwanda, the defendant Jean-Bosco Barayagwiza boycotted the trial. Barayagwiza, also a lawyer by training like Saddam Hussein, was a high ranking board member of the Comité d'initiative of the RTLM and founding member of the Coalition for the Defense of Republic(CDR). He also held the post of Director of Political Affairs in the Ministry of Foreign Affairs.

Early on in the proceedings, not only did he boycott, but he did not want legal counsel or any assigned counsel. Barayagwiza sought the withdrawal of his first counsel citing reasons of "lack of competence, honesty, loyalty, diligence, and interest." He then declined to accept assigned counsel and instructed them not be attend the trial and represent him, based on his inability to have a fair trial. Nonetheless, the ICTR Trial Chamber ordered counsel to continue representing Barayagwiza, even after they filed a motion to withdraw. The ICTR Trial Chamber held Barayagwiza's behavior to be an attempt to obstruct proceedings, and that the judiciary must ensure the rights of the accused, taking into account what is at stake for him. The ICTR Trial Chamber further noted that assigned counsel represents the interest of the court to ensure that the accused receives a fair trial, efficient representation and adversarial proceedings. Eventually, the ICTR Trial Chamber directed the Registrar to withdraw their assignment and appoint new counsel for Barayagwiza because he had terminated their mandate.

Unlike the case of Milosevic and Barayagwiza, Saddam Hussein does not appear to be refusing counsel. Actually, it is quite the opposite, and from the looks of it, the interaction between his counsel and Judge Amin suggests the contrary. It appears as though his counsel is his trusted representative in court. If this is the case, this is just a one-day ploy, and not unheard of in international trials of such magnitude.

Who Won the Battle of Wills in the December Proceedings of the Saddam Trial?

By Cherif Bassiouni

I'm presently in Egypt where Arab television is covering the trial extensively. The problems I anticipated have materialized, and I'm afraid that the defendants and their lawyers will cause a lot of havoc.

I understand from my contacts in Iraq that this is turning into a spectator's sport, where people are keeping score on who is making points in the oral debates. Obviously, the ability of the defendants and their lawyers to cause difficulties in the proceedings is succeeding. My impression is that there are two distinct scenes that are playing out contemporaneously. The first is the witnesses' testimony which is touching people's hearts, and the defendants and their lawyers, which are playing on national pride since the trial is seen in part as being the U.S. vs. Saddam. In short, it is like having a two-ring circus.

Who Won the Battle of Wills in the December Proceedings of the Saddam Trial?

By Leila Sadat

As a matter of strategy, I think that Saddam does himself a disservice by not showing up, because with the Sunni insurgency, and at least some Iraqis and other Arabs, he is making good points about the legitimacy of the proceedings that he just cannot make if he doesn't appear. In fact, I think that he was doing quite well, although, as Cherif notes, there is also tremendous sympathy for the victim's of the crimes. What does he gain by not appearing? Very, very little, in my view, maybe a better suit, or cleaner clothes, but as a strategic matter, it doesn't make sense for him not to appear, making me wonder whose idea it really was.

Saddam's antics are of course legally irrelevant to the questions posed by the Dujail indictment, but the issues that his defense team is trying to raise about the legitimacy of the entire affair are completely relevant and unfortunately, will never really be aired. No one can feel sympathy for Saddam, particularly hearing the testimony of the survivors. But the question remains whether Iraqis might come to hate the United States and everything about it even more than they despise their former leader, and there is enough of a grain of truth in his categorization of the Iraqis participating in the trial as "collaborators" that he may ultimately win a great deal of public support for that position. Thus, there is a real risk that this trial may exacerbate rather than ameliorate that reality. Abu Ghraib, the alleged use of incendiary phosphorus again civilians, estimates as high as 100,000 Iraqi deaths (recall that the Nat bombing campaign had fewer than 500 total casualties, even by Serb estimates) these stories turn the U.S. effort to make this a real time morality play into hypocritical words, at best. It seems to me that most U.S. commentators on the trial simply brush aside the "technical" issue of the court's establishment by an occupying foreign power that killed thousands, maybe hundreds of thousands, of Iraqis in order to give Iraqis the "privilege" of putting their former leader on trial (at a cost of $U.S. 130 million). Yet the Iraqis live with that reality daily, which is why, even though so many of them hated Saddam, they sympathize with opponents of the U.S. (and the tribunal).

Having Saddam watch proceedings offstage, so to speak, will hurt the credibility of the proceedings, I believe, although David's comments about Sierra Leone suggest that perhaps that was not the case there (but as far as I can tell, the U.S. RCLO hasn't been leading "town meetings" as David did in Sierra Leone, to establish support for the court). At best, there will be an uneasy truce Saddam and his retinue will be executed, the U.S. will pull out, and Iraq will be poorer and less stable than before. Whether or not Ramsey Clark is involved in organizing the defense, I think the outbursts and antics are a logical approach for Saddam to use, given that he has been given no real legal forum in which to challenge the legality of the tribunal. Indeed, I note that proceedings have not been stayed so that the tribunal can consider the allegations of illegitimacy, presenting yet another striking difference between the conduct of these proceedings and international tribunal proceedings think about the carefully reasoned and very important decisions in the Tadic case on the question of jurisdiction.

In any event, as David Crane has noted, since the U.S. government decided this was to be the policy, we all have to live with it and hope for the best. Would that wiser and more experienced heads had prevailed.

What Will Happen if the Tribunal Finds That Saddam Hussein Was in Fact Tortured by His American Jailors?

By Michael P. Scharf

During the fifth day of the Saddam Trial, on December 21, 2005, Saddam Hussein interrupted the proceedings with the shocking claim that he and his co-defendants had been tortured by American prison guards several months before the start of the trial. Although the claim is extremely implausible, Presiding Judge Rizgar Amin wisely indicated that it would be fully investigated before the trial resumes on January 24, 2006.

If the investigation reveals that Saddam was in fact subject to "serious mistreatment" at the hands of his jailers, the Tribunal might have to dismiss the Dujail case and release him. Article 17 of the Statute of the Tribunal (entered into force on 18 October 2005) states that the judges are to be guided by the precedent of the International Criminal Tribunals for the former Yugoslavia and Rwanda (ICTY/R). This issue was addressed by the Appeals Chamber of the Yugoslavia and Rwanda Tribunal in Prosecutor v. Dragan Nikolic: Decision on Defense Motion on Illegal Capture (5 June 2003). In Nikolic, the ICTY/R Appeals Chamber stated that in cases in which treatment of the defendant rises to the level of serious human rights violations (i.e. torture or inhuman/cruel/degrading treatment), the Tribunal must dismiss the case since "it would be inappropriate for a court of law to try the victims of these abuses." Case No. IT-94-2-AR73, at para. 30. But the Court found that Nikolic's mistreatment was not serious enough to merit dismissal (he had been abducted in the middle of the night and roughed up but not permanently injured), stating that apart from the most "exceptional of cases," the remedy of setting aside jurisdiction would "usually be disproportionate" with respect to a defendant charged with crimes against humanity. Id.

If there were acts of mistreatment but they are not serious enough to merit dismissal, they may still lead the court to exclude Saddam Hussein's incriminating statements. Under Rule 59 of the Tribunal's Revised Rules of Procedure (adopted October 19, 2005), the Tribunal will rule evidence inadmissible if the statement was not voluntary or if the means by which it was attained casts substantial doubt on its reliability. This is equivalent to how U.S. courts apply the Constitutional due process right in criminal cases. Since it does not employ a jury, the Tribunal will enforce this exclusionary rule the way most European countries do, by prohibiting any mention of inadmissible evidence in the written judgment of the Tribunal, under Rule 58 of the Tribunal's Rules of Procedure. Thus, the judgment cannot refer to any pre-trial statements that Saddam Hussein provided that are found to have been induced by beatings or other forms of mistreatment, even if it falls short of torture.

There are several factors, however, that make it unlikely that the Tribunal will find that Saddam Hussein was in fact mistreated (seriously or otherwise) by his American jailers. First, American troops were reportedly instructed to exercise the utmost care not to mistreat Saddam Hussein and the other former leaders of his regime, given the grave political consequences that would ensue from any such incident. Second, in the first four days of the trial (October 19, November 28, December 5, and December 20), Saddam Hussein took advantage of the opportunity to freely air his grievances on several occasions, but his sole complaints of mistreatment were that he had not been provided a pen and paper with which to take notes, that he was given only six cigarettes a day (and did not like the brand), that he was required to wear the same suit for several days without a clean change of clothing, and that he was forced to walk up four flights of stairs rather than take an elevator. Had he been subject to acts of torture, he certainly would have mentioned it then, rather than confine his complaints to these minor inconveniences. Third, in the months leading up to the trial, Saddam Hussein confirmed on more than one occasion to the Investigating Judge, Ra'ad Juhi, that he had not been beaten while in detention. According to Judge Ra'ad, had any of the defendants complained earlier of torture or mistreatment, they would have been subject to contemporaneous medical examination to see if such claims could be substantiated. Fourth, Saddam's claim of torture followed harrowing testimony by victims of the torture endured at the hands of the Ba'ath party. Throughout the trial, Saddam has employed a number of gimmicks in an often successful attempt to distract media and public attention from the impact of such emotionally compelling testimony, including frequent outbursts, yelling at the judge to "go to hell," threatening to boycott the trial, and insisting on a break for prayer in the middle of a witness's testimony. Seen in this light, Saddam's allegations of torture are likely to be found to be no more than another tactic to distract, disrupt, and derail the trial.

A Changing of the Guard at the Iraqi Tribunal

By Michael P. Scharf

On January 17, the international press reported that Rizgar Mohamed Amin had decided to step down as Presiding Judge of the Saddam Hussein Trial in the face of criticism about how he has managed the proceedings. Judge Amin will reportedly be replaced by Judge Mohamed al-Hamash, who was one of the four other members of the panel trying the DuJail Case. One of the two reserve judges who have been observing the trial will fill the vacancy on the five-member bench created by Judge Amin's departure.

This changing of the guard should not be seen as a sign that Judge Amin had bungled the trial (as his critics have asserted). Despite the frequent (and sometimes successful) attempts by the defendants to disrupt and derail the proceedings, in just five trial days (October 19, November 28, December 5, December 21 and December 22), the prosecutor completed an opening statement, and fourteen witnesses testified and were cross-examined by the defense—a very efficient pace even by American judicial standards. With forty witnesses still to go, the prosecution has already proven the scale of the atrocities, the direct involvement of several of Hussein's co-defendants, and the command hierarchy—the key elements necessary for a conviction in this case. And especially for those who understand Arabic, the testimony of Saddam's victims has been both moving and compelling.

This does not mean that there was not room for improvement, and perhaps Judge al-Hamash is the man for the job. I remember Judge al-Hamash from the IHT training sessions in London last year. He's a Shi'ite, about ten years older than Judge Amin, and has a more outgoing and forceful judicial temperament.

Judge al-Hamash can use his new position to instill a greater degree of control on the proceedings. He can, for example, insist that for now on Saddam Hussein only speak through his lawyer, rather than address the court and the witnesses directly, except when it is the defendant's turn to testify as a witness on his own behalf. And Judge al-Hamash can enforce this by removing the microphones from the defendants' dock, so that the televised coverage does not pick up any disruptive outbursts.

Judge al-Hamash can also insist that only the lead Iraqi counsel for each defendant actively participate in the courtroom proceedings, rather than permit former U.S. Attorney General Ramsey Clark to continue to address the court as Judge Amin had allowed. This may prevent Clark from continuing Saddam Hussein's efforts to turn the trial into an indictment of U.S. foreign policy.

Moreover, Judge al-Hamash can use the fact that the lead attorneys are officers of the court to remind them that misbehavior can earn them sanctions, including fines and disbarment from the Iraqi Bar. And, following the precedent of the Yugoslavia Tribunal and Rwanda Tribunal, he can appoint standby defense counsel who would observe the proceedings and be available to step in if, for example, the defense counsel ever threaten another boycott or begin to act disruptively. This would enable the judge to better keep the defense counsel in line through the omni present possibility that they can be replaced at a moment's notice.

In taking such actions, Judge al-Hamash must be extremely careful not to appear too heavy handed. If Judge al-Hamash yells at the defendants, for example, as Judge Richard May did during the Milosevic trial at The Hague, it will only play into the defense strategy of trying to cast the proceedings as unfair and illegitimate. As Judge Amin understood, in the long run, it is far more important that the trial be seen as scrupulously fair than for the judge to be seen as winning the battle of the wills against Saddam Hussein.

* * *

On January 23, 2006, the press reported that judge Raouf Rashid Abdul-Rahman, rather than Judge Said al-Hamashi, would be replacing Judge Rizgar Amin as presiding judge of the Saddam Hussein Trial when it resumes on January 24. Judge Said al-Hamashi is under investigation by the Debathification Commission, which believes he may have been a former member of the Ba'ath party—something he continues to deny. Meanwhile, efforts are still underway to convince Judge Rizgar Amin to return to the bench.

Judge Raouf Rashid Abdul-Rahman is a 64 year-old distinguished Iraqi Judge of Kurdish ethnicity. I remember him as an active participant during the training sessions for the judges in London in October 2004. I think he is likely to be more forceful than Judge Rizgar Amin, but maybe a little lowered keyed than judge Sa'id al-Hamashi would have been. It is a positive development to have a Kurd like Judge Raouf rather than a Shi'ite like Judge al-Hamashi preside over this trial involving Sunni perpetrators and Shi'ite victims, since it provides a measure of objectivity.

The game of musical chairs that is unfolding at the Saddam Trial is bound to take its toll on local and world opinion about the legitimacy and efficacy of the proceedings in Baghdad. The Tribunal's credibility has taken a hit, but it is far from critically wounded by these latest developments. I think the Tribunal will push through this latest setback, as it has pushed through its other chalenges, including the assassinations of defense counsel in October and the resignation of one of the judges when it was disclosed on the first day of the trial that his family member had been tortured by the Ba'athist regime.

Resignation Casts Terrible Pall over Tribunal

By William A. Schabas

The resignation of the presiding judge casts a terrible pall over the ongoing trial of Saddam Hussein. The judge said he was resigning because of political interference or pressure.

For those of us who are used to living in a legal system with an advanced and sophisticated judiciary, it is difficult even to comprehend such a situation. Who ever heard of a senior judge in the United States, or in Europe, resigning in the midst of a high-profile trial because of political interference? Who ever heard of a senior judge in one of these jurisdictions even complaining about political interference?

I can recall a major scandal in Canada some years ago when a cabinet minister telephoned a judge, who was a personal friend, about some relatively insignificant matter. When this came to light, there was a tremendous outcry in Parliament and in the media, and the minister resigned, of course. Although some contributors to this book have waxed eloquently about the 'trial of the century', the resignation of the presiding judge shows what a poor excuse for justice is actually underway in Iraq. Note that in the Canadian example it was the minister who had administered the pressure who resigned in disgrace, and not the judge who was on the receiving end.

Will the problem in the Saddam trial be solved? Or will the presiding judge simply be replaced by a colleague with a thicker skin and a higher threshold of tolerance for political interference and pressure? Will this be treated as simply one more 'incident' in a process that has already seen the tragic assassination of defense lawyers?

When the Iraqi tribunal was being established, many expert commentators pointed to the need for some kind of international involvement in order to enhance the credibility of the Tribunal. And while the idea that the trial would be contracted out to foreigners was justly rejected as patronizing and even neo-colonialist, one thing that can be said of international experts is that they are relatively immune to pressures from domestic political actors. The resignation of a presiding judge in the middle of a trial because of political interference and pressure is unprecedented. It is a sad chapter in international justice.

This is a wake-up call to all who are concerned that the trial of Saddam Hussein be carried out fairly and impartially. It may well be that the current situation in Iraq, which borders on anarchy, is simply not conducive to proper justice being rendered. If that is the conclusion, the trial should be stopped, or it should be moved to a venue where justice can be done.

The Winds of Public Opinion

By David M. Crane

William O. Douglas declared in *Craig v. Harney* that: "Judges are sup-posed to be men of fortitude, able to thrive in a hardy climate." The resig-nation of Judge Rizgar is a set back to say the least for the trial of Saddam Hussein and his henchmen. Though I do not belittle his courage, and the circumstances he finds himself in to seek justice for the Iraqi people, this is a moral victory for the various indictees and a blow to the rule of law in Iraq.[144]

The back-bone and the Achilles heel of any international tribunal are its judges. The entire process succeeds or fails in large part on their professional and personal conduct. Public perception of the law inevitably is formed by how judges control their court rooms procedurally. Perceived personal or professional weak-ness on the part of a judge or a panel of judges in a chamber weakens confidence in the law by the victims, their families, indeed, in the very country the tribunal finds itself. I certainly saw this in spades with the Special Court for Sierra Leone.

The extant resignation shows a weakness, real or perceived. That weakness will be exploited legally, practically, and politically. It certainly brings into ques-tion the entire legitimacy of the process cobbled together by Iraq and the United States. I have not been shy about my concern about the way the Iraqi High Tri-bunal (IHT) was put together. Rightly or wrongly, it has been "snake-bitten" from the start. This resignation fosters that perception. The IHT exists in a part of the world where strength and perceived power matter. To this point, the IHT appears to be faltering in the eyes of the public, particularly the Iraqi people. In a devel-oping democracy, a lack of respect for the power of the law can be disastrous.

Legally, this tortuous process will move forward. As in Sierra Leone, a judge that leaves can be replaced. Politically its future is in doubt. Make no mistake about it; politics is like a red thread that runs through the trials. Ignore it and politics could unravel the whole process.

I wonder if an internationally recognized tribunal, such as a hybrid, put to-gether by the United Nations and the Iraqi government, placed regionally in a safe environ, would have had such trouble with politically cowed judges? The IHT will survive this resignation, but what happens when it really starts to get difficult during findings and sentencing?

Owen. M. Fiss stated: "That the function of a judge—a statement of so-cial purpose and a definition of role—is not to resolve disputes, but to give the proper meaning to our public values."[145] I pray that this public value is not backing down in the face of adversity.

A Changing of the Guard at the Iraqi Tribunal

By Michael A. Newton

The resignation of Judge Rizgar Muhammad Amin from the ongoing Dujail trial is far from the institutional catastrophe that some critics of the Iraqi-led process have postulated. The resignation is an intensely personal matter that has, of necessity, been a matter of extreme public curiosity and comment. The fact that the trial will resume on time with Judge Raouf Rashid Abdul-Rahman presiding is perhaps the strongest testimony to the resilience of this maturing institution.

The Rules of Procedure adopted by the Iraqis and published in the official gazette of Iraq envision the resignation of a judge and provide a mechanism for handling the resignation. Judge Rizgar displayed enormous personal courage in accepting the televised role as presiding judge. Day after day before millions of viewers from around the world, he demonstrated an unflappable judicial demeanor and navigated the unfamiliar terrain of a high profile trial in a way that strove to serve as a model of fairness even for observers who have no familiarity with Iraqi law or rules of procedure. The cornerstone of the Iraqi High Tribunal is that it functions as a wholly independent component of the Iraqi domestic justice system; there is no evidence whatsoever to suggest that Judge Rizgar's decision had anything to do with improper external attempts to manipulate the trial. Such judicial independence is the hallmark of a process that is fundamentally fair and legally defensible.

Institutional independence, however, should not equate to secrecy and justice conducted behind the veil of secrecy. The Iraqis understood that a televised trial would be a powerful demonstration of progress towards a society built on respect for law. At a minimum, the televised proceedings can contribute to a sense of societal restoration in the aftermath of the horrors endured by ordinary people under Ba'athist rule. These proceedings have thus far mesmerized the population and hence the politicians that seek the support of the Iraqi people. The process has, to date, been a trial by law based on evidence produced under the rules specified by law rather than a sham trial based on innuendo and emotion. In fact, it is precisely the public nature of the trial that generated such intense commentary and criticism that is the most visible validation of the faith that the Iraqi Higher Tribunal officials place in the process created under the Statute.

Though he worked at the center of the vortex of intense political and public interest, Judge Rizgar's efforts have demonstrated a process that to date has been fair and expeditious as required by Article 20 of the Statute. Judge Rizgar strove to perform his duties in the independent and impartial manner required by the Statute, as evidenced by the fact that both the defense and prosecution have grumbled about some of his decisions. He has bent over backwards to balance the right of those sitting in the dock to present a full defense, even as he strove to prevent defense gamesmanship from derailing the vital work of the court. When measured by the standards of similar high profile cases, the Dujail trial has moved along well and the evidence has been powerful. Nevertheless, one Iraqi newspaper commented that the resignation was "late" and criticized the judge for his "leniency" with Saddam Husayn.

No trial process is perfect and no trial can be perfectly pleasing from all perspectives. This trial in particular has riveted public and political attention. A free press and informed public is one of the benefits of democracy that is currently flourishing in Baghdad and across Iraq. In a free country, everyone is entitled to express their opinion. Judge Rizgar has apparently resigned in reaction to the flood of opinion surrounding his decisions during open court. In my opinion, those who believe in the rule of law should be vocal in thanking Judge Rizgar for his service and for his demonstrated commitment to the principles of justice and fairness

De-Baathification and Transitional Justice

By Mark Drumbl

Following the resignation of Judge Amin, and the controversy over Judge Hammash with regard to his alleged links to the Ba'ath Party, a new judge apparently has emerged as chief investigatory judge. This is Judge Rahman, a Kurd who already is on the panel.

With regard to the discrediting of Judge Hammash, I suspect the realities in Iraq bear some similarity to those in other societies trying to move beyond systemic human rights abuses, where purging is important to ensure credibility and produce the truth; but also can be used as a lever to denounce virtually anyone who occupied any position of authority. This might especially be the case in Iraq, where the authoritarian government ruled for many decades.

I found it telling that the NYT reports today that the Judge Hammash situation has "threatened to bring further disarray to a trial that has already seen its share of chaos." (Michael Scharf also seems to suggest that the debaathification situation also hurts the court's credibility). I would think that this controversy regarding the past life of Judge Hammash differs from the controversy with regard to the political pressure on Judge Amin, or my broader concerns that the trial, at present, might fuel instead of dissipate violence.

Discussion regarding the role of past officials in the future direction of the country—despite its risks of politicization and abuse—can be salutary, insofar as it is yet another vehicle to recognize accountability and create a discursive space. Perhaps that is naive and theoretical. Also, just because the Court's credibility is impaired doesn't mean that the credibility of transitional justice more generally in Iraq is impaired—once again, it simply could be that it is too soon to have a court, or that the weight of too much ambition has been placed on the court's shoulders.

An Assessment of Ra'uf Abdel-Rhaman's First Day As Presiding Judge— Chaos in the Courtroom: So What's New?

By David Crane

The antics by various accused and their counsel this past Sunday, 29 January, brought an interesting clash of the power of the rule of law with the power of greed, corruption, and a twisted arrogance towards that rule of law. Disruptive indictees in international tribunals are common in the early stages of a tribunal's work. It happened at Nuremberg, at the Hague, Arusha, Freetown, and now the internationalized domestic court in Baghdad. It will happen again. It is a painful realization for these accused that the law now controls them and not the other way around. The accused in Baghdad, like their predecessors in history, are going through an emotional process of tyrants being humbled publicly before those they terrorized and they don't like it.

Defense counsel resigning or refusing to go to court, ranting at the judges and the public gallery by the accused and counsel are manifestations of this emotional catharsis they are going through. Their antics and acting out are not signs of a court or tribunal in disarray. They are signs of the powerful realizing that the rule of law truly is more powerful than the rule of the gun.

The very same antics took place in Freetown just shortly after I gave my opening statements in the joint criminal trial against the leadership of the Civil Defense Force, as well as the joint criminal trial against the leadership of the Revolutionary United Front. Using the standing rules of procedure and evidence, the judges in those trial chambers, though initially flustered, took general control and followed the tribunal's rules. Within a month the ebb and flow of witnesses giving evidence began and the trials moved forward, in most instances without the accused, and at times with court appointed counsel from the Principle Defender's office. Defense counsel came and went, yet the trials continued justly forward under the rules. The rights of all of the accused were scrupulously followed. Such hi jinks are not surprising in Baghdad.

It is very instructive that the reaction of the Iraqi people who watched this on television on Sunday were generally impressed with the new chief judge. However, Judge Abdel Rahman needs to stay calm and collected and not joust with the accused. The respect of this court by the Iraqi people (and the international community) is tenuous at best. Firm and patient judging will most likely get the proceedings on track. It not, a grave injustice will have taken place and the role of the law in Iraq's future will be shaken indeed.

The Battle of the Wills—Part Two

By Michael P. Scharf

As expected, Judge Ra'uf Abdel-Rhaman has brought to the Saddam Trial a much firmer hand. Unlike Judge Rizgar Mohamed Amin, Judge Ra'uf has not hesitated to employ a number of tools at his disposal in an effort to assert greater control over the defendants and their lawyers.

Indeed, Judge Ra'uf began by reading the defendants the riot act, making it clear that he would not permit any further disruptive or disrespectful behavior during the remainder of the proceedings. Next, he appointed stand-by defense counsel, ready to step in if Saddam's lawyers once again attempted to derail the trial with a boycott. Later, he had some of the defendants and defense counsel removed from the courtroom when they attempted to disrupt the trial with offensive outbursts. And he told Saddam that he could watch the rest of the proceedings via close circuit video from his detention center when he tried to stage a walkout. The media focused almost entirely on the chaotic exchanges that ensued as Judge Ra'uf asserted his authority, but the fireworks only took up the first hour of the four and a half hours of the day's proceedings. Following Saddam's unceremonious departure, the trial proceeded quite smoothly with four of the eight defendants sitting quietly in the courtroom as three more witnesses completed their testimony.

The tools Judge Ra'uf's employed on his first day were field-tested by the international war crimes tribunals in The Hague, Arusha, and Freetown, and are considered to be consistent with internationally recognized due process and fair trial rights. The risk, however, is that if Judge Ra'uf completely shuts down the "Saddam show," the former dictator will refuse to return to the courtroom for the rest of the trial. Under such circumstances, he will have waived his right to be present, but a trial without the presence of Saddam (and his world famous attorneys) will still seem like a trial in absentia—a show trial without the star attraction. Such a situation would diminish the cathartic effect of the trial for victims who desire to see Saddam confronted by his accusers. The international and local media would quickly lose interest, and broadcasts would be reduced from gavel to gavel to a few highlights a day, thereby diminishing the educative function of the trial.

Two possible solutions exist to this problem. The first is to erect a sound-proof plexi-glass booth around the defense dock, and force Saddam Hussein to appear in court against his will. We'll call that the "Eichmann approach," made famous in Robert Shaw's acclaimed Broadway play and film, "The Man in the Glass Booth," about the trial of the former Nazi in Jerusalem. The second approach, a bit more innovative and less heavy-handed, is for the Tribunal to install a video camera so that the public can watch Saddam while he watches the trial from the detention center. By using cut-aways or split screen format (made famous in the Bush-Gore Presidential debates), the broadcasts could show Saddam's reactions to the proceedings as they unfold without necessitating that he be physically in the courtroom.

Despite the chaotic exchanges with the defendants and their lawyers, I give Judge Ra'uf high marks for his first day on the job—with one exception. I am concerned by the fact that he seemed to lose his temper in the face of the vitriolic insults that were hurled at him by the defendants. It is absolutely critical that Judge Ra'uf not play into the defendant's attempts to provoke him into an angry response. Since the judges serve as the jury in this case, shows of anger by the presiding judge will only fuel the perception that the proceedings are unfair, as was the case in the early months of the Milosevic trial. Judge Rizgar Amin may not have been as firm as some wished with the defendants, but he never lost his cool—an important lesson that Judge Ra'uf should take to heart.

A Turning Point in the Saddam Trial

By Paul Williams

In any country judges are subject to media and public criticism. While it is unfortunate that Judge Amin resigned, it is important to remember though that this is no ordinary trial, and that Judge Amin did not step down because he was biased, but because he realized he had lost control of his courtroom. I suspect in most other countries if a judge had clearly lost his ability to maintain order in his courtroom he too would resign in order to permit a new judge to assume the chair and to re-establish order in the court room. The change of judges also makes a bit more sense in light of the absence of traditional mechanisms like contempt of court citations frequently used to maintain order.

Sunday, January 29 marked a clear turning point in the Saddam trial. The approach of the previous Judge, Mr. Amin, had been to allow both Saddam and his lawyers great leeway in the courtroom. This was an appropriate approach given the need to create an environment conducive to a fair trial. The flexibility of the judge was taken as a weakness and was exploited by Saddam and his lawyers. The new judge Abdel-Rahman, who was originally scheduled to try the Anfal case, clearly saw it as his duty to regain control of the courtroom. Today's showdown was to be expected as Abdel-Rahman reasserted psychological and physical control over both Saddam and his lawyers.

The psychological contest in the courtroom mirrors the contest between the Iraqi government and the insurgents outside the courtroom. Within the trial chamber, as well as throughout Iraq, the new Iraqi institutions are trying to assert their control over the former Baathist forces. While chaotic, today's session was an important turning point for the Tribunal is it firmly reasserted control over the proceedings. The focus will hopefully now shift from Saddam's courtroom antics to the question of his culpability for the alleged crimes.

Despite the antics of Saddam, the Iraqi Tribunal has moved ahead at a pace comparable to trials conducted before the international tribunals for Yugoslavia and Rwanda. At the end of the day this is Iraqi justice for the Iraqi people. Most local commentators in Yugoslavia and Rwanda assert that while the international community has achieved some measure of justice, the victims have been forgotten and are detached from the trials being conducted in The Hague or Arusha. Despite the difficulties faced by the Iraqi Tribunal, the fact that it is being held in Iraq and that Saddam and others are being tried by Iraqis will contribute immeasurably to the healing process for victims, and to the sense among Iraqis that they are now in control of their own destiny

Can the Defense Team Be Held in Contempt of Court for Its Antics?

By Michael Newton

The very essence of a fair trial is the right to be judged based on the evidence produced in court rather than innuendo and emotion. Thus far, the defense antics in Baghdad have been the main obstacle to the calm and orderly consideration of evidence. I would daresay that there is no courtroom in the world that would tolerate a defendant hurling the insults at the bench that were heard in open court this week. No one who is seriously committed to justice and the provision of a fair and public hearing based on the evidence adduced in open court could expect the judge to smile politely and permit defendants to disrupt proceedings with extraneous insults and shouted denunciations. In fact, Iraqi criminal procedure law specifically empowers the judge to "prevent the parties and their representatives from speaking at undue length, or speaking outside the subject of the case."[146] After the defendant refused requests to come to order, Judge Raouf Rashid Abdul-Rahman restored order in the only way possible by directing the removal of Barzan al-Tikriti. As our own Supreme Court said in Pounders v. Watson, 521 U.S. 982, 987–988 (1997), when "misconduct occurs in open court, the affront to the court's dignity is more widely observed, justifying summary vindication." If one or more of the defendants refuses to attend open court, the proceedings can continue in accordance with international law and the accepted practice of international tribunals. For example, on April 19, 2005, Slobodan Milosevic absented himself from his trial in The Hague due to illness. The Trial Chamber simply proceeded in his absence and ordered that a video recording and a transcript of proceedings be delivered to his cell. The Iraqi High Tribunal has gone a step beyond that by making a closed circuit video available in the detention center for any of the defendants who refuse to participate in the proceedings in person.

In contrast to the narcissistic grandiosity of the defendants that has been on open display, the defense counsel should be held to the professional standards of acceptable practice as they represent the interests of their clients. This is one reason why Article 19 of the Statute of the Iraqi High Tribunal requires the principal lawyer for each defendant to be Iraqi. The lawyers who left the hearing without the permission of the bench could have immediately been detained for 24 hours or fined up to three dinars.[147] The Tribunal can initiate legal proceedings against counsel if, in its opinion, their conduct "becomes offensive or abusive or demeans the dignity and decorum of the Special Tribunal or obstructs the proceedings."[148] The International Criminal Tribunal for the Former Yugoslavia imposed (and later suspended for health reasons) a sentence of four months imprisonment on a witness who defiantly refused to answer questions and comply with the court's instructions.[149] Another panel of international judges wrote that "the purpose and the scope of the law of contempt to be applied by this Tribunal is to punish conduct which tends to obstruct, prejudice or abuse its administration of justice in order to ensure that its exercise of the jurisdiction which is expressly given to it by its Statute is not frustrated and that its basic judicial functions are safeguarded."[150] The practice of international judges has been to recognize that the pursuit of justice itself is the real victim of open and defiant contempt of court rather than the individual court or judge attempting to administer justice. In the face of persistent defense refusals to comport themselves with dignity and a seriousness appropriate to the enormity of the evidence, the judges in Baghdad should have no hesitation to order contempt proceedings for defense counsel who defy orders that are within their powers and appropriate in the circumstances.

What Can the Tribunal Do about Saddam Hussein's Hunger Strike?

By Michael P. Scharf

During the trial session on February 14, 2006, Saddam Hussein announced that he and his co-defendants were on day-three of a hunger strike to protest the appointment and actions of Presiding Judge Ra'uf Abdel Rhaman. This announcement must be viewed in the context of Saddam's other attempts to disrupt and discredit the trial, for example his allegation that U.S. prison guards had tortured him (later proved to be unfounded), his attempt to take prayer breaks in the middle of witness testimony (despite a psychological profile that indicates that he is not in fact a religious person), and his frequent offensive outbursts (including calling the judge "a son of a whore, a traitor, and a homosexual"). Indeed, the lead prosecutor Jaafar al-Moussawi immediately told the press that Saddam and the other co-defendants had eaten breakfast that very day. But what if Saddam really goes on a prolonged hunger strike? And what if this causes his health to seriously deteriorate? Would force-feeding be the appropriate response?

Worldwide, the hunger strike is a common tactic of defendants and prisoners who wish to protest their treatment. In the United States, convicted DC sniper John Allen Muhammad recently staged a hunger strike to protest for more access to legal papers. Suspected al Qaeda terrorists from Qatar, Yemen, Saudi Arabia, and Afghanistan held at Guantanamo Bay are currently staging a hunger strike to protest their prolonged confinement without trial. In Russia, Col. Yuriy Budanov, charged with murdering a Chechen girl, recently went on a hunger strike to protest what he viewed as the biased attitude on the part of the North Caucussus Military District Court. In Spain, former Argentine navy captain Adolfo Scilingo recently went on a hunger strike to protest Spain's attempt to exercise universal jurisdiction over him in relation to charges that he pushed hundreds of drugged political prisoners out of planes during Argentina's Dirty War. In Mauritania, coup leaders Major Saleh Ould Henenah and Captain Abderrahmane Ould Mini recently staged a hunger strike in an attempt to derail their trial for treason. In the United Kingdom, convicted animal rights activist/terrorist Barry Horne recently died of a hunger strike staged in an effort to protest his conviction and publicize his cause. And in India, villagers on trial for burning alive Australian missionary Graham States and his children recently went on a hunger strike in an attempt to have the judge removed from their trial.

The hunger strike can be a potent strategic weapon for a defendant determined to disrupt his trial, especially if it renders the defendant too ill to participate in the proceedings. Faced with that prospect, should a court order that the defendant be force-fed, or would that violate the defendant's fundamental rights? In the United States and elsewhere, courts have ordered force-feeding in such situations. Courts cite three interests in force-feeding a hunger-striking defendant: (1) concerns for the defendant's life; (2) concern for the orderly administration of justice; and (3) concern over the administrative costs and burden precipitated by the defendant's hunger strikes. Where a medical determination is made that continued fasting would seriously impair the health or jeopardize the life of a detainee, U.S. Federal and State Courts have consistently held that these interests outweigh defense arguments about the First amendment free speech right to protest and the Fourth Amendment privacy right to autonomy over one's body.[151]

There are three alternative methods of force-feeding a hunger-striking inmate: (1) nasogastric tube feeding, accomplished by inserting a tube down the nose through the esophagus and into the stomach; (2) intravenous feeding, accomplished by inserting a catheter into a major blood vessel leading to the heart; and (3) gastronomy, direct surgical access to the stomach. As photos demonstrating the nasogastric tube feeding approach employed on hunger strikers at Guantanamo Bay demonstrate, being subject to force-feeding is an extremely unpleasant experience—one that is sure to raise objections by the international human rights community notwithstanding the long judicial record supporting the practice. Nevertheless, Judge Ra'uf should make it clear to Saddam Hussein and his co-defendants that he can legally order force-feeding if their hunger strike threatens to derail the trial.

The Defense Boycott of the Defense Closing Arguments

By Michael Newton

The title of this issue seems at first glance like a misprint or an oxymoron. It is, nevertheless, the most recent development in what has been to date a trial process packed with surprises and interesting legal developments. From the outset, the defense strategy has been one of obstruction and obfuscation, as the lead attorney for Saddam Hussein indirectly confirmed in a recent New York Times interview. The erratic conduct by the defense team has been a major factor in disrupting the procedural predictability and overall dignity of the trial proceedings in the Dujail trial. In my personal opinion, the pronouncement by members of the defense team that they will not present closing arguments as the Dujail case nears its completion are an abdication of their ethical duty to diligently defend their clients. The defense team has stated that the boycott is a response to the June 21, 2006 murder of Khamis al-Obeidi, an Iraqi who was one of the team representing Saddam and his half brother Barzan al-Tikriti. The death of a third member of the defense team is a genuine tragedy, both in the symbolic sense that it represents a direct blow against the restoration of the rule of law and because it was completely avoidable. Prior to the onset of trial, and before the two previous murders, Tribunal officials worked with each member of the defense team to implement appropriate security arrangements. The members of the defense team turned down offers to live with their families in the security of the Green Zone, and chose the form of security that they preferred. The overall security environment has created a range of logistical, practical, and legal problems in the conduct of the prosecution and defense cases. Apart from the murder of defense attorneys, the defense has been unable to specify causal linkages that show a relationship between the challenges inherent in conducting such a high profile trial in the current environment and the conduct of the defense. In fact, Saddam Hussein attempted to take advantage of the security context by interspersing illegitimate exhortation to the insurgents outside the courtroom in the midst of appropriate illustration of defense perspectives. Overcoming these obstacles, approximately one hundred witnesses testified during the proceedings.

Press accounts of the recent letter to the bench announcing the defense boycott of the defense closing arguments indicate that it incorrectly asserts that the IHT lacks "the lawful proceedings that are well established in international and Iraqi law." The Statute and its implementing Rules of Procedure provide for the full range of individual rights reflected in acknowledged international standards for fair trial proceedings. Despite the challenges posed by the security environment, the defense has had every opportunity to present a fair and vigorous defense for those charged. The longest delay in the entire trial was granted to allow the defense team additional time to prepare for the beginning of the trial, despite the fact that the defense team received the investigative materials two months before trial was scheduled to begin. Significantly, the defense called almost precisely twice the number of witnesses as the prosecution, even though the bench cut short the presentation of a number of other witnesses deemed to offer testimony of redundant and limited probative value. If the defense has an articulable basis for concluding that the security environment has in some manner affected a procedurally fair process, the closing arguments would be precisely the appropriate forum to detail the legal and factual arguments forming the grounds that mitigate towards the innocence of their clients.

Rather than taking the occasion to state their legal case in public and on the record, the defense team has chosen to pack its portfolios and stay home. Given the obligation to represent their clients with vigor and legal precision, it was reasonable for Tribunal officials to presume at the beginning of trial that the defense team would participate in good faith in the judicial process. The defense team has, nonetheless sought to pierce the decorum in open court in ways that are unprecedented for a trial of this magnitude. The IHT Defense Office has worked to ameliorate the effects of the defense team's demonstrated disregard for the proceedings and their own ethical obligations. The defense closing arguments will proceed after a delay necessitated by the need for court-appointed counsel to prepare. The conduct of the defense in this first trial presents a troubling portent of even greater difficulties in the more complex and lengthy trials that lie ahead. If the defense simply refuses to engage in good faith adjudications based on the evidence and the legal evaluation of that evidence, there will be an inevitable corrosive effect on the procedural guarantees built into the IHT. Such conduct in future trials endangers the effort to demonstrate a fair and transparent trial process that exemplifies the rule of law in accordance with international standards for the Iraqi people and the wider regional audience.

Has the Iraqi Tribunal Learned the Lessons of the Milosevic Trial?

By Michael Scharf

At the conclusion of the Nuremberg Trial in 1946, Chief Prosecutor Robert Jackson said "Many mistakes have been made and many inadequacies must be confessed. But I am consoled by the fact that in proceedings of this novelty, errors and missteps may also be instructive to the future." Flash forward sixty years. Today (February 12, 2006) is the fourth anniversary of the start of the Slobodan Milosevic Trial at The Hague. As William Schabas and I document in our book "Slobodan Milosevic on Trial" (Continuum Press), the Milosevic proceedings have been subject to frequent disruptions due to difficulties obtaining witnesses, the outlandish behavior and health problems of the defendant, and the death of the presiding judge two years into the trial. During the training sessions for the Saddam Trial judges which I participated in last year, there were many discussions about the lessons from the Milosevic Trial. This essay assesses how well the Saddam Tribunal has learned from the major errors and missteps of the Milosevic proceedings.

Lesson #1: Keep in short.

The Milosevic trial involves a mega-case. The charges against the former Serb leader span atrocities committed in three conflicts (Croatia, and Bosnia, and Kosovo) over a period of a decade. Hundreds of witnesses have testified and thousands of documents have been admitted into evidence. After four years of proceedings, the end of the Milosevic trial may still be over a year away. Critics maintain that the trial has lost its focus and the world has lost interest as the proceedings in The Hague drag on and on.

In an attempt to avoid this problem, the Iraqi Tribunal decided to conduct a dozen mini-trials rather than one mega-trial for Saddam Hussein. The first case focused on a single atrocity—the retaliatory attack on the town of Dujail and the torture and murder of 143 inhabitants in 1982. This "air tight" case was expected to take no more than thirty court-days, and could be concluded in less than three months. But the Saddam Trial has been subject to a series of postponements to give the defense time to prepare its case, to provide better security to defense counsel and witnesses, to allow for national elections and religious holidays, and to deal with a recurring defense boycott. In over four months, the Tribunal has held only nine days of trial. Unless the pace begins to accelerate, this will be anything but the short trial that was envisioned, and collectively the trials of the Saddam Regime may drag on for years.

Lesson #2: Keep it fair.

The Milosevic Trial was presided over by Richard May, a judge from the United Kingdom, one of the countries that led the 1999 military intervention against Serbia. For many Serbs, the selection of a Brit to preside over the case was taken as a sign that the Tribunal would not be capable of fairly judging Milosevic, an impression that was magnified by the fact that Judge May sometimes responded to Milosevic's outbursts by shouting at the former Serb leader. Then, when Judge May died of a brain tumor, he was replaced by another British judge, who had not even been present for the first two years of the trial. Unlike Nuremberg, which had four alternate judges who observed the trial, to save money the Yugoslavia Tribunal had not appointed even a single reserve judge. Seen in this light, it should come as no great surprise that opinion polls have indicated that most Serbs view the Milosevic trial as unfair.

In an effort to achieve a greater perception of fairness in the Saddam Trial, the decision was made to select a Kurd to serve as presiding judge for the Dujail case, which involved Shi'ite victims and Sunni perpetrators. The man selected for the task, Rizgar Amin, was known for his calm judicial temperament. This was not a judge who could be provoked into yelling at the defendant. In addition, two reserve judges were appointed. Their job was to watch the proceedings and be ready to step in if any of the five judges had to step down for any reason. Unfortunately, Judge Rizgar resigned after five days of trial in the face of intense media and government criticism of his lenient judging style. He was replaced by Judge al-Hamashi, who in turn immediately resigned in the face of accusations that he had been a member of the Ba'ath party. Judge al-Hamashi was then replaced by Judge Ra'uf Abdul Rhaman, who had not been one of the reserve judges assigned to the Dujail case. And then last week, the media reported that Judge Ra'uf may have been tried in absentia and sentenced to life imprison by the Ba'ath regime for anti-governmental activity in the 1970s—an accusation that the Judge will have to address to avoid the appearance of bias. Within minutes of taking over, Judge Ra'uf was already yelling at the defendants and defense counsel, who he ultimately threw out of the courtroom—a move that has been subject to sharp criticism by human rights groups around the world. The damage all this has done to the credibility of the proceedings may be hard for the Tribunal to overcome, no matter how smoothly things run from here on out. And, with defendants and defense counsel who are committed to disrupting and derailing the trial, things are not likely to run smoothly.

Lesson #3: Keep it under control.

At the beginning of the Milosevic trial, Judge May ruled that Milosevic had a right to represent himself in the courtroom. Having so ruled, there was little Judge May could do to reign in the defendant as he used self-representation to make disparaging remarks about the Tribunal, to threaten and insult witnesses, and to turn the proceedings into a trial of the US/UK military action against Serbia. After judge May died midway through the trial, the Tribunal reversed his earlier ruling, and appointed a lawyer to step in if Milosevic's poor health or disruptive tactics threatened to disrupt the trial. Milosevic's behavior immediately improved, and the pace of the trial sped up considerably.

A year ago, I provided a 60-page memorandum to the Iraqi Tribunal, detailing why Saddam Hussein did not have an international right to self-representation, and explaining the risks of permitting Saddam to act as his own lawyer before the Tribunal. Consistent with my recommendation, in August 2005, the Iraqi National Assembly enacted a revised version of the Tribunal's Statute and Rules, which made clear that Saddam had to act through legal counsel, so that he could not use self-representation to turn the trial into a political stage from which to attack the United States and new Iraqi Government. In keeping with Iraqi legal traditions, however, Judge Rizgar and Judge Ra'uf have both allowed the defendants to pose questions to the witnesses following their cross examination by defense counsel. This has given Saddam an opportunity to make disparaging and offensive remarks about the witnesses, the Tribunal, the Iraqi Government, and the United States during the televised proceedings. Clearly, the proceedings would have run much more smoothly if the judges had taken the position that Saddam had to act through his appointed counsel and could not speak in the courtroom until such time as he took the stand to testify. Given the fact that Saddam has abused the traditional Iraqi privilege to participate in the questioning of witnesses, it is not too late for Judge Ra'uf to make a mid-trial correction … provided he can first get Saddam to return to the courtroom.

Judge Ra'uf's attempts to restore greater control over the proceedings were met by a walk-out by defense counsel. Judge Ra'uf responded by telling them "you can't walk out, you are fired," and by continuing the trial in their absence with court-appointed public defenders. Saddam and his co-defendants responded by refusing to return to the court. Although the trial sessions have run much more smoothly in the absence of the unruly defendants and their high-powered lawyers, the media and human rights groups have begun to criticize the proceedings as resembling an unfair trial in absentia. To answer this criticism, Judge Ra'uf must do a much better job of explaining his judicial decisions to the public, either by releasing written opinions or by taking a few minutes to do so orally at the beginning of each trial session. In particular, he needs to explain that the defense counsel have (at least temporarily) forfeited their right to continue to represent the defendants through their actions, and that public defenders have been appointed to replace them. He needs to explain that the actions of the defendants constitute a waiver of the right to be present in the courtroom, and that they will watch the proceedings and communicate with their new lawyers from the detention center if they refuse to come to court. And he needs to cite the precedents of the Yugoslavia Tribunal, the Rwanda Tribunal, the Special Court for Sierra Leone, and domestic courts, which indicate that his response to the situation is perfectly consistent with international due process and fair trial standards.

During the training sessions for the Saddam Trial judges last year, one of the judges (it may even have been Judge Ra'uf) asked whether the international trainers thought future war crimes trial judges in other parts of the world would be examining the precedents that were set in the Saddam Trial as we had been looking at the decisions of the Nuremberg and the Yugoslavia Tribunal. For good and bad, the answer is clearly yes.

Has the Iraqi Tribunal Learned the Lessons of the Milosevic Trial?

By David M. Crane

Over these past several weeks, tormented and shouting, Saddam Hussein and his henchmen have tried to turn their trial into political theater. To some extent they have. Yet, as we have seen in the past, from Nuremberg, The Hague, Arusha, and Freetown, eventually the calm deliberation of the law, administered by sober and serious judges will generally win the day. It has to or the proceedings will turn into a threat to peace, not a facilitator of peace in Iraq. On the fourth anniversary of another trial, far from Baghdad, in the Milosevic trial, we need to reflect on how we deliver international criminal justice so that the underlying theme of all tribunals, that the rule of law is more powerful than the rule of the gun, will continue to advance.

Professor Michael Scharf's three points are important for our consideration as they are keys to success—they were in Freetown during my tenure as the Chief Prosecutor and they will be in Baghdad. Lengthy court proceedings in this environment, charged with pain, suffering, and political intrigue need to be well planned, with a clear beginning and an anticipated end. Though the law must be seen to be fair, it also must be seen to be efficient and effective. Lengthy proceedings can leave that impression that it is not effective and undermine the respect for the tribunal itself. In my opinion, the longer the trial, the greater the chance for the entire process to unravel around the edges.

The law has to be seen as fair. That was what I told the victims in Sierra Leone at my many town hall meetings with them. Any appearance of bias against the accused on the part of the judges can be fatal. The Iraqi people are going to have to live with the result and if they perceive it as unfair they will not live with the result I can assure you.

I have a concern about an appearance of bias on the part of the new Chief Judge, currently presiding over this stage of the trial of Saddam. An Iraqi Kurd, who lived in a village destroyed by Saddam, a defendant, can give the appearance of just such a bias. This may bring a result that may appear to be unfair to this fledgling democracy. I am surprised that there has not been a stronger move to have the Chief Judge recused.

Despite the perceived bias that could bring the fairness of the proceedings into question, control of the court room is what will allow the proceedings to continue and the victims to come in and to tell the world what took place in their towns and districts. This is a must and must happen very quickly as the proceedings progress. Delay or keep the witnesses from testifying due to control problems and they will be intimidated. Thus another victim may be the truth, further bringing the fairness of the process into question.

All sides have an absolute right to present their case in a way that is fair, open, and efficient. Any one of these ingredients that are missing will show that perhaps in Iraq, the rule of the gun is more powerful than the rule of the law. It is early yet, it remains to be seen.

Comparing the Trial to International Standards of Due Process

By Kevin Jon Heller

As Saddam's trial draws to a close—and following the murder of a third defense attorney—it seems appropriate to catalogue the many ways in which the trial has failed to satisfy international standards of due process. Those failures are particularly unfortunate in light of the trial's historic importance; given that the evidence against Saddam is overwhelming, I am firmly convinced that a perfectly fair trial would be no less likely to result in a conviction.

Iraq is a signatory to the International Covenant on Civil and Political Rights (ICCPR), which guarantees criminal defendants "a fair and public hearing by a competent, independent and impartial tribunal established by law." According to Article 14 of the Covenant—which is paralleled, in large part, by Article 19 of the IHT Statute—a fair trial requires a defendant be provided, at a minimum, with the following rights:

- To be informed promptly and in detail ... of the nature and cause of the charge against him;
- To have adequate time and facilities for the preparation of his defense and to communicate with counsel of his own choosing ...
- To be tried in his presence, and to defend himself in person or through legal assistance of his own choosing ...
- To examine, or have examined, the witnesses against him and to obtain the attendance and examination of witnesses on his behalf under the same conditions as witnesses against him.
- As the discussion below demonstrates, Saddam's trial cannot be considered fair under Article 14. (Note that some of the points discussed below focus on the IHT in general. Although it is highly likely that most, if not all, of the due-process violations involved Saddam or his co-defendants, not enough information exists to make that claim categorically.)

Uncounseled Interrogations

U.S. investigators interrogated at least thirty high-value detainees, including most of the senior members of Saddam's regime, before the IHT became operational in December, 2004. At the time of those interrogations, the detainees were not represented by counsel. Although it appears that none of the uncounseled statements made by the detainees were introduced as evidence during Saddam's trial, it is impossible to know whether those statements led to incriminating evidence—the proverbial fruit of the poisonous tree. Indeed, the Court refused to guarantee Human Rights Watch that it would exclude incriminating evidence so obtained.

Uncounseled Court Appearances

Saddam was not represented by counsel during his arraignment, where he was informed of the general accusations against him (though not the formal charges in the Dujail case).

Interference with the Attorney-Client Relationship

- When the Dujail defendants were questioned by the investigative judge, their attorneys were given no advance notice of the questioning. On most occasions, the attorneys were not permitted to meet with their clients until after the questioning was completed.
- The most senior attorneys at Saddam's trial were not allowed to visit their clients until after the trial started.
- Saddam's attorneys were prevented from meeting with him for nearly a month after they were ejected from the courtroom in January, 2006.
- The attorneys for Saddam and his co-defendants were not allowed to meet with their clients in private for nearly two months during trial, including the entirety of the defense case.
- All meetings between defense attorneys and the Dujail defendants were conducted under audio and visual surveillance, and American officials reviewed all the materials the attorneys brought into the visiting room.
- On more than one occasion, a U.S official with knowledge of Arabic was present in the interview room when a defense attorney was conferring with his client.

Appointment of Inadequate Defense Counsel and Replacement Counsel

Two of Saddam's co-defendants have been represented by appointed counsel from the Tribunal's Defense Office. Those attorneys, who received only one or two training sessions in international criminal law prior to beginning work, have been completely incompetent: according to Human Rights Watch, they "were completely passive in court and did not ask a single question of witnesses, at any session between October 19, 2005, and January 29, 2006." In addition, one of the attorneys told Human Rights Watch in October 2005 that he had never met with his client, even though he had been appointed a month earlier.

The inadequacy of the attorneys working at the Defense Office also harmed the other defendants. After Chief Judge Abdel-Rahman ejected a number of defense attorneys for disruptive conduct, including one of Saddam's attorneys, the Court immediately replaced them—over the vehement protests of the defendants—with four new attorneys from the Defense Office. The Court appears to have decided to replace the defendants' chosen attorneys in advance; according to Human Rights Watch, the replacement counsel were waiting in a room next to the courtroom the whole time. Those attorneys proved little better than their appointed counterparts; during their tenure, they failed to cross-examine at least two prosecution witnesses and conducted sub-standard cross-examinations of the witnesses they did question.

Preventing the Defense from Monitoring the Investigation

Defense attorneys were not permitted to be present when the investigative judge interviewed witnesses and collected evidence, even though Article 57 of the Iraqi Code of Criminal Procedure permits their presence unless the investigative judge enters into the record an explanation of why counsel's presence was not permitted. No such explanation has ever been given.

The absence of defense attorneys during the investigative stage is particularly troubling, because Iraqi law provides that the dossier prepared by the investigative judge constitutes substantive evidence of a defendant's guilt. In this respect, the IHT lags behind international criminal law generally: the ICTY specifically held in Kordic and Cerkez that the wholesale admission of a dossier is inconsistent with the right to a fair trial; instead, the trial court must examine each category of evidence in the dossier, sensitive to the need to guarantee the evidence's authenticity and to the dangers of admitting evidence not tested by cross-examination.

Limiting Defense Access to the Evidence

Rule 40 of the IHT's Rules of Procedure and Evidence specifically provides that the defense is permitted "to inspect any books, documents, photographs and acquire these things, which are material to the preparation of the Defense, and also inspect any books, categories of, or specific documents, photographs and tangible objects in the accused custody or control which are intended for use by the Criminal Court as evidence at the trial." Nevertheless:

- Less than six months prior to trial, the defense had not been given an official version of the IHT's Rules.
- The defense was routinely denied access to documents and evidence during the investigative phase, and transcripts of judicial questioning were never made available, despite numerous requests.
- Defense attorneys were consistently denied sufficient time to review the investigative judge's dossier—and were often been forced to conduct even their limited review in public areas of the court.
- The defense was only provided with the prosecution's evidence a few days prior to trial, although Rule 40 requires the prosecution to disclose witness

statements and all other evidence 45 days earlier—itself a patently insufficient amount of time to prepare a defense to charges of crimes against humanity, which are very factually and legally complex. That violation of Rule 40 was in no way cured by the 40-day continuance granted the first day of trial; by comparison, when the prosecution in Kovacevic introduced 14 new genocide charges against the defendants, the ICTY Appeals Chamber held that a seven month continuance was reasonable.

Failure to Notify the Defendants of the Charges against Them

Judge Abdel-Rahman read the formal charging document at the end of the prosecution's case. Saddam and his co-defendants are charged with a number of crimes against humanity; the failure to inform them of the charges prior to trial thus significantly limited the defense's ability to effectively cross-examine the prosecution witnesses.

Preventing the Defendants from Presenting Their Case

- After three defense witnesses testified that some of the 148 Shiites allegedly executed in Dujail are still alive—evidence supporting the defense's claim that the documentary evidence regarding the events in Dujail could not be trusted—Chief Judge Abdel-Rahman had the witnesses arrested for perjury, along with a fourth defense witness who claimed that the Chief Prosecutor had tried to bribe him to testify against Saddam. The four witnesses later "confessed" that they testified falsely because they were either intimidated by Saddam loyalists or bribed by the defense. Two of those witnesses, who have since fled Iraq, told the Associated Press that they were beaten in detention to make them sign the confessions.
- The Court refused to allow the defense to enter video that allegedly showed the Chief Prosecutor at a 2004 ceremony in Dujail with several individuals who later became witnesses for the prosecution. The video was refused pending a written request, despite the fact that the Court had earlier allowed the prosecution to introduce video evidence with no advance notice.

Failure to Rule on Defense Motions

The Court has yet to rule on numerous defense motions, many of which were submitted prior to trial. Although some of those motions are likely frivolous—such as the one challenging the IHT's legitimacy—at least two are not. One is a motion to recuse Judge Abdel-Rahman on the ground that he cannot be impartial toward Saddam and his co-defendants, because he is from Halabja, where 5,000 people died in a chemical attack by Saddam's forces, and was once the president of a Halabja victims' society. Rule 11 of the IHT Rules of Procedure and Evidence specifically provide that "[a] Judge may not sit in any case in which he has a personal interest or concerning which he has or has had any personal association which might affect his impartiality."

The other motion sought to obtain the complete records of the Revolutionary Court trial that led to the 148 executions—obviously critical evidence, given that the prosecution's central contention is that the trial was a sham.

The Court has also failed to investigate defense claims that some of the 148 Shiites allegedly executed are still alive, even though Judge Abdel-Rahman ordered such an investigation.

Prejudicial Statements by Government Officials and IHT Judges

In an interview with Al-Iraqiya before the trial began, Iraqi President Jalal Talabani stated: "I received the investigating magistrate who is in charge of questioning Saddam. I encouraged him to continue his interrogation. He told me good news, saying that he was able to extract important confessions from Saddam Hussein." Talabani added that "Saddam signed these confessions," and that "Saddam Hussein is a war criminal and he deserves to be executed 20 times a day for his crimes against humanity."

Prior to trial, Abdul Aziz Hakim, head of the Supreme Council of the Islamic Revolution in Iraq (SCIRI), stated in an interview with Reuters that "there is no doubt that Saddam deserves more than just execution ... I am among those who are going to file a complaint for killing 64 members of my family. For these crimes alone he deserves 64 executions."

• In a 2005 film by Jean-Pierre Krief for Arte France, an IHT judge said that Saddam had "persecuted the Kurds. He killed them, wiped many of them out. He also used chemical weapons with the aim of committing genocide against this race, against this people, to eradicate them as a nation. He also went after the Shiites due to their religious beliefs."

• In the same film, another IHT judge called Saddam "one of the worst tyrants in history."

Political Interference with the Court

The original trial judge, Rizgar Amin, resigned after senior Iraqi government officials publicly criticized him for being too lenient with Saddam. Judge Amin cited those comments as one of the reasons for his resignation.

Judge Amin's replacement, Saeed al-Hammashi, a Shiite, was transferred out of the trial chamber after the De-Baathification Commission claimed that he had been a member of the Baath Party. Not only was Judge al-Hammashi the consensus choice of the IHT judges, the Chief Prosecutor at Saddam's trial was skeptical of the Commission's claims and insisted that it produce proof of al-Hammashi's Baathist past. The Commission refused.

Inadequate Standard of Proof

The IHT statute does not require the Court to find Saddam and his co-defendants guilty "beyond a reasonable doubt" in order to convict. Moreover, Paragraph 213 of the Iraqi Code of Criminal Procedure specifically provides that "[t]he court's ... verdict in a case is based on the extent to which it is satisfied by the evidence presented during any stage of the inquiry or the hearing"—obviously a much lower standard.

Failure to Provide for the Commutation of a Death Sentence

Article 27 of the IHT Statute prohibits any government authority, including the President of Iraq, from "granting" "a pardon or mitigating" the punishment issued by the Court." The article directly contradicts Article 6(4) of the ICCPR, which provides that "[a]none sentenced to death shall have the right to seek pardon or commutation of the sentence. Amnesty, pardon or commutation of the sentence of death may be granted in all cases."

Did the Dujail Trial Meet International Standards of Due Process?

By Michael P. Scharf

Introduction

According to an old adage, where one sits determines where one stands. As someone who helped train the Iraqi High Tribunal's judges, I acknowledge that my writing might naturally reflect an inclination to view the Tribunal sympathetically. In contrast, the writing of many critics of the Tribunal appears shaped by a desire to discredit the institution at every turn as a way of saying: "See, we told you so; Saddam should have been tried by an international tribunal, not an Iraqi court!"

We should not be surprised that expert commentators would have such divergent perceptions of the job the Iraqi High Tribunal has done in its first trial. After all, every major war crimes trial, from the Nazis at Nuremberg to Slobodan Milosevic at The Hague, has been vehemently lambasted as unfair by critics. For an eye-opening example, one need look no further than Senator Robert Taft's 1946 derisive remarks about the (now venerated) Nuremberg Tribunal, which were reproduced in John F. Kennedy's Pulitzer Prize-winning 1956 book, "Profiles of Courage."

Unique Challenges

Moreover, due to the defense tactics in this case, the challenge of ensuring a fair trial while at the same time maintaining order in the courtroom was enormously daunting. Saddam's chief lawyer, Khalil al-Dulaimi, gave an interview to the New York Times a few days ago in which he explained the unusual defense strategy. According to al-Dulaimi, the defense was convinced that Saddam would be found guilty and that Saddam's best chance was to use the proceedings to inflame the insurgency and to stretch the trial out as long as possible, so that in the end the United States would agree to set Saddam free in return for his help in restoring peace to Iraq.[152]

What would even the most distinguished American jurist do, if faced with a defendant and his lawyers whose trial strategy was to be as disruptive as possible, provoke the judge at every opportunity, and continuously attempt to turn the trial into political theatre? For an answer, one need only turn to the recent proceedings against accused al-Qaeda terrorist Zacarias Moussaoui, who was thrown out of court by U.S. District Judge Leonie Brinkema four times in one day, and then temporarily banned from returning to court, due to his disruptive and belligerent outbursts. Newspapers reported that the consensus of legal experts was that Judge Brinkema acted appropriately; in contrast, critics of the Iraqi High Tribunal decried that Judge Ra'ouf Abdel-Rhaman violated international fair trial standards when he did the same exact thing.

Harmless Error

What was truly amazing about the Saddam Trial is that it was televised gavel-to-gavel in Iraq, and the international media broadcast daily highlights with translations. This means that observers around the world had the chance to watch justice unfold over 35 trial days in Baghdad, warts and all. It is worth stressing that few countries in the world have had the courage to go to such lengths to ensure transparency of judicial proceedings, including the U.S. Federal Courts which continue to this day to ban cameras from criminal trials. True, this was among the messiest trials in history, and many mistakes were made for all to see—and for TV commentators including many of our experts to dissect. But as the United States Supreme Court has often said: "We do not live in a perfect world, and a criminal defendant is not guaranteed a perfect trial, just a fair one." Bruton v. United States, 391 U.S. 123 (1968).

In assessing whether the Iraqi High Tribunal's errors and missteps resulted in a miscarriage of justice, it is significant that the Dujail trial (much like the Nuremberg trial) turned out to be based almost entirely on the Ba'ath Regime's own documents, whose authenticity was proven in court and confirmed by the statements of Saddam Hussein in his infamous "I am responsible" testimony in court on March 1, 2006. If Saddam is convicted on the strength of these documents, even an American court would likely dismiss Professor Kevin Jon Heller's catalogue of alleged judicial blunders as "harmless error."

Not an American Court

But we also have to keep in mind that this is not an American court. Although the Iraqi High Tribunal Statute and Rules adopt the fundamental due process safeguards enumerated in Article 14 of the Covenant on Civil and Political Rights, they also make clear that the Tribunal is to be governed by Iraqi Criminal Procedure, which is based on the civil law model prevalent in the

Middle East. While we may not be accustomed to a system that does not provide for disposition of preliminary motions until the final Judgment, that allows the defendant to conduct cross examination along side his lawyer, or that issues a detailed charging instrument at the end of the prosecution's case—that does not mean the IHT process violates international fair trial standards.

Take, for example, Professor Heller's assertion that the trial is unfair because the Tribunal's Statute does not require the Court to find Saddam and his co-defendants guilty "beyond a reasonable doubt." Instead, Article 19 of the IHT's Statute merely provides that "the accused is presumed innocent until proven guilty before the Court." Although the Statute does not spell out the test for proving guilt, the Statute must be read together with the Iraqi Criminal Code and practice, under which a Judge must be "satisfied of a defendant's guilt"—the traditional standard which civil law judicial systems (like France and Holland) employ, and a phrase that the IHT judges told me is functionally equivalent to the American "beyond reasonable doubt standard." It should also be noted here that the U.S. Supreme Court has refused to define what "beyond reasonable doubt" means and has held that American courts do not have to provide any definition of this amorphous phrase in their instructions to a jury in a criminal case.[153]

Moreover, "different" does not always mean "worse." Indeed, in one important respect, the Iraqi High Tribunal improves upon the American judicial model: The IHT Statute requires the Court to produce a written reasoned opinion, explaining in detail the factual and legal basis of its judgment—something that is not required of an American jury verdict which emerges from a proverbial "black box."

Allegations Based on Misleading Press Reports

Reading Professor Heller's essay, I was reminded of how inadequate and at times misleading the reporting has been about this trial in the major newspapers. For trial details, I watch the daily proceedings via Court TV's Webcast, I read English translations of Middle Eastern newspapers which devote a great deal of space to the proceedings, and as a reality check, I talk to the Department of Justice trial observers in Baghdad.

Here are but a few examples of Professor Heller's factual misconceptions:

Professor Heller is critical of Judge Ra'ouf Abdel-Rahman's decision to eject a number of defense attorneys for disruptive conduct, and to replace them with attorneys from the Tribunal's Defense Office, who Heller asserts were incompetent and unprepared. In fact, in January of 2006 the Court ejected only one attorney, after he screamed at the court and insulted the Chief Judge, and one defendant, Barzan Al-Tikriti, who called the Court "the daughter of a whore." The remaining defense attorneys, over Judge Ra'ouf's orders, walked out of Court, abandoning their clients (in a death penalty case) without excuse, and refused to return unless the Court acceded to a set of unreasonable demands including recognizing Saddam Hussein as the President of Iraq. During their boycott, Judge Ra'ouf continued the proceedings with IHT Public Defenders. Not only did the Public Defenders vigorously cross examine witnesses (some press reports said they did a far better job than the retained lawyers), but they were assisted by an international law adviser at all times. Moreover, these Public Defenders were intimately familiar with the trial as they had sat in court every day, reviewed the investigative file before trial began, witnessed the proceedings as they unfolded and remained prepared to step into court at a moment's notice should the privately retained defense attorneys prove unable or unwilling to defend the interests of their clients. There was no preordained decision to eject the privately retained attorneys from the Court and to replace them with IHT Public Defenders, as Professor Heller asserts. The privately retained defense attorneys voluntarily walked out of the courtroom and the Court did what was necessary to keep the trial on track and at the same time protect the defendants—by immediately appointing competent counsel who were prepared to defend their clients in full accordance with Iraqi and international law.

Professor Heller writes: "The Court refused to allow the defense to enter a video that allegedly showed the Chief Prosecutor Ja'afar" at a 2004 ceremony in Dujail with several individuals who later became witnesses for the prosecution." In fact, the Tribunal did permit the Defense to play this video in court and allowed three defense witnesses to testify that the man in the video offered them money to testify against Saddam. After this video was shown, the Prosecution brought the person who was actually shown on the tape, which the defense team had alleged was Prosecutor Ja'afar, into open court. Everyone present, including the defense attorneys, immediately grasped that, despite some resemblance, Prosecutor Ja'afar was not the person shown on this video tape. Those following the proceedings closely got to see the defense counsel profusely apologizing to the Court for this misunderstanding, acknowledging that the testimony that Ja'afar had tried to bribe the witnesses was clearly false.

As a final example of the disconnect between reporting and reality that underlies Professor Heller's conclusions, Professor Heller criticizes Judge Ra'ouf for arresting three defense witnesses for perjury after they testified that they personally knew some of the 1984 Dujail Trial execution victims, who they claimed were actually still alive and well in Iraq. Heller adds that two of these witnesses, who have since fled Iraq, told the Associated Press that they were beaten in detention to make them confess that they had lied to the Court. Heller fails to point out, however, that during these witnesses' testimony, Judge Ra'ouf asked the three whether they could (without the aid of a written piece of paper which they had carried into the witness box) state the names of any of the alleged victims who had not actually been executed. When the witnesses could not, Judge Ra'ouf asked them whether they could write the names on a piece of paper which was separate from the one they carried into court. When the witnesses could not do that either, Judge Ra'ouf asked them to see the list of names which they each were carrying. When presented with the lists, Judge Ra'ouf asked the witnesses whether the names on the list were written in their own hand. All three witnesses admitted in open court that another source had given them the lists of names. They were imprisoned for perjury after, not before, they freely made this admission.

A more thorough rebuttal of Professor Heller's numerous contentions is warranted but space limitations prevent me from doing that here. Suffice it to say, the trial is not over and much (including closing arguments, judgment, and appeal) must occur before one can conclusively opine whether the Dujail trial met international standards. But just as the IHT must be fair, so too must we be fair in judging the Court.

Fixing the Legitimacy Deficit in the Saddam Hussein Trial

By Leila Sadat

The theatrics of the Saddam Hussein Trial have confirmed many onlookers worst fears that the trial is political theater, rather than serious legal process. Even prior to the trial's beginning, the manner in which the Court was established, its funding, operation, jurisdiction, substantive law and procedural rules all raised some very serious issues regarding its legitimacy. In spite of Saddam Hussein's recent dramatic confession that he was responsible for (but not guilty of) the killings at Dujail, and the very moving testimony of several prosecution witnesses, the proceedings over the last few months since the opening day on October 19, 2005 appear to raise more questions than answers. Indeed, the balance sheet (so far) is far from positive: So far the total is one judge dead; one court employee and two defense lawyers killed; the rest of the defense team either excluded or periodically boycotting the proceedings (depending on whom one believes), and being replaced by Court appointed lawyers; the presiding judge forced to resign, only to be replaced by a judge who was then forced to resign and who was himself replaced by a Kurdish judge from the town of Halabja, the northern Iraqi town which was the situs of one of Saddam's regimes worst chemical weapons attacks; and two, and maybe more accused, threatening hunger strikes, including the Court's top defendant, Saddam Hussein.

Of course, high profile trials of former leaders are bound to be dramatic, and were the theatrics the only difficulty one might dismiss them as par for the course. Yet very serious questions remain regarding the legitimacy of the overall endeavor, as well as it's potential for assisting Iraq's transition to the rule of law, and at least three major problems persist.

Should Judge Rahman Be Recused?

Accusations of bias directed towards a judge are serious matters, and should be thoughtfully considered. Michael Scharf argues that Serbs may have believed that Judge Richard May was biased against Slobodan Milosevic because he was a British national, and NATO (a nineteen-country Regional Security Organization) conducted military operations to repel Milosevic's incursion into Kosovo. Yet that standard does not comport with rules for the recusal of judges in either international or national tribunals. (Indeed, accepting this argument would have disqualified judges from each of the nineteen countries of NATO including the United States, whose current Judge, Theodor Meron, has presided over the Appeals Chamber of the Court (and heard appeals in the Milosevic case) for the last several years). So clearly, the nationality or ethnicity of a particular judge is not enough, without more, to support otherwise unfounded allegations of bias. Indeed, if the test for recusal were that broad, almost any judge could be disqualified for a variety of reasons including social class (biased against or for the poor) or religion. So, the mere fact that the presiding judge in the Saddam trial is Kurdish should not and does not disqualify him. More disquieting, however, is that the judge hales from Halabja, and has family members who were killed by the attack there that was allegedly ordered by Saddam. Under the rules governing International Tribunals, the question is whether Judge Rahman can be said to have a "personal interest in the case,"[154] because members of his family were the victim's of one the defendant's alleged crimes, even if it is not the crime charged in the instant case. Although hearing the Dujail case might pass this test, cases involving Kurdish victims, particularly from Halabja, clearly would not. Of course, there may not be any future trials, in which case the victims of Halabja will have to content themselves with experiencing justice vicariously through the active participation of Judge Rahman.

Will the Sunni's Accept the Judgment of the Court?

In a recent television appearance, Iraq's Deputy Ambassador to the United Nations stated that Iraqi's believe that justice is being done by the Saddam Hussein trial. Yet it is clear that this position does not reflect Sunni public opinion. What the Sunni's see is a trial presided over by a Kurdish judge of a claim involving Shiite victims. Of course, just as German public opinion was initially negative towards the Nuremberg trials, and Serb public opinion is mixed towards the Milosevic trial, perhaps it is unrealistic to expect individuals that share the ethnicity or nationality of the defendant to immediately embrace the proceedings. Yet if they are ever to do so, the proceedings must be seen as fair, which these proceedings do not appear to be. While the prosecution has done a good job introducing evidence of Saddam's potential culpability for Dujail, the defense team, at least until now, has not been allowed to raise real issues regarding the jurisdiction of the Court and the charges against the accused, and when it has asked for a change of venue—a completely reasonable request given the killings, threats and daily insecurity that surrounds the Court proceedings—it's requests have been summarily dismissed.

Under Saddam's regime, defense lawyers received the file of their clients the morning of the trial. This attitude appears to persist in the Iraqi High Tribunal. Unless Saddam's defense team is allowed to put forward an effective defense, which might require that the proceedings be moved out of Iraq for security reasons, the trial will never appear fair to the Sunnis—now or twenty years from now. Additionally, the judges need to issue written, reasoned decisions on preliminary motions relating to jurisdiction, venue, and particular defenses. Otherwise their out of hand dismissal of these motions—even if correct on the facts and the law—appear to be arbitrary and partial, rather than judicious and impartial. Finally, of the five initial judges sitting on the Saddam trial, three have now been replaced. This suggests political interference with the Court that is unlikely to sit well with constituencies already inclined to be skeptical about the proceedings. Further tinkering with the composition of the bench needs to stop if the proceedings are to retain any semblance of credibility.

Will the More Significant Cases Ever Be Tried So That an Accurate Historical Record Is Made?

A trial of the Dujail killings will presumably result in the conviction of Saddam and the other accused—it is hard to imagine, given the short shrift the defense team has received thus far that any other outcome is possible. Under article 27(B) of the Court's Statute, punishments must be executed within 30 days of the date when the judgment becomes final and non-appealable. It is difficult to imagine that the Dujail trial can conclude without the Court imposing a sentence upon the accused (which could be the death penalty); and although it has been argued that this is only the first of many cases that will be brought against Saddam Hussein and the other accused, it would seem inconsistent with the Court's statute to permit serial trials of the same accused for other offenses. Additionally, even if article 27(B) was interpreted not to apply, or the Court simply refrained from imposing a sentence in order to avoid its application, what kind of due process would the accused receive in subsequent proceedings if a death sentence had already been imposed or threatened in a prior proceeding? And what would be his incentive (or his lawyers) to zealously defend against the charges presented? The Court therefore has two unpleasant alternatives: Not to try the other cases against these accused, meaning that the most significant crimes—Halabja, the invasion and occupation of Kuwait, the suppression of the 1991 uprising, the draining of the southern marshes, the ethnic cleansing of ethnic Persians from Iraq to Iran, and the unlawful killing of political opponents—will never be heard. Alternatively, to try them in what would probably be labeled show trials. In neither case will the kind of historic record be made that can ensure that Saddam Hussein is remembered as a war criminal, rather than a martyr.

Looking Beyond Due Process

By Mark A. Drumbl

Michael Scharf and Kevin Jon Heller engage in a vigorous debate whether the Hussein trial, thus far, accords with internationalized notions of due process. I have two responses. First, although this is an interesting debate, what I believe more relevant is to consider the effects of process on the narrative that emerges from the trial. Second, I worry that much of the energies of external observers are caught up in the minutiae of due process and technocratic assessments, instead of looking at a broader picture likely much more relevant to Iraqis. This broader picture involves judging the full record of Saddam's abuses and, further, the relevance of retrospective justice during a tragic period of ongoing violence and injustice.

Iraqi High Tribunal judges demonstrate considerable vigilance in controlling the courtroom. On the one hand, tight control is necessary for managerial and bureaucratic reasons, to streamline process, dissipate inflammatory controversy, and preserve judicial authority. The need for such control arises from Hussein's antics, designed to turn the proceedings into farce. On the other hand, though, levels of control that become too tight may strangle the judicial record and thereby incur credibility costs. To the best of my knowledge, the Iraqi High Tribunal judges have not yet formally responded to defense motions that pertain to the Tribunal's jurisdiction and the legality of its creation. Whereas debate over the formation of the Tribunal may be unnecessary, embarrassing, or technical to U.S. officials, this debate may be construed differently by Iraqis insofar as it goes to the heart of the U.S. occupation and continuing U.S. control over important political decisions in Iraq, including the decision to put Hussein on trial and invest large sums of money to that end. This presents a contrast with the ICTY, whose interlocutory opinion on jurisdiction in the Tadic matter flaws notwithstanding grappled with the institution's own legitimacy.

As I have previously written, Iraqi High Tribunal prosecutors elected to proceed through a series of mini-trials instead of, as had been the case with Milosevic, one overwhelming omnibus proceeding. The first mini-trial involved the deaths, at the hands of the Iraqi state, of 148 residents of the Shiite village of Dujail. Although a grievous act, the Dujail massacre remains a very small part of Hussein's atrocities, which involved the deaths of at least 300,000 Iraqis (exclusive of those who perished in wars conducted against Iran and Kuwait). Notwithstanding that the Dujail proceedings permits the opportunity to judge the Revolutionary Court as a whole for applying the law in the service of oppression, their overall performativity is of relatively modest value. Other Tribunal mini-trials involve a higher-stakes context. This is the case with imminent proceedings related to the Anfal campaign. By proceeding sequentially, Iraqi High Tribunal prosecutors ensure cyclical episodes of gratification and closure. They thereby reduce the risks that long-term proceedings may lead to a deferred all-or-nothing outcome. This is a prudential move. However, it is not without its own drawbacks. It results in a dramaturgical methodology in which the narrative is related through iterated vignettes. Tribunal officials need to be diligent that the digestible parts add up to a compelling, overarching whole. If discontinuous lower-stakes convictions remain narratively fragmented, then the Tribunal may, in the name of prudence, have forsaken the opportunity to leave a hardier historical footprint.

Finally, the choice to prosecute Saddam Hussein (and other defendants) and to showcase this trial as an instrument for transitional justice was made at a time of ex ante optimism about the ability to maintain order in Iraq. At present, however, Iraq is wrought with pervasive insecurity. There are daily reports of bombings, death, and sectarian violence. The Tribunal itself has been plagued by violence. Several individuals associated with the Tribunal (including a judge and three defense lawyers) have been assassinated. Any accountability process must reasonably guarantee the safety of its participants and its audience. Iraqis wonder why so much effort is dispensed to punishing twenty-five year old crimes while such limited effort is dispensed to punish yesterday's sectarian crimes.

Section 3: Issues of Proof

Does Saddam Hussein Have a Viable Defense Based on the Necessity to Combat Insurgents and Terrorists?

By Michael P. Scharf

In the first trial of the Iraqi High Tribunal scheduled to start on October 19, 2005, Saddam Hussein and several of his lieutenants will be prosecuted for the attack on the Iraqi town of Dujail in 1982 — an attack which involved the killing of 150 townspeople, the destruction of their homes and businesses, and the burning of the surrounding date palm groves. Under the headline, "Saddam Expects to Prove Innocence, Lawyer Says," (USA Today, October 13, 2005), Saddam Hussein's lawyer, Khalil al-Dulaimi, is quoted as saying: "Saddam Hussein was on a visit to this village [Dujail], and he was subject to an assassination attempt. Punishing those who carried it out is justifiable all over the world. Any president in the position of Saddam would do the same thing." Wiping a town out in retaliation for an assassination attempt is not a legitimate defense, but wiping a town out to root out terrorists and suppress an insurgency may be another matter.

To prove this line of defense, Dulaimi could call former U.S. President Bill Clinton or other members of his administration to testify in Baghdad or through video link from the United States. After all, in 1993, Clinton ordered the launch of 23 cruise missiles to strike the Iraqi Intelligence Service Headquarters in downtown Baghdad when the U.S. learned that Iraq was behind an attempt to assassinate former President Bush during a visit to Kuwait. Cruise missiles are a blunt instrument when fired into a populous residential area, and numerous civilian casualties were reported. "If Clinton's action was justified in response to an assassination attempt," Dulaimi will ask, "why wouldn't Saddam's be?"

Or Dulaimi could call U.S. General George Casey, who currently commands the U.S. forces in Iraq. Just last week, (October 4, 2005), General Casey ordered the U.S. military to launch a major offensive against three small towns in the Euphrates River valley (Haqlaniyah, Parwana and Haditha), which were reportedly being used by insurgents and members of the al Qaeda terrorist organization as a base of operations in Iraq. The attack, code-named "River Gate," involved air strikes from U.S. warplanes and helicopters, followed by an assault by 2,500 U.S. and Iraqi government soldiers. Most of the buildings in the towns were destroyed, and hundreds of Iraqi casualties were reported, including civilians who were "unavoidable collateral damage." Similar operations have been conducted across Iraq in an effort to "uproot" terrorists and insurgents, and to "suppress" terrorist and insurgent attacks in the months leading to the vote on the Iraqi Constitution. In the context of this aggressive campaign against Iraqi terrorists and insurgents, the Iraqi Department of Health has reported that the U.S. and Iraqi armed forces have been responsible for twice as many civilian casualties than those caused by insurgent and terrorist attacks. "If civilian casualties are acceptable collateral damage for General Casey's troops in their effort to stamp out al Qaeda and suppress insurgency in Iraq in 2005," Dulaimi will ask, "why not for Saddam Hussein's troops facing the same type of threat in 1982?"

These will be tough questions for the prosecution to respond to, and certainly the line of questioning will raise questions of moral equivalence that may be embarrassing for the Bush Administration. For an answer, the Prosecution is likely to turn to the 1969 case of *United States v. Calley*, one of the most important war crimes trials of the Vietnam war era. The Defendant, Lt. William Calley was charged with commanding troops which executed 102 civilians at the South Vietnamese town of My Lai in 1968. In defense, Calley said that he had received orders by radio to destroy the town, which was being used as a base of operations by the Viet Cong, and to kill all the townspeople since it was impossible to distinguish Viet Cong insurgents from innocent civilians. This was in essence, the same exact argument that Dulaimi is likely to make on behalf of Saddam Hussein and the other defendants in the Dujail case. The Court rejected Calley's obedience to orders defense, finding that an order to kill all of the townspeople, including babies, children, and frail elderly persons, was a manifestly illegal order. The Court reaffirmed that under international law, a person can be held criminally liable for ordering such an atrocity, and that subordinates have a duty to disobey such an illegal order or they too can be held liable for carrying it out.

Can the Defendants Raise the "Tu Quoque" Defense?

By Michael P. Scharf

"Tu Quoque," Latin for "you also," is a defense in which the defendant argues that since the other side committed the same crimes, it is not legitimate to prosecute the defendants of those crimes. In the case of Saddam Hussein, the defense might be raised in three contexts. First, the defense may seek to

argue that since the United States provided financial support and material assistance to aid the Ba'athist Regime's war efforts against Iran, with knowledge
of the actions the regime took against Iraqi Kurds and Shi'ites who supported
Iran, that it would be unfair for an American-created Tribunal to prosecute
the defendants for such actions. Second, the defense may try to argue that
since the United States invaded Iraq without Security Council authorization
or a legitimate claim to self-defense, it is unfair for an American-created Tribunal to prosecute the defendants for the crime of aggression against Iran or
Kuwait. And third, the defense may seek to claim that since the United States
has argued that the necessity defense justifies its aggressive actions against
towns in Iraq and Afghanistan suspected of being a base of operation for terrorists, that an American-created Tribunal should be estopped from denying
the right of the Ba'athist Regime to take actions for the same reason against
the northern Kurds and the southern marsh Arabs.

The Tu Quoque defense is a cousin of the equitable "clean hands doctrine,"
which provides that one who comes to court for help must come with unsoiled
hands. The International Criminal Tribunal for the Former Yugoslavia stated
in *Prosecutor v. Kupreskic* (2000), that the Tu Quoque defense has been "universally rejected" and that "there is in fact no support either in State practice
or in the opinions of publicists for the validity of such a defense." But precedent for applying the doctrine can be found in the case law of the Federal
Supreme Court of Germany which held in a 1960 war crimes case that "no
State may accuse another State of violations of international law and exercise
criminal jurisdiction over the latter's citizens in respect of such violations if it
is itself guilty of similar violations against the other State or its allies."[155] Based
on this precedent, we must ask: Did the U.S. government's involvement in establishing the Iraqi High Tribunal open the door for the defendants to argue
the Tu Quoque defense?

The first answer is that although the United States' CPA initially established
the Iraqi High Tribunal in December 2003, the IHT is not a U.S. court. The
Tribunal and its judges were approved on August 11, 2005, by the Iraqi National Assembly, and the judges and prosecutor are Iraqi, not American.
Moreover, under the IHT Statute the judges and prosecutor are independent
and are prohibited from taking guidance from any government. Since the
Judges and Prosecutors represent the Iraqi people and not the United States,
their hands are not soiled by the actions of the United States, and there is no
equitable bar to prosecuting the defendants

Secondly, Courts that have examined the Tu Quoque defense in the past have
held that a guilty State's involvement in creating a Tribunal does not open the
door to the Tu Quoque defense where the Tribunal's bench does not include

judges from the guilty State. The issue arose in two cases before the post-World War II U.S. Military Tribunal at Nuremberg, where the defense argued that the Tribunal could not legitimately convict the defendants of the crime of aggression when the Soviet Union, which cooperated in the establishment of the Military Tribunal, had also engaged in a war of aggression in complicity with Germany. In the "High Command Case",[156] the Military Tribunal ruled that "Under general principles of law, an accused does not exculpate himself from a crime by showing that another committed a similar crime, either before or after the alleged commission of the crime by the accused." And in the "Ministries Case,"[157] the Tribunal stated: "But even if it were true that the London Charter and Control Council Law No. 10 are legislative acts, making that a crime which before was not so recognized, would the defense argument be valid? It has never been suggested that a law duly passed becomes ineffective when it transpires that one of the legislators whose vote enacted it was himself guilty of the same practice."

Thus, the Iraqi High Tribunal should reject the defendants' attempts to elicit evidence of American actions in an attempt to prove a Tu Quoque defense. There is, however, one argument that the defense can make based on American actions that would be relevant. At Nuremberg, defendant Grand Admiral Carl Doenitz argued that he could not be convicted of waging unrestricted submarine warfare in the Atlantic since American Admiral Chester Nimitz had admitted that the United States had done the same thing in the Pacific. But the defense was not arguing that American violation of international law rendered it unfair to convict the German Admiral for the same acts. Rather, the defense was arguing that the American actions indicated that it was not a violation of international law to conduct unrestricted submarine warfare. Thus, Defense Counsel Kranzbuehler told the Tribunal: "The stand taken by the Prosecution (which had argued against recognition of the Tu Quoque defense) differs entirely from the conception on which my application is based. I in no way wish to prove or even to maintain that the American Admiralty in its U-boat warfare against Japan broke international law. On the contrary, I am of the opinion that it acted strictly in accordance with international law."[158] The Nuremberg Tribunal was persuaded by this argument, and did not convict Doenitz of the charge.

Drawing on the Nuremberg precedent, defense counsel before the Iraqi High Tribunal may legitimately seek to prove that the international community's mixed reaction and the absence of a General Assembly resolution condemning the 2003 invasion of Iraq, as well as the lack of consensus on a definition of aggression for use by the International Criminal Court, indicate that there does not presently exist sufficient international agreement on the crime of aggression to fairly prosecute the defendants of the charge. Similarly, defense counsel may legitimately seek to prove that the international community's lack of condemnation of American aggressive actions to root out terrorists and insurgents from towns in Iraq and Afghanistan indicates that it was not against international law for Saddam Hussein to take similar action against the town of Dujail in 1982. The prosecution may counter with evidence that the defendants' actions were unnecessary or disproportionate to the threat, but this will ultimately be a question that the Tribunal will have to decide based on the evidence. It is not an argument foreclosed by virtue of the international rejection of the Tu Quoque defense.

When Witnesses Get Cold Feet—
Manage Your Witnesses

By David M. Crane

On, 13 February 2006, we saw two key witnesses get cold feet. This is not unusual in criminal trials throughout the world. However, at the international level, what appears to be routine or normal is being viewed through a prism that is anything but normal. Already the Iraqi High Tribunal suffers from credibility problems, a reluctant judiciary, hysterical defendants, and now witnesses that "can't remember". This is not good.

In my mind, having prepared and worked with several hundred witnesses in proving our joint criminal trials against the leadership of various combatant groups in the civil war that devastated Sierra Leone, witness management is absolutely essential. There should be no surprises, as we have just seen, if one works with their witnesses. Like Iraq, witnesses in Sierra Leone live and work in and around the crime scenes and the relatives and colleagues of the indictees. Witness management becomes critical in ensuring their safety, security, as well as their comfort level in coming forward to tell the truth.

In West Africa, we developed an extensive witness management program that ensured that the local victims and other witnesses living in a society transitioning from war to peace, with the rule of law fragile and uncertain, could testify at the international level and provide sustainable and creditable testimony. We had few surprises, despite the initial reluctance and fear at times of some witnesses giving evidence against very powerful and dangerous men who have great influence outside their detention cells.

Our program, designed by the Chief of Investigations, Dr. Alan White and his team, in conjunction with our Chief of Prosecutions, Luc Cote, and the

Victims and Witness Support Unit of the Special Court for Sierra Leone, was designed to take an identified witness from initial assessment, interviews, background checks, trial preparation, into the trial chamber ready and willing to tell the truth. For child victims and gender crime witnesses this could take as much as 1–2 years. For witnesses who could testify directly implicating the accused from a political or policy point of view, our witness management program ensured anonymity, family security, and in some instances protection for an extensive period of time after their testimony was taken.

Regardless of importance, every witness was monitored regularly, briefed periodically on their status, with trial counsel checking their testimony, and our witness management team, their security. Each witness was classified based on importance to the case and the threat to their safety. This was reviewed by our witness management team constantly. I met every week with the witness management team going over each and every witness, particularly our witnesses who were political. The bottom-line here is that our witnesses in West Africa gained a comfort level as to the process, their status, the part they would play in the case, and when they would testify. We gave them no surprises and in large measure they gave us no surprises.

Saddam's Admission: I Am Responsible

By Paul Williams and Brianne McGonigle

Saddam Hussein's latest in court declaration, accepting accountability for his action as Iraqi's former leader in relation to the current charges against him, is interesting for two important reasons. First, never before during the history of modern war crimes trials has a former leader requested that he alone should be held responsible for the actions of his regime and his subordinates.

At trial on 1 March 2006, Saddam intervened near the closing of the day's session in which the Prosecution presented evidence that implicated Saddam and his co-defendants in the killing of 148 Shia Muslims from Dujail. He claimed responsibility for razing the farms of those convicted of trying to assassinate him in the town of Dujail in 1982 and for their subsequent deaths, stating further that his co-defendants are not criminally responsible for his decisions as leader.

Although Saddam Hussein, like other leaders who have stood trial for war crimes, submits that his actions were legal, his request of the court to release the other defendants for simply "following orders" is unprecedented. There have been numerous defendants at the International Criminal Tribunal for the former Yugoslavia (ICTY) and at the International Criminal Tribunal for Rwanda (ICTR) who have formally pled guilty to the charges against them. However, none have ever asserted that they alone should bear the burden of the blame, and none held such a senior position as Saddam Hussein.

Currently, at the trial of Kosova Liberation Army members at the ICTY, the defense is asserting that two men subordinate to the primary accused, Haradinaj, are willing to plead guilty to the charges against them by asserting that Haradinaj did not issue any orders contrary to international law, thereby attempting to clear him of command responsibility. In contrast to what happened at the IHT today, where a leader claims responsibility to clear subordinates, at the ICTY it is the subordinates attempting to take responsibility to clear a leader.

While Saddam's statement accepting blame is an interesting tactic on behalf of his Defense team, likely increasing his popularity among his supporters, it is unlikely to aid his defense or the defense of his co-defendants. Instead, his admissions have essentially proven two-thirds of the prosecutor's case against him. As for his co-defendants, following orders has been a common defense employed by many accused, but it does not relieve a defendant of guilt. Article 7(4) of the ICTY Statute, which deals with individual criminal responsibility provides:

"The fact that an accused person acted pursuant to an order of a Government or of a superior shall not relieve him of criminal responsibility, but may be considered in mitigation of punishment if the International Tribunal determines that justice so requires."

Erdemovic, the first defendant to formally plead guilty to war crimes in a modern international criminal court, was also found to have followed orders under duress of being killed himself. Nonetheless, he was held responsible for his actions. The fact that he was following orders out of fear for his own life was only taken into consideration at his sentencing. The Trial Chamber applied the ruling of the Appeals Chamber in Erdemovic that "duress does not afford a complete defense to a soldier charged with a crime against humanity and/or a war crime involving the killing of innocent human beings." Instead, it may only be taken into account when mitigating the sentence. It is expected that the IHT will reach a similar conclusion in regards to Saddam and his co-defendants. Moreover, Saddam's assertion that his actions were in accordance with Iraqi law, a defense also employed by Nazis accused of war crimes, will likely have little impact.

Second, Saddam's assertion of responsibility is interesting because of the change from present tense to past tense in regards to his leadership role in Iraq. In the past he spoke of himself as a leader in the present tense rather than in past tense. For example, in October of this past year, a defiant Saddam Hussein, challenging the legitimacy of the Iraqi court, declared, "I am the president of Iraq," and "I will not answer to this so-called court." Juxtapose that statement with the statement made this week, in which Saddam declared, "I am Saddam Hussein. I was in charge, and just because things have changed, I am not going to say someone else was responsible." He went on to say, "They [his co-defendants] were not presidents, there was only one." Although he concluded in the present tense, the damage was already done. Despite the statement's success in rallying his supporters, Saddam also made some other principal errors during his outburst. When speaking on his prerogative as leader to prosecute those he felt were responsible for the attack on his life, Saddam stated:

"If I had wanted, I wouldn't have referred them [those accused of the attempted assassination] to the Revolutionary Court. I did refer them to the Revolutionary Court. And they were tried according to the law, just as you are trying [us]. So Awad [Bandar, former head of the court and a co-defendant] tried them according to the law, he had the right to try or to acquit according to the law and according to his own judgment."

In essence, Saddam declared that just as he had a right, while the leader of Iraq, to try individuals he felt were guilty of attempted assassination, the IHT now has the legitimacy to try him under the rule of law of the current Iraq. Saddam's outbursts this past week, while highly unlikely to help his legal defense, have proved interesting for their unprecedented nature and for their indication of his reluctant acceptance of the tribunal's role in regards to administering law.

Saddam's Admission: I Am Responsible

By David M. Crane

As I've stated in the past publicly, these indictees are behaving in as "classical" war crimes indictees who rant and rave at the system, defy the Court, and then eventually simmer down and the trial moves forward. This happened to Goering (Nuremberg), Milosevic (Yugoslavia), Norman (Sierra Leone) etc.

It is important to understand that, in general, the rules of procedure and Iraqi law allow defendants to do and say things unlike common law, where a defendant does not have to make any statement or give testimony and the burden is entirely on the prosecution to prove the case against an accused, usually beyond a reasonable doubt.

Saddam and others are making fairly incriminating statements that are to the benefit of the prosecution. I would be surprised indeed that they were doing this on advice of their counsel. The only reason I would offer is that many of these indictees feel strongly that they were above the law and believe that what they are saying or were doing was not breaking the law. Their attitudes in Iraq, Yugoslavia, Sierra Leone, Rwanda are: "I am the supreme ruler/tyrant and I made the law or interpreted/used the law as I felt necessary for the good of the people or nation."

As a former international prosecutor, my perspective is that this has been a good few days for the Iraqi prosecutor. But most importantly, Saddam is now being seen (by the people of Iraq) as having finally submitted to the rule of law. Let's hope this continues.

Saddam Can Handle the Truth— The Tyrant Takes Full Responsibility for the Actions of His Government

By Gregory S. McNeal

Saddam Hussein made a dramatic courtroom admission reminiscent of the movie A Few Good Men. In the film, young Navy defense attorney Lt. Daniel Kafee (Tom Cruise) needs to prove that Colonel Nathan Jessup (Jack Nicholson) ordered Kafee's clients to execute a "Code Red" which resulted in the accidental death of a fellow Marine. The order was key to proving that the defendants did not act on their own with the intent to kill and that true responsibility lay with the commander. One piece of dialogue between Kaffee and his co-counsel explains the defense theory:

> Kaffee: *Our clients followed the order. The cover-up isn't our case. To win, Jessup has to tell the jury that he ordered the code red.*
> Sam: *And you think you can get him to just say it?*
> Kaffee: *I think he wants to say it. I think he's pissed off that he's gotta hide from us. I think he wants to say that he made a command decision and that's the end of it.*

Kaffee puts Jessup on the stand, rattles him, and in a dramatic shouting match asks Jessup if he ordered the Code Red. Jessup screams "You're goddamn right I did!" Thus proving a large part of the defense.

Saddam did a similar favor for the prosecution by brazenly admitting command responsibility and setting the stage for the conclusion of the prosecutor's case. The current proceeding, known as "the Dujail case," is the first in a series of trials planned against Saddam and his co-defendants. The charges stem from a failed July 1982 assassination attempt against the former dictator in the town of Dujail, north of Baghdad. In retaliation, Saddam and his seven co-defendants are alleged to have ordered and carried out the aerial bombardment of the town, the burning of its groves of date palm trees, the destruction of its water supply, the bulldozing of the its houses, and the imprisonment, torture, and execution of hundreds of the town's inhabitants.

The keys to proving Saddam guilty are: first, proving that the crimes occurred, a nearly indisputable fact for which substantial evidence has been admitted; second, proving that the defendants were tied to and responsible for the crimes, and finally addressing the defendants' affirmative defense that their actions were justified. The prosecutors, with Saddam's admission, all but proved the second element.

In the trial's morning session prosecutors presented before and after satellite photos of the farmlands around Dujail. On the left was a shot taken before the attempted assassination of Saddam in July 1982. It showed green farmlands. On the right was a satellite photo of the same land, taken on July 31, 1983. In the newer photo the land was brown from the demolition of the orchards. The evidence proved the fact that someone committed the war crime of destroying the village's crops. But like all evidence in the case, the prosecution still needed to tie the evidence to Saddam. Fortunately for the prosecutors, Saddam would have his Jack Nicholson moment.

As the afternoon session drew to a close, Saddam took the stand and stunned the court, admitting "I demolished the orchards. That was a Revolutionary Council decision to modernize the orchard, and I signed that order." He argued that Iraqi law allowed him to seize land and boldly stated "Where is the crime? Where is the crime?" Saddam went on, speaking about his other crimes, "If trying a suspect accused of shooting at a head of state—no matter what his name is—is considered a crime, then you have the head of state in your hands. Try him."

History will regard Saddam's admissions as a significant turn in the trial. With the hardest part of the case now proven, it is likely that the prosecution will soon rest.

As the former dictator stated, "I am Saddam Hussein, and at the time of leadership, I am responsible. It is not my habit to rely on others. I signed that decision, and nobody forced me to sign that decision." Did Saddam order the massacre at Dujail? You're goddamn right he did.

Hussein: "I'm Responsible" An Admission of Control but Not of Guilt

By Michael P. Scharf

Just before the close of the Iraqi High Tribunal's proceedings on March 1, 2006, Saddam Hussein asked to address the Court. Hussein, who was known for the brutal micromanagement style of his role-model, Soviet Premier Joseph Stalin, was apparently uncomfortable with the line of argument the defense was beginning to develop in its cross examinations that day, namely that the abuses at Dujail were the responsibility of subordinates who had acted outside the scope of their orders.

Hussein stood and told the court that he had ordered the destruction of the orchards and homes, and that he had ordered the arrest, interrogation, trial, and execution of the townspeople. "If I hadn't wanted to, I wouldn't have sent them to the Revolutionary Court. But I did," he said of the villagers. "And they were charged according to the law, just like you charge people according to the law.... When the person says he's responsible, why go to others and search? Saddam Hussein was a leader and says, 'I'm responsible.' "

With these words, Hussein proved about one-third of the Prosecutor's case. He proved that he was in effective control of the perpetrators, which is the legal standard required for liability under the principle of command responsibility. He also proved that he ordered their actions, thereby proving direct responsibility. Now, the Prosecution doesn't have to spend time proving the command structure and power hierarchy in the Iraqi Government, and is thus likely to rest its case when the trial resumes on March 12 or soon thereafter.

Perhaps Hussein's psychological makeup[159] made it impossible for him to maintain that his subordinates were acting outside his orders or control. He seemed to want the world to know that he was in full control of everything in Iraq during his reign, and that included the actions against the town of Dujail. But his admission of control was not an admission of guilt.

Hussein and his lawyers will still argue during the second phase of the trial that his actions against Dujail were lawful under international and Iraqi law. In doing so, they will make some interesting comparisons to recent American military actions against towns across Iraq and Afghanistan, in which the United States has bombed buildings and rounded up, interrogated, and detained hundreds of suspected terrorists and insurgents. The difference, which the Prosecution will presumably point out during its cross examinations and closing argument, is that the United States didn't round up eight- and eleven-year-old children as Hussein's subordinates did at Dujail; one third of the people subject to interrogation by the United States did not die from torture as they did at the hands of Hussein's subordinates in the 1980s; and the United States never ordered executions without a trial as Saddam Hussein did to the citizens of Dujail.

The submission of the "execution documents" together with Hussein's admission of control represents a major turning point in the trial. With this important point now proven, the media and public's attention has begun to focus on the evidence and legal principles and not just Hussein's antics.

What Is the Significance of the Documents Entered into Evidence by the Prosecution?

By Michael A. Newton

Saddam's outburst at the conclusion of the court session on Wednesday might be the most important few minutes of the entire trial because the judges are now in a perfect position to assess his words and demeanor in light of all the other evidence found in the referral packet and introduced during the court proceedings. As far as the actual documents that were introduced formally into evidence, it is important to remember that they were contained in the original referral packet collected by Judge Ra'id and provided to the defense team back in August 2005. The relevant exhibits have been in the referral packet and in the possession of the defense team and are being publicly explored at the appropriate time. The documents point to crimes against humanity that go well beyond the murders of the civilians in the aftermath of the attempted assassination in Dujail. The problem of weaving together documentary evidence, video and film evidence, and live witness testimony into a compelling and complete trial narrative has been shared by all of the major tribunals applying international norms since Nuremberg. The Iraqis have learned the lessons of past tribunals and are reading some into evidence, allowing others to come in as written drafts, and as in the past two days, putting some into digital form for viewing in open court—pretty sophisticated—the message is that the trial itself cannot be fairly judged in its various pieces, but its true procedural adequacy can only be properly assessed as a holistic matter—the prosecutor promised these documents in the opening statement and now has presented them.

In legal terms, the documents are a powerful supplement to the testimony of the numerous witnesses in establishing a joint criminal enterprise by the Ba'athist leadership, up to and including Saddam. The modern doctrine of a joint criminal enterprise under international criminal law was first clarified by the International Criminal Tribunal for the Former Yugoslavia Appeals Chamber in the Tadic case and its legal contours have been shaped in a number of subsequent cases.[160] According to settled jurisprudence, the required actus reus for each form of joint criminal enterprise comprises three elements, each of which Saddam helped establish with regard to the crimes alleged in al-Dujail with his outburst in open court. First, a plurality of persons is required. They need not be organized in a military, political or administrative structure. Second, the existence of a common purpose which amounts to or involves the commission of a crime provided for in the Statute is required. The cases in other tribunals are clear that there is no necessity for this purpose to have been previously arranged or formulated. It may materialize extemporaneously and be inferred from the facts introduced during trial. Third, the participation of the accused in the common purpose is required, which involves the perpetration of one of the crimes provided for in the Statute. This participation need not involve commission of a specific crime under one of the provisions (for example, murder, extermination, torture, or rape), but may take the form of assistance in, or contribution to, the execution of the common purpose. The criminal theory of joint criminal enterprise is different from merely aiding and abetting a crime as the ICTY Appeals Chamber clarified in Kvocka et al,. Judgment (AC), 28 February 2005, para. 90 (Where the aider and abettor only knows that his assistance is helping a single person to commit a single crime, he is only liable for aiding and abetting that crime. This is so even if the principal perpetrator is part If a joint criminal enterprise involving the commission of further crimes. Where, however, the accused knows that his assistance is supporting the crimes of a group of persons involved in a joint criminal enterprise and shares that intent, then he may be found criminally responsible for the crimes committed in furtherance of that common purpose as a co-perpetrator.) Under some limited circumstances, the theory of joint criminal enterprise may even extend to the crime of genocide in its various forms provided that the requisite intent is present. Rwamakuba, Decision on Interlocutory Appeal Regarding Application of Joint Criminal Enterprise to the Crime of Genocide (AC), 22 October 2004, para. 31.

The evidence that underage victims were murdered and that their bodies were secretly disposed of was particularly chilling, and especially powerful because those documents and Saddam's reaction to them attest to the knowledge and approval of President Hussein himself. Perhaps most importantly, there is absolutely no evidence that any of the victims actually received a trial before they were sentenced to death and murdered at the command of the Revolutionary court pursuant to Saddam's signed orders; this evidence strikes at the very heart of the efforts of the legal professionals working in the Iraqi High Tribunal to punish those who subverted the rule of law in Iraq. It is no accident that the Iraqi lawyers demanded that the domestic crime of "manipulating the judiciary or influencing the judiciary" in Article 14 of the Statute be included in the Tribunal's jurisdiction right alongside the crimes of genocide, war crimes, and crimes against humanity in the Statute for the Higher Criminal Court. Furthermore, it is very symbolic that Judge Awad Bandar normally sits beside Saddam Hussein in the courtroom because he was the actor subjected to the demands of politically motivated murder wrapped in the cloak of justice. The judges in Baghdad are now positioned to draw reasonable inferences from the evidence contained in the referral packet and shown in open court and supplemented by the outbursts of the defendants that a common criminal purpose existed to commit crimes against the civilians in al-Dujail.

Execution Order #3, Documentary vs. Testimonial Evidence?

By Mark Drumbl

The Saddam proceedings are adjourned until March 12. From the perspective of the prosecutors, the proceedings adjourned on a high note: the introduction into evidence of a decree allegedly bearing Saddam's signature mandating the execution of 148 Shiite men and boys, some as young as 11, in the Dujail massacre. This massacre was initiated after a failed assassination attempt on Saddam in 1982. Saddam's response to this evidence was more subdued than has hitherto been the case. He admitted he ordered trials of those eventually executed, but intimated that this was legal in light of their having been involved in an assassination attempt against a head of state. This response becomes less plausible to the extent the execution orders exceeded the actual attackers.

This development demonstrates the power of documentary evidence. One of many reasons the Nuremberg proceedings went relatively smoothly was because of the Nazis' propensity to document their evil. Then, nearly two decades later, it became possible for proceedings such as those involving Adolf Eichmann in Jerusalem District Court to unfurl around the axis of witness testimony. With the foundations of the criminality having been established documentarily, witnesses became able to recount their own harrowing stories, thereby serving important cathartic and pedagogical functions. This put a human face on the suffering instead of merely sterile prose of placidly authorized extermination.

In the event further documentary evidence in the Saddam case becomes authenticated, then perhaps this can settle the proceedings somewhat and make them more routinized. This suggests that the Prosecution might prefer (if possible) to introduce (and build) a case around documents instead of testimony. However, as sectarian violence in Iraq tragically escalates and the architecture of security crumbles, it seems to me that the trial is increasingly becoming remote from the daily lives of Iraqis. That said, justice in Iraq will be multigenerational. It may be that showing the paper trail first, and hearing the voices later, is a surer path to safeguard the legitimacy of the proceedings in very troubled times. But, on the other hand, this may dampen some of the expressive and didactic possibilities of the trial, assuming that these ever were realistic.

Is the Execution Order the Prosecution's "Smoking Gun" against Saddam?

By Kevin Jon Heller

During the February 28 trial session, the Chief Prosecutor, Jafaar al-Moussawi, presented a presidential order allegedly signed by Saddam Hussein approving the execution of the 148 Dujail villagers whose deaths are the centerpiece of the case against Saddam and his co-defendants. Earlier, Al-Moussawi had presented a document signed by Awad al-Bandar, the former Chief Justice of the Iraqi Revolutionary Court, announcing that the villagers had been sentenced to death and listing them by name.

There is no question that the execution order is critical to the prosecution's case, because it provides the first documentary link between Saddam and the executions. But is it the proverbial "smoking gun"?

At the outset, it is important to note that we do not know the precise charges that have been brought against Saddam—the Iraqi High Tribunal ("IHT") has not made his indictment public. Nevertheless, it is safe to assume that he has been charged, inter alia, with the crime against humanity of "Willful Murder," a violation of Article 12(1)(A) of the IHT Statute. It is that crime I will focus on here.

According to the IHT's Elements of Crimes, which "shall assist" the IHT in interpreting Articles 11, 12, and 13 (i), Willful Murder has three elements:

1. The perpetrator willfully killed one or more persons;
2. The conduct was committed as part of a widespread or systematic attack directed against a civilian population; and

3. The perpetrator knew that conduct was part of or intended the conduct to be part of a widespread or systematic attack directed against a civilian population.

Although Saddam did not personally kill the villagers, Article 15(2)(B) of the IHT Statute provides that a person who orders the commission of a crime is no less criminally responsible for it than the actual perpetrators. The real question, then, is whether the execution order satisfies the elements of Willful Murder under Article 12(1)(A).

Given the evidence that has been presented at trial thus far, it seems clear that it does. The first element is satisfied, because the order led directly to "one or more persons"—148, in fact—being killed. "Willful" here is synonymous with "intentional" (ii) and simply reflects the IHT Statute's general requirement that the defendant must have "meant ... to cause a particular consequence" when he committed the act in question (iii). Saddam obviously intended for the condemned villagers to be killed, so there is no question that he acted intentionally for purposes of Article 12(1)(A).

The second element is also satisfied. "The widespread nature of the attack can be derived in particular from the number of the victims" (iv). 148 executions most likely qualify as a "widespread" attack under this standard; although no international court has ever specified a minimum number of victims, the International Law Commission's commentary to the relevant provision speaks only of a "multiplicity" of victims (v). Moreover, even in the unlikely event that the IHT were to hold that 148 executions are not sufficient to satisfy the "widespread" requirement, the executions would still clearly qualify as a "systematic" attack. In the context of crimes against humanity, "systematic" simply refers to "the organized nature of the acts of violence and the improbability of their random occurrence" (vi). It is difficult to imagine a more organized, less random series of acts than Saddam's brutal reprisal against the Dujail villagers following the attempt on his life.

Finally, the third element is easily satisfied. Saddam personally ordered the executions; insofar as they qualify as a widespread or systematic attack, therefore, he clearly knew and intended his conduct to be part of that attack.

The second and third elements of Willful Murder, of course, require the attack be directed "against a civilian population." Saddam has argued that the villagers were executed because they had participated in the attack on his life—actions that would arguably have deprived the villagers of their civilian status (vii). Nevertheless, it should not be difficult for the prosecution to show that most of the executed villagers did not take part in the assassination attempt; after all, the doomed group contained at least 10 minors, including a child who was 11 years old. The distinction is critical, because the presence of a small number of combatants among an otherwise non-combatant population does not deprive that population of its civilian status (viii).

Saddam has also argued—more centrally to his defense—that the death sentences were lawfully imposed by the Iraqi Revolutionary Court and that, as the President of Iraq, he had every right to order them carried out. That argument seems to have impressed various observers of the trial; a representative of Human Rights Watch, for example, commented: "What we saw today was not Saddam admitting guilt, but admitting to the fact that he acted in accordance with his official duties and powers."

With all due respect to Human Right Watch, that simply isn't accurate. Although Paragraph 223 of the Iraqi Penal Code of 1969 prescribes death for murdering the President of Iraq, Paragraph 31(1) expressly provides that the punishment for attempting a felony punishable by death is not death but life imprisonment. As a result, Saddam did not have the authority to order the executions even if they were involved in the assassination attempt—the order was nothing more than an ultra vires act neither legitimated nor justified by his authority as President of Iraq.

It is difficult to overstate the importance of the ultra vires nature of the execution order. If Saddam could not lawfully have ordered the villagers to be executed, the execution order is, in fact, the prosecution's "smoking gun." It does not matter whether Saddam properly referred the villagers' cases to the Iraqi Revolutionary Court. It does not even matter whether, as al-Moussawi contends, the death sentences were imposed after "imaginary" trials. By signing the execution order, Saddam essentially admitted that he committed Willful Murder as that charge is defined by the Article 12(1)(A) of the IHT Statute—and most likely signed his own execution order, as well.

Show Trial or Real Trial?— A Digest of the Evidence Submitted during the Prosecution's Case-in-Chief

By Michael P. Scharf and Gregory S. McNeal

After five months—but just a dozen "trial days"—the Prosecution is about to rest in the first Saddam Hussein Trial. Nearly obscured by the media's focus on controversial judicial rulings, assassinations of defense counsel, resignation of judges, scathing outbursts, allegations of mistreatment, hunger strikes, and even underwear appearances—is the fact that the Prosecution has been meticulously building a compelling case against Saddam and his seven co-defendants.

This essay provides a detailed précis of the evidence submitted during the Prosecution's case-in-chief. It includes an analysis of the testimony of the three-dozen witnesses, the surprising admissions of defendants Saddam Hussein and Barzan al-Tikriti, and the numerous Exhibits that have been admitted into evidence.

The material is divided into four categories: The first is evidence of control, knowledge and intent. This category includes testimony and documents proving that Saddam and the other defendants are legally responsible for the atrocities done to the town and people of Dujail because they issued orders or in the alternative because they were in control of the perpetrators and had knowledge of their crimes.

The second category is evidence that the attack on Dujail rose to the level of armed conflict, which is a prerequisite for finding that the actions of the defendants were war crimes.

The third category is evidence that the actions taken against the town and people of Dujail constituted a widespread and systematic attack against a civilian population which is necessary to prove the actions of the defendants were crimes against humanity.

The final and by far most extensive category is the evidence of the prohibited acts perpetrated by those under the Defendants' command and control—acts such as the destruction of Dujail's orchards, homes, and wells; and the arrest, torture, and execution of innocent civilians including young children. Taken together, this evidence demonstrates that the attack on Dujail was not a legitimate effort to route out terrorists responsible for an assassination attempt, but rather an act of retaliation and retribution against persons who were in no way involved in the attack on Saddam's convoy.

Control, Knowledge or Intent

- A Video CD was introduced showing the visit of Saddam Hussein to Dujail and his return back to Dujail after the attack on his convoy. Saddam is seen interviewing detainees after their arrest. SIGNIFICANCE: It shows Saddam's personal involvement in the post-incident detainments; Saddam's remarks also show that he knew that it was only a small number of people involved in the assassination attempt.

- A report from July 13, 1982 from the Director of the Iraqi Intelligence Service (Barazan Al Tikriti) to the Chairman of the Revolutionary Command Council (Saddam Hussein) summarizing the results of the investigation of the Dujail incident; allegedly contains Saddam's notes. SIGNIFICANCE: It confirms Barzan's supervision of operations after the incident and indicates that Saddam knew that only 10 people were involved in the actual assassination attempt.
- July 31, 1982 official paperwork awarding some of the Iraqi Intelligence Service officers for their roles in the Dujail investigation; documents contain the signature of Saddam Hussein; one of the officers recognized was Wadhah Ismail Al Shaikh (interviewed by the Iraqi High Tribunal in hospital as a witness in the case shortly before his death). SIGNIFICANCE: It confirms Wadah's role in the Regime's actions at Dujail; the documents also indicate knowledge by Saddam in approving the award.
- Documents from September and October 1982 in which the Iraqi Intelligence Service discusses plans for the disposal of the land owned by those arrested in the Al Dujail investigation. SIGNIFICANCE: Plans for land confiscation began well before the supposed "trial" took place in 1984.
- Revolutionary Command Council Decision Number 1283 dated October 14, 1982 and signed by Saddam Hussein; the decision directs that land in Dujail and Balad be retitled to the Ministry of Agriculture. SIGNIFICANCE: The Decree contains Saddam's signature and directly ties him to the land confiscation.
- 1984 memorandum from Saddam Hussein referring the Dujail victims to the Revolutionary Court; the memorandum directs that they should be prosecuted according to Articles 49, 50, 53, 156 and 175 of the Iraqi Civil Law. SIGNIFICANCE: Reaffirms Saddam Hussein's role in the handling of the case. By this time, many of the people named in the referral have already died during interrogations.
- A June 14, 1984 sentencing decision issued by the Revolutionary Court against the Dujail defendants. Defendant Awad Bandar sentences 148 people to death by hanging, along with confiscation of their movable and immovable estates. SIGNIFICANCE: Document is signed by defendant Awad Bandar.
- Presidential Decree 778, dated June 16, 1984 approving the execution of those condemned to death by Revolutionary Court Judge Awad Bandar; Presidential Decree 778 is signed by Saddam Hussein, commensurate with his role in approving all death sentences from the Revolutionary Court. SIGNIFICANCE: Demonstrates Saddam's personal involvement in the decision to execute 148 individuals, even though only 10 were involved in the actual assassination attempt.

- March 12, 1985 order of execution from the Presidential Diwan's office for the condemned in the case according to the Presidential Decree # 778 for the year 1984.
- March 2, 1985 order for the immediate execution of the 148 condemned in the Dujail case; by name request to carry out the death sentences immediately.
- March 23, 1985 report from the execution committee confirming that the executions of the 148 had been carried out; some of the named people were mistakenly released instead of being executed; other prisoners, not on the list, were executed by mistake.
- June 8, 1985 Iraqi Intelligence Service correspondence about one of the condemned whom the executioners originally missed, but still prepared a death certificate for.
- January 16, 1989 document indicating that the death sentences for ten persons scheduled to occur March 23, 1985 were delayed and not carried out until 1989; the letters indicated that the bodies of the executed are to be buried in secret.
- April 5, 1987 report from the Iraqi Intelligence Service (IIS), noting the conviction of 148 persons in the Dujail case and their execution by hanging; families were released by an order from Saddam Hussein on April 13, 1986. Two of the condemned were released by mistake and were not executed; the IIS suggestion is to issue these two a forgiveness decree given their old ages. SIGNIFICANCE: Confirms that Saddam received an after-action report by the IIS, stating the facts of the regime's treatment of Dujail residents. Although he pardoned Dujail family members, this only occurred after 4 years of detention and mistreatment without being charged or tried.
- Presidency Bureau letters discussing whether to add the names of those mistakenly executed to the execution order. SIGNIFICANCE : Demonstrates that regime could not even execute the correct people that it had "tried" in the Dujail case and then made efforts to cover up the mistaken executions after the fact. Also demonstrates that the death toll in the Dujail case is more than just the 148 names listed on the execution order.
- 14 September 1988 letter from Iraqi Intelligence Service to clarify why a certain family was detained. The letter states that they contacted an officer who previously worked in the investigation sector, who stated that Barzan directly followed the case. SIGNIFICANCE: Shows Barzan's personal involvement in the case.
- The joint committee by the presidency of Hussein Kamil introduced a final report to Saddam Hussein on the botched executions. The report mentions that Hussein Kamil met 10 intelligence officers—one of them was Wadhah Ismail Al Shaikh. The report concludes that the statements of accused were

written without their attendance and Al Thawra court (RCC court) issued execution orders against the accused without a trial. The number of the persons who executed by mistake were 5 persons. SIGNIFICANCE: The former regime has already concluded that Awad Bandar ran an illegitimate court.

- Saddam stated: "I signed that decision," he continued, "and nobody forced me to sign that decision." "I am Saddam Hussein, and at the time of leadership, I am responsible," he said. "It is not his (Saddam's) habit to rely on others."
- Witness testified that Barzan, was the one who directly issued orders regarding the investigations that were carried out. The inspection of the groves and the deployment of military forces in the area were also under orders from Barzan.
- Witnesses testified that Barzan was present at their interrogation and participated in their torture
- Barzan stated "Had I not gone to Al-Dujayl then, the inhabitants of Al-Dujayl would have been eliminated, for the extremists and those who wanted to cover up their mistakes and laxity would have killed people to cover up their mistakes." He said he ordered that anyone arrested then without adequate evidence be released.
- A witness testified that she saw Taha Yasin Ramadan when the orchards were bulldozed and that he was present wearing a military uniform, and that she recognized him.

Use of Military/Armed Conflict

- Witness testified that Barzan, was the one who directly issued orders regarding the investigations that were carried out. The inspection of the groves and the deployment of military forces in the area were also under orders from Barzan.
- A Witness testified that a few days after the attack on Saddam "We heard heavy fire. There was indiscriminate fire. And then 12 helicopter gunships began to bomb the orchards. The houses in Dujail are built in the middle of the orchards. My father built our house in his orchard. The bombing was directed at the orchards. There was a curfew and forces gathered as if there was war."
- A witness said that Taha Yasin Ramadan supervised the removal of the plantations. The prosecuting judge asks the witness to identify the persons who were killed as a result of helicopter gunship shelling of the plantations. The witness says the dead he saw were the same nine persons he mentioned earlier. He then names those nine persons again.

- The prosecuting attorney then asks the witness whether anybody was killed as a result of the practices of the intelligence officers of the former regime. He says yes and names those who died as a result of torture during interrogation.
- A witness testified that one of his sons was killed in an aerial bombardment of Dujail. Three other sons were also killed. He said that he was held for four years in the Abu Ghraib.
- A witness testified that the Popular Army killed and tortured people.
- Ali Hasan Muhammad al-Haydari al-Dujayl testifies that troops began to beat citizens and that intelligence agents and others wearing civilian clothes raided houses in the town, including his house and that helicopters were involved.
- A female witness testified that planes and army personnel took part in the attack on Dujail, and that the planes opened fire on the orchards.

Widespread Unlawful Conduct

- Minutes of a December 28, 1982 joint committee from the Iraqi Intelligence Service and the General Security Service discussing the transfer of Dujail detainees to the Muthana governorate; the minutes discuss a total of 687 people; the minutes divide the detainees into two groups: men and children over the age of 9 years total 293 persons, women and other children total 394 persons. SIGNIFICANCE: Proves the overwhelming number of people detained; the minutes also confirm that children were detained.
- April 5, 1987 report from the Iraqi Intelligence Service (IIS), noting the conviction of 148 persons in the Dujail case and their execution by hanging; families were released by an order from Saddam Hussein on April 13, 1986. Two of the condemned were released by mistake and were not executed; the IIS suggestion is to issue these two a forgiveness decree given their old ages. SIGNIFICANCE: Confirms that Saddam received an after-action report by the IIS, stating the facts of the regime's treatment of Al Dujail residents. Although he pardoned Al Dujail family members, this only occurred after 4 years of detention and mistreatment without being charged or tried.
- The prosecution presented a before/after satellite photo exhibit of the farmlands around Dujail. On the left was a shot of greenery before the attack against Saddam. On the right was a satellite photo of brownish land that the prosecution said was taken on July 31, 1983.

Prohibited Acts

- Undated portions of Intelligence Service letters concerning the detainment location of nine boys under the age of 18. The boys are 11, 14, 14, 12, 16,

17, 15, 14, and 17 years old. SIGNIFICANCE: Shows the punishment of children as part of the Regime's retaliation for the assassination attempt.

- The June 14, 1984 report from the Revolutionary Court reporting its decision to convict the Al Dujail defendants, who are described as "Talib Abed Al Jawad and his group;" written and signed by defendant Awad Al-Bandar, the report states that all the defendants appeared in the court; the documents also states that the defendants were represented by attorneys; the report lists 147 names that are convicted for joining the Al Dawa party and attacking Saddam's convoy in Al Dujail. SIGNIFICANCE: This was written by defendant Awad Bandar, who states that the court "listened to the accused" and that the accused confessed; in actuality, many of those convicted by Bandar had already been killed; two survivors from Bandar's list of those convicted have testified that they never attended a trial.

- A decision issued by the intelligence court to condemn the intelligence officer who executed 4 persons by mistake whereas he was entrusted to execute total of 148 persons in 1984. The real number executed was 96 persons as a result of the deaths that happened during the investigation (some of them dead in the prison). The intelligence court decided to jail the intelligence officer for four years.

- Witness accounts tied Taha al-Ramadan to the destruction of the orchards and parts of the town of Dujail.

- Saddam stated: "I demolished the orchards, that was a Revolutionary Council decision to modernize the orchard and I signed that order. Where is the crime?"

- Witness testimony that the families of those suspected of attacking Saddam, mainly civilians, peasants, and others, were moved to the sectors assigned for them in Abu-Ghraib prison.

- Witness testimony that Taha yasin Ramadan, led the committee responsible for razing the groves in Al-Dujayl and Balad, and dealt with the detained families, Among the committee members were Muhammad Ulaywi and Sa'dun Sabri.

- Witness testimony indicating that he observed the misbehavior with and ridicule of the detainees.

- Witness testimony that only 12 people were involved in the attack against Saddam.

- Witness testimony that after the attack on Saddam several persons were executed inside the groves by the bodyguards of Saddam. The persons killed were relatives of an intelligence officer, named Muhammad Mut'ib. They were considered martyrs when it was revealed that they had no role in the shooting on the motorcade.

- A witness described the use of a meat grinder as a torture device "On my left I saw a machine that looked like a grinder with coagulated blood and human hair. What I saw could not be removed from my mind."
- The witness says: "Interrogation began on Saturday. Those who went down on their feet were carried back on blankets. The age did not matter, whether you are 70 or 14 years. They were all tortured. I was 15 years at that time. They detained me on Friday and I stayed Saturday, Sunday, and they took me down at 1900 Monday and they brought me back at 0200. Was it possible for me to topple a regime? They treated me as an cunning politician who has a command and a party and who could bring down regimes. That was how I was treated. The blindfold that they placed on my head kept slipping all the time because I was so young. Many women were tortured in front of me. You have arrested me and you arrested my injured brother. All right. But why do you take my sisters?"
- A witness described how they were deprived of food while in detention, they originally received two pieces of bread, but in response to complaints their meals were adjusted down to only one piece of bread, and a bowl of rice for eight-twelve inmates.
- A witness said that they brought a detainee Salih Muhammad Jasim, born in 1950 and they shot him twice in his foot during the interrogation. Another, Qasim Abd Ali al-Ubaydi, born in 1959, was "burned with electric shocks."
- "Husayn Ya'qub Majid had his hand and leg broken during interrogation." He says that Jasim Muhammad Latif died under torture. They broke all his bones because he was a deserter and he died under torture.
- A witness told of his friend Khamis Kazim Ja'far, Karim's brother, as telling him "that he was arrested on Thursday, the same day he himself was arrested. He cites Khamis as saying Saddam was with the Ba'th Party unit at the detention center and they brought him to Saddam and told him that this was Khamis, brother of Karim, from a family that opposes the regime. Saddam asked him: Do you know me? He said: Yes. Saddam said who am I? He told him: Saddam because I did not know how to tell him: Mr President. I was only a boy. He asked me three times who he was and each time I replied: Saddam. He says that Saddam then hit him with an ashtray on his head and wounded him very badly."
- A Witness testified that he saw a man hit by the guards who died instantly. He was 65 and he had a heart attack after he was hit. They never brought his body to his relatives and nobody knew where they took his body. He says: "I saw this with my own eyes." He also said that members of a "committee from the presidential office" that visited the center as saying: "You, the people of Al-Dujayl. We have made you an example for the Iraqis. We taught you a lesson."

- A witness testified that an 11-years old girl, Batul Muhammad Hasan, was "shot in the foot by indiscriminate fire by the intelligence and the guards." He says that the girl and her grandmother were imprisoned for four years and then died.
- A witness described torture and displacement stating "They moved the families in groups. We did not know that they were in the desert; we thought they were released. We did not know. We stayed at Abu Ghurayb the entire 1983. The torture continued and guards changed. Every 21 days they brought four new guards. They were butchers."
- A witness says several persons died under interrogation, and he names several.
- A witness says that she was beaten with hoses and prodded and tortured with electricity to confess. She details how her brother was brought for interrogation, and how children, elderly people, and families were taken to Abu Ghraib for interrogation. She spoke about the horrible conditions in the prison, and how they had to be resourceful to get their basic needs, such as making needles to be able to sow clothes for the children. She says that her younger brother was beaten by people she cannot identify.
- Ali Hasan Muhammad al-Haydari al-Dujayl recounted how he was taken in a car to an unidentified location and was tortured by electric shock, burning, and other methods.

The Case against the Lesser-Known Defendants

By Michael P. Scharf and Kevin Pendergast

It is not surprising that nearly all of the focus in the Dujail trial has been on Saddam Hussein, his half-brother Barzan Ibrahim (former head of the Mukhabarat intelligence agency), and Awad al-Bandar (the head of Saddam's Revolutionary Court). This essay analyzes the legal case against Saddam's lesser known co-defendants—Mizhar Abdullah Ruwayyid, Abdullah Kazim Ruwayyid, Ali Dayih and Mohammed Azawi Ali, residents of Dujail charged with informing on their neighbors who later either died in prison or were sentenced to death.

According to the evidence submitted in the Dujail trial, a few hours after the July 8, 1982, assassination attempt against Saddam, these lesser known co-defendants wrote letters to the Ba'ath regime informing on villagers with familial connections to a Shiite opposition group called the Dawa party. The letters both identified those families as disloyal to Saddam's regime and provided information as to their whereabouts. The people named in the letters—including women and children—were subsequently rounded up, tortured, sentenced to death in a sham trial, and executed in retaliation for the assassination attempt.

In helping Saddam's agents identify and locate the residents who would soon become detainees, torture victims, and casualties, the informants served as aiders and abettors to one of the most serious of international crimes: the crime against humanity. Under Article 15 of the IHT Statute, a person who "aids, abets, or otherwise assists in the commission" of a crime against humanity subjects himself to criminal liability, even if he only "provides the means" for the principal crime. Several of the post-World War II war crimes trials confirmed that civilians and low-level officials can be held criminally liable for informing on neighbors who were opposed to the Nazi regime or were part of the underground resistance, where such neighbors were immediately thereafter arrested, tortured and executed without trial.[161]

For a conviction, the Iraqi High Tribunal must merely conclude from the evidence that the informers knew or should have known that a crime against humanity would befall the neighbors on whom they informed. The documents and video entered into evidence show that Saddam's forces rampaged through the town of Dujail and conducted their investigation with indiscriminate violence. The house-to-house intrusions and beatings occurring in al Dujail on the day of the informing constitute all the circumstances necessary for the Tribunal to infer the informers' knowledge.

The defendants may assert the defense that as local Ba'ath party officials, they were required by the Iraqi Penal Code to report information important to the government. In other words, they were merely following the law. This defense has failed too often in past war crimes trials to be taken seriously.

Saddam's co-defendants are obviously small fish compared to the three primary figures. But tyrannical regimes do not succeed without the sycophantic support of such underlings. It is therefore just as important that such persons be brought to justice.

The Case against the Lesser-Known Defendants

By Mark Ellis

In response to the essay by Michael Scharf and Keven Pendergast, I would like to propose a counter argument: the Court has failed to show the required intent by the four lesser-known defendants in committing crimes against humanity.

Case law emerging from recent decisions of the international tribunals establishes that the requisite *mens rea* for crimes against humanity is intent to commit the underlying acts, combined with the knowledge of the broader context in which the occurs. It is this knowledge that transforms the into a crime against humanity i.e., that the defendants were aware of the greater dimensions of crimes committed.

This "knowledge" requirement makes sense because of the definition of crimes against humanity: "an act committed as part of a widespread or systematic attack against any civilian population with knowledge of the attack." Thus, since these crimes cannot consist of isolated or sporadic acts but must form part of a systematic plan or widespread atrocities, the four lesser-known defendants must be aware of the link between their misconduct and the plan or widespread abuses. The defendants must have knowingly committed crimes against humanity in the sense that they must have understood their acts were part of something "bigger."

The evidence would have to show that the four lesser-defendants had knowledge, either actual or constructive, that their acts were occurring and were part of a widespread or systematic basis as set forth by Saddam and his government. I don't think it is sufficient to simply show that the defendants knew that an "additional crime" (e.g. torture) "would befall the neighbors on whom they informed." The evidence would have to show that the defendants had knowledge that the "additional crimes" were, in fact, part of a widespread or systematic attack on the neighbors. If these defendants facilitated the arrest of their neighbors without this knowledge, they may have committed ordinary crimes under Iraqi law, but they did not commit a crime against humanity.

The witnesses who appeared last week on behalf of the four defendants painted a picture of defendants who are low-level, bureaucratic Baath party officials with little knowledge of the "big picture." In fact, as we now know, one of the defendants (Mohammed Azawi Ali) is illiterate, and was dismissed by the Baath party because his cousins were members of the opposition Dawa party. In fact, the evidence presented earlier by the Court showed that the acts by the four lesser-known defendants, following orders from Baghdad, occurred immediately after the assassination attempt on Saddam Hussein. This undermines the argument that the defendants had knowledge that their acts were part of a widespread or systematic plan, since it is likely that Saddam and his cohorts were still constructing their overall policy of retribution against the Dujal residents.

I agree that even lower level perpetrators should be held accountable for their criminal involvement with the atrocities. There is little doubt that under the Iraqi criminal code, they would be liable for committing ordinary crimes. However, it does not mean that they have committed crimes against humanity.

The Court should be careful not to undermine or lessen the seriousness of crimes against humanity by casting an unsubstantiated wide-net over lower level defendants who have not shown the requisite knowledge of crimes against humanity.

The Significance of Defendant Al-Bandar's Testimony—Judgment at Nuremberg Revisited

By Michael P. Scharf

The defendant who sits immediately to the right of Saddam Hussein in the IHT courtroom every day is Awwad Al-Bandar, the former Chief Judge of Saddam's Revolutionary Court. The placement is no coincidence, as next to Saddam, Al-Bandar is the most important man on trial. He is charged with crimes against humanity in connection with ordering the execution of 148 Dujail townspeople after an unfair trial. He is the first judge since the Nuremberg-era Alstoetter case, which was made into the Academy Award-winning Movie "Judgment at Nuremberg," to be tried for using his court as a political weapon.

On March 13, 2006, Al-Bandar took the stand to testify on his own behalf. Al-Bandar acknowledged that he presided over the 1984 Dujail trial, and that he sentenced all 148 defendants in that case to death after a trial that lasted only two weeks. "They attacked the president of the Republic and they confessed," he told the IHT. He said that their confessions were verified by the intelligence department's investigative judge, and added that the Dujail defendants also admitted their responsibility on radio and television. Moreover, Al-Bandar said that the case file had established that weapons and incriminating documents, proving the Dujail defendants' affiliation with the Iran-allied Al-Da'wah Party, were found in their hideouts in the Dujail orchards. He said that the Dujail defendants were represented by court-appointed counsel, and that his court issued the ruling in accordance with the law and without the interference or influence of any side. He admitted that the trial was a short one given the number of defendants, but said that due to the war with Iran and the defendants' confessions the trial could not be delayed, stressing that "these were extraordinary events, as the president was targeted." When confronted with documents showing that 46 of the 148 Dujail defendants had actually died during interrogation before the 1984 trial, Al-Bandar replied: "Is it so strange for someone to die during interrogation," asserting that that five of his fellow former Ba'ath party leaders have died in U.S. custody since 2003. Al-Bandar then read from a prepared statement, saying "according to the law, a judge cannot be arrested or tried unless he carries out a proven crime." He added that at the time of the Dujail trial, Iraqi law stated that any member of the Al-Da'wah Party was to be executed, and also required the death sentence for any person who attempts to kill the head of state. "Therefore, the court had no choice but to sentence the Dujail defendants to death."

Al-Bandar's testimony raises difficult moral and legal questions: should a judge be held criminally liable for presiding over an unfair trial if it comported with the domestic law then in effect? And should departures from normal fair trial norms be permissible with respect to alleged insurgents or terrorists in times of war? In considering these questions, it may be helpful to consider a few of the most memorable passages from the movie "Judgment at Nuremberg."

Prosecutor's Opening Statement: "Your Honor, the case is unusual in that the defendants are charged with crimes committed in the name of the law. These men are the embodiment of what passed for justice in the Third Reich. As judges on the bench you will be sitting in judgment of judges in the dock. This is how it should be. For only a judge knows how much more a court is than a courtroom. It is a process and a spirit. It is the House of Law. The defendants knew this too. They knew courtrooms well. They sat in their black robes. And they distorted and they perverted and they destroyed justice in Germany. They are, perhaps more than others, guilty of complicity in murders, tortures, atrocities—the most cruel and devastating this world has ever seen. Here they will receive the justice they denied others."

Defense's Opening Statement: "If the defendant is to be found guilty, certain implications must arise. A judge does not make the law. He carries out the laws of his country, be it a democracy or a dictatorship. The statement, 'My country right or wrong,' was expressed by a great American patriot. It is no less true for a German patriot. Should the defendant have carried out the laws of his country? Or should he have refused to carry them out and become a traitor?"

Judgment: "This trial has shown that under a national crisis, ordinary, even able and extraordinary men can delude themselves into the commission of crimes against humanity. How easily it can happen. There are those in our own country too that today speak of the protection of country, of survival. A decision must be made in the life of every nation, at the very moment when the grasp of the enemy is at its throat; then it seems that the only way to survive is to use the means of the enemy, to wrest survival on what is expedient, to look the other way. Only the answer to that is … survival as what? A country isn't a rock; it's not an extension of one's self. It's what it stands for. It's what it stands for when standing for something is the most difficult. Before the people of the world, here in our decision, this is what we stand for—justice, truth, and the value of a single human being."

Like its Hollywood counterpart, the real-life Nuremberg Tribunal found the Nazi judges guilty of crimes against humanity, concluding that "the dagger of the assassin was concealed beneath the robe of the jurist." The Tribunal rejected both the necessity defense and the notion that the judges should be absolved because they did not make the law, they only carried it out—the very arguments Al-Abandar has made before the IHT. For sixty years, the Alstoetter judgment has served as a warning to judges and other government officials. A conviction in the Al-Abandar case would reaffirm the continuing vitality of this precedent, and send an important message not just to those in the new Iraqi government, but also to those in governments around the world (including the United States) who might be tempted to argue that in time of war the law must be silent.

The Significance of the Testimony of Tariq Aziz— Not Just Another Witness

By Michael Scharf

May 24, 2006, will likely be remembered as the high water mark for the defense in the Saddam Hussein Trial. On that day, Tariq Aziz, the Foreign Minister of Iraq during the Ba'ath Regime, took the stand to testify on behalf of the defense.

Even more than Saddam himself, Tariq Aziz is the Iraqi face most recognized by Westerners. Known for his white hair, glasses, expensive suits, and articulate statements in fluent English, Aziz has appeared frequently at the United Nations, foreign capitols, and on the international media during the past two decades. Many of us expected that the seventy-year-old former diplomat, who has been in custody since 2003, would end up testifying against Saddam in a plea deal, and that he would provide the crucial insider's view that would nail the lid on the case against Saddam. Instead Aziz testified passionately for his former boss. "I wanted to come and witness for President Saddam Hussein, because I know he has not committed any crime in relation to Dujail," Aziz confidently told the Iraqi High Tribunal judges.

Building on one of the main themes of the defense, Aziz asserted that the Iraqi government had reacted lawfully during what he described as a period of attacks by Iranian-allied terrorists and insurgents against Iraqi government officials, including an attempt on his own life at Mustansariye University a short time before the incident at Dujail in 1982. "No one is guilty of anything," Aziz opined. "The President of the State in any country, if faced with an assassination attempt during a time of war, is entitled to take procedures to capture and punish those who were involved." He added that there was nothing personal about the response to the Dujail assassination attempt.

Aziz compared the conflict in the 1980s to the instability in Iraq today, pointing out that the people in Dujail were treated no differently than the Americans have treated people in places like Falluja. In concluding, Aziz contended that Saddam was being prosecuted selectively as the fallen leader of a country whose new rulers include members of the very group—the Dawa party—which was responsible for the 1982 assassination attempt against Saddam. To highlight this point, as Aziz walked passed the former Iraqi leader on the way out of the courtroom, he respectfully said: "Goodbye, Mr. President."

The problem for the Prosecution is not just that the distinguished former diplomat made a compelling witness, but more importantly that the comparisons Aziz made between Ba'athist and American anti-terrorism/anti-insurgency tactics are not really all that far off the mark. In fact, at the very moment Aziz was testifying in the IHT courtroom in Baghdad, a thousand miles away in Kabul his point was being driven home when Afghan President Hamid Karzai announced an official inquiry into a U.S. military raid of a southern Afghan village suspected of hiding Taliban fighters, which reportedly ended up killing at least sixteen innocent civilians, including some at a religious school. And just a few days after Aziz had appeared before the IHT, the international press broke the story of the November 2005 massacre at the Iraqi town of Haditha, in which U.S. marines reportedly went on a retaliatory killing spree, resulting in two dozen Iraqi civilian deaths a few hours after a makeshift bomb killed one of their comrades outside the town. In the last two years, the largely Sunni town has been the periodic target of a series of anti-insurgent raids by American troops (Operation River Gate, Operation Scimitar, and Operation River Blitz), in which numerous homes and building have been destroyed and scores of non-combatants have become "collateral damage."

Similarly, earlier in the trial, one of the defendants compared the lawfulness of the detention, interrogation, and torture of the Dujail townspeople by the Ba'ath regime to the much criticized U.S. detention and interrogation practices at Abu Ghraib and Guantanamo Bay, saying "everyone knows during interrogation of terrorists these things happen, it's unavoidable."

But are such comparisons legally relevant? In two earlier essays I explained that this line of argument is not foreclosed by the historic rejection of the "tu quoque" (you too) defense under international law. At Nuremberg, defendant Grand Admiral Carl Doenitz argued that he could not be convicted of waging unrestricted submarine warfare in the Atlantic since American Admiral Chester Nimitz had admitted that the United States had done the same thing in the Pacific. It was significant that Doenitz was not arguing that American violation of international law rendered it unfair to convict the German Admiral for the same acts—an argument that would have been rejected as "tu quoque." Rather, the defense was arguing that the American actions indicated that it was not a violation of international law to conduct unrestricted submarine warfare. Thus, Defense Counsel Kranzbuehler told the Nuremberg Tribunal: "The stand taken by the Prosecution (which had argued against recognition of the Tu Quoque defense") differs entirely from the conception on which my application is based. I in no way wish to prove or even to maintain that the American Admiralty in its U-boat warfare against Japan broke international law. On the contrary, I am of the opinion that it acted strictly in accordance with international law."[162] The Nuremberg Tribunal was persuaded by this argument, and did not convict Doenitz of the charge. Similarly, it is perfectly legitimate for the defense to argue (as Tariq Aziz did on May 24) that what Saddam did to the town and people of Dujail was lawful, and as evidence of its legality draw comparisons to contemporary U.S. actions to route out insurgents and terrorists in towns across Afghanistan and Iraq and to detain and interrogate such persons at the Abu Ghraib and Guantanamo Bay detention centers.

In response, the Prosecution should draw three critical distinctions between the two situations. First, Saddam's disproportionate response to Dujail (destroying the houses, burning down the orchards, rounding up 399 people including young children) suggests that his intent was to retaliate against the town and use it as an example to deter future acts of insurgency, rather than simply to route out the terrorists involved in the assassination plot. Second, rather than prosecute and punish his subordinates, documents and witness testimony indicate that Saddam issued medals of honor to the security forces who tortured and killed 49 of the Dujail detainees during interrogation. Third, two years after the assassination attempt, when any threat they posed had long passed, Saddam ordered 148 of the Dujail detainees summarily tried en mass before the Revolutionary Court and executed at the end of a patently unfair proceeding.

While I expect the Tribunal to be swayed by these distinctions, the Dujail case may end up providing an enduring lesson to the United States as well as to Iraq—a lesson about what tactics cross the line in its global war on terror.

What Must the Prosecution Successfully Address in Its Closing Argument to Win the Case?

By Michael Scharf

The Prosecution's Closing Argument in the first trial before the Iraqi High Tribunal is scheduled to begin on Monday, June 19, 2006. Since the IHT did not conduct preliminary hearings on procedural matters nor produce written opinions on such matters, presumably these will be dealt with in the final judgment and therefore the Prosecutor must make relevant procedural as well as substantive arguments during its closing. This essay addresses the ten points the Prosecution must successfully address to win its case.

First, the Prosecution must respond to the Defense arguments that the IHT is not a legitimate judicial body. In particular, the Defense has asserted that the creation of the IHT by an Occupying Power (the United States) violates the Geneva Conventions. They have also argued that the Presiding Judge, Ra'uf Abdel-Rhaman, was biased (due to past membership in an anti-Ba'athist organization) and should have been removed.

Second, the Prosecution must deal with the issue of whether prosecution of Saddam Hussein in an Iraqi Court is barred by head of state immunity under Iraqi law, and whether the Iraqi National Assembly legitimately revoked such immunity by approving the Statute of the IHT in August 2005.

Third, the Prosecution must respond to the Defense arguments that certain rulings by the IHT denied the defendants a fair trial. Specifically, the Prosecution must address the propriety of waiting until half-way through the trial to announce the detailed charges, the practice of frequently expelling defense counsel and defendants from the courtroom for disruptive behavior, the use of court-appointed counsel when the Defense Counsel were boycotting the proceedings or were expelled from the courtroom, and the Tribunal's refusal to permit the Defense to call a number of their remaining witnesses. The Prosecution must also address the defendants' claims that they were physically abused while in custody, as under international precedent such abuse could constitute a ground for dismissal of the case.

Fourth, the Prosecution must explain how the various acts carried out by the Ba'ath Regime, which were described in the testimony and documents admitted into evidence during the trial, constitute crimes against humanity.

These acts included the shelling and strafing of the town of Dujail via heli-copter gunships; the destruction of the town's homes, water supplies, and or-chards; rounding up 399 townspeople, including young children, for interro-gation; employing torture and causing the deaths of 50 people during interrogation; ordering 148 people summarily tried en masse before the Rev-olutionary Court; and ordering all of these people executed after the trial which lasted a single session. To establish crimes against humanity under Ar-ticle 12 of the IHT Statute, there must be proof of widespread and systematic mistreatment, torture, and/or killings of civilians. Related to this, the Prose-cution must answer the claim by several defense witnesses that many of the alleged victims are actually still alive in Iraq.

Fifth, the Prosecution must address issues of authenticity. The trial turned out to be much more document-based than was anticipated. Some of the most important documents included Saddam's order for the execution of the Dujail townspeople, and his order that medals of honor be awarded to the security forces involved in their apprehension and interrogation. The Defense has chal-lenged the authenticity of these and other documents, and argued that the court-appointed experts who affirmed Saddam's signature on them cannot be trusted as independent because they all have links to Iraq's interior ministry. In particular, the defense strenuously argued that the document indicating that Saddam Hussein approved the execution of people under the age of eighteen was forged.

Sixth, the Prosecution must respond to the Defense claims that certain wit-nesses were offered money and/or threatened with bodily harm by the chief prosecutor to give false testimony. The Prosecution should explain how the documentary evidence and the in-court admissions of the defendants cor-roborate the testimony of key witnesses.

Seventh, the Prosecution must respond to the Defense argument that the Defendants' actions were lawful based on the necessity to combat/suppress the terrorists and insurgents operating in Dujail who tried to assassinate Sad-dam. Related to this is the question of whether comparisons between the Ba'ath Regime's actions in 1982 and the way the United States has conducted its current war on terrorism (namely by attacking towns in Afghanistan and Iraq and imprisoning suspects at Abu Ghraib and Guantanamo Bay) are legally relevant. Since the Tribunal may conclude the comparisons are rele-vant, the Prosecution needs to distinguish American actions from those of the Ba'ath Party in terms of necessity, proportionality, and treatment of sub-ordinates who committed crimes. In this light, the Prosecution also needs to address the testimony of Saddam's bodyguards who said that Saddam ordered them not to return fire after the assassination attempt in case innocent people might be hurt, and the testimony of former Ba'ath party officials who said that routine procedures were followed in responding to the Dujail assassination attempt.

Eighth, the Prosecution must respond to the defense witness testimony that the proceedings before the Revolutionary Court were fair under the circumstances. The Prosecution must spell out in detail those attributes of a fair trial that were lacking in the Revolutionary Court case against the Dujail townspeople.

Ninth, the Prosecution must explain how each of the eight defendants can be held criminally responsible for the alleged crimes. Under principles of direct responsibility and command responsibility, Saddam Hussein and his half-brother Barzan Ibrahim (former head of the Makhubarat intelligence agency) can be found responsible either for issuing orders (to attack the city, to round up hundreds of townspeople for interrogation, to try them before the Revolutionary Court, and to order their execution), or for failing to prevent or punish subordinates for unlawful acts (such as destroying the Dujail water supply, burning down the orchards, and/or torturing and killing the DuJail detainees). Under the precedent of the Nuremberg-era Alstoetter Case, defendant Awad al-Bandar (the head of Saddam's Revolutionary Court) can be held responsible if he ordered the executions of the Dujail defendants knowing that the Dujail trial was patently unfair and that his court was being used as part of a systematic attack against the civilian population of Dujail. To warrant a conviction of the four lesser known co-defendants—Mizhar Abdullah Ruwayyid, Abdullah Kazim Ruwayyid, Ali Dayih and Mohammed Azawi Ali— the Prosecution must explain how the evidence proves these informers knew or should have known that a crime against humanity would befall the neighbors on whom they informed.

Finally, the Prosecution must address the issue of whether the death penalty is the appropriate sentence for any or all of the defendants, in light of the relative gravity of the crimes charged, the defendants' position in the hierarchy of power, and their personal involvement in the crimes.

The Defense will get their chance to rebut the Prosecution's arguments during their Closing Argument a few days later, and then the five judges of the IHT will adjourn to consider and write their judgment. That judgment will be appealed to the 9-member Appeals Chamber, which will bring the case to a final conclusion sometime in the fall.

An Assessment of the Prosecutor's Closing Argument

By Michael Scharf

There were three noteworthy aspects of the Prosecutor's closing argument in the Saddam Trial:

First, it was very significant that the Prosecutor asked the Tribunal to drop charges against one of the lesser-known co-defendants and to be lenient on the other three lesser-known co-defendants. The Prosecutor is obviously hoping that this move will show that the proceedings are fair. Experts who have been following the trial had opined that there was very little evidence against these four and wondered if it was a mistake to include them in the case. I think there is a parallel here to the Nuremberg trial, in which three of the defendants were acquitted. Supporters of the Nuremberg Tribunal said that proved the Tribunal was fair, while critics asserted that it was a travesty of justice that the three were ever made to stand trial in the first place.

Second, compared to other recent war crimes trials, this was a remarkably short Closing Argument. Closing Arguments at The Hague, Arusha and Freetown have been known to go on for days, not hours. The brevity here reflected the strength of the Prosecutor's case. Like Nuremberg, the Dujail trial turned out to be based mostly on documents, whose authenticity was confirmed, rather than the testimony of witnesses, whose credibility could be called into question. These documents, proved that Saddam ordered the assault on Dujail and the destruction of its buildings, palm groves, and water supply, that he ordered the rounding up of 399 townspeople, that he ordered their interrogation and detention at Abu Ghraib, that he gave medals of honor to the security forces that tortured and killed the townspeople, that he ordered their summary trial en mass before the Revolutionary Court, and that he signed the order of execution for 148 of the townspeople. Even Saddam confirmed during the trial that he was responsible for these acts. In light of the strength of the documentary evidence, all the Prosecutor really had to do in his Closing Argument was argue "res ipsa loquitur," Latin for "the thing speaks for itself." The Prosecutor did a competent job of summarizing the evidence, and explaining the legal case for why the proven acts constituted crimes against humanity, defined as a systematic attack on a civilian population. However, I would have liked to have seen the Prosecutor do a better job of rebutting Saddam's argument that the acts against the people of Dujail were justified and were no different than American actions taken to root out terrorists and insurgents in Afghanistan and Iraq in the context of its war on terrorism, for this will turn out to be the most important legal question of the trial.

Third, the Prosecution asked for the death penalty for Saddam Hussein and his half brother, the Security Chief, Barzan Tikriti. If the judges find that the two defendants are responsible for the detention, torture, and mass murder of 148 innocent civilians as retribution for a failed assassination attempt, the death penalty may well be warranted, even if it means that Saddam will not be around to stand trial for the more serious offenses, such as the killing of 200,000 Kurds in the Anfal campaign in 1988 or the killing of 500,000 Southern Marsh Arabs in 1991. It was significant that the Prosecutor also requested the death penalty for co-Defendant Judge Awad al-Bandar, the Revolutionary Court Judge who in 1984 had sentenced the 148 townspeople to death after an allegedly unfair trial. Judge al-Bandar and several of the defense witnesses argued that the 1984 trial process was not unreasonable given that the defendants had all signed confessions before trial, that the trial was conducted in the middle of the Iran-Iraq war, and that the defendants were assigned a defense counsel, all according to the prevailing law at the time. If convicted, Judge al-Bandar will be the first judge since the Nuremberg Alstoetter case (made famous in the Academy Award-winning movie Judgment at Nuremberg) to be held criminally responsible for presiding over an unfair trial in which the law was used as a political weapon against opponents of the regime. Unlike Judge al-Bandar, the Nazi judge was accused of presiding over a whole series of unfair trials, of receiving large financial rewards for his politicized rulings, and of sentencing people to death for such crimes as "racial pollution" which were inherently discriminatory and unjust. While the case against the four underlings was extremely weak, and the case against Saddam and Barzan was extremely strong, I believe the real question will be how the judges decide the case against Awad al-Bandar.

Response to Professor Scharf's Analysis of Closing Arguments

By Mark Ellis

I would like to respond to Professor Scharf's essay regarding the Prosecutor's closing arguments. I agree with Professor Scharf's position that the Prosecutor, during his closing arguments, will likely restate the substantive case presented against the defendants during the trial. I believe the Prosecutor will also set forth how these acts constitute crimes against humanity. However, I do not think that the Prosecutor needs to address the procedural elements of the case.

Iraqi law is based on a civil law system and the Iraqi High Court is following Iraq's own criminal procedure code, supplemented by the Rules of Procedure and Evidence, created specifically for the Court under the direction of the CPA. Thus, even though the Prosecutor has played a much greater role in this trial than would generally occur in a civil law criminal case, it is still the Court (i.e., the judges) that has the burden of determining all procedural legal matters.

Under Iraqi law, once the Investigative Judge presented the Court the dossier containing evidence for a prima facie case against the defendants, the judges, and particularly the Chief Judge, took full control over the trial. This included the Chief Judge's very active role in examining and cross-examining witnesses, as well as the Court arbitrating, on its own, issues relating to procedural law. In many ways, this is neither the Prosecutor's case nor the defendants' case; it is simply a case before the Court. The Prosecutor is there to "walk" the Court through the evidence contained in the dossier. Therefore, it is not the Prosecutor's responsibility to respond to, nor argue for or against, any of these procedural issues. He does not have the "burden to prove" procedural issues. In truth, he doesn't actually have the burden to prove the substantive elements either. This evidence is already contained in the dossier and it is up to the Court to make that determination.

Therefore, I would submit that the Prosecutor does not need to proffer his opinion on issues such as the Court's legitimacy, head of state immunity, the expulsion of defense counsel and defendants, the authenticity of documents, nor witness tampering by the defense. These are issues solely within the domain and jurisdiction of the Court and it alone carries the burden of addressing them. The Court is not looking to the Prosecutor to "make a case" on any of these issues. The Prosecutor will likely focus on succinctly summarizing the evidence presented in the case.

The Prosecutor will, however, be able to address any perceived procedural errors made by the Court during the appeals process.

Section 4: Issues of Impact

What Is the Relationship between the Saddam Trial and the Level of Violence in Iraq?

By Mark Drumbl

The Washington Post and other news outlets reported this morning that, over the past two days, 11 U.S. troops and at least 182 civilians have been killed in Iraq. The violence springs from many sources and is influenced by many factors. What I have not (yet) seen is discussion of the relationship, if any, between prosecutions at the Iraqi High Tribunal and the security situation in general. Some writers have been concerned, rightfully, with how the prosecution triggers security concerns to court personnel (i.e. with regard to the murders of defense lawyers/personnel and death threats to others) and whether the process can continue when it is a site for violence. But I am worried that the prosecution (even though still just in a preliminary stage) itself may exacerbate insecurity at a cost that might transcend, at least in the short term, the benefits of justice. The choice to prosecute Saddam and to see his trial as promoting justice and establishing a historical record was made at a time of ex ante optimism about the ability to maintain security in Iraq. Although peace and justice aren't viewed as incommensurable by international lawyers such as ourselves, what might the purpose be of proceeding with the Saddam trial amid such great instability (and it is unclear to me whether relocating internationally would help)? To be sure, given where we are, just incapacitating Saddam indefinitely also may fracture security.

What Is the Relationship between the Saddam Trial and the Level of Violence in Iraq?

By Michael P. Scharf

Drawing on the historic precedent of the post WWII Nuremberg trial of the Nazi leaders, many advocates of the Saddam Hussein trial hoped that the televised proceedings would establish a historic record of abuses that would pierce the propaganda and discredit the former regime. And this in turn would suppress popular support for the insurgency within the Sunni Iraqi community.

But a closer examination of the Nuremberg experience indicates that such high expectations for the educational role of the Saddam Hussein trial are misplaced.

Contrary to Chief Prosecutor Robert Jackson's claim that the Nuremberg Tribunal's greatest success was that it "established incredible events with credible evidence," recently de-classified opinion polls conducted by the U.S. Department of State from 1946 through 1958 indicated that over 85 percent of West Germans considered the Nuremberg proceedings to be nothing but a show trial, representing victor's justice rather than real justice, and believed that the Nazi leaders were not really guilty of the crimes for which they had been convicted.[163]

Two generations later, the German people largely have a favorable view of the Nuremberg Tribunal and are overwhelmingly convinced of the guilt of the Nazi leadership. This might simply suggest that war crimes trials take twenty years or more to influence target populations. But it is more likely that German popular opinion was influenced by: (1) the aggressive "reorientation" program which the United States imposed on Germany in the decade after the end of the second world war; (2) the fact that government-required history books in use in German elementary and secondary schools for the past sixty years have portrayed the Nuremberg Tribunal positively and the Nazi leaders negatively; and (3) the fact that Germany has aggressively enforced its law criminalizing denial of the holocaust.

In any event, the lesson of Nuremberg is that in the short run, those who support Saddam Hussein (including most Sunni Iraqis) are likely to view the Saddam trial as illegitimate and will be convinced of his innocence no matter the testimony and evidence that is elicited during the proceedings. Those that oppose him (including most Shi'ites and Kurds), are likely to view the Tribunal as confirming what they already believe. Thus, as Mark Drumbl observes above, in the short-term the Saddam trial may well have more of a divisive than peace-engendering impact in Iraq.

Opinion polls taken during the ongoing war crimes trial of Slobodan Milosevic in The Hague, on the other hand, may yet give cause to be hopeful about the role of the Saddam Trial in drying up support for the Iraqi insurgency. In the early months of the Slobodan Milosevic trial, the popularity of the former Serb leader among Serbs steadily rose, as he used his televised trial to repeatedly attack the 1999 NATO intervention that destroyed the Serb infrastructure and the UN sanctions that wrecked the Serb economy. But support for Milosevic began to erode midway through the trial when the Prosecution presented evidence of Milosevic's involvement in the assassination of popular Serb politicians such as Ivan Stambolic and Zoran Djindjic, and popular support for the Milosevic in Serbia plummeted when the Prosecution showed a particularly horrific video of the Srebrenica massacre, which was subsequently played repeatedly on Serb television. Anecdotal accounts of Sunni Iraqis watching the Saddam trial indicate that the testimony of victims of the Ba'ath party abuses may be having a similar effect among the Sunni population.

What Historical Narratives Are the Iraqi Trials Developing?

By Mark Drumbl

The October 2005 version of the Statute of the Iraqi High Tribunal identifies its "justifying reasons" in a postscript as follows:

- to expose the crimes committed in Iraq;
- to lay down rules and punishments to condemn the perpetrators after a fair trial;
- to form a high criminal court;
- to reveal the truth, agonies, and injustice;
- to protect the rights of Iraqis; and
- "alleviating injustice and for demonstrating heaven's justice as envisaged by the Almighty God."

The "justifying reasons" therefore encompass all the ambitious goals generally placed upon the shoulders of atrocity trials, although lean more than is the case with other institutions toward what I would call the narrative function: namely, truth-telling, authenticating a historical record, and expressivism.

How have the proceedings fared thus far in terms of this narrative function?

In response to the Milosevic trial, the Iraqi High Tribunal decided to implement its proceedings through a series of mini-trials. The first of these involved the violence at Dujail. In 1982 this was the site of a failed assassination attempt on Saddam. In response, in 1984 the Iraqi Revolutionary Court ordered the execution of 148 townspeople.

The Prosecution case against Saddam for Dujail recently closed. It ended on a high note. Documentary evidence was proffered and admitted by the Court that implicates Saddam, as well as the Revolutionary Court, in sentencing and ordering executions of Shiites not plausibly connected to any assassination attempt against him in 1982. One document is a memo from the Revolutionary Court announcing that 148 suspects had been sentenced to death by hanging, in 1984, with a list of names, and signed by codefendant Awad al-Bandar (former chief judge of the Revolutionary Court). Then, two days later, Hussein signed a document approving all 148 sentences. Some involved boys. Prosecutors did an effective job displaying these signed documents through audio-visual technology in the courtroom. A third document, signed by Barzan Ibrahim al-Tikriti, Saddam's half-brother and former chief of intelligence (the Mukhabarat service), then was displayed. This document ordered the executions to be carried out. Many individuals died under torture before they could be executed.

These documents corroborated the often moving victim testimony. They also prompted Saddam's admission of responsibility for the Dujail village killings, accompanied with his disclaimer of guilt based on the argument that any leader targeted by an assassination attempt would have done the same.

However, and not to minimize the suffering of victims, Dujail remains a relatively minor thread in a broader tapestry of atrocity. The performativity of a Dujail conviction will be of relatively low value; other than the fact that it might permit the opportunity to judge the Iraqi Revolutionary Court as a whole for applying the law in the service of oppression—like the Altstoetter (jurists) trial by the United State Military Commission at Nuremberg. Awad al-Bandar, proffers the defense that the Dujail defendants were given a proper trial and legitimately sentenced to death for having endeavored to assassinate Saddam, during a time of war with Iran.

Dujail was chosen as the first of a dozen or so of these mini-trials owing to perceptions it was a water-tight case. Subsequent mini-trials will occur in a higher-stakes context.

Other commentators have inquired about technical-legal aspects of a Dujail conviction. To build on their observations: if a low-stakes conviction overshadows the rest of the charges, on much fierier accusations—including repression of Kurds by chemical weapons, draining of the marshes, and crushing of the 1991 Shiite uprising in the south by Sunni tribes of the west (under Saddam's alleged order)—then the Court will, in the name of conservatism, have forsaken its ability to make a hardier historical footprint. Paradoxically: in striving to avoid one of the major shortcomings of the now terminated Milosevic trial, namely an overarching but unwieldy and unduly lengthy narrative, the iterated vignettes of atrocity planned by the Saddam trial may create a situation where closure with regard to the first vignette may overshadow and perhaps strip the meaning of the subsequent vignettes keyed to much more serious allegations. These subsequent vignettes then become deflating anticlimaxes.

In another note: to what extent does the artificial reductionism of the criminal trial shield much deeper inquiries? Such inquiries might include international and foreign complicity in Saddam's abuses, such as the selling of weapons (some of which has come to light in alternate proceedings, such as the verdict in the Netherlands against Frans van Aaraat); the role of the U.S. in providing financial support and material assistance to aid the Ba'athist war against Iran; the U.S. exhortation of uprising in 1991 and subsequent failure to support those who rose up; complicity and involvement by ordinary Iraqis in totalitarianism; the toll U.N. sanctions took on ordinary Iraqis and how these sanctions may have paradoxically strengthened Saddam's control over power by weakening his opposition; and the legality of Operation Iraqi Freedom.

I do not raise these as tu quoque defenses. These issues have no bearing on determinations of the individual guilt of the defendants before the Court. Admittedly, defendants have exploited these to embarrass the Court. Nonetheless, these are historical truths that may be squeezed out by application of the modern rules of evidence and, therefore, fail to appear on the pages and transcripts of judicialized truths, notwithstanding the fact that these truths form an important part of Iraqis' perceptions of their current reality and of the very legitimacy of the Court in the first place.

The current chief judge, Judge Rahman, has been praised for his tight control over the courtroom, in contradistinction to Judge Rizgar, his predecessor, who was subject to considerable criticism from politicians for his having accorded Hussein too much leeway (some say he in fact had lost control over the courtroom). On the one hand, tight control is necessary for managerial and bureaucratic reasons, to streamline process and dissipate inflammatory controversy, and to preserve the authority of the Court. The need for such control arises from defendants' antics, designed to turn the proceedings into farce. These include outbursts, allegations by Saddam Hussein that the U.S. had tortured him, taking prayer breaks during witness testimony, hunger strike, a brawl, dismissal of defense attorneys, chief of intelligence (and half-brother) showing up in pajamas. Examples of this tight control—a valuable lesson learned from the Milosevic proceedings include in the Dujail proceedings shutting out political speeches and controlling audio output. However, there is a cost to managerial effectiveness in terms of the resonance of the trial to wider audiences in Iraq and whether the full story of the multi-causal origins of Saddam's grip on power is told. There is a balance between risk-management and uncovering the truth.

In particular, by thus far refusing to respond to defense motions that pertain to the Court's jurisdiction and the legality of its creation, the Court may weaken its own credibility. This presents a contrast with the ICTY, whose decision in the Tadic matter flaws notwithstanding grappled with important issues of legitimacy. I'm not sure what convincing rationalization the Court can proffer regarding the legitimacy of its own creation, but engaging with the issue is preferable to leaving it as the elephant on the table.

What Happens to the Saddam Trial if Civil War Consumes Iraq?

By David Scheffer

In the event civil war or sectarian violence consume Iraq—and that day already may have arrived—the fate of the Iraqi High Tribunal and the trials of Saddam Hussein and his regime's top leaders will hang in the balance. Security issues will dominate the proceedings, even more so than they have during the last six months. Although Presiding Judge Ra'uf Abdel Rahman can cut off Saddam Hussein's microphone at will, the fact remains that Saddam can use the Dujail trial, as currently managed, and any later trials to stoke the violence outside the Green Zone and encourage its threat to the courtroom itself. The immediate alternative is closed trials which will endanger the fairness of the process and anger large numbers of Iraqis (particularly Sunnis) demanding public access to the trials. Indeed, the original justification for holding the trials in Iraq will be largely defeated if that happens. Whether the trials remain open or closed, witnesses increasingly will fear giving testimony. One can imagine the threats to judges, prosecutors, and defense counsel rising and, with their families at risk, many may abandon their important roles in the trials or be killed or wounded trying to fulfill their duties. Even journalists will find it very difficult to cover the trials each day, particularly if their editors and producers deploy them to cover the civil war and a potentially crumbling government, or pull them out of Iraq all together for their own safety. Trial delays will multiply. As the American security umbrella begins to fold, security will become increasingly problematic.

When the International Criminal Tribunal for the Former Yugoslavia was established in 1993, war continued to rage in Bosnia-Herzegovina and Croatia and there was good reason to locate the court in The Hague where security could be assured and the benefit of distancing the judicial process from the violence could be realized. The downside was how remote it seemed (despite televised coverage) to the perpetrator and victim populations alike, but that was a price that had to be paid at the time. The International Criminal Tribunal for Rwanda was established only months after the genocide that swept that country and, at the time, security was a paramount concern regarding the location of the court. While its location in Arusha, Tanzania, has created some difficulties and the occasional obstruction of the Rwandan Government, the fact remains that the trials have proceeded in a secure environment and its judgments well received in Kigali and globally. An important compromise was to locate the Office of the Prosecutor in Kigali, an arrangement that worked fairly well despite mismanagement problems in both locations during the early years. The Special Court for Sierra Leone was not physically established in Freetown until the United Nations was satisfied that the civil war there had essentially ended and security could be supplemented with the presence of U.N. peacekeepers. The agreement between the United Nations and Sierra Leone establishes the authority to move the court to a foreign jurisdiction "if circumstances so require ..." The Extraordinary Chambers in the Courts of Cambodia, located near Phnom Penh, has begun its operations in a peaceful country long after the demise of the Khmer Rouge. All of these tribunals, of course, have enjoyed intensive U.N. engagement and the support of the international community. All of that has been lacking with the Iraqi High Tribunal.

The discredited optimism of the Bush Administration during and after Operation Iraqi Freedom and the Anglo-American occupation of Iraq included a good faith effort to build a court on Iraqi soil to investigate and prosecute more than a quarter century's atrocity crimes of genocide, crimes against humanity, and war crimes under the regime of Saddam Hussein. If all else had proceeded well—creating a secure environment that would have saved the lives of an estimated 30,000 Iraqis who have now perished, maintaining the Iraqi army and police largely intact, launching a successful reconstruction program, fully restoring and improving essential services like electricity and sewage treatment and the crippled oil industry, and preventing the killing, torture, or abusive treatment of detainees and civilians by U.S. personnel and contractors which has shattered American credibility within Iraq and across the Islamic world—than the Iraqi High Tribunal might have had a fighting chance. But such progress never occurred and now, as with so much else in Iraq, we are where we are and we must cope with the consequences.

Three outcomes must be guaranteed. First, the Dujail trial must proceed in accordance with international standards of due process. Otherwise, it will constitute defective justice that will undermine the rule of law in Iraq and threaten civil order. The judges (or some other competent Iraqi court) must rule in writing and with professional reasoning as soon as possible on defense motions regarding the legitimacy of the Iraqi High Tribunal and of its jurisdiction over the Dujail case, as well as whether there is any conflict of interest for Judge Rahman or any other judge. The security risks and occasional chaos of the Dujail trial might subside somewhat, and key due process fundamentals would be observed, if those rulings were delivered.

Second, the death penalty must be removed, de facto if not de jure, as a possible sentence in the Dujail trial in the event Saddam Hussein is found guilty. No one can predict accurately the consequences of such a penalty being carried out in the near future, but one has to assume the worst case scenario in the violent circumstances of contemporary Iraq. A death penalty likely will make Saddam a martyr for the insurgency and much of the Sunni population. Why invite that probability? Furthermore, Saddam Hussein must be kept alive for many years in order to be prosecuted for far more significant atrocity crimes for which his alleged responsibility is the fulcrum of forthcoming trials covering, at a minimum, the Anfal campaign, the chemical gassing at Halabja, the invasion and occupation of Kuwait, the brutal suppression of the Shi'a and Kurdish uprisings following the Gulf War, the draining of the southern marshes, and the political persecutions of Saddam's regime. Iran also looks for justice regarding Saddam's alleged war crimes during the Iran-Iraq war of the 1980's. If Saddam sits in the dock with a death penalty already imposed but temporarily suspended, he will have nothing to lose by using subsequent trials as his platform to inspire domestic violence. If Saddam is executed following the Dujail trial, there is a strong likelihood that the air will be sucked out of the later mega-trials (if they are held at all). Justice and the historical record would not be served well. The millions of victims and their families in Iraq, Kuwait, and Iran would look back at the Dujail trial as an obscenity.

Third, someone has to have the foresight and courage to plan for the transfer of the Dujail trial or at least the subsequent trials to a location outside Iraq where security can be guaranteed and a process undertaken over many years to bring Saddam Hussein and his colleagues to justice. That plan not only must be initiated, it must be known to be underway so that the forces of violence in Iraq understand that justice will not be derailed or denied whatever the outcome within Iraq politically or militarily. That requires a far more energetic diplomatic effort by the United States and Iraqi authorities to discuss and negotiate judicial options in foreign jurisdictions and even under United Nations authority. Pride needs to be swallowed and reality embraced. In the end, if all of the trials can take place in Iraq in a secure environment and observant of international standards of due process, then the plan would be an obscure footnote to Iraq's emergence from the Saddam era. But without such a plan in a country sliding towards civil war, the Dujail trial may become the main act burying credible justice in modern Iraq.

Section 5: The Next Trials

Did the Anfal Operations Constitute Genocide?

By Dominique Callins, Heather Johnson and Jennifer Lagerquist

The Iraqi constitution recognizes and protects the separate nationality of the Kurdish population within the Iraqi state. Military activities by the Iraqi government conducted from February through September of 1988 ("Operation Anfal") along the Iranian border ("cordon sanitaire") under the leadership of Saddam Hussein, nevertheless targeted certain Kurdish population centers and subjected them to gross violations of human rights

Estimates from Human Rights Watch indicates that upwards of 100,000 Kurdish men, women, and children were killed by mass executions, chemical attacks against dozens of Kurdish villages, systematic firing squads, the destruction of approximately 2,000 villages near to the border of Iran and elsewhere in Iraq, the destruction of residential structures in civilian areas, looting of civilian property and farm animals, arbitrary arrest of villagers captured in designated "prohibited areas," and mass deportations and relocations from the northern part of Iraq to camps located in non-Kurdish areas of Iraq.

These actions not only denied particular groups of Kurdish Iraqis security within Iraq's borders, but affirmatively victimized them in particular, as a regional population. Article II of the convention on the Prevention and Punishment of Genocide ("Genocide Convention" or "Convention"), defines genocide: In the present Convention, genocide means any of the following acts committed with intent to destroy, in whole or in part, a national, ethnical, racial, or religious group, as such:

(a) Killing members of the group;
(b) Causing serious bodily or mental harm to members of the group;
(c) Deliberately inflicting on the group conditions of life calculated to bring about is physical destruction in whole or in part;
(d) Imposing measures intended to prevent births within the group;
(e) Forcibly transferring children of the group to another group.

Article three of the Convention makes the international crime punishable.

Although it is clear that numerous human rights abuses occurred within the cordon sanitaire, the prosecution of genocide is complicated by the lack of a coordinated national policy by the Iraqi government to persecute the Kurds as a nationality through the territory of Iraq. Indeed, evidence tends to show that people initially placed into relocation centers were subsequently released to their families, and that others who complied with Iraqi Government orders were left unharmed. The various Anfal Operations appear somewhat limited to the rural border regions between Iraq and Iran with major population centers remaining mostly unscathed.

The Kurds, as a distinct minority nationality within Iraq, should be protected as a group by the Genocide Convention. Likewise, the acts of the Iraqi government in the cordon sanitaire (mass exterminations, etc.) appear to be actus reus within the definition of genocide. For the actors to be liable for apparent human rights abuses under the Genocide Convention in particular, however, they must have had the specific genocidal "intent to destroy, in whole or in part, a national, ethnical, racial, or religious group, as such." This is the most difficult analysis because it involves both subjective and objective determinations.

Preliminary to the finding of specific genocidal intent, judges sitting for the Iraqi Tribunal considering cases of genocide will need to first define objectively, the group that was allegedly targeted. In this case, Iraqi Kurds as a national group would clearly be protected groups within the Convention, and may have been victimized "in part." Iraqi Kurds of the cordon sanitaire might also be recognized as an "ethnical" sub-group of the larger Kurdish nationality. Multiple ethnical sub-groups might exist in the region, and this finding might lead to different conclusions of whether smaller groups were targeted "in whole" or "part". Once the group has been defined, judges will assess the specific intent of alleged perpetrators.

The intent must be to destroy the group "in part." The numbers of intended victims must be substantial, either quantitatively or qualitatively. The quantitative analysis might consider a raw numeric total of victims, or a proportional one assessed in relation to the total number of individuals of the group under the control of the perpetrators. The qualitative assessment would focus on whether the target for destruction was picked because of its importance to the group such that its elimination would be likely to destroy the group. It will be for the judges to determine in light of the examples presented by Rwanda and Yugoslavia, whether substantial destruction, either qualitatively or quantitatively, occurred.

Finally, intent must be directed towards the group "as such." That a separate motive exists for the persecution of the group is irrelevant, as long as it is membership in the group that drives the destruction, and that the destruction was committed because of its tendency to destroy the group.

Finding that genocide occurred in Iraq will be an exhaustive consideration of the facts of each case; any consideration of genocidal intent must be carefully considered based on a totality of the circumstances.

The Significance of the Anfal Campaign Indictment

By Michael A. Newton

The April 4, 2006 referral of the Anfal case for trial in the Iraqi High Tribunal is a sign of a maturing institution that is willing to confront the most difficult cases and apply the most modern jurisprudence. The Anfal case will encompass a series of military campaigns directed against Kurdish civilians from February to August 1988.[164] Saddam Hussein appointed Ali Hassan Al-Majid as the Head of the Northern Bureau Command through Revolutionary Command Council Decree 160 in March 1987, and the campaign against Kurds began the next year. Saddam and six other senior Ba'athists are charged with destroying between 2,000 and 4,000 Kurdish villages, including Qala Dizeh which had 70,000 residents. As many as 100,000 Kurds died during Anfal, almost entirely non-combatants, while an equal number disappeared, and another 500,000 were forced into hastily constructed and barren concrete "collective towns." According to the Institute for War and Peace Reporting, Iraqi forces used chemical weapons against civilians in at least 40 separate attacks. Paraphrasing Justice Jackson's assessment of the International Military Tribunal at Nuremberg, "no history of the era of Iraq under Ba'athist rule will be 'entitled to authority' if it ignores the factual and legal conclusions that will be presented in open court in the IHT."[165]

An accurate and comprehensive record of the history associated with the Anfal will be one of the most important long-term legacies of the High Criminal Court. Justice Jackson also wrote that: "We have documented from German sources the Nazi aggressions, persecutions, and atrocities with such authenticity and in such detail that there can be no responsible denial of these crimes in the future and no tradition of martyrdom of the Nazi leaders can arise among informed people." However, the prosecution of the Anfal campaign is an ambitious undertaking that would stretch the resources and capacity of almost any judicial body around the world. Properly trying the Anfal case will be a major accomplishment and a validation of the vision that justice is best served by an Arabic speaking court undertaken by Iraqi judges on behalf of the Iraqi people. To that end, the Trial Chamber should consider three ways of balancing the right of the defense and the need for the Iraqi people to witness a full trial based on the facts adduced in open court, with the potential for judicial paralysis and exhaustive inefficiency that could seriously undermine other important cases.

Prior to the beginning of the trial, the judges should work to develop and publish a binding trial calendar applicable to both the defense and prosecution. The establishment of such a trial schedule would have the collateral benefit of giving due notice to the defense team before trial of the intended scope of trial evidence. As a result, no defense delays should be granted during the trial except those perhaps based on a showing of very good cause. The result would be to minimize the disruptions and delays inherent in such a difficult and emotionally charged case. To prevent the Anfal trial from becoming a confusing quagmire, court officials should carefully weigh the balance between documentary evidence, witness testimony, and sworn affidavits in building the case. In the context of the ICTY, Rule 73bis was adopted to assist the Trial Chamber in adjudicating extremely complex factual and legal campaigns similar to the Anfal case. Under the ICTY Rule, the Trial Chamber may hold a Pre-Trial conference to specify (i) the number of witnesses the Prosecutor may call; and (ii) the time available to the Prosecutor for presenting evidence. In addition, the Trial Chamber may specify a discrete number of crime sites or incidents related to the charges in respect of which evidence may be presented by the Prosecutor. Limiting the scope of testimony implicates the important interests of the victims across Iraq, and should be reached only after evaluation of the relevant circumstances, including the scope of crimes during Anfal, as well as their classification and nature, the places where they are alleged to have been committed, their scale and the need to be reasonably representative of the entire pattern of criminality.

Secondly, the Trial Chamber in the Anfal case should consult with the Dutch judges who recently tried the case against Frans Van Anraat. On December 23, 2005, a court in Amsterdam convicted Van Anraat of complicity in war crimes and sentenced him to 15 years imprisonment for providing the raw materials for the chemical weapons used against Kurdish civilians. The Dutch court obtained personal jurisdiction over the defendant after he fled Iraq following the end of the regime, but acquitted him of genocide on the basis that there was insufficient evidence to establish that he knew of the genocidal intent of the regime. The IHT Statute mirrors other tribunals in requiring any conviction for the crime of genocide to be based on a specific intent to destroy the Kurdish population in whole or in part. Significantly, the Dutch court held that the overall campaign amounted to genocide against Kurds. Both Saddam Hussein and Ali Hassan Al-Majid are charged with genocide, while all of the accused are charged with war crimes committed during an armed conflict not of an international character and crimes against humanity. Review of the Van Aanrat trial, and its presentation of evidence would prove instructive for the judges and perhaps indicate other sources of relevant evidence that should be presented during the Anfal trial.

Finally, in considering the judicial plan for presenting the evidence in the Anfal case in a fair and efficient manner, the Trial Chamber should consider that it "may admit any evidence which it deems to have probative value."[166] NGOs and other organizations around the world have compiled a veritable mountain of evidence related to Anfal. For example, Human Rights Watch obtained audio tapes from inside Iraq that document key conversations between the defendants in the Anfal case and has made some of them public. In one audio tape, Ali Hassan Al-Majid comments on Iraqi Kurds and exclaims: "I will kill them all with chemical weapons! Who is going to say anything? The international community? *#*@ them! The International community and those who listen to them." Tribunal officials should pursue such additional evidence provided that they can be satisfied of its authenticity and any other circumstance that might shed doubt on its reliability. The Trial Chamber should specifically issue opinions for each piece of evidence considered from other sources that specify the criteria of Rule 59 (Fifth) of the Court Rules.

The Anfal trial will be one of the most visible and challenging trials in the history of the Iraqi High Tribunal, just as the campaign in 1988 scarred Iraqi society. The Trial Chamber should proceed in a calibrated manner to ensure the needs of justice while preserving the long term record in a way that does justice to those Kurdish civilians whose remains have been found in the mass graves of the north

The Significance of the Anfal Campaign Indictment

By Michael P. Scharf

As the Dujail trial was nearing an end, on April 4, 2006, the Iraqi High Tribunal announced the referral of its second case to the Trial Chamber. The case concerns the Anfal campaign, a series of eight military operations launched against the Northern Kurds in 1988, which resulted in an estimated 100,000 deaths.

The IHT had been criticized for beginning with the Dujail Case, which involved 150 casualties, rather than the far more weighty Anfal case, whose casualty figures were 100 times greater. Since many experts were opining that Saddam would be promptly executed following the verdict in the Dujail trial, comparisons were made to the 1931 trial of Chicago mob boss Al "Scarface" Capone, who was prosecuted for tax evasion rather than for the thousands of murders he orchestrated in a series of gang wars in the 1920s. While Saddam might pay the ultimate price for Dujail, his victims would be robbed of seeing him face justice for his much greater atrocities.

The announcement of the Anfal referral changed all that. Since the Anfal case is scheduled to begin immediately after the close of the Dujail trial (while the Dujail verdict is being appealed to the Appeals chamber of the IHT), this means that whatever the Dujail verdict, Saddam Hussein will be available to face his accusers in the Anfal trial.

The Anfal referral is important in a second respect. The IHT announced that Saddam and his co-defendants, including Ali Hassan Al-Majid ("Chemical Ali"), would be charged with the crime of genocide. Genocide has been called "the crime of crimes." It is the worst crime known to humankind, and it is the hardest crime to prove. Charging Saddam with genocide suggests that his atrocities rank with those committed by Adolf Hitler, Pol Pot, Idi Amin, and Slobodan Milosevic.

The problem, however, is that it will be extremely difficult to prove the genocide charge in relation to the Anfal campaign, and thus there is a great risk that Saddam will be acquitted, leaving the world to wonder whether he was no more than a petty thug as opposed to a genocidal dictator, after all.

The 1948 Genocide Convention defines genocide as mass killing and other similar actions "committed with intent to destroy, in whole or in part, a national, ethnical, racial or religious group, as such." It is significant that the drafters of the Genocide Convention deliberately excluded acts directed against "political groups," or "opponents of the regime" from the definition of Genocide. This exclusion was due to the fact that the Convention was drafted during the height of the cold war, during which the Soviet Union and other totalitarian governments feared that they would face interference in their internal affairs if genocide was defined to include such acts. Thus, history has not labeled the murder of four million Russians in Stalin's purges (1937–1953) or of five million Chinese in Mao's Cultural Revolution (1966–1976) as acts of genocide.

With their distinct language and culture, the Iraqi Kurds obviously constitute an ethnic group under the Genocide Convention. Moreover, the large number of victims in a distinct geographic area is more than sufficient for a finding of genocide. The challenge for the Tribunal will be finding the necessary "specific intent" to destroy the Kurds "as such"—in other words for no predominant reason other than because they are Kurds. As described below, there are two alternative theories, having nothing to do with ethnocentrism, xenophobia, or hatred of Kurds, for why Saddam ordered the Anfal operations.

First, in 1986, the two main Kurdish parties, the KDP and PUK, united with the help of Iran (which was then at war with Iraq), to attempt to topple Saddam's government. Thus, the Anfal campaign may have been aimed at punishing the Kurds for their acts of treason and at suppressing the continuing threat of an Iranian-backed insurgency. It is noteworthy that Kurds who cooperated with Iraqi officials, dissociated themselves from Kurdish nationalists, and accepted deportation to southern Iraq, were not otherwise persecuted.

Second, parts of Kurdistan in northern Iraq contained vast quantities of oil that Saddam's government desired. The Kurdish claims to these oil fields in the 1980s would have been perceived as a significant threat that required a response. It is significant in this regard that the Anfal campaign did not target all Kurdish populated towns throughout Iraq, just those in oil-rich Kurdistan in northern Iraq, and that the people killed in the Anfal campaign included non-Kurds, as well as Kurds, who refused to vacate the targeted towns.

These motivations would not absolve Saddam for liability for crimes against humanity and war crimes (for using chemical weapons and indiscriminately killing mass numbers of Kurdish civilians). But if the Tribunal concludes that the Anfal operations predominantly reflected Saddam's intent to retaliate against the Kurds for treason, to suppress insurgency, or to gain access to oil, Saddam must be acquitted of the genocide charge. Thus, the genocide charge represents an ambitious but risky move for the Tribunal.

The Significance of the Anfal Campaign Indictment

By Mark A. Drumbl

The "riskiness" of the Anfal genocide charge can be seen from a different light, as well. Michael Scharf is right to point out that there may be a risk that an acquittal on genocide charges might diminish the expressive value of the trial by leaving a historical footprint of Saddam as "just" a thug and not a genocidal mastermind. However, there also is a risk that a conviction on the charge of genocide might further dilute the heinousness of the purported "crime of all crimes."

To be sure, this discussion is entirely speculative, as I do not have a sense of the precise nature of the evidence that the Prosecutor will adduce. It may well be that there is evidence that solidly meets the dolus specialis of genocide in the case of the Anfal campaign against the Kurds. However, it seems to me that the prosecution of Saddam on genocide forms part of a trend in international criminal law toward what appears to be a more flexible and capacious understanding of genocide.

One example of this trend is from the International Criminal Tribunal for the Former Yugoslavia, whose 2004 Appeals Chamber decision in the Krstic Case confirmed that the slaughter of 7,000 Bosnian Muslim men and boys in Srebrenica was related to the intended destruction of the Srebrenica Bosnian Muslims as a target group which, in turn, was connected to the intended destruction of the protected group, namely Bosnian Muslims. Another example might be the draft instruments of the Extraordinary Chambers for Cambodia which, to the best of my knowledge, are minded to have jurisdiction to prosecute genocide.

As the threshold for genocide may lower, the crime of genocide may become more blurred with certain crimes against humanity such as persecution and extermination. This may permit capture of a broader number of perpetrators as "genocidaires" but, as well, may obscure the singularly heinous nature of genocide as the most reprehensible of the major international crimes.

I appreciate that this may be a somewhat technical discussion to the Kurdish population that was so victimized by Saddam, but individual prosecutions of individual defendants must be placed in the context of their overall effects on the structures of international criminal law.

Shouldn't Saddam Hussein Be Prosecuted for the Crime of Aggression?

By William Schabas

Back in 1990, U.S. President George Bush and UK Prime Minister Margaret Thatcher spoke of bringing Hussein to an international court for the illegal invasion of Kuwait. The idea later gained some purchase within the EU, before fading. Accounts of the birth of the International Criminal Tribunal for the former Yugoslavia refer to these aborted proposals to try Hussein for aggression as evidence of the impending revival of the concept of international prosecution.

But in 2003, when lawyers for the U.S. and the UK were setting up the Iraqi High Tribunal, Bush and Thatcher's idea of prosecuting Hussein for aggression had disappeared from the radar screen. Some commentators have suggested that because aggression has not yet been defined for the purposes of the Rome Statute of the International Criminal Court, that it is not punishable under international law.

The crime of aggression (or 'crimes against peace') was punishable at Nuremberg, where it was defined as 'planning, preparation, initiation or waging of a war of aggression ... or participation in a common plan or conspiracy for the accomplishment' of such a war. The International Military Tribunal responded to the charge that this was retroactive criminalization by saying that aggression had been an international crime as a matter of customary international law prior to 1939. Famously, the judges said it was the 'supreme international crime'.

If it was customary law in 1939 and 1946, has anything changed? Before joining the U.S. invasion, British Prime Minister Blair obtained a legal opinion from his Attorney-General, Lord Goldsmith. It warned Blair that although the possibility was 'remote', there was an arguable case for prosecution for the crime of aggression. 'Aggression is a crime under customary international law which automatically forms part of domestic law', noted Lord Goldsmith in his 7 March 2003 opinion.

So why shouldn't Saddam Hussein be tried for the 'supreme international crime', instead of an isolated massacre, as seems currently to be the case? The answer is straightforward enough. Any prosecution of Saddam Hussein for aggression would invite analogies with the aggression committee by the U.S. and the UK in early 2003, against Iraq.

Intriguingly, the argument that Saddam committed aggression in Kuwait is somehow joined at the hip with the argument that the U.S. and the UK were justified in invading Iraq 13 years later. Security Council Resolution 678, adopted following the first Gulf War, mandated the coalition forces to use all necessary means to force Iraq to withdraw from Kuwait and to restore peace and security to Iraq. Over the years, the U.S. and the UK used force against Iraq on this basis on several occasions.

But the fundamental justification for the 2003 invasion, Iraq's possession of weapons of mass destruction, has proved to be a canard, as everyone now knows. The realization that the legal justification of the invasion was hollow did not, however, seem to be sufficient to provoke the invaders into immediate withdrawal of their armed forces.

This comment is not the place to debate whether or not the U.S. and the UK committed aggression. What a pity that this important question, too, cannot be the subject of a trial. Alas, there is no forum for such a debate. The issue seems inseparable from what is the ultimate hypocrisy. Nazis were convicted at Nuremberg by U.S. and UK judges for the 'supreme international crime' of aggression. Yet Iraqis, including Saddam Hussein, will not be tried for the same crime, despite ample evidence that the waging of aggressive war was one of the central tenets of his despotic regime, as the country's neighbors, Kuwait and Iran, know only so well. And this despite the appeals, in 1990, by Bush and Thatcher.

It is all so reminiscent of Nuremberg, when Admiral Dönitz was acquitted of illegal submarine warfare because he had produced an affidavit from U.S. Admiral Nimitz saying he had done the same thing. Or when the Soviet massacre of Polish officers at Katyn was ignored in the final judgment. It doesn't do the credibility of international or internationalized justice any good to have such inconsistencies, and such double standards.

PART IV

LOOKING FORWARD: THE TRIAL
IN A BROADER CONTEXT

Is the Saddam Hussein Trial One of the Most Important Court Cases of All Time?

By Michael P. Scharf

The term "Trial of the Century" has been employed with respect to the major international war crimes trials of our time, including the 1945 Nuremberg Trial, the 1961 Adolf Eichmann Trial, the 1987 Klaus Barbie Trial, the 1989 Nicolae Ceausescu Trial, and most recently the 2002–2005 Milosevic Trial. There are five criteria, which the Saddam Hussein Trial meets, which suggest that it is likely to rank among these seminal cases.

The first criterion is the scale of the atrocities. Saddam stands accused of the worst crime known to human kind—genocide. He is alleged to have ordered the use of poison gas against the Northern Iraqi Kurds, to have dammed rivers in order to starve out the Southern Marsh Arabs, and to have deported, detained, tortured, and executed thousands of opponents of the Ba'ath regime. Altogether, there are said to be nearly one million victims of his regime.

The second criterion is the status of the accused. At Nuremberg, Hitler escaped trial by committing suicide, leaving his second in command, Herman Goering to be prosecuted as a proxy. Eichmann and Barbie were merely sycophantic underlings. Ceausescu was a petty dictator. And Milosevic has proved to be less of a monster than Bosnian Serb leader Radovan Karadzic and Bosnian Serb General Ratko Mladic, who are still at large. Saddam Hussein, in contrast, was the top official responsible for the actions of the Ba'ath regime, and he is said to have maintained extraordinary control over the Iraqi military and security forces.

The third criterion is the level of interest of the international community. Because a broad coalition fought against Saddam Hussein with U.N. approval in 1991, Saddam Hussein is extremely well known throughout the world and the level of media and public interest in his trial is immense.

The fourth criterion is the legal precedent that the trial will set. As the world's first "internationalized domestic tribunal," the Iraqi High Tribunal is likely to serve as a new kind of model for bringing former leaders to justice throughout the world, which will complement other options such as trial before the International Criminal Court or before Hybrid International-Domestic tribunals like the Special Court for Sierra Leone. Moreover, the Iraqi High Tribunal's use of international definitions of crimes and standards for due process will serve as a model for the ordinary Iraqi courts, as well as courts throughout the Middle East.

The final criterion is the likely effect of the trial. If the Saddam Hussein trial is viewed as fair and if the evidence convinces most Iraqis of his guilt, this will discredit his followers and quell support for the ongoing insurgency. If, on the other hand, the trial is a train wreck, it may ignite an Iraqi civil war, which could spill over to neighboring countries. The stakes couldn't be higher. For these reasons, it is fair to say that the Saddam Hussein case merits the title "mother of all trials."

Is the Saddam Hussein Trial One of the Most Important Court Cases of All Time?

By Leila Sadat

In arguing that the Saddam Hussein trial is a "Trial of the Century," Professor Scharf appears to be suggesting that media interest is tantamount to success, importance and legitimacy. This is a mistake. Criminal trials, whether of important and notorious individuals, or of small-time offenders accused of petty crimes, are nothing more than show trials, unless three criteria are met: The judges must be independent, well-qualified and impartial; the accused must be properly and effectively represented; and the proceedings must be fair. Using these criteria, it is difficult not to be skeptical about the fairness, and therefore the ultimate significance, of the trial of Saddam Hussein.

As I have noted in one of my earlier essays the judges of the Iraqi High Tribunal were originally chosen under U.S. occupation, and several media reports suggest that they are all of Kurdish or Shiite ethnicity. Moreover, there have been attempts to "purge" the court of former Baath party members including, most recently, Judge Juhi, the Tribunal's chief investigative judge.

This in and of itself does not automatically indicate that the judges are not "independent, well-qualified and impartial," but it suggests that it is perhaps very soon for a country that has been without an independent judiciary for many years to quickly reinvent itself. It is difficult to imagine how a few weeks training in London under the tutelage of a handful of U.S. lawyers can overcome 35 years of living under the regime of Saddam Hussein. Recall that the French courts that tried and heard appeals from Klaus Barbie, and the Israeli Courts that tried and heard appeals from Adolf Eichmann were not established for the sole purpose of doing so. Instead, they were for the most part ordinary civil courts staffed by professional judges who were tasked to participate in extraordinary events. The judges of the IHT, in contrast, are newly-minted, sit on an extraordinary court created by a foreign occupying power that is still waging a military campaign within the country, and are themselves subject to threats of violence. Without opining as to whether they are qualified or not (and one can only wish them "good luck" in their endeavors), it is undeniable that they face challenges that would try the most seasoned, phlegmatic and experienced of jurists.

At the same time, the qualifications of the judges are probably the least problematic aspect of the proceedings before the IHT, which are significantly more deficient on the question of representation of the accused and fairness of the proceedings. Although the right to counsel is granted by IHT rules of procedure, counsel is not mandated to be present at many stages of the proceedings, meaning that Saddam and other accused have been interrogated without defense counsel present. Indeed, Iraqi President Jalal Talabani recently stated on Iraqi State television that a judge had been "able to extract confessions" from Saddam Hussein. Although it is unclear at what point defense counsel (or those who claim to be representing Saddam) were given the file, there is no doubt that there is an extraordinary imbalance between the resources of prosecution and defense counsel. The Prosecution is being staffed by U.S. lawyers working behind the scenes, and funded by the United States, to the tune of U.S. $ 128 million. Many of the Tribunal's rules also appear to have been shaped to suit U.S. rather than Iraqi interests, particularly the absence of IHT jurisdiction over non-Iraqi defendants. Many defense lawyers have argued that they are not safe in Iraq because they do not (unlike the Prosecution team) receive U.S. military protection. Saddam's lead Iraqi attorney, Khalil al-Dulaimi has stated that he has not been able to speak privately with his client without "severe" American monitoring, and that he has not been given sufficient time to prepare for the trial. There also appears to be no requirement that guilt be proved beyond a reasonable doubt.

The creation of ad hoc courts with special jurisdiction is inevitably fraught with peril, and is never the best option. The accusation of "victor's justice" is ever-present, which is one of the reasons why the world has now established a permanent international criminal court, rather than resorting to ad hoc adjudication in each case. Sometimes ad hoc or extraordinary courts are a necessary evil, but because their legitimacy is inherently fragile, it is particularly important that the process by which an accused is tried before them is beyond reproach. What made the Nuremberg trials so significant wasn't just the importance of the accused and the extraordinary nature of the atrocities (two of Professor Scharf's criteria), but the fairness of the proceedings. When Admiral Karl Dönitz was accused of waging unrestricted submarine warfare, his lawyer was permitted to introduce an affidavit from U.S. Admiral Chester Nimitz to the effect that the U.S. was doing the same thing in the Pacific. As Justice Robert Jackson stated in his opening address to the International Military Tribunal at Nuremberg, "[w]e must summon such detachment and intellectual integrity to our task that this trial will commend itself to posterity as fulfilling humanity's aspirations to do justice." For the IHT's legacy to be enduring, its personnel must do the same.

Lessons from the Saddam Trial

By Michael P. Scharf

It is often said that just as courts try cases, so too do cases try courts. As the first trial before the Iraqi High Tribunal, the Dujail Case was the test-run for this novel judicial institution, which I have characterized as an "internationalized domestic tribunal."

The Iraqi High Tribunal (IHT) joins the War Crimes Chamber of the Court of Bosnia and Herzegovina as the first of a new breed of domestic tribunals that combine elements of international and domestic war crimes courts. Although it sits in Baghdad and its judges are (currently) all Iraqi, the IHT is independent from the ordinary Iraqi court system, it is assisted by international advisers, and its constituent instruments incorporate the definitions of crimes and due process rights contained in the statutes of the existing international war crimes tribunals and stipulate that the precedent of those tribunals are to guide the decisions of the IHT. In the future, internationalized domestic tribunals like the IHT may play an increasingly important role in the growing accountability web for atrocity crimes that also includes the International Criminal Court, the Security Council-created ad hoc war crimes tribunals for the former Yugoslavia and Rwanda, the U.N.-created hybrid war crimes tribunals for Sierra Leone, East Timor, and Cambodia, and ordinary national courts.

In the previous essays, our experts have debated every facet of the Iraqi High Tribunal and Dujail trial—from the issue of whether it was a mistake to hold the trial in Baghdad to the question of whether the trial met international standards of due process. The general perception from media reports was that the Dujail trial was extremely messy, a bit out of control, and rather unfair. While I would not go as far as some who characterize the Dujail trial as a "judicial train wreck," clearly, there is much room for improvement.

After the Nuremberg Trial sixty years ago, Chief Prosecutor Robert Jackson reported to President Truman that despite the many errors and missteps that occurred during the proceedings, he was consoled by the fact that the lessons from the WWII war crimes tribunal would be instructive for the future. While the views expressed by our experts have diverged on many issues, we all agree that much can be learned from the way the Dujail trial unfolded, and that these lessons can help improve the way the Iraqi High Tribunal tackles its upcoming trials, as well as the way the international community can help domestic prosecutions of former leaders accused of atrocities in other parts of the world. These concluding essays therefore analyze some of the major lessons learned from the Dujail trial. My own "top ten" list would include the following:

Lesson #1: Further internationalize the Tribunal.

Like the Statute of the War Crimes Chamber of the Court of Bosnia and Herzegovina, the IHT Statute provided for the appointment of one or more foreign judges to join the Iraqi judges on the bench, but without explanation none were ever appointed. Such an appointment of a distinguished Arabic-speaking judge from the region—someone like Egyptian Judge Georgese Abi-Saab who had served with distinction on the Yugoslavia Tribunal during the 1990s—would greatly promote the perception of the IHT as a fair and competent judicial institution, without sacrificing the essential Iraqi character of the tribunal. In addition, the Statute provides for the appointment of international advisers to assist the judges, prosecutor, and defense team. To date, the identities of the non-U.S. advisers working with the Tribunal have been kept confidential for their protection, but this has led to the misperception that the only foreign advisers are members of the U.S. Department of Justice Regime Crimes Liaison Office, which in turn makes the Tribunal appear to be an American-controlled enterprise. In future trials, more advisors selected by respected NGOs such as the International Bar Association should be recruited to assist the Tribunal, and their contribution (if not their identities) needs to be made public.

Lesson #2: Ensure visible gender representation on the Tribunal.

In recognition of the fact that many of the victims of the atrocities of the Ba'ath regime were women and that women jurists would bring important perspectives to the gender-crimes that the Tribunal would be prosecuting, several women were appointed as IHT judges. But there was no mention of a female judge serving as a member of the IHT bench during the Dujail trial. The IHT was designed not just to prosecute the leaders of the Ba'athist regime, but also to serve as a model for the newly emerging Iraqi judicial system by employing international rules for the protection of the rights of the defendant and standards of due process. It should also serve as a model of gender equality, by appointing women to serve a visible role as judges in future trials. At a very minimum, in the future the IHT should disclose the gender representation of each trial bench, along with other basic information about the qualifications and experience of the judges (but not put them at risk by disclosing their identities). Just as it is important that prominent members of the new Iraqi government be women, so too should women be seen playing a prominent role in the Iraqi judiciary, beginning with the IHT.

Lesson #3: Appoint a sufficient number of alternate judges.

While the Nuremberg Tribunal had four alternate judges, the Yugoslavia Tribunal had none, which created a huge problem when the judge presiding over the Milosevic case died of a brain tumor half way through the trial. The IHT split the difference and appointed two alternate judges. But that number turned out to be inadequate, as three judges had to be replaced during the Dujail trial—one resigned when he found out that a relative had been a victim at Dujail, one resigned under pressure for not being tough enough with the Defendants, and one resigned when the de-Ba'athification Commission announced that he was under investigation for past membership in the Ba'ath Party. Judge Ra'uf, who replaced the first Presiding Judge on day five of the trial, had not even been in the courtroom for the first four trial sessions, creating concerns about the fairness of the proceedings. Given the length and importance of the upcoming trials, there should be at least three alternate judges for every case, who sit in the courtroom throughout the trial, ready to step in at a moment's notice if the need arises. When that event occurs, this will enable the trial to continue without delay and without the perception of unfairness.

Lesson #4: Guarantee better security.

The international community has recognized that when they are practicable, domestic trials have many inherent advantages over international trials. Indeed, the International Criminal Court's "complementarity" provisions are founded on that assumption. The Dujail case was certainly not the first trial in history conducted in a dangerous climate, and the security situation in Baghdad was not so grave to justify relocation of the trial outside of Iraq, with all the disadvantages that would have entailed. But when Defense Counsel initially rejected the offer of U.S. and Iraqi security, the apparent attitude of the U.S. and Iraqi government could be summed up as: "Fine, it's your funeral." With the assassination of two defense lawyers during the first week of the trial, it became obvious that that was a completely inadequate response. The deal that was worked out in October 2005 for the Defense Counsel to use IHT funds to arrange for their own, hand-selected, personal security guards, and to move their families into the Green Zone or out of Iraq, was an appropriate compromise. But the assassination in the closing days of the trial of a third Defense Lawyer, who had elected not to have his security guards at his house the morning of the attack, indicates that even more must be done. For the IHT process to work, one way or another the Defense team has to be protected to the same extent as the judges, prosecutors and witnesses—whether they desire such protection or not. In addition, there should be a high level international investigation into who committed the three assassinations, similar to that recently conducted with respect to the assassination of the Prime Minister of Lebanon.

Lesson #5: Resolve pre-trial issues as they arise.

The Defense made a host of pre-trial motions that the Tribunal merely filed away until its final judgment. Such motions challenged everything from the legitimacy of the tribunal to the bias of the chief judge, from the physical mistreatment of the defendants to the expulsion of the defense lawyers. Rather than dispose of these issues in written reasoned opinions at the beginning of the trial (following the precedent of the international tribunals), the IHT decided to wait to deal with them until the end of the trial, leading to the misperception that the Tribunal did not take these issues seriously. While the IHT's approach did not violate international fair trial standards, in future trials the IHT should make it a practice to issue written opinions addressing such issues as they arise, consistent with the normal practice of Iraqi courts and the international war crimes tribunals.

Lesson #6: Keep the trial short.

In an attempt to avoid one of the greatest blunders of the Milosevic trial, the IHT began with an uncomplicated case that focused on a single atrocity (the 1982 Dujail incident), thereby providing "a snapshot of evil" rather than trying to prove the entire history of the crimes committed by the Ba'ath Regime in a single mega-case. With its narrow focus, the Dujail trial was designed to last about a month, but dragged on for eight. Many of the delays can be attributed to official holidays, security problems, defense boycotts, and difficulties locating witnesses. But the length of the resulting delays seemed disproportionate to these challenges, and many of the recesses seemed to be related to the personal predilections of the Presiding Judge, who made frequent trips home to Kurdistan during the trial. The future IHT trials, which will be far more expansive in scope than the Dujail trial, need to move along at a much faster pace, with procedural matters handled before the trial begins or in the margins of the trial sessions. Any necessary recesses should be at most a few days long, rather than lasting several weeks, and trial proceedings should normally be conducted eight hours a day, five days a week.

Lesson #7: Do not permit the defendant to cross-examine witnesses after his lawyer has done so.

Consistent with international law and in an effort to decrease the possibility that the defendants would attempt to hijack the trial, in August 2005 the democratically elected Iraqi National Legislature amended the IHT Statute to make clear that the defendants had to act through a lawyer in the courtroom—and Saddam and the other seven defendants in the Dujail trial were represented by superb lawyers, including former U.S. Attorney General Ramsey Clark. But both the first and second presiding judges—Rizgar Amin and Ra'uf Abdul Rahman—inexplicably circumvented and undermined that decision by ruling that Saddam and the other defendants could conduct their own cross-examinations of witnesses and address the court each day after their lawyers had done so. This opened the door for Saddam Hussein to brow-beat witnesses, make disrespectful statements about the presiding judges and prosecutors, and to frequently make speeches inciting violence against U.S. military forces and the new Iraqi government—leading to widespread criticism that the judges were losing the battle of the wills with Saddam. In the future, the defendants should only be allowed to speak in court at the end of the trial when they take the stand to testify in their own defense. At all other times, it is their lawyers who should do all the talking.

Lesson #8: Appoint distinguished stand-by counsel.

As anticipated, the defense lawyers were not the model of decorum in this trial. At times their disrespectful and disruptive conduct resulted in their expulsion, and at other times they boycotted the proceedings. In these instances, the trial continued on with stand-by-counsel—public defenders which were appointed at the beginning of the trial by the IHT, and trained and assisted by international advisors. The use of such stand-by counsel had been successfully employed at the Yugoslavia Tribunal, Rwanda Tribunal, and Special Court for Sierra Leone. The very existence of such stand-by public defenders can deter misconduct by the Defense, since the defense lawyers know they can be replaced if necessary at a moments notice. But the public must be convinced that the stand-by Counsel are up to the challenge. The IHT can accomplish this by better explaining the role of the stand-by counsel, releasing biographic information about their qualifications and experience, and by offering them the same type of extensive international training as was provided to the IHT judges and prosecutors.

Lesson #9: Take action to deter disruptions.

Trying former leaders is always a messy affair, especially when a decision has been made to televise the proceedings gavel-to-gavel, and the Defendants' avowed intention is to disrupt the trial, distract public attention from the evidence against them, and turn the televised trial into a political stage. To ensure decorum and protect the integrity of the process, the IHT judges should be prepared to take a number of steps, which have been undertaken successfully by other Tribunals. As mentioned above, the disruptive behavior of the defendants and their lawyers can be minimized by requiring the defendants to act through counsel and by appointing expert public defenders who can step in place of the defendants' chosen lawyers when necessary. If defendants insist on acting disruptively in the courtroom (such as jumping out of their seat and shouting profanities at the bench), they should be placed in a sound-proof booth (like Adolf Eichmann had been in his trial in Jerusalem) or in remote locations tied to the trial by two-way video. Because Counsel of record must be members of the Iraqi Bar, the Tribunal should not hesitate to hold them in contempt of court and subject them to appropriate disciplinary sanctions for conduct that would merit such action in an ordinary court. In such cases, the Presiding Judge needs to dispassionately explain in open court why the steps taken were warranted.

Lesson #10: Expand the Tribunal's public outreach.

As evidenced by the decision to televise the proceedings, the IHT was designed in part to serve an educative function. But the procedural decisions of the IHT were usually shrouded in mystery, as little attempt was made to clarify the many public misconceptions as they arose during the Dujail trial. If the Iraqi people are ever going to feel ownership over the IHT proceedings, and if the international community is ever going to accept the Tribunal as legitimate and fair, they need to fully understand what is going on in the courtroom, and the message should not have to be filtered through the press. To remedy this problem in the future, the Presiding Judge should explain procedural decisions in open court, even if this is not traditionally done in Iraqi trials. In addition, the IHT should appoint one of its judges to act as Press Officer (a role eventually undertaken by Chief Investigating Judge Ra'id). The IHT Press Officer should issue an official statement every day of the trial (in both Arabic and English), explaining what went on that day and answering the questions that the public and press are likely to have about the day's proceedings. Such official press statements, together with trial exhibits and transcripts, should be posted (in both Arabic and English) on the Tribunal's website on a daily basis for world-wide viewing.

The Trial of Saddam Hussein, Lessons Learned Thus Far

By David M. Crane

As the closing arguments by the defense echo about the chamber at the Iraqi High Tribunal in Baghdad, what have we learned thus far related to the trials of Saddam Hussein, former President and ruling tyrant of Iraq, and his henchmen?

First, perception trumps reality.

Born of suspicion, the Iraqi High Tribunal moved forward in seeking a type of just end to a tragic episode in the decades long reign of terror. It was a tough first round as the trial wound its way around practical and legal landmines all under the shadow of suspicion that this was a "fixed trial", a "done deal". The tragedy of all this is that it is probably is not, but the doubt lingers in the corners that somehow the United States is pulling the legal and procedural strings to ensure the appropriate result. Whether this is true remains to be seen. The perception by the international community that it is a show trial certainly trumps the reality that it is not a done deal and that the statute and rules will permit a fair trial. History will tell. I am skeptical.

Second, tyrants need to be faced down.

Despite the way the court was created, Saddam Hussein and his co-defendants are on trial for war crimes and crimes against humanity in an Iraqi domestic court being held accountable for what he has done to the people of the region. The world is being shown the facts about what took place in Iraq. There is an accounting and that is a step in the right direction in facing down the beast of impunity that continues to feed around the periphery of civilization.

Third, peace first—then justice.

In the situation where war continues to rage around the region, particularly a guerilla war, justice should wait in the wings until there is a stable and relatively peaceful society. In Iraq they should have waited a year or so before going to trial. They had Hussein and his henchmen in custody. The significance and public impact of the trial is lessened as the society in which the victims and their families struggle daily for a sense of normalcy. The wave of sectarian violence may wash away any good that is done at the trial itself. The United States and Iraq jumped the gun, which raises the specter of a show trial.

Fourth, security is important.

Part in parcel to peace first, justice second, is the issue of a secure environment to hold the trial. The security problems faced by all of the brave men and women at the Iraqi High Tribunal are overwhelming and are a detractor in ensuring a fair trial. The sober and deliberate consideration of law and fact so fundamental to a fair trial is hampered when officers of the court are murdered and the threat of future violence remains. Everyone is looking over their shoulder and thinking who is next. The focus should be on the law and a fair trial rather than whether one will live to the end of the day.

Fifth, a death sentence makes a martyr.

This is the first in a series of trials. The result could be a finding of guilty and a sentence of death. If Hussein and his co-defendants are executed they could become martyrs rather than convicted and fairly judged war criminals. Because there is the perception of unfairness, their execution only exacerbates the problem.

It is always dangerous to play "armchair quarterback" in the extreme circumstances of conducting a war crimes trial in the midst of an ongoing conflict. However, the five lessons learned above beg comment. The stakes are too high, the legacy too important to allow passive observation. The trials will move forward, attended to by brave and heroic jurists, with the outcome certain, the results set. It is unfortunate that a mega-murderer such as Saddam Hussein will be tried questionably and then dies a martyr.

The Saddam Trial—
Lessons in International Justice

By Mark S. Ellis

As the world awaits a verdict in the Saddam Hussein trial, the Iraqi High Court is itself under scrutiny for lessons learned in the conduct of a high-profile war crimes trial. In the future, given the limited jurisdiction of the new International Criminal Court, domestic war crimes courts will continue to play a key role in administering justice under international law. These courts must possess a basic capacity to undertake trials consistent with international standards of independence, fairness and impartiality. To meet this standard, the following lessons should apply:

First, there should be a presumption *against* undertaking domestic war crimes trials in countries languishing in a conflict environment. In the best of circumstances, managing international criminal trials is arduous. In a country plagued by sectarian violence and devoid of reliable security mechanisms, the undertaking of such a trial is reckless and potentially futile. In Iraq, it resulted in the killing of three Iraqi defense attorneys and one investigative judge. A more responsible and viable option would be to utilize a neutral jurisdiction, as when the trial of former Liberian President Charles Taylor was moved to The Hague.

Second, post-conflict countries that do undertake domestic war crimes trials need unbiased international assistance. It is a misnomer to refer to the Iraqi High Court as a 'domestic' court. Behind the scenes, the United States played a crucial role in drafting the Court's Statute, collecting evidence to be used by the prosecution, and providing both security and financing to the Court. Although the United States, as an occupying force, should not have been the one to play this role, international assistance for these courts is indispensable.

Third, the international community should provide substantial training in international criminal law to jurists, including defense attorneys, serving on domestic trials. An international perspective on substantive and procedural law concerning crimes of genocide, war crimes, and crimes against humanity is essential. Experience shows, however, that even the best and brightest jurists may lack sufficient knowledge in these areas. The result is a natural struggle to comprehend the myriad of complex issues involved with these challenging court proceedings. This was true for the Iraqi Court, and highlights the need for significant training to fill the gap.

Fourth, domestic war crimes courts should be judicious in deciding the charges brought against a defendant, particularly a Head of State. The Iraqi Court was correct in selecting, as its first case against Saddam Hussein, a relatively straightforward incident of criminality. The Dujail case was manageable and the documentary evidence was remarkably strong. This enabled the Court to more directly focus its case.

Fifth, domestic war crimes courts should create a media outreach office to provide regular briefings on trial developments. Not only would this enhance public knowledge about Court proceedings, it would impede the constant speculation, misinformation, and rumors that so often overwhelm high-profile trials. The Iraqi Court failed to create an effective media office. Consequently, Iraqi citizens and the international community were essentially left to use their imaginations when judging the Court's proceedings.

Sixth, the Saddam trial is a lesson in how *not* to deal with trial motions. Consistent with Iraqi and international law, Saddam's defense counsel filed a series of motions addressing issues such as the impartiality of the judges and access to witnesses and documents. One of the most glaring shortcomings of the Court was its failure to articulate a response to these motions. The Court's silence significantly weakened its transparency and undermined the credibility of the judicial process.

Finally, an independent and impartial court is a fundamental prerequisite for meeting international standards of fairness in a trial. Any appearance of government influence is a damning indictment of a court's independence. During the Saddam trial, there were several instances in which the government made inappropriate comments and attempted to interfere with the proceedings. If history judges the trial to be unfair, the government's indiscretion will be central to that determination.

The trial of Saddam Hussein offers a unique glimpse into the challenges and imperfections of administering international justice on a domestic stage. Whatever the final verdict, it will be history's judgment of the trial itself that will echo for years to come. Before future domestic war crimes trials begin, the international community should heed the lessons from Iraq.

Lessons from Al Dujail:
The First, but Not Final, IHT Trial

By Michael Newton

As the trial phase in the Al Dujail moves towards its imminent conclusion it is appropriate to reflect on the lessons learned. There are two important caveats to any observations made at this point of the proceedings: 1) for western observers, the Arabic official language has obscured the actual interchanges between the bench and the counsel, as well as the testimony of witnesses and the active participation of the defendants, and 2) prior to issuance of a detailed legal judgment, it is somewhat premature to engage in finely tuned legal analysis of the ultimate adequacy of the overall trial because its outcome and the legal rationale for its decisions yet lies in the future. Just as the ad hoc tribunals made many adjustments to rules, procedures, and trial practices as they experienced the uncertainties inherent in conducting such complex and emotional trials, it is reasonable to expect that the IHT judges, prosecutors, and defense attorneys have been keen observers of this trial and will adjust their practice based on their own conclusions. Many of the admonitions and perceptions related to this process may well turn out to be unfounded based on the actual detailed record in light of the ultimate judgment and judicial opinion. While I concur with a number of the observations already presented and will not rehash points already raised, I'd add the following comments.

Lesson #1: Keep the Endstate in mind.

The very fact that there is a structure applying international law in combination with domestic norms is a monumental development in this region. The Iraqis who worked to create the IHT as an autonomous structure within the Iraqi judiciary, and those who now serve in its various offices share an aspiration that it will serve as the doorway through which international norms permeate the fabric of Iraqi society. The essence of this trial process is to bring justice based on law to elites who previously acted as though they WERE the law. Each of the witnesses who testified of the suffering in Al-Dujail or the now grown men who talked of being imprisoned as children spoke on behalf of thousands of victims, which is why their testimony was so gripping for average citizens. The images of once mighty Ba'athist officials being subdued to the authority of the law in the person of a judge and established procedures has left an indelible imprint on this culture and on these people. This is a trial based on evidence and testimony and law, not a sham or fabrication. The IHT process stands in sharp contrast to the fact that 148 average citizens of Dujail either died while being tortured or were sentenced as a group to die based on what were, according to defense testimony, "trials" conducted by one defense attorney and allegedly lasting sixteen days.

Lesson#2: The importance of the Tribunal Defense Office.

The Tribunal Defense Office has had an important and often overlooked effect in securing the rights of the defendants in this process. As the retained counsel have engaged in courtroom demeanor that would be inexcusable in most courtrooms around the world, the bench has generally accorded them wide latitude, and has often overlooked defense violations of the Rules of Procedure. Given the dignity of the proceedings and the significance of the judicial process, no court should be held captive to the capricious demands of defense counsel, particularly in matters that are often unrelated to the presentation and consideration of actual evidence. The IHT Defense office has been fully prepared to step in on those occasions when retained counsel have refused to come to court, or have been ejected by the bench for inappropriate and disrespectful courtroom conduct. Just like the *amici curiae* in the Milosevic case, the IHT Defense Office has served as a necessary backstop to give effect to the procedural rights of these accused. They have conducted cross examinations, and at the last trial session were asked by the bench to be prepared to conduct closing arguments if retained defense counsel are unprepared. In future trials, it may well become axiomatic that the staffing and funding of the Defense Office rises in direct proportion to the proximity of the trials and the overall security environment. In this context, those lawyers have striven to protect the rights of these defendants.

Lesson #3: Trials happen in court not in the TV studio.

The very essence of a fair trial is that the judgment and sentence are based on the application of established law to facts and inferences drawn from the record of what transpired in court and on the record. The media dimension of this process has been both predictable and tragic. The initial Iraqi decision to televise the trial was a courageous demonstration of its transparency and its intent to serve the people. For the western world, the media coverage of the trial has focused on no more than a few minutes of each day's events and given scant attention or analysis of the hours of trial testimony. This has permitted wild misstatements of what is happening in the courtroom and in some circles held the IHT hostage to preconceived notions. The IHT press outreach to correct errant impressions has thus far been spotty and its goal of creating a useful website as an authoritative source for press statements and official documents remains unfulfilled. The defense team has attempted to raise a number of legal arguments in the media that have either been omitted in the actual trial proceedings or very scantily developed in arguments. The erratic conduct by the retained defense counsel has also undercut their effectiveness in raising their legal arguments, which in turn has prompted them to use media outlets as an alternative for the vigorous in court representation that their clients expected when they agreed to pay them. In retrospect, the written opinions will serve a critical purpose in illuminating the relevant facts drawn from the referral file and trial testimony, in addition to the vital application of the relevant law to those facts.

Lesson #4: The merger of Iraqi procedure and law with international norms.

Like any of the nations that have ratified the ICC Statute and are incorporating international law into domestic practice, the IHT has the character of a domestic court applying domestic law and procedure in conjunction with substantive international law when appropriate. This aspect of the trial is important because it has resulted in a process that is far from the American controlled process panned by IHT naysayers. Any Arabic speaker who wishes to watch the lengthy exchanges among witnesses, defendants, counsel and judges has seen

Iraqi judges and lawyers subject to the professional standards of their craft. While on the one hand, this has resulted in rulings from the bench rather than the detailed written pretrial motions common in other practice, the IHT has been recognizable to the people as reflective of their experience in courtrooms around this country. In addition, the trial testimony that some Iraqi defense lawyers conspired to fabricate testimony and threaten witnesses and their families may subject them to sanctions in their domestic system in a manner that would not be feasible in a purely international *ad hoc* trial. The essentially Iraqi character of the proceedings also explains Judge Rizgar's early decision to permit each defendant to cross examine witnesses in addition to that of their counsel (which practice was continued by Judge Ra'ouf). That practice carried over from domestic practice and has allowed each of the defendants at times to become active participants in the presentation of their perspectives. The practice of allowing both defense attorneys and the defendants to raise defense perspectives related to witnesses and evidence (sometimes for hours) is a unique feature of this trial that should serve to enhance its truth-seeking function. While the world has seen Saddam use that opportunity for illegitimate exhortation to the insurgents outside the courtroom, the fact is that all of the defendants have raised some of the most effective points made in their own defense. While their lawyers have repeatedly stormed out in protest or defiance of the bench, the defendants have been able to participate actively in their own defense. Conversely, when the defendants have chosen to stay out of the trial, they have been in holding cells watching the trial on closed circuit TV similar to the practice in the *ad hoc* international tribunals.

Post-Conflict Justice in Iraq: Is the Glass Half-Full, Half-Empty, or Is It a Phyrric Achievement?

By M. Cherif Bassiouni[167]

The Iraqi High Tribunal (IHT), formerly called the Iraq Special Tribunal (IST), has faced many difficulties since its inception. The past instructed the present, and shaped the future of an institution that was much needed, but so far has yielded few positive results.

Prior to the establishment of the IST in 2003, there was a great deal of ambivalence in the US and among Iraqi expatriates about whether there should be an international tribunal established by the Security Council like the ICTY and ICTR, a hybrid international/national tribunal like that of Sierra Leone, or a purely national tribunal, which is part of the ordinary Iraqi system of justice. The Department of State (DoS) Future of Iraq Project's Working Group on Justice dealt with these three options, on the basis of a study I prepared comparing the merits of the three models, including a complete statute for an international model. The National Security Council (NSC) however, for political reasons, did not circulate the DoS report, and the insights and recommendations of the Future of Iraq Project's Working Group on Justice were unused by the Administration. This loss had something to do with the subsequent errors made in connection with the IST's establishment and statute.

Some government and UN experts, academics, and NGOs favored the internationalized approach through the Security Council's establishment of a tribunal to prosecute major Iraqi offenders. Others from these categories favored a hybrid tribunal which would balance international concerns and Iraqi legal tradition. Few favored the use of Iraq's national criminal justice system because they thought that system incapable of producing fair and impartial prosecutions. I did not share these views. My reasons were that a national institution would advance the goals of the Rule of law in Iraq and help sustain a new era for the Iraqi legal system, provided the judges, investigating judges, and prosecutors received adequate training, the institution to be well-staffed and well-funded. I also thought it would be cost-effective and provide for the death penalty as the Iraqi legal system permits, because no one in that country would have tolerated the possibility of Saddam and his cronies leading a fairly comfortable life in some international prison. This was the same issue faced at Nuremberg, where it was resolved to apply the death penalty. It is noteworthy, however, to recall Winston Churchill's argument to Franklin Roosevelt and Joseph Stalin at the Moscow Summit of 1943, when he argued against the prosecution of major Nazi war criminals, urging instead that they should be given a short summary court martial and then lined up and shot. In the end of course, the longer-lasting wisdom and beneficial effect of the Nuremberg prosecutions proved their merit and value.

The debate over which model was to apply took some time to settle, but the Administration gave it low priority though it favored the national model, if for no other reason than it felt it could control it. I also suspect that at the time, namely, between January and December 2003, some in the Administration thought that national proceedings conducted by a "special" tribunal under US control would not only work fast and efficiently, but would also emphasize the brutally repressive nature of that regime over the last 30 years, thus justifying the US invasion in the eyes of American and world public opinion.

By analogy to the Eichmann trial in Israel in 1960, which established the existence and extent of the Holocaust, the prosecution of Saddam and his cronies was expected to establish the extent and scope of Saddam's brutal regime, including the use of chemical weapons against Iran and the Iraqi people, thus implying the possibility of the use of similar weapons which the US claimed was the basis for its invasion.

The US managers of Iraqi post-conflict justice who were at the NSC, Department of Defense (DoD) and Department of Justice (DoJ) failed to see that "special" tribunals have the connotation of exceptional tribunals, which are in violation of international human rights law and thus smack of illegitimacy. Not only the name, but other aspects of the IST's statute which remained unchanged in the modification brought about in the IHCC in 2005, are in violation of international principles of legality, which Iraqi law also embodies. This applies to the definition of the crimes within the jurisdiction of the tribunal and also to several other provisions of the statute. The statute that US drafters developed was so influenced by American thinking that it had the fingerprints of the foreign occupying power all over it. It also had glaring violations of Iraqi law. This was followed by a decision to establish the IST through the Governing Council, a politically-appointed body by the US—a foreign occupying power in Iraq. Moreover, the selection of judges, investigating judges, and prosecutors by the GC was in violation of Iraqi laws on judicial appointments. All of this cast a dark shadow on the tribunal's legitimacy and legality, which continued even though a name change and minor modifications occurred in 2005.

Since Iraq was subject to the exclusive control of the Coalition Provisional Authority (CPA) run by US Ambassador Paul Bremer, the IST statute was promulgated by Bremer on December 10, 2003, by CPA Order No. 48, thus confirming the "made in America" label of the institution. Moreover, the IST judges, investigating judges and prosecutors were formally approved by Bremer. The US, acting through the Department of Justice and its Regime Crimes Liaison Office (RCLO), controlled the Tribunal, conducted and directed its investigative activities, collected and stored the evidence, directed its operations, funded it, and had the seat of the Tribunal within the "Green Zone." In time, the judges, investigating judges, and prosecutors whose salaries were paid by the RCLO moved into the Green Zone where everything was concentrated under US protection. There was little doubt about who owned the IST. Some things changed after 2005, particularly, the Iraqis taking ownership of the process, but the rest remained as it was.

The choice of this post-conflict justice modality was dictated by US political considerations, supported by Iraqi expatriates. It is the right choice, though by no means should it have been limited to a tribunal, and certainly not to one whose statute had so many infirmities. The Administration and its Iraqi expatriate collaborators approached the tribunal's drafting of the statute without enough knowledge or respect for the Iraqi legal system, and without much experience in international criminal justice precedents. More importantly, they ignored the first lesson of post-conflict justice, namely, to keep politics at a minimum and make sure the legalities are at a maximum. In the IST's case, it was the reverse.

During the period of time in which I was involved in earlier drafts of the statute, namely 2002–3, and before the IST's promulgation in December 2003, I had advocated the establishment of a truth commission and a victim compensation scheme. Both I thought would be indispensable support to the prosecutions, and would round out the post-conflict justice process. Taken together, these three modalities would have had synergies and produced reciprocal positive reinforcements.

The national truth commission I had contemplated was to become the rallying point for all Iraqis to join together in producing a record of the Saddam crimes. This would have been a national unifying effort, and it could have avoided turning future prosecutions into a forum for sectarian victimization politics, as it turned out to be. Moreover, experience with international and national prosecutions for international crimes evidences that such trials are not the adequate means by which to record history. A trial is against one or more persons, dealing with a certain number of facts within a limited frame of time, and its purpose is to determine the responsibility of the accused through a fair and impartial process. It cannot be artificially broadened in scope to record historic or contextual facts, or facts unrelated to the nature of the charges brought against the individual. Thus, the Dujail case, a simple, straightforward murder case without external political implications, hardly reveals the many crimes and depredations committed by Saddam and his regime against the Shi'a over the years. Similarly, the forthcoming Halabja case dealing with the use of chemical weapons against the Kurds hardly reveals the extent of the crimes and brutality that the Kurds suffered. However, because of the present Iraqi politics of victimization, there will be no cases involving crimes against the Sunni, thus omitting this category of victims. A truth commission would have filled the gaps left open by selective prosecutions, and avoided the charge that the prosecutions are selective, as they necessarily are. Critics often charge that selectivity is unfair, though in my opinion, selectively charging persons whose conduct objectively warrants prosecution is not inherently unfair.

The victim compensation scheme I proposed was a way to engender public participation and support for the prosecutions by having people come forth, record their histories, and receive some compensation. While this may have provided some measure of comfort to the victims, as well as provided them some economic support that many needed, it would have also provided a wide popular basis in support of prosecutions which now does not exist. Surely if over 100,000 persons would have come forth with their stories, it would have been difficult to criticize the establishment of the tribunal as being American or as "victor's vengeance" by the Shi'a or the Kurds, as is now the case. Moreover, since these victims would have likely been from all Iraqi religious and sectarian groups, critics of the prosecutions would not have been able to claim that it was set up to satisfy only some of these groups to the exclusion of others, namely, the Sunni.

Since the tribunal's work was driven by US prosecutors with experience in US federal criminal prosecution, but with little or no experience in international criminal justice, and since the NSC and others in the White House and DoD working on Iraq had other political objectives, these two mechanisms were ignored. This meant that all of post-conflict justice in Iraq was to rest on the tribunal, which would necessarily be limited to a few selected defendants and to a few cases. This left the demand for more prosecutions unsatisfied, history unrecorded, and victims' thirst for justice to turn into revenge manifested through sectarian violence.

As a result of much effort on my part, including extensive discussions with the judges, investigating judges and prosecutors of the IST during a training session I conducted for them at the International Institute for Higher Studies in Criminal Sciences in Siracusa, Italy, as well as with members of the RCLO, the IST statute was slightly amended. This was not what I had urged in a book published in Arabic for the purposes of helping the Iraqi jurists and politicians make the necessary changes to give the tribunal more legality and legitimacy. The ill-fated name of the IST was changed to the IHT, some minor amendments were made to some of the statute's provisions, and there was an overall editing process. The latter was direly needed because, absurd as it may sound, the IST statute was drafted in English and translated into Arabic, and the translation was quite poor. Even more absurd was the provision in the IST statute that the English text would control. How anyone could think that a national tribunal, even a "special" one in a country that had a well-established legal system and legal traditions, could be drafted in a foreign language and then translated into the official domestic language with the foreign text controlling, is beyond hubris.

Among the statute's shortcomings is the drafter's confusion as to the role of the investigating judge and prosecutor under Iraqi criminal procedure, which is essentially an inquisitorial model. The American drafters sought to graft the adversary/accusatorial model on the inquisitorial one, producing an unhappy mixture. In an uncanny way, however, that which could have been a serious flaw impeding the effectiveness of the tribunal, turned out not to be the case. The reason was the pragmatic approach of the judges, investigating judges and prosecutors who simply reverted to the practice of criminal law and procedure as they knew it from the Iraqi Code of Criminal Procedure (1971) and the Criminal Code (1969). More surprising was the fact that the defense, even though repeatedly challenging the legitimacy of the tribunal insofar as it was established by a foreign occupying power and subsequently legitimized in form by the re-promulgation of its statute under a law dated October 18, 2005, nonetheless failed to raise many of the issues of legality with the tribunal's statute, as well as the inconsistencies between procedural provisions in the statute and the 1971 Code of Criminal Procedure. Why this occurred may well be due to the fact that some defense lawyers were not Iraqis, while local counsels may not have been up to the technical task. In any event, the combination of these factors rendered the issue moot in practice. However, legal historians will surely revert to these infirmities to critique the statute and the tribunal's processes. *De facto*, the more troublesome technical legal issues with the tribunal were bypassed by actual practice.

Even the modest effort of re-naming the IST as the IHT and the minor changes in the statute took some time. When the new text was ready for Iraq's President's signature, the first prosecution, namely the Dujail case, was already in progress. This case started under the IST and was continued for 30 days because that was the time required for a new law to be published in the Official Gazette in order to enter into effect. When the case resumed, it was under the new IHT statute. To the best of my knowledge, only totalitarian regimes have changed laws during the course of a trial and applied the new law retroactively. This is in clear violation of the internationally recognized principles of legality, also required by Iraqi law. However, even this glaring violation of the principles of legality was given short shrift by the judges, thus adding another layer of illegitimacy to a process already encumbered by infirmities.

By October of 2005, when the Dujail trial proceedings started, a sectarian civil war was increasing in tempo. The threats to the Court's personnel and to the defense increased, and in fact several of them were subsequently killed, adding to the complex political contextual backdrop of the tribunal and the prosecutions. Nevertheless, the Iraqi judges, investigating judges, and prosecutors continued to demonstrate courage and commitment. They have since then taken ownership of the process, and this in itself is an accomplishment which has to be applauded.

The highly politicized context in which the IST, later the IHT began and then proceeded, was not conducive to a detached and sober judgment of the institution and how it worked. Admittedly, the tribunal did not work too well, but that should not have come as a surprise to anyone who follows the history of new legal institutions. The assessment of many observers was also colored by their judgments concerning the legality or advisability of the invasion of Iraq and its subsequent occupation. While a large segment of the IST/IHT critics would have never been satisfied with the institution, its statute and processes, regardless of whether it was fair and impartial, because of political considerations, another segment of critics seemed to focus exclusively on the technical and legal infirmities of the statute and on the imperfections of its proceedings evidenced throughout the Dujail trial. It is worth mentioning, however, that any similar institution in its inception, particularly during its first trial with an obstreperous defendant like Saddam, would surely face some of the same problems that this trial displayed. Suffice it to recall that Hermann Goering ran away with the proceedings of the IMT in Nuremberg for three days while he was on the stand, and that for nearly four years, Slobodan Milosevic was able to cause periodic havoc during his trial before the ICTY. Those who follow similar trials at the domestic level will remember similar problems, one of which was the Chicago Seven conspiracy trial in 1968 where the defendants literally ran amok of the proceedings for a number of days until one of them was ordered by the judge to be bound and gagged, while sitting in a chair in the courtroom.

Saddam's antics at the Dujail trial should not have come as a surprise, nor should they in any way be enough to judge the tribunal and its proceedings on the basis of these occurrences. In fact, the leeway given to Saddam is evidence of the Tribunal's deference to the defense's rights, even though many other defense rights were sharply curtailed. The point here is not to defend the validity or propriety of the proceedings, but to show the narrow focus of critics who tended to lose sight of the big picture.

Symbolically, the fact that Saddam Hussein and his Ba'athist cronies have been brought to trial for even some of the crimes they committed during their 30-year reign must be considered an achievement. By way of analogy, it was less important for Augusto Pinochet to be extradited from the UK to Spain than to have been held extraditable, just as it was more important for Slobodan Milosevic to have stood for trial for four years than to have been found guilty, had he not died before his trial's end.

The very importance of the Iraqi proceedings has made the shortcomings of the establishment of the tribunal and its work that much more unfortunate. These shortcomings were the product of errors in judgment that could have been avoided had it not been the lack of knowledge and hubris of the American handlers who also elected to choose Iraqi collaborators to work on this process based on political considerations, as opposed to high-level competence. Above all, these US officials and their Iraqi collaborators lost sight of the deeper and far-reaching significance and implications of these proceedings on the future of the rule of law in Iraq and in the Arab world. Admittedly, all concerned were well-intentioned and acted in good faith, but sometimes this is not enough. The ability to exercise power can never be a substitute for knowledge and wisdom. In the end, the judgment of history will be that this was a missed opportunity to advance international criminal justice and to advance the rule of law in Iraq and in the Arab world.

The mistakes made in light of what was at stake were monumental, and in my judgment, unforgivable because they could have been avoided. The mistake of the US not to have complemented the tribunal with a concurrent truth commission and victim compensation scheme was also significant.

Before all is said and done, however, it is possible that the process may somehow redeem itself, as has already been evidenced in the last stages of the Dujail trial which started to proceed with some regularity and propriety. What is more important is that the Dujail case has not turned Saddam and his cronies into martyrs, though for his followers, other detractors of the tribunal, and opponents of the US invasion and occupation of Iraq, he will always be a martyr.

Regrettably, however, the victims in Iraq do not feel that the present proceedings are meaningful to them. The few prosecutions still contemplated will not record the full extent of the crimes committed by that repressive regime. The foreseeable conviction and death sentence likely to be imposed upon Saddam and some of his cronies will hardly leave a legacy of justice. Like the prosecution, conviction and execution of General Yamashita who was tried in the Philippines in 1946 by an American military commission which was deemed a miscarriage of justice, the IST/IHT prosecutions will also be marred by a lack of legality and legitimacy.

If nothing else, however, the Iraqi prosecutions will still be a precedent. By analogy, the Leipzig trials in Germany 1923 after WWI were a failure, even though the judges behaved impeccably, and the proceedings were orderly and properly conducted. Nevertheless, the Leipzig trials remained a historic precedent for post-WWII prosecutions, irrespective of the negative substantive outcomes with respect to the defendants on trial, as well as with respect to the thousands who were to be prosecuted and who never were. History has a strange way of legitimizing failures when the need for valid precedent becomes pressing.

Appendix

Glossary of Key Legal Terms

Abetted, see Aided and abetted.

Actus reus. The material or objective element of a crime, from the Latin for "guilty act." The Prosecutor must establish that the accused was responsible for the material act or actus reus that is involved in the crime, but also that the offender had knowledge of the relevant facts and intent to commit the act (known as *mens rea*).

Additional Protocols to the Geneva Conventions of 1977. Two treaties adopted to bring the 1949 Geneva Conventions up to date, particularly in light of post-World War II conflicts like the Vietnam War. Protocol I deals with international armed conflict, while Protocol II deals with non-international armed conflict. Serious violations of the two Protocols can be prosecuted as "violations of the laws or customs of war" under Article 3 of the ICTY Statute.

Admissibility. Refers to whether or not the Trial Chamber will allow evidence to be part of the record. Statements that are not voluntary or evidence gathered in a way that raises questions about the integrity of the proceedings are inadmissi-

ble, and will not be referred to in the Trial Chamber's written judgment.

Adversarial system, see Common Law.

Affidavit. A written statement taken while the affiant, deponent or witness has sworn an oath to tell the truth. Strict common law rules of evidence do not allow affidavit evidence in a criminal trial as a general rule. But at Nuremberg, affidavits were widely admitted as a replacement for live testimony, a subject of much criticism. Where the content is not particularly controversial, they can be admitted before the IHT.

Aggravating factors. Factors to be taken into account in sentencing that tend to lengthen a sentence. Examples include a superior or commanding position in a hierarchy, and evidence of premeditation where this is not a specific element of the crime itself. The opposite of Mitigating factors.

Aided and abetted. Also known as "complicity." An individual is responsible for a crime even if he or she does not actual commit the physical criminal act. The accomplice must either aid, by performing a material act that assists the principal perpetrator, or abet, by encouraging the perpetrator.

Amicus curiae. Literally, a "friend of the court." The IHT Trial Chamber and Appeals Chamber can consider briefs produced by expert groups as amicus curiae, in addition to those of the defense and prosecution on major issues pending before the Tribunal.

Appeals Chamber. A nine-judge panel with the authority to overturn decisions of the Trial Chamber and to order an acquittal or a retrial, or to revise a sentencing judgment. It is the court of last resort, because there is no "supreme court."

Armed conflict. The resort to armed force between States or protracted armed violence between governmental authorities and organized armed groups or between such groups within a State. International humanitarian law distinguishes between international and non-international armed conflict.

Binding Order, see Order.

Chambers. A collective reference to the judges of the tribunal. The IHT is divided into several Trial Chambers and one Appeals Chamber.

Charter of the United Nations. The constitution of the United Nations organization, proclaimed on the stage of the San Francisco Opera in June 1945. Article 2(4) of the United Nations Charter prohibits use of force against another State unless (1) in self defense in response to an armed attack pursuant to Article 51 of the Charter, or (2) when authorized by a Chapter VII resolution of the Security Council.

Civil Law system, see Romano-Germanic system.

Civil Law. A commonly used expression to describe the procedural regime used in criminal trials in continental Europe and many other parts of the world, including Iraq, characterized by an inquisitorial approach rather than the adversarial framework of the common law.

Civil war, see Non-international armed conflict.

Civilian population. Crimes against humanity must consist of an attack on a "civilian population." The adjective civilian is defined broadly, and is meant to emphasize the collective nature of the crimes amounting to crimes against humanity rather than strictly the status of the victims. It covers not only civilians in a strict sense but also all persons who were no longer combatants, whether due to injury or because they were while the crimes were committed.

Closing argument. Trial takes place in two phases, the first involving the production of evidence, the second in which the two sides attempt to draw conclusions about issues of law and fact and explain the theory of their case to the judges. The Prosecutor goes first, followed by the Defense.

Command responsibility. A legal technique by which a commander or superior may be convicted of crimes committed by his or her subordinates, even if the prosecution cannot prove that the commander or superior actually knew of the crimes or in some way ordered or incited them. In effect, the commander or superior is punished for providing negligent supervision of subordinates. The concept was first developed in post-World War II trials, and was later codified in Protocol Additional I to the Geneva Conventions of 1977.

Common design. This is a form of complicity where offenders have a common design, that is, they possess the same criminal intention to commit a specific act and formulate a plan to carry it out, although each co-perpetrator may play a different role within it.

Common Law. The procedural system that first developed in England and then spread to its colonies, almost all of whom kept the system with some modifications after de-colonization. The common law treats Prosecutor and Defense as adversaries who in effect duel before relatively passive judges. Each side takes strategic decisions aimed at winning its case rather than approach the trial as a forum where the truth of the allegations is to be determined in an objective sense.

Compensation. The Tribunal itself cannot order compensation to victims, but its judgments may facilitate claims for compensation by victims under Iraqi national legislation.

Competence. This term is sometimes used as a synonym for jurisdiction. It refers to the power or authority of the Tribunal to judge cases, rather than to its expertise.

Complicity. Participation in a crime for which the main physical act is committed by another. Accomplices general participate by "aiding and abetting" the commission of specific acts. But an accomplice may also be held liable for acts of other participants that are reasonably foreseeable when there is an overall plan or common design to carry out a criminal act.

Concurrent jurisdiction. War crimes, genocide and crimes against humanity can be prosecuted both by the IHT and by the Iraqi national courts, but in case of conflict, the IHT takes precedence under the principle of "primacy."

Concurrent sentences. If two or more convictions are registered by the Trial Chamber it may impose distinct sentences for each crime yet order that they be served concurrently, especially if they relate to the same general fact situation or criminal transaction. In practice, then, the convicted person serves the longer of the two sentences. Alternatively, the Trial Chamber may specify that the sentences be served consecutively. There is no limit in the Statute as to the length of sentences.

Conspiracy. An agreement between two or more persons to commit a crime.

Contempt. Misconduct before the Tribunal may be punished by it as "contempt." Contempt includes such acts as "contumaciously" refusing or failing to answer a question, violating Orders of the Tribunal, and tampering with witnesses.

Counsel. A defendant in proceedings before the IHT has a right to counsel of choice, provided that lead counsel is a member of the Iraqi Bar.

Crimes against humanity. The concept of crime against humanity was first recognized at the Nuremberg trial. It filled a major gap in humanitarian law, which hitherto had regarded what a state did to its own population as being its own concern, in contrast with what a state did to populations of occupied territories or soldiers of another belligerent, who were already protected. Crimes against humanity consist of an underlying "ordinary crime," like murder, that is committed as part of a widespread or systematic attack on a civilian population.

Cruel treatment. A grave breach of the Geneva Convention and a violation of common article 3 of the Convention, involving infliction of severe physical or mental pain or suffering upon one or more persons.

Cumulative convictions. Although the Prosecutor is free to charge an accused with several different crimes with respect to the same act, if there is a conviction, the Tribunal will only enter a finding of guilt with respect to one if there is sufficient overlap.

Customary international law. A source of international law derived not from written treaties but rather from unwritten rules developed over the ages. Customary law is established by proof of constant practice by states indicating the existence of a legal rule, coupled with some indication (other than the practice itself) that they consider themselves to be bound by such a rule.

Customs of war. Half of the expression "laws or customs of war." International law is an amalgam of customary law (see Customary law) and treaties. These two sources are reflected in the concept "laws or customs of war."

Decision, see Order.

Defense. The accused or the accused's counsel.

Deportation. A crime against humanity involving the forced displacement of a civilian population by expulsion or other coercive acts from the area in which it is lawfully present.

Deposition. Testimony by a witness taken out of court, sometimes by videoconference, but for use during the trial as if the witness were actually present. The Trial Chamber can authorize a deposition in cases where a witness cannot physically attend, or for other reasons deemed acceptable.

Disclosure. Prior to trial, the Prosecutor is required to disclose or make available to the Defense copies of witness statements of those who will be called to tes-

tify, copies of sworn statements, books, documents, photographs and tangible objects which are material to the defense.

Disqualification. Removal of a judge assigned to a case because the judge has a personal interest or has or has had any association which might affect his or her impartiality.

Double jeopardy, see *Non bis in idem*.

Due process. Ancient term of the common law referring to the right to a fair trial.

Duress. A defense invoked by the accused during trial whereby the commission of the criminal act is admitted, but it is claimed that the perpetrator had no moral choice because he or she was threatened with death or some other dire consequence.

Enslavement. A crime against humanity involving the exercise of any or all of the powers attaching to the right of ownership over a person, such as by purchasing, selling, lending or bartering such a person or persons, including the exercise of such power in the course of trafficking in persons, in particular women and children.

Equality of arms. Concept developed in human rights law whereby a fair trial requires that both sides, Prosecution and Defense, have a certain equivalence in terms of resources.

Ethnic group. One of the groups protected by the prohibition of genocide. It is similar in many respects to a national or racial group.

Expert witness. A witness who ventures an opinion about a matter that is beyond the expertise of the judges themselves.

Extermination. A crime against humanity by which a particular civilian population is targeted for death, either by killing or being otherwise subjected to conditions of life calculated to bring about the destruction of a numerically significant part of the population.

Extradition. Process by which an accused is sent from one state to another in order to stand trial.

Geneva Conventions. Four international treaties adopted in 1949 to deal with the protection of victims of armed conflict: wounded soldiers and sailors, prisoners of war and civilians. In principle applicable only to international armed conflict, each of the four conventions includes one provision, known as "Common Article 3," addressing the protection of victims of non-international armed conflict.

Genocide. The intentional destruction of a national, ethnic, racial or religious group, in whole or in part. The definition of genocide in the IHT Statute is taken essentially word for word from the 1948 Convention for the Prevention and Punishment of the Crime of **Genocide**. It has been described by judges as the "crime of crimes" and is, arguably, the most severe of the categories of crimes within the jurisdiction of the Tribunal. Genocide is in many ways an extreme form of the crime against humanity of persecution, to which it is closely related.

Grave breaches. Grave breaches consist of particularly heinous violations of the 1949 Geneva Conventions and of Additional Protocol I. They are punishable under the IHT Statute. Grave breaches can only be committed in international armed conflict. All states have an obligation to investigate grave breaches and see that their perpetrators are brought to justice, wherever the crimes have been committed.

Habeas corpus. A remedy by which a person who is detained challenges the legality of the detention. Defendants before the IHT are not permitted to seek habeas relief before the national courts of Iraq.

Hague Convention. International treaty adopted in 1907 that concerns the laws or customs of war. It largely codifies important customary legal rules dealing with means and methods of war, the protection of prisoners and the rights of civilians in an occupied territory. Though not designed as a criminal law treaty, its prohibitions were taken as the basis of individual criminal responsibility by the Nuremberg Tribunal. Violations of the Hague Convention are included in the IHT Statute.

Head of State or Government. Many countries grant their own heads of state or government a form of immunity from criminal prosecution, at the very least while they are still in office. However, no similar immunity was recognized at Nuremberg in the case of international prosecution. Moreover, governments can revoke a former head of state's immunity as Chile has done with its former President, Augusto Pinochet.

Human rights law. Body of international law developed since World War II in such instruments as the Universal Declaration of Human Rights, the Convention for the Prevention and Punishment of the Crime of Genocide and the international human rights covenants. The IHT may be guided by the precedents from regional human rights bodies like the European Court of Human Rights, particularly with respect to fair trial issues.

Humanitarian law. Sometimes called "international humanitarian law" or "IHL," this is the body of law that regulates armed conflict that is both international and non-international. The core of humanitarian law comprises the four Geneva Conventions of 1949, the two Additional Protocols of 1977, and the Hague Convention of 1907. Violations of humanitarian law are war crimes within the jurisdiction of the IHT.

Imprisonment. A crime against humanity consisting of severe deprivation of liberty, usually involving inhumane conditions.

In camera proceedings. Proceedings that are not public.

Incitement. Incitement to commit genocide can be prosecuted by the IHT even if nobody is actually incited to commit the crime. Defendants and Defense Counsel can be ordered not to make statements which would incite imminent violence.

Indictment. The indictment is prepared by the Investigative Judge and sets out the charges against the accused. It must be in sufficient detail so as to indicate the points that are at issue, and not to take the accused by surprise at trial.

Inhumane acts. A crime against humanity involving infliction of great suffering, or serious injury to body or to mental or physical health, by means of any act similar in nature to those set out in the list of crimes against humanity, such as murder, sexual violence, torture and beatings.

Inquisitorial system, see Romano-Germanic system.

Intent. It is a requirement for any criminal conviction that the prohibited act be committed with intent and knowledge, often referred to by the Latin expression mens rea or guilty mind.

Interlocutory motion. An issue contested during the proceedings, usually on procedural or evidentiary issues, and on which one of the parties seeks an immediate ruling.

Internal armed conflict, see Non-international armed conflict.

International armed conflict. Resort to armed force by two or more states. Certain violations of international humanitarian law that are within the jurisdiction of the IHT can only be prosecuted if it can be shown that there was an international armed conflict.

International Court of Justice. Located in The Hague, the International Court of Justice hears cases between sovereign states.

International Criminal Court, see Rome Statute.

Internationalized Domestic Tribunal. The IHT is sometimes referred to as an internationalized domestic tribunal since its statute and rules are derived from those of the international tribunals, it is independent of the domestic legal system, and it is assisted by international experts, but at the same time its judges and prosecutor are Iraqi and it sits in Baghdad.

Iraqi High Tribunal. Known by its initials the "IHT," the Iraqi High Tribunal was established in 2003 and approved by the democratically elected Iraqi National Assembly in 2005 to prosecute Saddam Hussein and other top figures of the former Iraqi Government for crimes against humanity, war crimes, genocide, aggression, corruption of the judiciary, and wastage of natural resources in Iraq.

Joinder. Persons accused of the same or different crimes committed in the course of the same transaction may be jointly charged and tried. In the first trial, Saddam Hussein is being jointly tried with seven other defendants for crimes against the inhabitants of the town of Dujail in 1982.

Joint criminal enterprise. A venture by two or more persons to effect a criminal result, in which each member is held responsible for the specific acts perpetrated by the other members of the enterprise, but only to the extent these acts were likely to lead to such an act. Where a defendant is charged with a crime committed by another participant that goes beyond the agreed object of the joint criminal enterprise, the Prosecutor must establish that the crime was a natural and foreseeable consequence of the enterprise, that the accused was aware of this when he or she agreed to participate in the enterprise.

Joint trial. A trial of two or more accused.

Judgment. Ruling by the Judges of the Trial Chamber or by a majority of them at the conclusion of the trial on the question of guilt or innocence. The final determination of an Appeal by the Appeals Chamber is also called a Judgment.

Judicial notice. As a general rule, if the judges are to take facts into account in their deliberations such facts must be proven in open court. But some facts are so notorious and well-accepted that judges may take "judicial notice" of them.

Jurisdiction. The limits that circumscribe the power of the Tribunal. See also: Subject matter jurisdiction, Personal jurisdiction, Temporal jurisdiction and Territorial jurisdiction.

Killing, see Murder.

Laws of war. Historic rules governing means and methods of warfare, and the treatment of the wounded, prisoners and civilians. Many of them date back to the age of chivalry, and they are regularly referred to in classical Greek histories as well as in the plays of Shakespeare. The first great modern codification is the Hague Convention of 1907. They were referred to as part of the expression "laws or customs of war" in article 6(b) of the Charter of the Nuremberg Tribunal.

Lawyer-client privilege. Communications between lawyer and client are privileged, and cannot be disclosed at trial without the consent of the client, unless the client has voluntarily disclosed the content of the communication to a third party, and that third party then gives evidence of that disclosure.

Martens clause. So-named after its author, a Russian diplomat, who insisted that a clause be added to the preamble of the 1907 Hague Convention, recognizing that inhumane acts, even those not codified by the treaty, remain prohibited: "Until a more complete code of the laws of war has been issued, the High Contracting Parties deem it expedient to declare that, in cases not included in the Regulations adopted by them, the inhabitants and the belligerents remain under the protection and the rule of the principles of the law of nations, as they result from the usages established among civilized peoples, from the laws of humanity, and the dictates of the public conscience."

Material element, see Actus reus.

Mens rea. The mental or subjective element of a crime, from the Latin for "guilty mind." A guilty act (or actus reus) is only punishable as a crime if the offender had knowledge of the relevant facts or circumstances and actually intended to commit the act. But this should not be confused with motive, which is the reason why the act was committed. For most crimes, the Tribunal does not require proof of motive, although it may find such evidence to be helpful in clarifying any doubts about whether or not the accused actually committed the crime. But in the case of the crime against humanity of persecution, the Prosecutor must establish that he did this on "political, racial and religious grounds" or, in other words, for a discriminatory motive.

Military necessity. A justification for the commission of war crimes, in certain circumstances. For example, wanton destruction of cities, towns or villages, or devastation is a violation of the laws or customs of war, but only to the extent it is not justified by military necessity.

Mitigating factors. So that the punishment actually fits the crime, an accused may invoke a range of personal circumstances, including age, infirmity and mental illness in order to reduce the sentence that might otherwise be imposed.

Moot questions. A legal or factual issue that is no longer of any consequence with respect to the result of the case.

Motion to acquit. At the conclusion of the Prosecutor's evidence, the Defense may ask the Trial Chamber for an immediate acquittal on the grounds that the Prosecutor has not even proven all of the essential elements of the charge. If the motion is dismissed, the Defense must decide whether or not to call evidence.

Motion. An application to the Tribunal that normally takes place prior to or during the trial, asking the judges to make a ruling on a specific issue. Motions may deal with the admissibility of evidence, or with a variety of procedural questions. A motion is not generally subject to appeal to the Appeals Chamber.

Motive. The reason why a crime is committed, as opposed to the intent, which is quite a distinct concept. Several people may all intend to commit a crime, but for different motives. Generally, motive is not an element to be considered in assessing guilt or innocence, although judges tend to be more easily convinced of guilt when they can understand why a person committed a crime, and equally perplexed about guilt when they see no reason why a person committed a crime. The Statute introduces a motive requirement with respect to the crime against

humanity of persecution, which must be committed on "political, racial and religious grounds."

Murder. The Statute refers to both "murder" and "killing." This is for historical reasons, because the crimes defined in the Statute are derived from various texts that use slightly different terminology. But the Yugoslavia and Rwanda Tribunals have concluded that the grave breach and genocidal act of "killing," and the crime against humanity of "murder," amount to the same thing: intentional homicide.

National court. A court that is part of the ordinary Iraqi justice system. The IHT is independent of the national courts of Iraq, including the Supreme Constitutional Court.

National group. A category of group protected by the prohibition of genocide. Kurds may either be a national group or an ethnic group.

Nicaragua decision. Reference to a 1985 ruling of the International Court of Justice dealing with involvement of contras backed by the United States in civil war within Nicaragua. It established a criterion of "effective control" in determining whether acts of armed bands acting within a country could be imputed to a foreign power. In a case dealing with the level of control that the Federal Republic of Yugoslavia exercised over Bosnian Serb forces, the Appeals Chamber of the Yugoslavia Tribunal ruled that Nicaragua set too narrow a standard, and that the better test was "overall control."

Non bis in idem. Latin expression for what is known in the common law as "double jeopardy." An accused cannot be tried by a national court if he or she has already been tried by the Tribunal. This also works in the other direction, but subject to important exceptions, such as sham trials held to shield someone from international prosecution.

Non-governmental organizations. The IHT has received assistance and training by several NGOs including the International Bar Association based in London, the International Legal Assistance Consortium based in Stockholm, the International Association of Penal Law based in Paris and Siracusa Sicily, and the Public International Law and Policy Group based in DC and Cleveland. Other NGOs, such as Human Rights Watch, are participating as trial observers during the IHT proceedings.

Non-international armed conflict. In popular parlance, a civil war. But international humanitarian law takes care to distinguish between non-international armed conflict and situations of internal disturbances and tensions, such as riots, isolated and sporadic acts of violence or other acts of a similar nature. There may also be a requirement that there be evidence of protracted armed violence between governmental authorities and organized armed groups or between such groups within a State. Serious violations of the laws or customs of war committed during non-international armed conflict include violations of Common Article 3 of the Geneva Conventions, as well as some serious violations of Additional Protocol II. They are punishable under the IHT Statute. A non-international armed conflict may become "internationalized" if another State intervenes in that conflict through its troops, or alternatively if some of the participants in the internal armed conflict act on behalf of that other State.

Notice of appeal. Written declaration, followed after Judgment, indicating a party's intent to appeal.

Nullum crimen sine lege. Latin for, literally, "no crime without law." This is the prohibition of retroactive crimes.

Office of the Prosecutor. The organ within the IHT that is responsible for preparing prosecutions and presenting them to the Tribunal at trial.

Official position. Official position is not a defense. In the past, tyrants alleged that they were merely acting on behalf of a state, and that they could not be held responsible individually for criminal offenses. The Pinochet judgment of the English House of Lords rejects this view, and it is set out clearly in the Statute of the IHT, which says official position "shall not relieve such person of criminal responsibility nor mitigate punishment."

Opening statements. Before presentation of evidence by the Prosecutor, each party may make an opening statement. The defense may, however, elect to make its statement after the conclusion of the Prosecutor's presentation of evidence and before the presentation of evidence for the defense.

Order. A ruling by a Judge or a Trial Chamber that relates to the preparation of the trial, transfer of suspects, protection of witnesses and other trial participants, televising the proceedings, and similar matters.

Pardon. An executive act that cancels a conviction and leads to the release of the convict.

Persecution. A crime against humanity consisting of the deprivation of fundamental rights, and are acts that are not inherently criminal but that may nonetheless become criminal and persecutorial if committed on political, racial and religious grounds.

Personal jurisdiction. The IHT only has personal jurisdiction over persons of Iraqi nationality.

Plunder. Archaic term used to describe appropriation of property by force during armed conflict.

Precedent. A previous decision of a court that resolves a legal issue. The IHT Statute provides that the Tribunal will be guided by the precedent of the International Criminal Tribunal for the Former Yugoslavia and the International Criminal Tribunal for Rwanda. Judgments of post-World War II war crimes tribunals, international judicial bodies like the International Court of Justice and the European Court of Human Rights, and even rulings of national courts, may also be invoked by the judges of the IHT as they interpret the Statute.

Preliminary motion. An application to the Tribunal by one of the parties made prior to the trial itself in order to resolve issues that affect the future proceedings, such as the joinder of defendants, or details about the indictment.

Presiding judge. Each of the Trial Chambers elects a Presiding Judge who directs the proceedings.

Prima facie. Latin expression indicating that there is sufficiently credible evidence to sustain a conviction if not contradicted by the accused. During the trial, if the Defense makes a motion to acquit at the end of the Prosecution's evidence, the Trial Chamber must grant the motion if the Prosecution has not made out a prima facie case.

Primacy, see Concurrent jurisdiction.

Prisoner of war. A prisoner of war is a captured enemy combatant who wears a distinctive sign, carries arms openly and does not violate the laws or customs of war. Prisoner of war status is presumed upon capture, but may be contested before a court. Prisoners of war status is regulated by the third Geneva Convention of 1949.

Proprio motu. Latin for "on its own initiative." In an adversarial system, like that of the common law countries, the initiative is left to the Prosecution and to the Defense. But in the IHT, the judges may intervene proprio motu even where the Defense and the Prosecutor are silent. For example, the Trial Chamber may, on its own initiative, issue such orders, summonses, subpoenas, warrants and transfer orders as may be necessary for the purposes of an investigation or for the preparation or conduct of the trial.

Prosecutor, see Office of the Prosecutor.

Protected person. Categories of persons protected by the Geneva Conventions, namely former combatants who can no longer fight because they are wounded or taken prisoner, and civilians. Grave breaches of the Geneva Conventions, other serious violations of the Geneva Conventions, and violations of Common Article 3 to the Geneva Conventions must be committed against such protected persons.

Protocols Additional, see Additional Protocols

Racial group. Archaic term used to describe what we now know as "ethnic groups." One of the four groups protected by the prohibition of genocide.

Rape. Several of the crimes within the jurisdiction of the IHT can be committed by the underlying act of rape. There is no international definition of rape, so the Tribunal has attempted to distill the various definitions from national legal system. It considers that rape involves nonconsensual sexual penetration of the vagina or anus of the victim by the penis of the perpetrator or any other object; or sexual penetration of the mouth of the victim by the penis of the perpetrator. The offender must intend to effect the sexual penetration and know that it occurs without the consent of the victim.

Rebuttal. When the Defense has closed its case, the Prosecutor is entitled to rebut the case by introducing a limited amount of new evidence in order to rebut new matters that arose from the Defense evidence and that it could not reasonably have anticipated.

Record on appeal. The appeal is not a new trial and as a general rule it does not consider evidence that was not initially presented to the Trial Chamber during the trial. The Appeals Chamber bases its decision exclusively on the "Record on appeal," consisting of transcripts of the testimony at the trial, documents and other material evidence entered in evidence, and the various written proceedings of the court file.

Recusal, see Disqualification.

Rejoinder. Prosecution evidence that is introduced in "Rebuttal," that is, to answer the Defense case, may itself be contested by the Defense with the production of "Rejoinder" evidence.

Religious group. A group protected by the prohibition of genocide. Intentional destruction of a religious groups is a form of genocide. The category was included in the prohibition to ensure that disputes as to whether Jews or Muslims, for example, were not an ethnic but rather a religious group would not provide a loophole for defendants.

Romano-Germanic system. A system of criminal procedure widely used in continental Europe and other parts of the world, including Iraq, sometimes also called the "civil law system" or the "inquisitorial system." Unlike the "common law system," where this is done by prosecution and defense lawyers, it is a judge (known as the investigating or instructing magistrate) who prepares the case for trial.

Rome Statute. The treaty that creates the International Criminal Court. Adopted by a diplomatic conference in July 1998, it came into force in mid-2002. Much like the IHT, the Court can prosecute genocide, crimes against humanity and war crimes. It has jurisdiction over crimes committed on the territory of countries that have ratified the Rome Statute, or by their nationals. Iraq has not ratified the Rome Statute. But the United Kingdom has, and complaints have been filed before the ICC about war crimes allegedly committed by UK personnel in Iraq during the 2003 invasion. Because the UK has prosecuted such cases domestically, the complementarity principle prevents the ICC from pursuing the matter further.

Rules of Procedure and Evidence. Detailed rules guiding the operation of the Tribunal. They were approved, along with the IHT Statute, by the Iraqi National Assembly on August 11, 2005. The Rules are to be supplemented by the Iraqi Criminal Code, but in cases of conflict, the IHT Rules prevail.

Sentence. If the Tribunal decides to convict, it can impose an appropriate sentence, ranging from a term of years, life imprisonment, or capital punishment. Any evidence or arguments that the Defense wishes to submit in order to mitigate sentence must be produced during the trial itself, before the Trial Chamber has ruled on the issue of guilt.

Severance. Where an indictment deals with two or more accused persons, it may be necessary to "sever" the cases of specific defendants in order to ensure a fair trial. Severance may also occur if an indictment deals with two or more quite separate and distinct fact situations, with no obvious relationship between them.

Statute. The legal basis for the operations of the IHT. It was first promulgated by the CPA on December 10, 2003, and later re-promulgated with revisions by the Iraqi National Assembly on August 11, 2005.

Subject matter jurisdiction. The crimes which the ICTY is empowered to try, namely, grave breaches of the Geneva Conventions, violations of the laws or customs of war, genocide, crimes against humanity, aggression against an Arab country, corruption of the judiciary, and wastage of natural resources. In legal Latin, ratione materiae jurisdiction.

Subordinate, see Command responsibility.

Subpoena. An order issued by a Judge or a Trial Chamber directing a person to testify in person or to produce a document that is under their control.

Superior orders. A classic defense in war crimes trials, in which the obedient soldier admits committing a war crime but says "I was only following orders." Even in post-World War II trials, superior orders was rejected as a defense in cases where the order was manifestly unlawful. To avoid any debate on this point, the IHT Statute simply prohibits the defense. But the Tribunal can take the issue into account in mitigation of punishment.

Suspect. A person concerning whom the Prosecutor possesses reliable information which tends to show that the person may have committed a crime over which the Tribunal has jurisdiction.

Temporal jurisdiction. The Tribunal can only punish crimes committed within its temporal jurisdiction, that is, from 1968 to 2003. In legal Latin, this is ratione temporis jurisdiction.

Territorial jurisdiction. The IHT can punish crimes committed within the Territory of Iraq or within neighboring States, such as Iran or Kuwait. In this way, it's jurisdiction is more expansive than the Yugoslavia Tribunal or the Rwanda Tribunal.

Torture. Torture can be prosecuted as a grave breach of the Geneva conventions, a serious violation of the laws or customs of war, or a crime against humanity. It consists of the intentional infliction of severe pain or suffering, whether physical or mental, upon a person in the custody or under the control of the accused. Torture must be conducted for a prohibited purpose, such as obtaining information or a confession, punishing, intimidating, humiliating, or coercing the victim or a third person, or discriminating, on any ground, against the victim or a third person.

Transaction. A number of acts or omissions whether occurring as one event or a number of events, at the same or different locations and being part of a common scheme, strategy or plan.

Trial brief. In other war crimes tribunals, such as the Yugoslavia Tribunal and Rwanda Tribunal, both Prosecutor and Defense are required to set out their legal and factual arguments in writing. First, they must submit a "Pre-trial brief," outlining the factual and legal issues, including a written statement setting out "the nature of his or her case." Then, after the evidence has been presented, both sides are also expected to present a "trial brief" prior to making their closing arguments.

Trial Chamber. Five judges of the Tribunal, led by a Presiding Judge, who actually hear the case and rule on guilt and in-nocence. The Trial Chamber also has some responsibilities over pre-trial matters.

Tu quoque. Latin for "you too," tu quoque is an argument used in war crimes trials in which the defense argues that "since you have committed the same crime, you cannot legitimately prosecute me." The tu quoque argument was rejected as an ille-gitimate defense by the Nuremberg Tri-bunal and by the Yugoslavia Tribunal.

Universal jurisdiction. As a general rule, national courts only prosecute crimes committed on their territory or by their nationals. But for certain serious crimes, of which war crimes, genocide and crimes against humanity are the best ex-amples, it is well recognized that any state may prosecute anyone, no matter where the crime was committed.

War crimes. This general expression refers to grave breaches of the Geneva conventions and other serious violations of the laws and customs of war. In 1995 the Yugoslavia Tribunal's Appeals Cham-ber ruled that war crimes could be com-mitted in non-international armed con-flict as well as in international armed conflict, a principle that was later codified in the Rome Statute.

Willful blindness. Where it is estab-lished that a defendant suspected that a fact existed, or was aware that its exis-tence was highly probable, but refrained from finding out whether it did exist so as to be able to deny knowledge, this is deemed to be equivalent to real knowl-edge for the purpose of establishing the mental element or mens rea of the of-fense.

Indictments of Saddam's Co-Defendants

Indictment of Defendant Barzan Ibrahim

English Translation of the Charges against Barzan Ibrahim

Accusation Document
Scene of the Crime: Al-Dujayl Town/Salah-al-Din
Governorate/Baghdad
Date of the Crime: July 8, 1982 until January 16, 1989

I, Judge (Ra'uf Rashid 'Abd-al-Rahman), the Presiding Judge of the First Criminal Court of the Iraqi High Tribunal accuse you, (Barzan Ibrahim Al-Hasan), of the following:

When you occupied the position of the Head of the Intelligence System and was in charge of the Security Protection of the President of the Republic (former), and after the accused (Saddam Hussein) had visited the village of (Al-Dujayl) on July 08, 1982 and under the claim that gun shots were fired in the direction of the cars that were escorting his motorcade, you issued orders to the Intelligence System members, the security and military authorities, the peoples' army, and the Al-Ba'th Party organizations (disbanded) in Al-Dujayl, to launch a wide scale, systematic attacks to shoot and use all kinds of weapons and helicopters to kill, arrest, detain, and torture large numbers of the residents of Al-Dujayl (men, women, and children).

Afterwards, you issued orders to remove the orchards and demolish their houses. Based upon these orders these forces killed (nine) people on that day and the following day. Groups of families adding up to (399) people were apprehended and detained at the Investigation and Interrogation Directorate (Al-Hakimiyyah) of the Head of the Intelligence System (disbanded) which was under your command. According to the records attached to the case documents, in view to the fact that the detainees were subjected to torture by the use of the electric current, beating on the head with metal objects, and in other ways. Some of them were killed and the rest of them were transferred to (Abi-Ghurayb) under the supervision of the Intelligence System (disbanded). There the torture continued and some were killed using different ways of torture. A number of them died.

Others were transferred to the desert Complex of (Layyah) which was intended to accommodate the Bedouin nomads and their livestock in Al-Samawah Area, were they were detained for a period of (four years) they were subjected to torture, poor health conditions, and hard living conditions which resorted from lack of nutrition and medicine and mainly in the desert, where one was killed, and several other members of the families that were detained died. Then the Investigation and Interrogation Directorate (Al-Hakimiyyah) of the Intelligence System, referred (148) names which include the names of those who were killed due to torture during their interrogation at (Al-Hakimiyyah Intelligence) and Abi-Ghurayb prison and a number of names of juveniles whose ages are less than (eighteen years), to the Security Affairs Department in the Presidential Diwan (disbanded).

They were then referred to the Revolutionary Court (cancelled) headed by the accused ('Awwad Hamad Al-Bandar) who issued an irrevocable sentence to hang them all till death, in a brief trial which lasted one session, in accordance to resolution number 944/ Criminal/984 on June 14, 1984, where some people were convicted without being tried and had originally been killed during interrogation in the Investigation and Interrogation Directorate (Al-Hakimiyyah) of the Intelligence due to torture. In addition to that is that some of those who were sentenced to death and the sentence was implemented were juveniles who were not yet (eighteen years) old. This was in violation of the article (79) of the Penal Code number (111) for 1969 (amended) and the in-force Juvenile Care Code number ( ) for the year 1983 and in violation to the articles of the procedures that are stipulated in the Code of Procedure for Criminal Trials number (23) for 1971 (amended), and in violation to the article (6) clause (5) of the international Declaration on the Civil and Political Rights dated December 16, 1966 and in force since March 23, 1976 and ratified by the Iraqi Republic on February 18, 1969 and which stipulates that (it is inadmissible to sentence to death for crimes committed by people less than 18 years old) The corpses of the dead were hidden and they were not handed over to their families. The fate of some of those who were apprehended to include six juveniles are still unknown.

Based on that and since you are one of the former regime pillars as Head of the Intelligence System and directly in charge of imprisoning those detainees in the Intelligence Department which was under your supervision and since the accused were under interrogation.

Based on that, you have committed crimes to which the following apply: paragraphs: A, D, W, H, U, I of clause (First) of Article (12) of the Iraqi High Tribunal Law number 10 of 2005 and which stipulates the following: For legal purposes, crimes against humanity mean any of the below mentioned actions when these actions are committed in a widespread or systematic attack against a civilian population, and knowledge of such an attack:

A: Murder
D: Relocation of the population or its compulsory transportation
H: Imprisonment and severe deprivation in any other way of physical freedom in contrast with basic regulations of the international law

W: Torture

U: compulsory concealment of people

I: Other inhumane acts that are of similar characteristics and that deliberately cause severe suffering or serious damage to the body or mental or physical health

In reference to paragraphs (First, Second and Third) of the article (15) of the Iraqi High Tribunal Code which stipulates the following:

First. The person who commits a crime which is within the jurisdiction of the court, is responsible for it in his personal character and will be subject to penalty according to the stipulations of this code

Second. The person is considered responsible according to the stipulations of this code and to the stipulations of the penal code if he commits the following:

a- If the person commits the crime personally, in participation, or via another person regardless if this person is criminally responsible or not

b- Ordering the committing of a crime that was in fact committed, initiated, or urged and perpetrated to be committed.

c- Contributing with a group of people in a collaborative criminal intention to commit a crime or to start committing it, provided that this participation is deliberate

Third. The official title of the accused is not a reason to exempt him from penalty or to commutate the penalty whether the accused is the president of the state, a member in the Revolutionary Command Council, a prime minister or a member in the Cabinet or member in the Ba'th Party Command. It is inadmissible to use the immunity as a pretext to be relieved from the responsibility of the crimes mentioned in the articles (11), (12), (13), and (14).

Fourth. The Supreme President is not exempted from the criminal liability of the crimes committed by his subordinates, if the President is aware or has reasons to be aware that his subordinate has committed or is about to commit these acts and the President did not take the necessary and suitable measures to prevent these acts or submit the case to the competent authorities for interrogation and trial.

Indictment of Defendant Taha Yassin Ramadan

English Translation of the Charges against Taha Yassin Ramadan

Accusation Document
Scene of the Crime: Al-Dujayl Town/Salah-al-Din
Governorate/Baghdad
Date of the Crime: July 8, 1982 until January 16, 1989

I, Judge (Ra'uf Rashid 'Abd-al-Rahman), the Presiding Judge of the First Criminal Court of the Iraqi High Tribunal accuse you, Taha Yasin Ramadan, of the following:

At the time you were a member of the (disbanded) Revolutionary Council Command, the Vice President of the Republic of Iraq, and the (former) General Commander of the People's Army, and when the defendant (Saddam Hussein Al-Majid) had visited (Al-Dujayl) Town in July 08, 1982 claiming that fire shots were launch against the cars escorting his convoy, and considering that you were the General Commander of the People's Army and the Head of the Security Committee that was formed in 1982 July 08, in charge of investigating in this issue, and that met in the same day at the (former) National Council building, you issued orders for your forces to orderly and widely attack to kill, arrest, detain and torture large number of Al-Dujayl inhabitants (men, women and children), where nine persons were killed at that day and the next day, as well as arresting and detaining groups of families, which contain (399) members, at the Interrogation and Investigation Department (Al-Hakimiyyah) of the (disbanded) Head of Intelligence Service that was commanded by the defendant (Barzan Ibrahim Al-Hasan) according to the documents attached to the case's file.

The arrested people were tortured by the Intelligence Officers. during the interrogation and due to torture by electricity, battering the head with metal rods, and other torture methods, some of them died. Then, another group was transferred to (Abi Ghrayb) Prison that was supervised by the (disbanded) Intelligence Service, where their torture continued and other people died due to the use of several means of torture. Another group of them (men, women and children) was taken to Liyyah Desert Compound in Al-Samawah, which is designed to lodge the wandering nomads and their cattle, where they were detained there for (four years), during which they were subject to torture, harsh medical and living conditions in the desert that hugely lacked food and medicine, and as a result one person was killed, and other members of the detained families died.

The Interrogation and Investigation Department (Al-Hakimiyyah), which is related to the Intelligence Service, then transferred the names of (148), including the names of those killed due to torture during interrogating with them in Interrogation and Investigation Department (Al-Hakimiyyah) of the Intelligence Service, and in (Abi-Ghrayb) Prison. Also included, were some juveniles who are less than 18 years old, and who were transferred to the National Security Affairs Department of the (disbanded) Presidential Diwan, and then transferred to the (disbanded) Revolutionary Court that was presided by the defendant ('Awad Hamad Al-Bandar) who issued an irrevocable death sentence against all of them, in a brief trial that took one session, according to Decision number 944/Criminal/1984 in June 14,1984 where several people were convicted and weren't exposed to a trial. They were killed in the Interrogation and Investigation Department (Al-Hakimiyyah) due to torture, in addition to that, some of the persons sentenced to death were juveniles who didn't complete their 18 years old, and that violated the article (79) of the Penal Code number (111) for 1969 (amended) and the in-force Juvenile Care Code, and violates the articles of the procedures that are stipulated in the Code of Procedure for Criminal Trials number (23) for 1971 (amended), and violates the article (6) clause (5) of the International Declaration on the Civil and Political Rights dated December 16, 1966 and in force since March 23, 1976 and ratified by the Iraqi Republic on February 18, 1969 and which stipulates that (it is inadmissible to sentence to death in the crimes committed by juvenile people).

You, as a member of the (disbanded) Revolutionary Council Command Decision, participated in issuing Decision number (1283) in 1982 October 24 to confiscate the agricultural lands and orchards that belong to the Al-Dujayl inhabitants, and you personally supervised the removal of the orchards and trees inside Al-Dujayl Town and its surrounding, based upon direct orders issued by the defendant (Saddam Hussein Al-Majid), as mentioned in the audio tapes attached to the lawsuit documents. The bodies of the dead were also hidden and weren't delivered to their parents, and the fates of several persons remain unknown.

Therefore, you have participated in committing a crime that is applicable to the stipulations of the clause A, D, W, H, U, I of the paragraph (First) of the article (12) of the Iraqi High Tribunal Code number (10) for 2005 and which stipulates the following:

First: the crimes against humanity mean, in the law purposes, any of the below listed acts if committed in a widespread or systematic attack against a civilian population, and knowledge of such an attack:

A: Murder
D: Relocation of the population or its compulsory transportation

H: Imprisonment and severe deprivation in any other way of physical freedom in contrast with basic regulations of the international law

W: Torture

U: Compulsory concealment of people

I: Other inhumane acts that are of similar characteristics and that deliberately cause severe suffering or serious damage to the body or mental or physical health

In reference to paragraphs (First, Second and Third) of the article (15) of the Iraqi High Tribunal Code which stipulates the following:

Fifth. The person who commits a crime which is within the jurisdiction of the court, is responsible for it in his personal character and will be subject to penalty according to the stipulations of this code

Sixth. The person is considered responsible according to the stipulations of this code and to the stipulations of the penal code if he commits the following:

a- If the person commits the crime personally, in participation, or via another person regardless if this person is criminally responsible or not

b- Ordering the committing of a crime that was in fact committed, initiated, or urged and perpetrated to be committed.

c- Contributing with a group of people in a collaborative criminal intention to commit a crime or to start committing it, provided that this participation is deliberate

Seventh. The official title of the accused is not a reason to exempt him from penalty or to commutate the penalty whether the accused is the president of the state, a member in the Revolutionary Command Council, a prime minister or a member in the Cabinet or member in the Ba'th Party Command. It is inadmissible to use the immunity as a pretext to be relieved from the responsibility of the crimes mentioned in the articles (11), (12), (13), and (14).

Eighth. The Supreme President is not exempted from the criminal liability of the crimes committed by his subordinates, if the President is aware or has reasons to be aware that his subordinate has committed or is about to commit these acts and the President did not take the necessary and suitable measures to prevent these acts or submit the case to the competent authorities for interrogation and trial.

Indictment of Defendant Awad al-Bandar

English Translation of the Charges against Awad al-Bandar

Accusation Document
Scene of the Crime: Baghdad
Date of the Crime: May 28, 1984 until January 16, 1989

I, Judge (Ra'uf Rashid 'Abd-al-Rahman), the Presiding Judge of the First Criminal Court of the Iraqi High Tribunal accuse you ('Awwad Hamad Al-Bandar) of the following:

At the time you were the Head of the Revolutionary Command Council (canceled), and after the accused (Saddam Hussein Al-Majid) visited (al-Dujayl) area on 1982 July 08 and under the claim that gun shots were fired against the cars escorting his convoy, and after arresting inhabitants from Al-Dujayl and interrogating them at the General Intelligence Department under the presidency of the accused (Barzan Ibrahim Al-Hasan), the National Security Affairs Department in the Presidential Diwan (disbanded) referred to you on May 27, 1984 (one hundred and forty eight) names to include the names of some people who died during the interrogation because they were subject to torture by the Intelligence Officers in the Interrogation and Investigation Directorate (Al-Hakimiyyah) of the Intelligence Service and in (Abu Ghurayb) prison.

Among those arrested people are also minors who did not complete their (eighteenth) year old and are as their serial numbers are indicated in the sentence issued against each one of them. During a quick session formed by the (disbanded) Revolutionary Court, an irrevocable sentence to hang them all until death was issued, according to the resolution number 944/ Criminal/1984 on June 14, 1984 which was ratified by the accused (Saddam Hussein) as President of the republic by virtue of the presidential decree number (778) dated June 16, 1984 and upon which the hanging till death was implemented against those who were still alive. This was in violation of the article (79) of the Penal Code number (111) for 1969 (amended) and the in-force Juvenile Care Code, and in violation of the articles of the procedures that are stipulated in the Code of Procedure for Criminal Trials number (23) for 1971 (amended), and in violation of the article (6) clause (5) of the international Declaration on the Civil and Political Rights dated December 16, 1966 and in force since March 23, 1976 and ratified by the Iraqi Republic on February 18, 1969 and which stipulates that (it is inadmissible to sentence to death in the crimes committed by people under the age of eighteen). Whereas this issue is considered as a complementary part of the methodical and wide-scale attack operation that was carried out against the inhabitants of Al-Dujayl town for the purpose of annihilating the largest number of inhabitants and destroying the properties and the lands

Therefore, you have participated in committing a crime that is applicable to the stipulations of the clause (A) of the paragraph (First) of the article (12) of the Iraqi High Tribunal Code number (10)for 2005 and which stipulates the following:

First:—The crimes against humanity mean, in the law purposes, any of the below listed acts if committed in a widespread or systematic attack against a civilian population, and knowledge of such an attack:

A. Killing on purpose

In reference to the article (15) paragraphs (First, Second and Third) of the Supreme Iraqi Criminal Court Code which stipulates the following:

First. The person who commits a crime which is under the jurisdiction of the court, is responsible for it in his personal character and will be subject to penalty according to the stipulations of this code

Second. The person is considered responsible according to the stipulations of this code and to the stipulations of the Penal Code if he commits the following:

a. If the person commits the crime on a personal level, in participation or via another person regardless if this person is criminally responsible or not responsible

b. If the person orders the committing of a crime that was in fact committed, started or even urged and perpetrated to be committed.

c. If the person participates in any other way with a group of people in a collaborative criminal intention to commit a crime or to start committing it, provided that this participation in on purpose

Third. The official title of the accused is not considered as a reason to exempt him from penalty or to decrease the penalty whether the accused is a president of the state, a member in the Revolutionary Command Council, a president or a member in the Cabinet or member in the Ba'th Party Command. It is inadmissible to use the immunity as a pretext to be relieved from the responsibility of the crimes mentioned in the articles (11), (12), (13), and (14) of this code as well as in reference to the article 44 of the Iraqi High Tribunal Code number 10 of 2005.

Indictment of Defendant Mizhar Abdullah Ruwayyid

English Translation of the Charges against Mizhar Abdullah Ruwayyid

Accusation Document
Scene of the Crime: Al-Dujayl Town/Salah-al-Din
Governorate/Baghdad
Date of the Crime: July 8, 1982 until January 16, 1989

I, Judge (Ra'uf Rashid 'Abd-al-Rahman), the Presiding Judge of the First Criminal Court of the Iraqi High Tribunal accuse you (Muzhir 'Abdallah Kazim) of the following:

At the time you were a member of the (disbanded) Ba'th Party and after the visit of Saddam Hussein Al-Majid) to Al-Dujayl on 1982 July 08, and under the and under the claim that gun shots were fired against the cars escorting his motorcade and in implementation of the orders that were issued to you by the accused (Saddam Hussein), (Barzan Ibrahim Al-Hasan), (Taha Yasin Ramadan), and from the other accused fugitives against whom separate lawsuits were raised, you contributed in the systematic, organized, and wide scale attack which was launched by the Intelligence Service, the Security, the Popular Army, the military troops, and the (disbanded) Ba'th Party organization by arresting Al-Dujayl residents and pointing them out for the purpose of arrest by the security organizations.

The residents were then detained and tortured during interrogation in the Investigation and Interrogation Directorate (court of the intelligence service) of the disbanded Intelligence Service, in Abi-Ghurayb Prison, and the Liyyah desert compound, whereas you contributed to the arrest and detention of said along with their families. As a result of the torture that was carried out by the Intelligence Officers and the harsh living and health conditions, some of those detainees died, in addition to that, a juvenile was one of those sentenced to be executed by hanging by the (cancelled) Revolutionary Court and which was headed by the accused ('Awwad Hamad Al-Bandar), by virtue of the resolution number 944/ (SATTS J)/1984, dated June 14, 1984 after a brief trial, which issued an irrevocable sentence after one session. Indeed, they were executed in a later period after the accused (Saddam Hussein) ratified the sentence decision, by virtue of the presidential decree number (788), dated June 16, 1984.

You have also participated in sweeping and confiscating the orchards and agricultural lands of the residents of Al-Dujayl.

Thus, you have committed crimes that correspond to provisions of clauses A, H, W, T, Y paragraph (1st) of article (12) of the law of Iraqi High Tribunal No.10, for the year 2005, and which stipulate the following:—

For legal purposes, crimes against humanity mean any of the below mentioned actions when these actions are committed in a widespread or systematic attack against a civilian population, and knowledge of such an attack:

A: Premeditated murder
H: Imprisonment and severe deprivation in any other way of physical freedom in contrast with basic regulations of the international law
W: Torture
U: Compulsory concealment of people
I: Other inhumane acts that are of similar characteristics and that deliberately cause severe suffering or serious damage to the body or mental or physical health

In reference to paragraphs (First, Second and Third) of the article (15) of the Iraqi High Tribunal Code which stipulates the following:
First. The person who commits a crime which is within the jurisdiction of the court, is responsible for it in his personal character and will be subject to penalty according to the stipulations of this code Second. The person is considered responsible according to the stipulations of this code and to the stipulations of the penal code if he commits the following:

a. If the person commits the crime personally, in participation, or via another person regardless if this person is criminally responsible or not
b. Ordering the committing of a crime that was in fact committed, initiated, or urged and perpetrated to be committed.
c. Contributing with a group of people in a collaborative criminal intention to commit a crime or to start committing it, provided that this participation is deliberate

Fifth: In case any accused individual commits any action in implementation of an order issued by the government or the person in charge of him, this will not exempt him from criminal liability.
However, the commutation of punishment could be considered if the court perceives it as an aid to achieve justice.

Indictment of Defendant Ali Dayih Ali

English Translation of the Charges against Ali Dayih Ali

Accusation Document
Scene of the Crime: Al-Dujayl Town/Salah-al-Din
Governorate/Baghdad
Date of the Crime: July 8, 1982 until January 16, 1989

I, Judge (Ra'uf Rashid 'Abd-al-Rahman), the Presiding Judge of the First Criminal Court of the Iraqi High Tribunal accuse you, 'Ali Dayih 'Ali, of the following:

When you were a member of the (disbanded) Ba'th Party, and after the accused (Saddam Hussein Al-Majid) visited the town of Al-Dujayl on 1982 July 08, under the claim that shots were fired towards the cars that accompanied his motorcade, and considering that you are a member of the Popular Army, with your Party rank, and implementing the orders that were issued to you by the accused (Saddam Hussein), (Barzan Ibrahim Al-Hasan), (Taha Yasin Ramadan), and from the other accused fugitives against whom separate lawsuits were raised, you contributed in the systematic, organized, and wide scale attack that was launched by Intelligence Service, the Security, the Popular Army, the military forces, and the (disbanded) Ba'th Party by arresting citizens of the Al-Dujayl residents and by pointing them out and by writing the party report dated 1982 July 08, titled (Security Information Report), and sent to the Member of the State Command of the (disbanded) Ba'th Party and the (former) Minister of Interior (Sa'dun Shakir), that contained the names of citizens and families of the Dujayl residents.

This resulted in their arrest by the security authorities, and then detaining and torturing them during the interrogations in the Investigation and Interrogation Directorate (Al-Hakimiyyah) of the (disbanded) Intelligence Service, in (Abi Ghurayb) prison, and in the desert (Layyah) compound. As a result of the torture that was practiced by the Intelligence officers, who used electricity, fire shots, and metal objects in the Intelligence Department, two individuals were killed. In addition to that, as a result of the harsh living and health conditions and other unlawful actions, a number of detainees died in addition to the individuals you mentioned in your party report. The mentioned were among the individuals who were sentenced to death by hanging by the (cancelled) Revolutionary Court, according to the sentence decision numbered 1984/(SATTS J)/944, dated June 14, 1986. The sentence was promptly implemented after the accused (Saddam Hussein) ratified the irrevocable sentence in accordance to the Presidential Decree numbered 778 in June 16, 1984. Juveniles who have not reached the age of eighteen were among those who were killed as a result of the death sentence issued against them. You also contributed in removing and confiscating the orchards and the agricultural lands of the residents of Al-Dujayl.

Based on that, you have committed crimes to which the following apply: paragraphs A, H, W, U, I of clause (First) of article (12) of the Iraqi High Tribunal Law number 10 of 2005 and which stipulates the following:

Second. For legal purposes, crimes against humanity mean any of the below mentioned actions when these actions are committed in a widespread or systematic attack against a civilian population, and knowledge of such an attack:

> A: Murder
> H: Imprisonment and severe deprivation in any other way of physical freedom in contrast with basic regulations of the international law
> W: Torture
> U: Compulsory concealment of people
> I: Other inhumane acts that are of similar characteristics and that deliberately cause severe suffering or serious damage to the body or mental or physical health

In reference to paragraphs (First, Second and Fifth) of the article (15) of the Iraqi High Tribunal Code which stipulates the following:

First. The person who commits a crime which is within the jurisdiction of the court, is responsible for it in his personal character and will be subject to penalty according to the stipulations of this code

Second. The person is considered responsible according to the stipulations of this code and to the stipulations of the penal code if he commits the following:

> d. If the person commits the crime personally, in participation, or via another person regardless if this person is criminally liable or not
> c. Aiding, perpetrating, or assisting in any other way for the purpose of facilitating the committing of the crime or initiating it, to include providing the means to commit it
> d. Contributing with a group of people in a collaborative criminal intention to commit a crime or to start committing it, provided that this participation is deliberate

Fifth: In case any accused individual commits any action in implementation of an order issued by the government or the person in charge of him, this will not exempt him from criminal liability. However, the commutation of punishment could be considered if the court perceives it as an aid to achieve justice.

Indictment of Defendant Mohammed Azzawi Ali

English Translation of the Charges against Mohammed Azzawi Ali

Accusation Document

Scene of the Crime: Al-Dujayl Town/Salah-al-Din
Governorate/Baghdad
Date of the Crime: July 8, 1982 until January 16, 1989

I, Judge (Ra'uf Rashid 'Abd-al-Rahman), the Presiding Judge of the First Criminal Court of the Iraqi High Tribunal accuse you, Muhammad 'Azzawi 'Ali, of the following:

When you were a member in the (disbanded) Ba'th Party, and after the defendant (Saddam Hussein Al-Majid) visited Al-Dujayl Town in 1982 July 08, and because of the shooting that took place toward the vehicles accompanying his convoy, and as being considered one of the (disbanded) Ba'th Party members in Al-Dujayl, and for implementing the orders issued for you by the defendants (Saddam Hussein), (Barzan Ibrahim Al-Hasan), (Taha Yasin Ramadan), and the two other accused fugitives against whom separate lawsuits were raised, you participated in the methodical, organized, and broad attack by the Intelligence authorities, Security, People's Army, Military Forces, and the (disbanded) Ba'th Party in the town, where you arrested some of Al-Dujayl's citizens and pointing them out, which caused their detention by the security organizations, hence, they were detained and tortured while interrogated in the Investigation and Interrogation Directorate (Al-Hakimiyyah) that is related to the disbanded Intelligence Service, Abu Ghrayb Prison, and in the desert Liyyah Compound, where you participated in the arrest and detention of a group of people and their families, and as a result of the torture performed by the Intelligence officers, the rough living and unhealthy conditions, in addition to the other illegal actions, some were murdered and others died, including children. Among the children, was among those who were sentenced to death by the former Revolutionary Court which was headed by the defendant ('Awwad Hamad Al-Bandar) according to irrevocable verdict decision number 944/ (SATTS J)/ 1984 in June 14, 1984 in a brief trial. Later, the verdict was actually implemented against them after the defendant (Saddam Hussein) had ratified the verdict decision according to the Republican Decree number 778 in June 16,1984. You have also participated in sweeping and confiscating the orchards and agricultural land belonging to the citizens of Al-Dujayl.

Hereby, you have committed crimes that conform to the verdicts of the clauses A, E, F, and I of the first paragraph of law number (10) of the Iraqi High Tribunal for the year of 2005, which states the following:

For legal purposes, crimes against humanity mean any of the below mentioned actions when these actions are committed in a widespread or systematic attack against a civilian population, and knowledge of such an attack:

A: Intentional murder
H: Imprisonment and severe deprivation in any other way of physical freedom in contrast with basic regulations of the international law
F: Torture
I: Kidnap
J: Other similar actions against humanity that deliberately caused extreme sufferance or hazardous harm against the body, mental or physical health.

In reference to the article (15) paragraphs (First, Second and Third) of the Supreme Iraqi Criminal Court Code which states the following:

First: The person, who commits a crime which is under the jurisdiction of the court, is personally considered responsible for it and will be subject to penalty according to the verdicts of the law

Second: The person is considered responsible according to the verdicts of this code and to the Penal Code if he commits the following:

A. If the person commits the crime on a personal level, in participation or via another person regardless if this person is criminally responsible or not responsible.
C. Aiding, perpetrating, or assisting in any other way for the purpose of facilitating the committing of the crime or initiating it, to include providing the means to commit it
D. If the person contributes in any other way with a group of people in a collaborative criminal intention to commit a crime or to start committing it, provided that this participation in on purpose

Indictment of Defendant Abdallah Kazim Ruwayyid

English Translation of the Charges against Abdallah Kazim Ruwayyid

Accusation Document

Scene of the Crime: Al-Dujayl Town/Salah-al-Din
Governorate/Baghdad
Date of the Crime: July 8, 1982 until January 16, 1989

I, Judge (Ra'uf Rashid 'Abd-al-Rahman), the Presiding Judge of the First
Criminal Court of the Iraqi High Tribunal accuse you, 'Abdallah Kazim
Ruwayyid, of the following:

At the time you were a member in the Al-Ba'th party (disbanded), and
when the accused (Saddam Hussein Al-Majid) visited the Al-Dujayl town on
1982 July 08 and under the claim that gun shots were fired in the direction of
the cars that were escorting his motorcade, and for being a member of the
people's army, an attribute to the party and implementing the orders issued to
you, by the accused (Saddam Hussein), (Barzan Ibrahim Al-Hasan), and (Taha
Yasin Ramadan), and other accused fugitives against whom separate lawsuits
were raised. You participated in the systematic, organized, and wide scale attack that was launched by the Intelligence Service, the security, the people's
Army, the Military forces, and the Al-Ba'th party organization (disbanded) in
the town, in arresting members of Al-Dujayl inhabitants, in pointing them
out, and in writing the party's report dated in 1982 July 08, titled (Security Information Report), which was addressed to the member of the state command
of the Al-Ba'th party(disbanded), the (former) Minister of the Interior (Sa'-
dun Shakir), in which you listed names of inhabitants and families form Al-
Dujayl which lead to their apprehension by the security system, and then their
detention, and torture during interrogation in the Investigation and Interrogation Directorate (Al-Hakimiyyah), of the Intelligence Service (disbanded),
and in (Abi-Ghurayb) Prison, and in the (Liyyah) desert complex.

Due to the torture that was implemented by the Intelligence officer, by
means of the electrical current, gun shots, and metal objects in the Intelligence Department, two individuals were killed. Moreover and as a result of
the hard living conditions, poor health conditions and other actions violating
the law, more of the detainees died, besides those whom you listed in your
party report were among those who were sentenced to death by hanging till
death by the Revolutionary Court (cancelled), which was headed by ('Awwad
Hamad Al-Bandar), who issued an irrevocable sentence to hang them all till
death in accordance to resolution number 944/ Criminal/984 on June 14, 1984
in a brief trial which lasted one session. The sentence was in fact implemented

on them later on, after the ratification by the accused (Saddam Husayn), on the sentence decision by virtue of the Presidential Decree numbered (778), on June 16, 1984. Among those who were killed for being sentenced to death were juveniles who did not complete their 18 years of age, as two juvenile names were mentioned in your party report. You also participated in the extraction and confiscation of the orchards and the agricultural lands that belong to the Al-Dujayl citizens.

Based on that, you have committed crimes to which the following apply: paragraphs A, D, W, H, U, I of clause (First) of article (12) of the Iraqi High Tribunal Law number 10 of 2005 and which stipulates the following:

For legal purposes, crimes against humanity mean any of the below mentioned actions when these actions are committed in a widespread or systematic attack against a civilian population, and knowledge of such an attack:

A: Murder
H: Imprisonment and severe deprivation in any other way of physical freedom in contrast with basic regulations of the international law
W: Torture
U: compulsory concealment of people
I: Other inhumane acts that are of similar characteristics and that deliberately cause severe suffering or serious damage to the body or mental or physical health

In reference to the article (15) paragraphs (First, Second and Third) of the Iraqi High Tribunal Code which stipulates the following:

First. The person who commits a crime which is under the jurisdiction of the court, is responsible for it in his personal character and will be subject to penalty according to the stipulations of this code

Second. The person is considered responsible according to the stipulations of this code and to the stipulations of the Penal Code if he commits the following:

a. If the person commits the crime on a personal level, in participation or via another person regardless if this person is criminally responsible or not responsible
b. If the person orders the committing of a crime that was in fact committed, started or even urged and perpetrated to be committed.
c. If the person participates in any other way with a group of people in a collaborative criminal intention to commit a crime or to start committing it, provided that this participation in on purpose

In case any accused individual commits any action in implementation of an order issued by the government or the person in charge of him, this will not exempt him from criminal liability. However, the commutation of punishment could be considered if the court perceives it as an aid to achieve justice.

English Translation of the 2005 IHT Statute

Resolution No. (10)

In the Name of the people
The presidency Council
Pursuant to what has been approved by the National Assembly and in accordance with Article No. (33) Paragraphs A and B and Article No. (30) of the Law of Administration for the State of Iraq for the Transitional Period.
The presidency Council decided in the session of October 9, 2005 to promulgate the following resolution:

Law No. (10) 2005
Law of
The Iraqi High Tribunal

SECTION ONE
The Establishment and Organization
Of the Court

PART ONE
Establishment

<u>Article 1</u>:
<u>First</u>: A court is hereby established and shall be known as The Iraqi High Tribunal (the "Court"). The Court shall be fully independent.
<u>Second</u>: The Court shall have jurisdiction over every natural person whether Iraqi or non-Iraqi resident of Iraq and accused of one of the crimes listed in Articles 11 to 14 below, committed during the period from July 17, 1968 and until May 1, 2003, in the Republic of Iraq or elsewhere, including the following crimes:
A. The crime of genocide;
B. Crimes against humanity;
C. War crimes
D. Violations of certain Iraqi laws listed in Article 14 below.
<u>Article 2</u>:
The Court shall have its main office in the city of Baghdad and may hold its sessions in any governorate, on the basis of a proposal by the Council of Ministers pursuant to a proposal from the President of the Court.

PART TWO
Organizational Structure of the Court

Article 3:

The court shall consist of:

First:

A. A Cassation Panel, which shall specialize in reviewing the provisions and decisions issued by one of the criminal or investigative courts.

B. One or more criminal courts.

C. Investigative judges.

Second: Public Prosecution.

Third: An administration, which shall provide administrative and financial services to the Court and the Public Prosecution.

Fourth:

A. The Cassation Panel shall be composed of nine judges who shall elect a president for amongst them. The president of the Cassation Panel shall be the senior president of the court and shall supervise its administrative and financial affairs.

B. The felony court shall be composed of five judges who shall elect a president from amongst them to supervise their work.

Fifth:

The Council of Ministers may, if deemed necessary, based upon a proposal by a President of the Court, appoint non-Iraqi judges who have experience in conducting criminal trials stipulated in this law, and who are of very high moral character, honest and virtuous to work in the Court, in the event that a State is one of the parties in a complaint, and the judges shall be commissioned with the help of the International Community and the United Nations.

PART THREE
Selection of Judges, Public Prosecutors and their retirement

Article 4:

First: Judges and public prosecutors shall be of high moral character, integrity and uprightness. They shall possess experience in criminal law and shall fulfill the appointment requirements stipulated in the Judicial Organization Law No. 160 of 1979 and the Public Prosecution law No. 159 of 1979.

Second: As an exception to the provisions of paragraph (First) of this Article the candidates for the positions of judges at the Cassation Panel, the Criminal Court, the investigative judges and public prosecutors do not have to be active judges and public prosecutors. Retired judges and members of public prosecution may be nominated, without restrictions age requirement and Iraqi lawyers who possess a high level of experience, competence and efficiency and of absolute competence, in accordance with the Legal Profession Code No. 173 of 1965 and have served in judicial, legal and the legal profession fields for no less than (15) years.

Third:

A. The Supreme Juridical Council shall nominate all judges and public prosecutors to this Court. The Council of Ministers after approving their nomination shall issue their appointment order from the Presidency Council and will be classified as class (A) judges, in an exception to the provisions of the Judicial Organization Law and the Public Prosecution Law. Their salaries and rewards shall be specified by guidelines issued by the Council of Ministers.

B. The judges, public prosecutors and the employees appointed in accordance with the provisions of law before this legislation shall be deemed legally approved starting from the date of their appointment according to the provisions of paragraph (Third/A) of Article (4) taking into account the provisions of Article (33) of this law.

Fourth: The Presidency Council in accordance with a proposal from the Council of Ministers shall have the right to transfer Judges and Public Prosecutors from the Court to the Higher Judicial Council for any reason.

Fifth:

The term of service of a judge or a public prosecutor covered by the provisions of this law shall end for one of the following reasons:

1. If he is convicted of a non-political felony.

2. If he presents false information.

3. If he fails to perform his duties without a legitimate reason.

Article 6:

First: A committee comprised of five members elected from among the Judges and public prosecutors shall be established in the Court under the supervision of the Cassation panel of the Court and they shall select a President for a term of one year. This committee shall be called "Judges and Public Prosecutors Affairs Committee". The Committee shall enjoy the authorities stipulated in the Judicial Organization Law and Public Prosecution Law. It shall consider disciplinary matters and the service of Judges and the members of the public prosecution. Its decisions shall be appealable before the extended panel of the Federal Court of Cassation if it decides to terminate the service of the judge or a member of the public prosecution.

Second: The committee shall submit a recommendations, after the appeal before the extended panel of the Federal Court of Cassation is denied, to the Council of Ministers to pass a resolution from the Presidency Council terminating the service of a judge or a public prosecutor, including the chief justice in case the provisions of Article (6) of this Law are met.

Third: At the end of the Court's work, the judges and the Public Prosecutors shall be reassigned to the Higher Judicial Council to work in the Federal Courts. Those reaching the legal age for retirement shall be retired in accordance with the Law.

PART FOUR
Presidency of the Court

Article 7:

First: The president of the court shall:

A. Chair the proceedings of the Cassation Panel.

B. Name the original and alternate judges of the Criminal Courts.

C. Name any of the judges to the Criminal Court in case of absence.

D. Accomplish the Court's administrative work.

E. Appoint and end the service of the Administrative Director, security director, public relations director and archive and documents keeping director in the court.

F. Name the official spokesman for the Court from among the judges or public prosecutors.

Second: The President of the Court shall have the right to appoint non-Iraqi experts to act in an advisory capacity for the Criminal Court and the Cassation Panel. The role of the non-Iraqi nationals shall be to provide assistance with respect to international law and the experience of similar Courts (whether international or otherwise). The paneling of these experts is to be done with the help from the International Community, including the United Nations.

Third: The non-Iraqi experts referred to in paragraph (Second) of this Article shall also be persons of high moral character, uprightness and integrity. It would be preferable that such non-Iraqi expert should have worked in either a judicial or prosecutorial capacity in his or her respective country or at the International War Crimes Court.

PART FIVE
Investigative Judges

Article 8:

First: Sufficient number of Investigative Judges shall be appointed.

Second: The Court's Investigative Judges shall undertake the investigation with those accused of crimes stipulated in paragraph (Second) Article (1) of this law.

<u>Third</u>: The Investigative Judges shall elect a Chief and his deputy from amongst them.

<u>Fourth</u>: The Chief shall refer cases under investigation to investigative judges individually.

<u>Fifth</u>: Each of the Investigative Judges' Offices shall be composed of an investigative Judge and qualified staff as may be required for the work of the investigative judge.

<u>Sixth</u>: An Investigative Judge shall collect evidence from any source he deems appropriate and question all relevant parties directly.

<u>Seventh</u>: An Investigative Judge shall act independently in the court since he is considered as a separate entity from the court. He shall not fall under nor receive requests or orders from any Government Department, or any other party.

<u>Eighth</u>: The decisions of the Investigative Judge can be appealed in cassation before the Cassation Panel within fifteen days from the date of receipt of notification or from the date notification is considered received pursuant to law.

<u>Ninth</u>: The Chief Investigative Judge, after consulting with the President of the Court, have the right to appoint non-Iraqi nationals experts to assist the Investigative Judges in the investigation of cases covered by this law, whether international or otherwise. The Chief Investigative Judge can commission these experts with help from the International Community, including the United Nations.

<u>Tenth</u>: The non-Iraqi experts and observers referred to in paragraph (<u>Ninth</u>) of this Article are required to be persons of high moral character, honest and virtuous; it is preferred that the non-Iraqi expert and observer had worked in either a judicial or prosecutorial capacity in his or her respective country or in the International War Crimes Court.

PART SIX
The Public Prosecution

<u>Article 9</u>:

<u>First</u>: Sufficient number of prosecutors shall be appointed.

<u>Second</u>: The Public Prosecution shall be composed of a number of public prosecutors who shall be responsible for the prosecution of persons accused of crimes that fall within the jurisdiction of the Court.

<u>Third</u>: Public prosecutors shall elect a Chief and his Deputy from amongst them.

<u>Fourth</u>: Each office of public prosecution shall be composed of a prosecutor and such other qualified staff as may be required for the work of the Public Prosecutor.

Fifth: Each prosecutor shall act with complete independence since he is considered as a separate entity from the Court. He shall not fall under, nor receive instructions from, any government department or from any other party.

Sixth: The chief prosecutor shall assign individual cases to a prosecutor to investigate and to try in court based on the authority granted to the public prosecutors pursuant to the law.

Seventh: The Chief Public Prosecutor, in consultation with the President of the Court, shall have the right to appoint non-Iraqi nationals to act as experts helping the public prosecutors in the investigation and prosecution of cases covered by this law whether in an international context or otherwise. The Chief Prosecutor can commission these experts with the help of the international community, including the United Nations.

Eighth: The non-Iraqi experts, referred to in Paragraph (<u>Seventh</u>) of this Article are required to be persons of high moral character, honest and virtuous. It is preferred that such non-Iraqi experts had worked in a prosecutorial capacity in his respective country or in the International War Crimes Court.

PART SEVEN
The Administration Department

Article 10:

First: The Administration Department shall be managed by an officer with the title of Department Director who holds a bachelor degree in law and have judicial and administrative experience. He shall be assisted by a number of employees in managing the affairs of the department.

Second: The Administration Department is responsible for the administrative, financial and service affairs of the court and the Public Prosecution.

SECTION TWO
The Court Jurisdictions

PART ONE
The Crime of Genocide

Article 11:

First: For the purposes of this law and in accordance with the International Convention on the Prevention and Punishment of the Crime of Genocide dated December 9, 1948 as ratified by Iraq on January 20, 1959, "genocide" means any of the following acts committed with the intent to abolish, in whole or in part, a national, ethnic, racial or religious group as such:

A. Killing members of the group.

B. Causing serious bodily or mental harm to members of the group.

C. Deliberately inflicting on the group living conditions calculated to bring about its physical destruction in whole or in part.

D. Imposing measures intended to prevent births within the group.

E. Forcibly transferring children of the group to another group.

Second: The following acts shall be punishable

A. Genocide.

B. Conspiracy to commit genocide.

C. Direct and public incitement to commit genocide.

D. Attempt to commit genocide.

E. Complicity in genocide.

PART TWO
Crimes against Humanity

Article 12:

First: For the purposes of this Law, "crimes against humanity" means any of the following acts when committed as part of a widespread or systematic attack directed against any civilian population, with knowledge of the attack:

A. Willful Murder;

B. Extermination;

C. Enslavement;

D. Deportation or forcible transfer of population;

E. Imprisonment or other severe deprivation of physical liberty in violation of fundamental norms of international law;

F. Torture;

G. Rape, sexual slavery, forcible prostitution, forced pregnancy, or any other form of sexual violence of comparable gravity;

H. Persecution against any specific party or group of the population on political, racial, national, ethnic, cultural, religious, gender or other grounds that are impermissible under international law, in connection with any act referred to as a form of sexual violence of comparable gravity.

I. Enforced disappearance of persons.

J. Other inhumane acts of a similar character intentionally causing great suffering, or serious injury to the body or to the mental or physical health.

Second: For the purposes of implementing the provisions of paragraph (First) of this Article, the below listed terms shall mean the stated definitions:

A. "Attack directed against any civilian population" means a course of conduct involving the multiple panel of acts referred to in the above paragraph "First" against any civilian population, pursuant to or in furtherance of a state or organizational policy to commit such attack;

B. "Extermination" means the intentional infliction of living conditions, such as the deprivation of access to food and medicine, with the intent to bring about the destruction of part of the population;

C. "Enslavement" means the exercise of any or all of the powers attached to the right of ownership over a person and includes the exercise of such power in the course of human trafficking, in particular women and children;

D. "Deportation or forcible transfer of population" means forced displacement of the concerned persons concerned by expulsion or other coercive acts from the area in which they are lawfully present, without grounds permitted under international law;

E. "Persecution" means the intentional and severe deprivation of fundamental rights contrary to international law by reason of the identity of the group or collectivity; and

F. "Enforced disappearance of persons" means the arrest, detention or abduction of persons by, or with the authorization, support or acquiescence of, the State or a political organization, followed by a refusal to acknowledge that deprivation of freedom or to give information on the fate or whereabouts of those persons, with the intention of removing them from the protection of the law for a prolonged period of time.

PART THREE
War Crimes

<u>Article 13</u>:

For the purposes of this Law, "war crimes" means:

<u>First</u>: Grave breaches of the Geneva Conventions of 12 August 1949, namely, any of the following acts against persons or property protected under the provisions of the relevant Geneva Convention:

A. Willful killing;

B. Torture or inhuman treatment, including biological experiments;

C. Willfully causing great suffering, or serious injury to body or health;

D. Extensive destruction and appropriation of property not justified by military necessity and carried out unlawfully and wantonly;

E. Compelling a prisoner of war or other protected person to serve in the forces of a hostile power;

F. Willfully denying the right of a fair trial to a prisoner of war or other protected person;

G. Unlawful confinement;

H. Unlawful deportation or transfer; and

I. Taking of hostages.

Second: Other serious violations of the laws and customs applicable in international armed conflicts, within the established framework of international law, namely, any of the following acts:

A. Intentionally directing attacks against the civilian population as such or against individual civilians not taking direct part in hostilities;

B. Intentionally directing attacks against civilian objects, that is, objects which are not military objectives;

C. Intentionally directing attacks against personnel, installations, material, units or vehicles used in a peacekeeping missions in accordance with the Charter of the United Nations or in a humanitarian assistance missions, as long as they are entitled to the protection given to civilians or civilian objects under the international law of armed conflicts;

D. Intentionally launching an attack in the knowledge that such attack will cause incidental loss of life or injury to civilians or damage to civilian objects which would be clearly excessive in relation to the concrete and direct overall military advantages anticipated;

E. Intentionally launching an attack in the knowledge that such attack will cause widespread, long-term and severe damage to the natural environment, which would be clearly excessive in relation to the concrete and direct overall military advantage anticipated;

F. Attacking or bombarding, by whatever means, towns, villages, dwellings or buildings which are undefended and which are not military objectives;

G. Killing or wounding a combatant who, having laid down his arms or having no longer means of defense, has surrendered at discretion;

H. Making improper use of a flag of truce, of the flag or of the military insignia and uniform of the enemy or of the United Nations, as well as of the distinctive emblems of the Geneva Conventions, resulting in death or serious personal injury;

I. The transfer, directly or indirectly, by the Government of Iraq or any of its instrumentalities (which includes for clarification any of the instruments of the Arab Ba'ath Socialist Party), of parts of its own civilian population into any territory it occupies, or the deportation or transfer of all or parts of the population of the occupied territory within or outside this territory;

J. Intentionally directing attacks against buildings that are dedicated to religion, education, art, science or charitable purposes, historic monuments, hospitals and places where the sick and wounded are collected, provided they are not military objectives;

K. Subjecting persons of another nation to physical mutilation or to medical or scientific experiments of any kind that are neither justified by the medical, dental or hospital treatment of the person concerned nor carried out in his or her interest, and which cause death to or seriously endanger the health of such person or persons;

L. Killing or wounding treacherously individuals belonging to the hostile nation or army;

M. Declaring that no one remained alive;

N. Destroying or seizing the property of an adverse party unless such destruction or seizure be imperatively demanded by the necessities of war;

O. Declaring abolished, suspended or inadmissible in a court of law, or otherwise depriving, the rights and actions of the nationals of the hostile party;

P. Compelling the nationals of the hostile party to take part in the operations of war directed against their own country, even if they were in the belligerent's service before the commencement of the war;

Q. Pillaging a town or place, even when it is taken by force;

R. Using poison or poisoned weapons;

S. Using asphyxiating, poisonous or other gases, and all analogous liquids, materials or devices;

T. Using bullets, which expand or flatten easily in the human body, such as bullets with a hard envelope, which does not entirely cover the core or is pierced with incisions;

U. Committing outrages upon personal dignity, in particular humiliating and degrading treatment;

V. Committing rape, sexual slavery, enforced prostitution, forced pregnancy, or any other form of sexual violence of comparable gravity;

W. Utilizing the presence of a civilian or other protected person to render certain points, areas or military forces immune from military operations;

X. Intentionally directing attacks against buildings, material and medical units, transport, and personnel using the distinctive emblems of the Geneva Conventions in conformity with international law;

Y. Intentionally using starvation of civilians as a method of warfare by depriving them of objects indispensable to their survival, including willfully impeding relief supplies as provided for under international law; and

Z. Conscripting or enlisting children under the age of fifteen years into the national armed forces or using them to participate actively in hostilities.

<u>Third</u>: In the case of an armed conflict, any of the following acts committed against persons taking no active part in the hostilities, including members of armed forces who have laid down their arms and those placed hors de combat by sickness, wounds, detention or any other cause:

A. Use of violence against life and persons, in particular murder of all kinds, mutilation, cruel treatment and torture;

B. Committing outrages upon personal dignity, in particular humiliating and degrading treatment;

C. Taking of hostages;

D. The passing of sentences and the carrying out of executions without previous judgment pronounced by a regularly constituted court, affording all judicial guarantees which are generally recognized as indispensable.

Fourth: Other serious violations of the laws and customs of war applicable in armed conflict not of an international character, within the established framework of international law, namely, any of the following acts:

A. Intentionally directing attacks against the civilian population as such or against civilian individuals not taking direct part in hostilities;

B. Intentionally directing attacks against buildings, materials, medical transportation units and means, and personnel using the distinctive emblems of the Geneva Conventions in conformity with international law;

C. Intentionally directing attacks against personnel, installations, materials, units, or vehicles used in humanitarian assistance or peacekeeping missions in accordance with the Charter of the United Nations, as long as they are entitled to the protection given to civilians or civilian targets under the international law of armed conflict;

D. Intentionally directing attacks against buildings that are dedicated to religious, educational, artistic, scientific or charitable purposes, and historic monuments, hospitals and places where the sick and wounded are collected, provided they are not military objectives;

E. Pillaging any town or place, even when taken over by assault;

F. Committing rape, sexual slavery, forced prostitution, forced pregnancy, or any other form of sexual violence of comparable gravity;

G. Conscripting or listing children under the age of fifteen years into armed forces or groups or using them to participate actively in hostilities;

H. Ordering the displacement of the civilian population for reasons related to the conflict, unless the security of the civilians involved or imperative military reasons so demand;

I. Killing or wounding treacherously a combatant adversary;

J. Declaring that no person is still alive;

K. Subjugation persons who are under the power of another party of the conflict to physical mutilation or to medical or scientific experiments of any kind that are neither justified by the medical, dental or hospital treatment of the person concerned nor carried out in his or her interest, causing death to such person or persons, or seriously endangering their health; and

L. Destroying or seizing the property of an adversary, unless such destruction or seizure is imperatively demanded by the necessities of the conflict.

PART FOUR
Violations of Iraqi Laws

<u>Article 14</u>:
The Court shall have the power to prosecute persons who have committed the following crimes:
<u>First</u>: Intervention in the judiciary or the attempt to influence the functions of the judiciary.
<u>Second</u>: The wastage and squander of national resources, pursuant to, item G of Article 2 of the Law punishing those who conspire against the security of the homeland and corrupt the regime No. 7 of 1958.
<u>Third</u>: The abuse of position and the pursuit of policies that were about to lead to the threat of war or the use of the armed forces of Iraq against an Arab country, in accordance with Article 1 of Law Number 7 of 1958.
<u>Fourth</u>: If the court finds a default in the elements of any of the crimes stipulated in Articles 11, 12, 13 of this law, and it is proved to the Court that the act constitutes a crime punishable by the penal law or any other criminal law at the time of its commitment, then the court shall have jurisdiction to adjudicate this case.

SECTION THREE
Individual Criminal Responsibility

<u>Article 15</u>:
<u>First</u>: A person who commits a crime within the jurisdiction of this Court shall be personally responsible and liable for punishment in accordance with this Law.
<u>Second</u>: In accordance with this Law, and the provisions of Iraqi criminal law, a person shall be criminally responsible if that person:
A. Commits such a crime, whether as an individual, jointly with another or through another person, regardless of whether that this person is criminally responsible or not;
B. Orders, solicits or induces the commission of such a crime, which in fact occurs or is attempted;
C. For the purpose of facilitating the commission of such a crime, aids, abets or by any other means assists in its commission or its attempted commission, including providing the means for its commission;
D. Participating by any other way with a group of persons, with a common criminal intention to commit or attempt to commit such a crime, such participation shall be intentional and shall either:

1. Be made for the aim of consolidating the criminal activity or criminal purpose of the group, where such activity or purpose involves the commission of a crime within the jurisdiction of the Court; or

2. Be made with the knowledge of the intention of the group to commit the crime;

E. In respect of the crime of genocide, directly and publicly incites others to commit genocide;

F. Attempts to commit such a crime by taking action that commences its execution, but the crime does not occur because of circumstances independent of the person's intentions. However, a person who abandons the effort to commit the crime or otherwise prevents the completion of the crime shall not be liable for punishment under this Law for the attempt to commit that crime if that person completely and voluntarily gave up the criminal purpose.

Third: The official position of any accused person, whether as president, chairman or a member of the Revolution Command Council, prime minister, member of the counsel of ministers, a member of the Ba'ath Party Command, shall not relieve such person of criminal penal, nor mitigate punishment. No person is entitled to any immunity with respect to any of the crimes stipulated in Articles 11, 12, 13, and 14 of this law.

Fourth: The crimes that were committed by a subordinate do not relieve his superior of criminal responsibility if he knew or had reason to know that the subordinate was about to commit such acts or had done so, and the superior failed to take the necessary and appropriate measures to prevent such acts or to submit the matter to the competent authorities for investigation and prosecution.

Fifth: The fact that an accused person acted pursuant to an order of the Government or of his superior, shall not relieve him of criminal responsibility, but may be considered in mitigation of punishment if the Court determines that justice so requires.

Sixth: Pardons issued prior to this law coming into force, do not apply to the accused in any of the crimes stipulated in it.

SECTION FOUR
Rules of Procedure and Evidence

Article 16:
The Court shall apply the Criminal Procedure Law No. 23 of 1971, and the Rules of Procedure and Evidence appended to this law, which is an indivisible and integral part of the law.

SECTION FIVE
General Principles of Criminal Law

Article 17:

First: In case a stipulation is not found in this Law and the rules made there under, the general provisions of criminal law shall be applied in connection with the accusation and
prosecution of any accused person shall be those contained in:

A- The Baghdadi Penal Law of 1919, for the period starting from July 17, 1968, till Dec. 14, 1969.

B- The Penal law no.111 of 1969, which was in force in1985 (third version), for the period starting from Dec.15, 1969, till May, 1, 2003.

C- The Military Penal Law no.13 of 1940, and the military procedure law no.44 of 1941.

Second: To interpret Articles 11, 12, 13 of this law, the Cassation Court and Panel may resort to the relevant decisions of the international criminal courts.

Third: Grounds for exclusion of criminal responsibility under the Panel Law shall be interpreted in a manner consistent with this Law and with international legal obligations concerning the crimes within the jurisdiction of the Court.

Fourth: The crimes stipulated in Articles 11, 12, 13, and 14 shall not be subject to limitations that terminate the criminal case or punishment.

SECTION SIX
Investigations and Indictment

Article 18:

First: The Investigative Judge shall initiate investigations ex-officio or on the basis of information obtained from any source, particularly from the police, or governmental and nongovernmental organizations. The Investigative Judge shall assess the information received and decide whether there is sufficient basis to proceed.

Second: The Court Investigative Judge shall have the power to question suspects, victims and witnesses, or their relatives to collect evidence and to conduct on-site investigations. In carrying out his task the Court Investigative Judge may, as appropriate, request the assistance of the relevant governmental authorities concerned, who shall be required to provide full co-operation with the request.

Third: Upon a determination that a prima facie case exists, the Investigative Judge shall prepare an indictment containing a concise statement of the facts of the crime with which the accused is charged under the Statute and shall refer the case to the criminal court.

PART ONE
Guarantees of the Accused

Article 19:

<u>First</u>: All persons shall be equal before the Court.

<u>Second</u>: The accused shall be presumed innocent until proven guilty before the Court in accordance with this law.

<u>Third</u>: Every accused shall be entitled to a public hearing, in pursuance with the provisions of this law and the Rules issued according to it.

<u>Fourth</u>: In directing any charge against the accused pursuant to the present Law, the accused shall be entitled to a just fair trial in accordance with the following minimum guarantees:

A. To be informed promptly and in detail of the content nature and cause and of the charge against him;

B. To have adequate time and facilities for the preparation of his defense and to communicate freely with counsel of his own choosing and to meet with him privately. The accused is entitled to have non-Iraqi legal representation, so long as the principal lawyer of such accused is Iraqi;

C. To be tried without undue delay;

D. To be tried in his presence, and to use a lawyer of his own choosing, and to be informed of his right assistance of his own choosing; to be informed, if he does not have legal assistance, of this right; and to have legal assistance and to have the right to request such aid to appoint a lawyer without paying the fees, case if he does not have sufficient means to pay for it; if he does not have the financial ability to do so.

E. The accused shall have the right to request the defense witnesses, the witnesses for the prosecution, and to discuss with them any evidence that support his defense in accordance with the law.

F. The defendant shall not be forced to confess and shall have the right to remain silent and not provide any testimony and that silent shall not be interpreted as evidence of convection or innocence.

SECTION SEVENTH
Trial Proceedings

Article 20:

<u>First</u>: A person against whom an indictment has been issued shall, pursuant to an order or an arrest warrant of the Investigative Judge, be taken into custody, immediately informed of the charges against him and transferred to the Court.

<u>Second</u>: The Criminal Court shall ensure that a trial is fair and expeditious and that proceedings are conducted in accordance with this Statute and the

Rules of Procedure and Evidence annexed to this Law, with full respect for the rights of the accused and due regard for the protection of the victims, their relatives and the witnesses.

Third: The Criminal Court shall read the indictment, satisfy itself that the rights of the accused are respected and guaranteed, insure that the accused understands the indictment, with charges directed against him and instruct the accused to enter a plea.

Fourth: The hearings shall be public unless the Criminal Court decides to close the proceedings in accordance with the Rules of Procedure and Evidence annexed to this Statue, and no decision shall be adopted under the session secrecy unless for extreme limited reasons.

Article 21:

The Criminal Court shall, in its Rules of Procedure and Evidence annexed to this Statue, provide the protection for victims or their relatives and witnesses and also for the secrecy of their identity.

Article 22:

Families of victims and Iraqi persons harmed may file a civil suit before this court against the accused for the harm they suffered through their actions constituting crimes according to the provisions of this Statue. The court shall have the power to adjudicate these claims in accordance with the Iraqi Criminal procedure Code No. 23 for the year 1971, and other relevant laws.

Article 23:

First: The Criminal Court shall pronounce judgments and impose sentences and penalties on persons convicted of crimes within the jurisdiction of the Court.

Second: The judgment shall be issued by a majority of the judges of the Criminal Court, and shall announce it in public. The judgment shall not be issued except pursuant to the indictment decision. The opinion of the dissenting Judges can be appended.

Article 24:

First: The penalties that shall be imposed by the Court shall be those prescribed by the Iraqi Penal Code No (111) of 1969, except for sentences of life imprisonment that means the remaining natural life of the person. With considering the provisions of Article (17) of this Statute.

Second: It shall be applied against the crimes stipulated in article (14) of this Statute the sentences provided under the Iraqi Penal Code and other punishable laws.

Third: The penalty for crimes under Articles 11, 12, 13 shall be determined by the Criminal Court, taking into account the provisions contained in paragraphs fourth and fifth.

Fourth: A person convicted of sentences stipulated under Iraqi Penal Code shall be punished if:

A. He committed an of murder or rape as defined under Iraqi Penal Code.

B. He participated in committing an of murder or rape.

Fifth: The penalty for any crimes under Articles 11, 12, 13 which do not have a counterpart under Iraqi law shall be determined by the Court taking into account such factors like the gravity of the crime, the individual circumstances of the convicted person, guided by judicial precedents and relevant sentences issued by the international criminal courts.

Sixth: The Criminal Court may order the forfeiture of proceeds, property or assets derived directly or indirectly from a crime, without prejudice to the rights of the bona fide third parties.

Seventh: In accordance with Article 307 of the Iraqi Criminal Procedure Code, the Criminal Court shall have the right to confiscate any material or goods prohibited by law regardless of whether the case has been discharged for any lawful reason.

SECTION EIGHT
Appeals Proceedings

PART ONE
Cassation

Article 25:

First: The convicted pr the public prosecutor has the right to contest the judgments and decisions before the Cassation Panel for any of the following reasons:

1. If a judgment issued is in contradiction with the law or there is an error in interrupting it.
2. An error in procedures.
3. Material error in the facts which has led to violation of justice.

Second: The Cassation Panel may affirm, reverse or revise the decisions taken by the Criminal Court or the decisions of the Investigative Judge.

Third: When the Cassation Panel issues its verdict to revoke the judgment of acquittal or release issued by the Criminal Court or the Investigative Judge, the case shall be referred back to the Court for retrial of the accused or for the Investigative Judge to implement the decision.

Fourth: The period of appeal shall be in accordance with the provisions of the Iraqi Criminal procedure Code No. 23 for the year 1971 that is in effect, in case there is no specific provision in that regard

PART TWO
Retrial

<u>Article 26</u>:

<u>First</u>: Where a new findings or facts have been discovered which were not known at the time of the proceedings before the Criminal Court or the Cassation Panel and which could have been a decisive factor in reaching the decision, the convicted person or the Prosecution may submit to the Court an application for a retrial.

<u>Second</u>: The Court shall reject the application if it considers it to be unfounded. If it determines that the application has merit, and for the purpose of reaching a modification of the court decision after hearing the parties in the case, may:

1. Send case back to the original Criminal Court that issued the ruling; or
2. Send case back to another Criminal Court; or
3. The Cassation Panel takes jurisdiction over the matter.

SECTION NINE
Enforcement of Sentences

<u>Article 27</u>:

<u>First</u>: Sentences shall be carried out in accordance with the Iraqi legal system and its laws.

<u>Second</u>: No authority, including the President of the Republic, may grant a pardon or mitigate the punishment issued by the Court. The punishment must be executed within 30 days of the date when the judgment becomes final and non-appealable.

SECTION TEN
General and Final Provisions

<u>Article 28</u>:

Investigative judges, Judge of the criminal courts, members of the public prosecution committee, the director of the administrative department and the court's staff must be Iraqi nationals with due considerations given to the provisions of Article 4 (Third) of this statute.

<u>Article 29</u>:

<u>First</u>: The Court and the national courts shall have concurrent jurisdiction to prosecute persons for those s stipulated in Article 14 of this statute.

<u>Second</u>: The Court shall have primacy over all other Iraqi courts with respect to the crimes stipulated in Articles 11, 12, and 13 of this statute.

Third: At any stage of the proceedings, the Court may demand of any other Iraqi court to transfer any case being tried by it involving any crimes stipulated in Articles 11, 12, 13, and 14 of this statue, and such court shall be required to transfer such case upon demand.

Fourth: At any stage of the proceedings, the Court may demand of any other Iraqi court to transfer any case being tried by it involving any crimes stipulated in Articles 13, 14, 15, 16 of this statue, and such court shall be required to transfer such case upon demand.

Article 30:

First: No person shall be tried before any other Iraqi court for acts for which the Court, in accordance with Articles 300 and 301 of the Iraqi Criminal Procedure Code, has already tried him or her.

Second: A person, who has been tried by any Iraqi court for acts constituting crimes within the jurisdiction of the Court, may not be subsequently tried by the Court except if the Court determines that the previous court proceedings were not impartial or independent, or were designed to shield the accused from criminal responsibility. When decisions are made for a retrial, one of the conditions contained in Article 196 of the Iraqi Civil Procedure Code and Article (303) of the Iraqi Criminal Procedure Code must be met.

Third: In determining the penalty to be imposed on a person convicted of a crime under the present Statute, the Court shall take into account the time served of any penalty imposed by an Iraqi court on the same person for the same crime.

Article 31:

First: The President of the Court, the Judges, the Court's Investigative Judges, the Public Prosecutors, the Director of the Administration Department and their staffs shall have immunity from civil suits in respect to their official functions.

Second: Other persons, including the accused, required at the seat of the Court shall be accorded such treatment as is necessary for the proper functioning of the Court.

Article 32

Arabic shall be the official language of the Court.

Article 33

No person who was previously a member of the disbanded Ba'ath Party shall be appointed as a judge, investigative judge, public prosecutor, an employee or any of the personnel of the Court.

Article 34

The expenses of the Court shall be borne by the State's general budget.

Article 35

The President of the Court shall prepare and submit an annual report on the Court activities to the Council of Ministers.

Article 36

The provisions of the civil service law No. (24) of 1960, Personnel law No. (25) of 1960, government and socialist sector employees disciplinary law No (14) of 1991 and civil pension law No.(33) of 1966 shall apply to the court's employees other than the judges and members of public prosecution.

Article 37

Law No. 1 for the year 2003 the Iraqi High Tribunal and the Rules of Procedure and Evidence issued in accordance with the provisions of Article (16) thereof are revoked from the date this statute comes into force.

Article 38

All decisions and Orders of Procedure issued under law No. 1 for the year 2003 are correct and conform to the law.

Article 39

The Council of Ministers in coordination with the President of the Court shall issue instructions to facilitate the implementation of this statute.

Article 40

This law shall come into force on the date of its publication in the Official Gazette.

Jalal Talabani Adil Abdul-Mahdi Ghazi Ajil Al-Yawir

President of the Republic Vice-President Vice-President

Justifying Reasons

In order to expose the crimes committed in Iraq from July 17, 1968 until May 1, 2005 against the Iraqi people and the peoples of the region and the subsequent savage massacres, and for laying down the rules and punishments to condemn after a fair trial the perpetrators of such crimes for waging wars, mass extermination and crimes against humanity, and for the purpose of forming an Iraqi national high criminal court from among Iraqi judges with high experience, competence and integrity to specialize in trying these criminals.

And in order to reveal the truth and the agonies and injustice caused by the perpetrators of such crimes, and for protecting the rights of many Iraqis and alleviating injustice and for demonstrating heaven's justice as envisaged by the Almighty God....

This law has been legislated.

English Translation of the Iraqi High Tribunal Rules of Procedure and Evidence

Justice is the Foundation of Governance

Al-Waqa'I Al-Iraqiya
The official Gazette of Iraq •

Rules of Procedure and Evidence
Of the Iraqi High Tribunal

No 4006 Ramadan 14, 1426 Hijri 47th year
October 18, 2005

Iraqi High Tribunal
Rules of Procedure and Evidence

Pursuant to the provisions of article 16, law No.10 of 2005, which was approved by article 48, transitional administrative law (TAL), it was decided to promulgate the following rules of procedure and evidence:

Part One
Definitions and general provisions

Rule 1: Definitions
In these Rules, unless the context otherwise requires, the following terms shall have the meanings ascribed to them below:
  1) Law: The Law No.10, 2005 of the Iraqi High Tribunal
  2) Judge: An Appellate Judge, Trial Judge or Investigative Judge.
  3) President: The President of the Iraqi High Tribunal.
  4) Appellate Judge: Any judge of the Appeals Chamber.
  5) Chief justice: The chief Judge of the Iraqi High Tribunal as referred to in the Law.
  6) Chief investigative judge: the chief investigative judge of the Tribunal.

7) Investigative Judge: The appointed judge.

8) Public Prosecution: The Prosecution appointed in the Tribunal.

9) Chief Prosecutor: The Chief Prosecutor as referred to in the Law.

10) Public prosecutor: The appointed prosecutor in the Tribunal.

11) Non-Iraqi Judges: Those Judges appointed pursuant to this law.

12) Experts: Those non-Iraqi nationals referred to in the Law.

13) Victim: A person against whom a crime over which the Special Tribunal has jurisdiction has allegedly or has been found to have been committed.

14) Suspect: A person concerning whom the Investigative Judge possesses reliable information which tends to show that he may have committed a crime over which the Special Tribunal has jurisdiction.

15) Operation: A number of acts or omissions, occurring as one event or a number of events, at the same or different locations, and are part of a common scheme, strategy or plan.

16) Investigation: All activities undertaken under the Law and these Rules for the collection of information and evidence, before or after issuing an indictment.

Rule 2: Measures taken outside the Tribunal

An investigative court or Judge may exercise its function outside Iraq, when necessary by a permission of the President. In so doing, audio or video-link technology, email or other available electronic instruments may be used; the Tribunal shall take the appropriate measures to apply this rule.

Rule 3: Non-compliance with the Rules

First: Objections on the ground of non-compliance with the Law or these Rules should be raised by a party at the earliest opportunity. The court may grant relief if it finds that the alleged non-compliance is proven.

Second: The relief granted under this Rule shall be such remedy as the Special Tribunal considers appropriate to compliance with the fundamental principles of fairness.

Rule 4: Time Limits

First: Unless otherwise mentioned in the law or these rules that time shall run to take any measure, a normal rules set forth in Iraqi laws shall be adopted.

Second: Unless otherwise ordered by a criminal court, any response to a motion must be filed within 14 days of the date of service of such motion on the responding party. Any reply to the response must be filed within 7 days of the date of service of the response.

Part Two
Cooperation and Judicial Assistance

<u>Rule 5</u>: Solicitations and Orders

Where an Investigative Judge is satisfied that an appointed government official or other individual has failed to comply with a request made in accordance with Article 18, he may take legal action against him and refer the matter to the Iraqi High Tribunal pursuant to the provisions of the Criminal procedures law.

Part Two
Organization of The Special Tribunal

Section One
The oath

<u>Rule 6</u>: Forms of the oath

<u>First</u>: The judges

All the judges shall take the oath before the president of the Federal Judicial Council as following:

"I swear by God to judge among the people with justice and to apply the law honestly"

<u>Second</u>: public prosecutors

Before starting their duties, all public prosecutors shall take the following oath before the president of the Federal Judicial Council:" I swear by God to perform the functions of my position and to apply the law honestly and loyally"

<u>Third</u>: Judicial investigators

Before starting their duties, judicial investigators shall take the following oath before the cassation panel:

"I swear by God to perform the functions of my position with justice and to apply the law honestly"

<u>Fourth</u>: The report of taking the oath should be kept in the records of the tribunal.

Section Two
The Judges

<u>Rule 7</u>:

<u>First</u>: Each Judge shall act independently and shall not be submitted to or response to the instructions or the directions issued by the presidency of the republic or the cabinet or from any other Governmental Department, or from any other source in his judicial functions.

Second: During an investigation, trial or appeal, Judges must perform their duties with impartiality.

Third: A Judge may not sit in any case in which he has a personal interest or concerning which he has or has had any personal association which might affect his impartiality.

Fourth: A Judge must withdraw from any case in which his impartiality or independence may reasonably be doubted.

Fifth: The President may assign another Trial Judge to sit in place of the withdrawn Trial Judge as necessary. The Chief Investigative Judge may assign another Investigative Judge to sit in place of the withdrawn Investigative Judge as necessary.

Rule 8:

Any party may file a request to the cassation panel, boosted by a legal evidence, for the disqualification of a Judge; the request must be answered within three days.

Rule 9: Absence and Termination of Service of Judges

First: Judges of the Special Tribunal shall perform their duties from the time they take their oath until such time as they are disqualified from holding office at the Special Tribunal or replaced by another Judge due to an expiration of the judge's term in office.

Second: A Judge who decides to resign shall give notice of his resignation in writing to the President, who shall forward such resignation to the cabinet of ministers.

Third: If a Trial Judge, for any reason, is unable to continue sitting in a case, the chief justice may, as appropriate, designate a judge to hear the case.

Rule 10: Seniority

First: Seniority of Judges appointed on different dates shall be decided according to the dates of their appointment. Judges appointed on the same date shall be decided according to age.

Second: In case of re-appointment, the total period of service as a Judge of the Special Tribunal shall be taken into account in deciding his seniority.

Third: All Judges are equal in the perform of their judicial functions, regardless of dates of appointment, age, period in service or nationality.

Section Three
The Presidency

Rule 11: The Vice-Presidency

The Vice-Presidency shall be delegated to the most senior Judge among the r members of the Cassation Panel.

<u>Rule 12</u>: Temporary replacements of the president and Vice-president.

If neither the President nor the Vice-President can carry out the functions of the Presidency, the next most senior judge in line shall assume, then the next, until the President or the Vice-President can carry out the function again, or until an alternative president is elected.

Section Four
Director of the Administration Department

<u>Rule 13</u>: Staff of the Administration Department

The Director shall assume appointing its annual staff as maybe required to perform administrative functions efficiently, such staff is a subject to the discussion and approval of the plenary body of the court.

<u>Rule 14</u>: Functions of the director of the administration department

(A) The Director of the Administration Department shall offer assistance to the Courts, the Plenary Meetings of the Special Tribunal, the Judges, the Prosecutors, and the Defense Office in the performance of their functions. The Director shall be responsible before the President for the administration and services of the Special Tribunal.

(B) The Director of the administration department, in the execution of his functions, may make oral or written statements to the Courts on any issue arising in the context of a specific case which affects or may affect the discharge of such functions, including that of implementing judicial decisions, he should take decisions necessary for notifying the parties where necessary.

(C) The Director is responsible for the conditions of detention of the accused. The Director, mindful of the need to ensure respect for human rights and fundamental freedoms, particularly the presumption of innocence prior to proof of conviction. He should be in consultation with the President to take necessary action or adopt and amend rules necessary to govern the detention of persons awaiting trial or appeal or otherwise detained in relation to proceedings that regulate detention of persons.

<u>Rule 15</u>: Victims and Witnesses Unit

<u>First</u>: The Director shall set up a Victims and Witnesses Unit which assumes specific functions, in accordance with the Statute and these Rules, and to implement orders of the Chief Investigation Judges and the Prosecutor General. This unit performs the following functions with respect to all witnesses and victims who appear before the Special Tribunal and others who are at risk because of testimony given by such witnesses. The following are among the functions performed by the unit for all victims and witnesses in accordance with their particular needs and circumstances:

(i) Provide recommendation to the Special Tribunal the regarding protection and security measures for victims and witnesses;

(ii) Provide the victims and witnesses with adequate protective measures and security arrangements, and establish long and short term plans and ensure development of plans for their protection and support;

(iii) Ensure that the victims and witnesses receive appropriate support, consultation and other appropriate medical assistance, physical and psychological rehabilitation, especially in cases of rape and sexual assault.

Second: The Unit staff shall include experts in trauma (or injuries) including trauma related to crimes of sexual violence. Where appropriate, the Unit shall cooperate with non-governmental and international governmental organizations.

Rule 16: Minutes of the Plenary Meetings

The Director and the administrative staff shall be responsible for taking minutes of the Plenary Meetings of the Special Tribunal and instructions of the Presiding Judge.

Section Five
The Chief Prosecutor

Rule 17: Selection of the Chief Prosecutor and his deputy

First: Subject to (Rule 9/fourth) of the law, the Chief Prosecutor and his deputy shall be selected for a term of one year. The Chief Prosecutor and his deputy may be re-selected.

Second: If the Chief Prosecutor ceases to be a Prosecutor, resigns, or is removed from his office before the expiration of his term, other appointed prosecution members shall select a replacement from among their number, in accordance with Article 9 (4) of the law for the remainder of the term.

Section Six
The Investigative Judges

Rule 18: Selection of the Chief Investigative Judge

First: The Chief Investigative Judge and his deputy shall be selected by a majority of the votes of the Investigative Judges. In the event that an equal number of votes are cast for the leading candidates, the candidate who has seniority according to Rule 10 of these rules will become the Chief Investigative Judge.

Second: The Chief Investigative Judge shall be elected for a term of one year. The Chief Investigative Judge may be re-elected for a subsequent term.

Third: If the Chief Investigative Judge ceases to be an Investigative Judge, resigns, or is removed from his office before the expiration of his term, the Investigative Judges shall elect from among their number a successor for the remainder of the term.

Rule 19: Functions of the Chief Investigative Judge

First: The Chief Investigative Judge shall coordinate the work of the Investigative Judges and exercise all the other functions conferred on him by the Statute and these Rules.

Second: The Chief Investigative Judge may after consultation with other Investigative Judges issue guidelines, consistent with the Statute and these Rules.

Rule 20: Functions of the Deputy Chief Investigative Judge

The Deputy Chief Investigative Judge shall exercise the functions of the Chief Investigative Judge in case the latter is absent or is unable to act.

Part Four
Non Iraqi Advisors/ Experts

Rule 21: Functions of Non-Iraqi Advisors/Experts

First: Non-Iraqi Advisors/Experts, appointed in accordance with the Statute, will be assigned to the Prosecution, Investigative Judges, the Trial Chambers and the Appeals. Each is a separate functional area. Anyone who is assigned as a Non-Iraqi Advisor/Expert to one functional area of the Special Tribunal may not concurrently act as an advisor to another functional area of the Special Tribunal. A Non-Iraqi Advisor/Expert may be reassigned from one functional area into another with the consent of the President. In the event of reassignment, Non-Iraqi Advisor/Expert may not take any part in providing advice in relation to a case in which that he previously participated in prior to reassignment.

Second: With the consent of the president, The Director shall provide the Non-Iraqi Advisors/Experts with all such access and facilities as required for them to fulfill their functions.

Third: Non-Iraqi Advisors/Experts appointed to the Defense Office under Rule 30 of these rules shall offer assistance for the administration of the Defense Office, including providing advice on any proposed amendments to these Rules or to any Rules related to code of Professional Conduct. They may not take any action that would involve them in any form of attorney-client relationship with a suspect or accused in any proceedings before the Tribunal.

Fourth: Any Non-Iraqi Advisor/Expert who is assigned to the Investigative Judges, a Trial Chamber or the Appeals Chamber will provide nonpartisan, confidential, non-binding expert advice and recommendations. Any Non-Iraqi Advisor/Expert assigned to the Prosecution Department or Defense Office will provide confidential, non-binding expert advice and recommendations.

Part Five
Investigations and Rights of The Accused

Section One
Initiation of Investigation

Rule 22: Initiation of an Investigation

First: Criminal proceedings under article 18 of this Statute are initiated by oral or written complaint filed to the Chief Investigative Judge.

Second: Such complaints may be filed to investigative judge of the Special Tribunal by Iraqi Ministries, government offices, investigative officers, or, international organizations, or any other appropriate agency or organization at the Iraqi High Tribunal.

Section Two
Investigation

Rule 23: Conduct Investigation

First: In the conduct of an investigation, an Investigative Judge may:

A- Review witness statements, summon and question suspects, interview victims and witnesses and record their statements, collect evidence and conduct on-site investigations;

B- Take all measures deemed necessary for the investigation, including special measures to ensure the safety of potential witness and sources;

C- Seek, with the concurrence of the Chief Investigative Judge, the assistance of any governmental agency or relevant international body including the International Criminal Police Organization (INTERPOLE);

D- Submit an application for deferral in accordance with the provocations of the law.

Second: An Investigation Judge shall collect the evidence of innocence. The prosecution may view all the evidences gathered by the Investigative Judge during his investigation.

Third: An Investigative Judge shall question the witness and the victims separate from public, with due consideration given to the provisions of the Criminal Procedures Code No. 23 for the year 1971 (amended). But this rule does not prohibit a suspect's Defense counsel from individuals interviewing witnesses and victims with undisclosed identities. A suspect or Defense counsel may provide evidence to an Investigation Judge. A suspect or Defense counsel may request an Investigative Judge to conduct any relevant and material witness interviews.

Rule 24: Provisional Measures

First: An Investigation Judge may order any relevant governmental authority to implement the order if he deems accordingly appropriate.

A. To arrest and place the suspect him in provisional detention in accordance with the IHT Statute and these Rules and such other provisions of Iraqi law as may be relevant;

B. To seize all physical evidence.

C. To take appropriate measures to prevent the escape of a suspect, an accused or without injury or intimidation of a victim or witness, or the destruction or the loss of evidence. An Investigative Judge must refer in this written order to the grounds on while he relied as well as to state the primary accusation along of a briefing with the foundation she relied on if he didn't want to question the suspect only. The Investigative Judge must specify the initial period for the temporary detention of the suspect.

If the accused was notified with this order, he must be informed of his rights as determined in this article and must be provided as soon as possible with a copy of the Investigative Judge's order.

Second: In deciding whether to issue such an order, the Investigative Judge must consider the following:

A. The existence of a reliable body of evidence that can be relied on and which shows that the suspect may have committed a crime within the jurisdiction of the Iraqi High Tribunal.

B. The conviction that the provisional detention is a necessary measure to prevent the escape of the suspect without injury to or intimidation of a victim or witness or the destruction or the loss of evidence.

C. The conviction that the provisional detention is necessary for the success of the investigation.

Third: The suspect must be released if:

A subsequent order issued by the Investigative Judge or the Iraqi High Tribunal dictates as such.

Rule 25: Provisional Detention Orders

First:

1. Initially no accused may be subject to a provisional detention period exceeding (90) days starting from the day following the suspect

placement in any detention unit of the Iraqi High Tribunal. The period of detention may be extended, by subsequent order by the Competent Judge, for an additional (30) day period extendable for the same periods but may not exceed (180) days in total.

2. The extension for the period that to exceed (180) days shall be ordered by the Competent Judge after receiving the consent of the President.

3. The decisions mentioned in paragraphs (first and second) above are appeal able.

<u>Second</u>: The provisions of the two paragraphs (35) and (36) of these rules shall be applied to the execution of the provisional detention of the suspect.

<u>Third</u>: The suspect shall be brought without delay, before the Investigative Judge who made the initial detention order, or before another Investigative Judge assigned by the Chief Investigative Judge. The Investigative Judge must be convicted that the right of the accused to counsel is respected. The accused has the right to be represented at his own expense by any Defense Counsel who is qualified under Rule (29) of these Rules. If the accused demanded from the Principle Defense to provide him with a Defense Counsel, the Investigative Judge must inquire into the accused's ability to pay for legal services and instruct the Defense Office to provide a Defense Counsel to the accused. The Defense Office shall charge the accused for any legal services provided; unless, a Trial Chamber Judge finds that the accused is indigent.

<u>Four</u>: With due consideration to Rules 59, an accused may be detained until the conclusion of his trial if necessary to ensure the accused's appearance at trial, or to protect any victim or witness, or to prevent the destruction or the loss of any evidence.

<u>Rule 26</u>: Preservation of Information and Evidence

<u>First</u>: The Investigative Judge, prosecutor or investigator shall send a copy of the information and physical evidence to the evidence and information collection unit that belongs to the tribunal. This unit must preserve the information and evidence received.

<u>Second</u>: The Investigative Judge must draw up an inventory of all materials seized, including documents, books, papers, and other objects, and must provide a copy thereof to the individual from whom the materials were seized. Materials that are of no evidentiary value must be inventoried and safeguarded until such time they can be returned.

<u>Third</u>: In a case the criminal court requests documents from the aforementioned unit, the unit must provide a secured place for their storage and transportation.

<u>Rule 27</u>: Rights of the Suspect during Questioning by an Investigative Judge
  <u>First</u>: A suspect who is questioned by an Investigative Judge shall have the following rights of which he must be informed by the Investigative Judge prior to questioning in a language he speaks and understands:
  A. The right to legal assistance of his own choosing, including the right to have legal assistance provided by the Defense Office if he does not have sufficient means to pay for it;
  B. The right to free interpreting assistance of if he cannot understand or speak the language used in questioning;
  C. The right to remain silent. In this regard, the suspect or accused must be cautioned that any statement he makes may be used against him in court.
  <u>Second</u>: An accused may voluntarily waive his right to legal assistance during questioning if the Investigative Judge determines that the waiver is voluntarily and knowingly made.
  <u>Third</u>: If an accused has exercised his right to legal assistance, questioning by an Investigative Judge may not be performed without the presence of counsel if the accused did not _____ his right, willingly and knowingly for the presence of his counsel. In a case of the waiver, if the accused later expressed his will to have legal assistance, accordingly the questioning must stop accordingly and must not resume except with the presence of counsel.
<u>Rule 28</u>: Recording the questioning of accused by an Investigative Judge
  If the Investigative Judge questioned the accused, he may record that questioning by audio, video or via a court reporter.

Section 3
Defense Counsel

<u>Rule 29</u>: Appointment of defense Counsel
  <u>First</u>: A Counsel engaged by an accused must file his power of attorney with the concerned Judge at the earliest opportunity. The judge must verify qualification of the counsel in accordance with the Iraqi law of lawyers.
  <u>Second</u>: In accordance with Articles 18(Third) and 20(Fourth) of the Statute, of the Iraqi High Tribunal an accused may consign one or more non-Iraqi counsel.
  <u>Third</u>: In the performance of his duties, a counsel must adhere by the relevant provisions whether they are of the Tribunal Statute, these Rules or any other rules or regulations adopted by the Special Tribunal. In addition, he must adhere by any codes of practice and ethics governing his profession.

Rule 30: Defense Office

First: The Director of the Administration Department. shall establish a Defense Office for the purpose of ensuring the rights of the accused. The Defense Office shall be headed by a Director from among the lawyers for a period of three years that is extendable. After conducting an appropriate investigation and getting the approval of the president, the Director may remove the Principal defense lawyer for good cause.

Second: The Defense Office, in accordance with the Statute of the Tribunal and these Rules, shall provide advice and assistance to:

A. The accused placed in provisional detention in accordance with Rule (22) of these Rules.

B. The accused being questioned by an Investigative Judge in accordance with Rule (27) including non-custodial questioning.

C. Accused persons before the Special Tribunal.

Third: The following are the function performed by the defense office.

A. Legal assistance to any accused who does not have sufficient means to pay or it, or as ordered by the Special Tribunal;

B. Assign or appoint a counsel locked within a reasonable proximity for the detention unit and the head of the Special Tribunal, to report the detention unit when summoned to provide legal assistance to a suspect or accused.

C. Adequate facilities to enable the counsel to use in the preparation of the Defense.

Fourth: The head of the defense office must, in providing for an effective Defense, select a highly qualified criminal Defense counsel.

Fifth: Defense Counsel must present his requests and his defense adequately.

Sixth:

A. In accordance with Rule 21 (Third) of these Rules and with the nominating by the head of the defense office, the Director may contract with Non-Iraqi Advisors and Experts to provide assistance and expertise to the Defense Office.

B. Non-Iraqi Advisors/Experts shall be selected based upon their criminal law experience in their respective countries, and should have extensive knowledge or experience in international war crimes trials and such Advisors/Experts must be of high moral character and integrity.

Rule 31: Misconduct of Counsel

First: A Judge or a Criminal Court may impose legal proceedings against counsel if, in its opinion, the Council's conduct becomes offensive or abusive or demeans the dignity and decorum of the Special Tribunal or obstructs the proceedings.

<u>Second</u>: A Judge or a Criminal Court may, with the approval of the President of the Court, communicate any misconduct of the Counsel to the professional body regulating the conduct of counsel in his State of admission

Part Six
Investigation Judge Proceedings

Section One
Multiplicity of Crimes.

<u>Rule 32</u>: Multiplicity of Crimes.

(A) The provisions of Article 132 of the Iraqi Criminal Procedure Law no. (23) Of 1971 should be applied in case of accused is alleged to have committed multiple crimes.

(B) Only one crime can be indicted in case of accused is alleged to have committed multiple crimes if those crimes are punishable pursuant to one article in one law.

<u>Rule 33</u>: Non-Disclosure of Indictment

(A) In exceptional circumstances and in the interests of justice, a Designated Judge may order the non-disclosure to the public of any documents or information until further order.

(B) A Criminal Court or Designated Judge may order that there be no disclosure of an indictment, or part thereof, or of all or any part of any particular document or information, if satisfied that the making of such an order is required to give effect to a provision of these Rules, to protect confidential information obtained by the Investigative Judge or the Chief Investigative Judge, or is otherwise in the interests of justice.

Section Two
Orders and Warrants

<u>Rule 34</u>: General Provisions

<u>First</u>: At the request of either party or the request of the complainant, an Investigative Judge may issue such orders, summons, subpoenas, and warrants as may be necessary in the interests of justice for the purposes of an investigation.

<u>Second</u>: At the request of either party or initially at the request of the complainant, a Designated Judge or a Criminal court may issue such orders, summons, subpoenas and warrants as may be necessary for the purposes of bringing the accused or the conduct of the trial.

Rule 35: Executions of Arrest Warrants

First: Pursuant to Rule 24, a warrant of arrest shall be signed by an Investigative Judge and shall bear the seal of the Special Tribunal. It shall be accompanied by a copy of the alleged criminal act, the legal article or the indictment, and a statement of the rights of the suspect or the accused. The Director shall transmit to the relevant authorities of Iraq three sets of certified copies of these documents.

Second: With due consideration given to the provisions of Rule 24, the Director of the Administrative Department shall request the following from the said Iraqi authorities:

A- To execute the arrest of the accused or the suspect and his transfer to the Court.

B- To serve a set of the aforementioned documents upon the suspect or the accused and cause the documents to be read to the accused in a language understood by him and to caution him as to his rights in that language; and.

C- To return a copy of the documents together with proof of service to the Iraqi High Tribunal.

Rule 36: Failure to Execute a Warrant of Arrest

First: When the competent authorities, to whom a warrant of arrest or orders under Rule 24 or others have been transferred, are unable to execute the warrant of arrest, they shall submit a report to the Director of the Administrative Department, stating the reasons for non-execution.

Second: If within a reasonable time after the delivery of the warrant of arrest or other orders to the relevant Iraqi authorities, no report is made on action taken, this shall be deemed a failure to execute the warrant of arrest and the orders. Upon his own initiative or at the request of an Investigative Judge, the Presiding Judge of a Criminal Court may refer the failure to the President of the Tribunal for appropriate action.

Rule 37: Procedure upon Guilty Plea

First: If an accused pleads guilty or requests to change his plea to guilty, the Criminal Court shall satisfy itself that:

A- The plea is made freely and voluntarily;

B- The plea is unequivocal; and there is a sufficient factual basis to establish the accused's culpability for the crime.

Second: Thereafter the Criminal Court may find him guilty in case the provisions mentioned in First of this Article are available and when the Criminal Court is satisfied to incriminate the accused regarding the action to which he actually pled guilty, the Criminal Court may enter a finding of guilt and set a date for the sentencing hearing.

Third:

A- If the Criminal Court is not satisfied as to any of the factors in subparagraph (First) above, or if, under applicable law, the is punishable by death, then the Criminal court shall enter a plea of not guilty and the case shall proceed to trial.

B- If the Criminal Court accepted the accused not guilty plea to an punishable by death and such answer is pursuant to Rule (38) and that the Prosecutor General is recommending a less severe sentence than the death penalty, and then the Criminal Court shall end the trial and issue the decision.

Rule 38: Agreements upon Guilty Plea

The pardon should be offered to the accused in ambiguous crimes in accordance with article 129 of Iraqi Criminal Procedure Law no.23 of 1971

Rule 39: Detention and bail

The detention and the bail should be in accordance with criminal proceedings law No.23 of 1971 provided that the accused shall be detained in the prison facilities of the Special Tribunal

Section Three
Production of Evidence

Rule 40: Disclosure of the Crime Materials by the Public Prosecutor

First: Pursuant to the provisions of Rule 33 and 51, the Prosecutor shall:

A- Disclose to the defense lawyer, at least 45 days prior to the commencement of trial, copies of the statements of all witnesses and all evidence. For purposes of this Sub-Rule, a "statement" of witnesses should be written statement signed, adopted, and approved by the accused, or a substantially verbatim recital of an oral statement made by the witnesses that was recorded contemporaneously with the making of the oral statement. The Criminal Court may order that additional copies of the statements of witnesses be made available to the Defense within a prescribed time.

B- At the request of the Defense, and pursuant to Rule (42), the Defense is permitted to inspect any books, documents, photographs and acquire these things, which are material to the preparation of the Defense, and also inspect any books, categories of, or specific documents, photographs and tangible objects in the accused custody or control which are intended for use by the Criminal Court as evidence at the trial.

Second: During the investigation and when informing the Prosecutor about the documents and information, the disclosure of which may prejudice further or ongoing investigations, or for any other reason may be contrary to the public interest or affect the general security interests of any State, the Prosecutor may apply to a Designated Judge sitting ex parte in private to be relieved from the obligation to disclose pursuant to Sub-Rule (A) of this Article. When making such an action the Public Prosecutor shall provide the information or materials that are sought to be kept confidential.

Rule 41: Reciprocal Disclosure of Evidence

First: Regarding reciprocal disclosure of evidence, the following should be done:

A- At least 45 days prior to the commencement of trial, the Prosecutor shall notify the Defense of the names of the witnesses that he intends to call to establish the guilt of the accused.

B- The Prosecutor shall be notified by the Defense of the names of the witnesses that the defense intends to call in rebuttal of any guilt of which the Prosecutor has received notice in accordance with Sub-Rule (Third) (A) of this Article, or any guilt in the Case Statement duration served under item (3) of (C) of this paragraph

C- At least 15 days prior to the commencement of the trial, the Defense shall notify the following to the Prosecutor before the trial commencement:

1. A defense of alibi, in which case the notification shall specify the place at which the accused claims to have been present at the time of the alleged crime and the names and addresses of witnesses and any other evidence upon which the accused intends to rely to establish the alibi;

2. Any special defense, including that of diminished or lack of mental responsibility, in which case the notification shall specify the names and addresses of witnesses and any other evidence upon which the accused intends to rely to establish the special defense;

3. In cases of sexual assault, to prove or demonstrate the case of the victim consent to the alleged acts committed by the accused;

4. Any books, documents, photographs, or tangible evidence, to be introduced at trial shall be provided to the Prosecutor to inspect or to copy.

D- At least 15 days prior to the commencement of the trial, the Defense shall notify the Prosecutor of the names of the defense witnesses that he intends to call.

Second: Failure of the Defense to provide such information under this Rule shall not preclude the accused from relying on the above defenses, at the discretion of the Special Tribunal.

<u>Third</u>: To assist the Prosecutor with his disclosure obligations pursuant to these rules, the Defense shall, at least 15 days prior to trial, provide the Prosecutor with a Defense Case Statement which should:

    A. Set out in general terms the nature of the defense of the accused.

    B. Indicate every matter on which he asked the prosecutor to take measure.

    C. State, in the case of each such matter, the reason why the prosecution took measure.

<u>Fourth</u>: If either party discovers additional evidence or information or materials which should have been produced earlier pursuant to these Rules, that party shall promptly notify the other party and the Trial Chamber of the existence of the additional evidence or information or materials.

Rule 42: Disclosure of Exculpatory Evidence

<u>First</u>: In extraordinary circumstances, according to a request of either party, and in the interest of justice, the trial Chamber or the chief of investigation judges may delegate one of the members or investigation judges of the tribunal to hear the testimony of the witness and organize a minuet for it.

<u>Second</u>: the Prosecutor shall disclose to the defense lawyer the existence of evidence known to the Prosecutor which in any way tend to suggest the innocence or mitigate the guilt of the accused or may affect the credibility of a prosecution witness or the authenticity of prosecution evidence. The Prosecutor shall disclose the grounds of the penalties continuously.

Rule 43: Matters not Subject to Disclosure

<u>First</u>: With due consideration given to the provisions of Rules 40 and 41, the reports, memoranda, or other internal documents submitted by a party, its assistants or representatives in connection with the investigation or preparation of the case, are not subject to disclosure or notification under the aforementioned provisions.

<u>Second</u>: If the tribunal is in possession of information which was provided to it, on a confidential basis and which has been used solely for the purpose of generating new evidence, that initial information and its origin — notwithstanding Rule 42 — shall not be disclosed by the tribunal without the consent of the person or entity providing the initial information.

<u>Third</u>: If, after obtaining the written consent of the person or entity providing information under this Sub-Rule (Second), the Prosecutor elects to present as evidence any testimony, document or other material so provided, the accused shall receive prior disclosure consistent with Rule 42. The Trial Chamber may not order either party to produce additional evidence received from a person or entity providing the initial information,

nor may the Trial Chamber for the purpose of obtaining such additional evidence itself summon that person or a representative of that entity as a witness or order their attendance.

<u>Fourth</u>: The right of the accused to challenge the evidence presented in the case shall remain unaffected subject only to the limitations contained in Sub-Rules (Third) and (Fourth) above.

Section Four
Depositions

<u>Rule 44</u>: Depositions

With due consideration given to provisions of rule (28) and at the request of either party, a Trial Chamber may, and in the interest of justice, order that a deposition be taken outside the court. The Trial Chamber shall delegate one of its judges or an investigative judge to preside over the writing of the deposition, and organize a record for it.

Part Seven
Proceedings of the Trial Chambers

Section One
General Provisions

<u>Rule 45</u>: Proceedings before Trial Chambers

Trial proceedings should comply with the provisions set forth in the Iraqi Criminal Procedure Law No.23 of 1971 and these rules.

<u>Rule 46</u>: Interveners

A Chamber may, if it considers it helpful for the proper determination of the case, invite any organization or person to make submissions on any issue specified by the Chamber.

<u>Rule 47</u>: Medical Examination of the Accused

A Trial Chamber may, or at the request of a party, order a medical, including psychiatric or psychological examination of the accused.

<u>Rule 48</u>: Measures for the Protection of Victims and Witnesses

<u>First</u>: A Chamber may, on its own initiative, or at the request of either party, the victim or witness concerned, or the Victims and Witnesses Unit, order appropriate measures to safeguard the privacy and security of a victim or a witness, provided that those measures are consistent with the rights of the accused. A Chamber may order measures to protect a victim or witness before any indictment is confirmed or at any other time.

Second: A Chamber may hold proceedings in private to determine whether to order:

    (A) Measures to prevent disclosure to the public or the media of the identity or whereabouts of a victim or a witness, or of persons related to or associated with a victim or witness by such means as:

        (1) Expunging names and identifying information from the Iraqi High Tribunal's public records;

        (2) Non-disclosure to the public any records identifying the victim or witness;

        (3) Not allowing he testimony o be photographed or voice-altering devices or closed circuit television, video link or other similar technologies; and

    (B) Hold closed sessions in accordance with Rule 71;

Third: A Chamber shall control the manner of questioning a witness to avoid any harassment or intimidation.

Fourth: When making a decision under Sub-Rule (First), a Chamber may wherever appropriate state whether the transcript of those proceedings relating to the witness shall be made available for use in other proceedings before the Special Tribunal.

Fifth: Once protective measures have been ordered in any proceedings before the Special Tribunal, such protective measures shall continue to have effect unless it needs to be changed in any subsequent proceedings before the Special Tribunal or rescinded, varied or augmented in accordance with the procedure set out in Sub-Rule (Seventh).

Sixth: In the case of subsequent protective measures, their variation or augmentation from those taken earlier, the following must applied:

    (A) The same protection continues in every trial chamber however constituted.

    (B) In case of an earlier protection discontinues, the trial chamber may stay the subsequent protection.

Seventh: Before determining an application under Sub-Rule (Sixth), the Chamber retaining of the subsequent protective measures shall obtain all relevant information from the earlier protection, and may consult with any Judge who ordered the protective measures.

Eighth: References in this Rule to a "Chamber" shall include "the Judge of that Chamber or a designated judge".

Rule 49: Solemn Declaration by Interpreters and Translators

Before performing any duties, an interpreter or a translator or an expert shall solemnly declare to do so faithfully, independently, impartially and with full respect for the duty of confidentiality.

Rule 50: Open Sessions

All proceedings before a Trial Chamber shall be open to public. Photography, video, or audio broadcasting or recording of proceedings for public showing shall be prohibited, except when authorized by the Trial Chamber and for recordings made by the Iraqi High Tribunal pursuant to Rule 57. All deliberations of the Chamber shall be private (closed).

Rule 51: Closed Sessions

First: A Trial Chamber may order the press and the public for be excluded from all or part of a proceeding when:

A. Information prejudicial to national security of Iraq is disclosed; or

B. It is necessary for the security of the Special Tribunal; or

C. It is necessary to protect the privacy of persons, as in cases of sexual s or cases involving children or women.

D. Publicity would prejudice the interests of justice.

Second: Unless otherwise ordered by the Chamber, no person may disclose information related to a closed session.

Third: If in the opinion of another sovereign State, disclosure of information would compromise its national security the reasonable steps including closed sessions, shall be taken by the Chamber to ensure that legitimate national security interests of that State are not compromised. If the State remains concerned about its national security interests after the decision of the Chamber, then it may appeal the decision and any such appeal must be submitted within 7 days of the date of the decision and must be considered urgent. This appeal will not stop the proceeding of the trial

Rule 52: Control of Proceedings

First: The Trial Chamber may exclude any person from the proceedings in order to protect the right of the accused to a fair and public trial, or to maintain the dignity and decorum of the proceedings.

Second: The Trial Chamber may not order an accused to be removed from the court from during proceedings unless he acted in disruptively. In the event of renewal, the proceedings continue until he can be present and the court should make him aware of the proceedings he missed.

Rule 53: Records of Proceedings and Preservation of Evidence

First: The Administrative and Service Director shall preserve a full and accurate record of all proceedings, including audio recordings, transcripts and, when deemed necessary by the Trial Chamber, video recordings.

Second: The Trial Chamber may order the disclosure of all or part of the record of closed proceedings when the reasons for ordering the non-disclosure no longer exist.

Section Two
Proceedings

<u>Rule 54</u>: Joint and Separate Trials

The provisions of the Iraqi Criminal Procedure Law No.23 of 1971 should be applied regarding the joint and separate trials.

<u>Rule 55</u>: Instruments of Restraint

The accused shall be brought to the Court without instruments of restraint and all the necessary measures shall be taken to keep order in the Court room.

<u>Rule 56</u>: Commencement of Trial

Except where expressly required by the law or these Rules, the trial will generally be conducted in accordance with the procedures in Article 167 of the Iraqi Criminal Procedure Law No.23 of 1971

<u>Rule 57</u>: Presentation of Evidence

<u>First</u>: With due consideration given to the provisions of Article (168) of the Iraqi Criminal Procedure Law, questioning and cross examination of the witness shall be allowed for each case by the opponents to refute his statements. The party calling for testimony shall conduct questioning or examining the witnesses. After cross-examination, the party calling a witness shall conduct re-examination. A judge may at any stage put any question to the witness. The accused may not directly question any witness except through the Trial Chamber.

<u>Second</u>: Evidence may be given directly in court via communications media (including video or satellite channels as the Trial Chamber may order.

<u>Rule 58</u>: Judgment

<u>First</u>: The judgment shall be pronounced in public on its scheduled session.

<u>Second</u>: If the Trial Chamber issues a convicted judgment and punishment against the accused, the Trial Chamber may order the forfeiture of any property, proceeds or other assets acquired unlawfully or by criminal conduct in accordance with Articles 101 and 117 of the penal Code,No.111 of 1969.

<u>Third</u>: The judgment shall be rendered by a majority of the five Trial Judges assigned to the Trial Chamber that heard the case. It shall be accompanied by a reasoned opinion in writing. Separate or dissenting opinions may be appended with the file of the case.

Section Three
Rules of Evidence

Rule 59: General Provisions

First: A Chamber shall apply the rules of evidence set forth in these Rules as well as the rules set forth in the Iraqi Criminal Procedure Law No.23 of 1971, and shall not be bound by rules of evidence used in any other forum.

Second: In cases there is no applicable legal stipulation for evidence, a Criminal Court shall apply rules of evidence which will best favor a fair determination of the matter before it and are consonant with the spirit and general principles of the law.

Third: A Chamber may admit any relevant evidence which it deems to have probative value.

Fourth: A Chamber may exclude evidence if its probative value is substantially outweighed by the potential for unfair prejudice, considerations of undue delay, waste of time, or needless presentation of cumulative evidence.

Fifth: The following factors should be considered when determining the admissibility of evidence under this rule:

A. The authenticity of evidence obtained out of court;

B. The selection of any statement and any circumstances that might verify or impugn the statement;

C. The respect of other scopes to the extent its content benefit the corroboration of the evidence and its trustworthiness.

D. Whether the means by which the evidence obtained casts substantial doubt on its reliability.

Rule 60: Testimony of Witnesses

First: Witnesses may give evidence directly, or as described in Rule 60. A Chamber may consistent with Rule 59(Fourth), permit the testimony of witnesses by telephone, audiovisual means, or other means; however, the Chamber shall consider the ability to test the veracity of that testimony in evaluating the weight to be given to the witness's testimony.

Second: A witness aged 15 years, before giving evidence, makes the solemn oath that he will say the truth and nothing but the truth, where as the witness below this age can be heard just for awareness without an oath.

Rule 61: False Testimony

If a Chamber has strong grounds for believing that a witness may have knowingly and willfully given false testimony, the Chamber may request the investigations Chambers to take the legal procedures against him.

Rule 62: Testimony of Expert Witnesses

First: Testimony may be received from a witness qualified as an expert by knowledge, skill, experience, training, or education, who has scientific, technical, or other specialized knowledge that will assist the Trial Chamber to understand the evidence.

Second: If any party wishes to provide a written statement of an expert witness in lieu of oral testimony, the full statement of the witness shall be disclosed to the opposing party as early as practicable.

Rule 63: Rules of Evidence in Cases of Sexual Assault

First: In cases of sexual assault and if there is reasonable cause, no corroboration of the victim's testimony shall be required.

Second: Consent shall not be allowed as a defense if the victim

A. Has been subjected to or threatened with or has had reason to fear violence, duress, detention or psychological oppression, or reasonably believed to be the victim, submittance, threat or fear.

Third: The evidence submitted by the accused should prove the victim's consent without shortcomings.

Section Four
Sentencing Procedure

Rule 64: Status of the Acquitted Person

First: If, at the time the judgment of acquittal or release is pronounced, the Prosecutor advises the Trial Chamber in the same session of his intention to file notice of appeal within the legal duration and to produce appeal statement later, the Trial Chamber may issue an order for the continued detention of the accused, pending the determination of the appeal.

Second: In case of acquittal or release, when the prosecutor has no intention to appeal pursuant to sub-Rule (First) above, and there is no other case against the accused, the Tribunal shall order the release of the accused.

Rule 65: Penalties

First: In determining a sentence, the Trial Chamber shall take into consideration the factors mentioned in Article 24 of the law, as well as such factors as:

A. Any aggravating circumstances;

B. Any mitigating circumstances including the substantial cooperation with the Chief Prosecutor or an Investigative Judge by the convicted person before or after conviction; and

C. Apply provisions of Article 30 (3) of the law.

Second: The Trial Chamber shall indicate whether multiple sentences of imprisonment shall be served consecutively or concurrently.

<u>Third</u>: Credit shall be given to the convicted person for the period, if any, during which the convicted person was detained pending his surrender to the Iraqi High Tribunal or pending trial or appeal. Such credit shall not be given for the period, if any, during which the accused was detained pursuant to the detention authority of another sovereign unless that sovereign was acting solely at the bequest of the Iraqi council of ministers or the successor government, taking into consideration the date of resuming the sovereign in June 1,2004.

<u>Rule 66</u>: The judgment Implementation

<u>First</u>: the judgment shall be implemented in accordance with these rules and the provisions of Iraqi Criminal Procedure law No.23 of 1971.

<u>Second</u>: If, by a previous decision of the Trial Chamber, the convicted person has been provisionally released, or is otherwise at liberty, and he is not present when the judgment is pronounced, the Trial Chamber shall issue a warrant for his arrest. On arrest, he shall be notified of the conviction and sentence, and the procedure provided in Rule 68 and article 151 of the Iraqi Criminal Procedure law No. 23 of 1971 shall be followed.

<u>Rule 67</u>: Forfeiture of Property

With due consideration given to article (307) of the Iraqi Criminal Procedure law No. 23 of 1971 and paragraph 7 of article 24 of the Iraqi High Tribunal Statue after a judgment of conviction containing a specific finding as provided in Rule 58(Second), the Trial Chamber, at the request of the Prosecutor or at its own initiative, may hold a special hearing to determine the matter of property forfeiture mentioned in the previous article if it did not decide to forfeiture.

<u>Rule 68</u>: The Appeal

The appellate proceedings and the time limit for the appeal should be consistent with the Iraqi High Tribunal law and Iraqi Criminal Procedure law No.23 of 1971.

(A) The judgment of the investigation Judge can be appealed before the cassation panel within15 days starting from the date when the judgment being or consider being notified.

(B) The appeal before the cassation panel should be in accordance with Iraqi Criminal Procedure Law No. 23 of 1971.

<u>Rule 69</u>: The Re-Trial

The procedures of re-trial should be consistent with the Iraqi High Tribunal law and Iraqi Criminal Procedure law No.23 of 1971.

<u>Rule 70</u>:

These rules shall be deemed as an annex to the Iraqi High Special Tribunal Law No. (10) of 2005.

Iraqi High Tribunal Elements of Crimes

Section 1
General Introduction

1. Pursuant to Section l(4) of Coalition Provisional Authority Order No. 48, Delegation of Authority Regarding an Iraqi Special Tribunal, (CPA/ORD/10 DEC 2003/48), the following Elements of Crimes shall assist the Iraqi Special Tribunal in the interpretation and application of Articles 11, 12, 13, and 14 of the Statute of the Iraqi Special Tribunal ("Statute"). The provisions of the Statute are applicable to these Elements of Crimes.

2. Unless otherwise provided, a person shall be criminally responsible and liable for punishment for a crime within the jurisdiction of the Court only if the material elements are committed with intent and knowledge. Where no reference is made in the Elements of Crimes to a mental element for particular conduct, consequence, or circumstance it is understood that:

   (a) intent shall mean that the person either meant to engage in particular conduct, to cause a particular consequence, or was aware that a particular consequence would occur in the ordinary course of events and

   (b) knowledge shall mean awareness that a circumstance exists or a consequence will occur in the ordinary course of events. Exceptions to this standard are indicated below.

3. Existence of intent and knowledge can be inferred from relevant facts and circumstances.

4. With respect to mental elements associated with elements requiring a value judgment, such as those using the terms "inhumane", "widespread" or "severe", it is not necessary that the perpetrator personally completed a particular value judgment, unless otherwise indicated.

5. Grounds for excluding criminal responsibility or the absence thereof are generally not specified in the elements of crimes listed under each crime.

6. The requirement of "unlawfulness" found in the Statute or in other parts of international law, in particular international humanitarian law, is generally not specified in the elements of crimes.

7. The perpetrator may not raise a defense of diminished mental capacity for any offense under Articles 11, 12 and 13 of the Statute of the Special Tribunal. For these offenses, the issue of the perpetrator's diminished mental capacity is only relevant as a mitigating factor for sentencing.

8. As used in the Elements of Crimes, the term "perpetrator" is neutral as to guilt or innocence.

9. A particular conduct may constitute one or more crimes.

10. The use of short titles for the crimes specified in the Statute has no legal effect.

Section 2
The Crime of Genocide: Article 11

1. Introduction
a. For the last element of each crime, the term "in the context of'" would include the initial acts in an emerging pattern.

b. The term "manifest" is an objective qualification.

c. Notwithstanding the normal requirement for a mental element provided for in Section 1, paragraph 2 above, and recognizing that knowledge of the circumstances will usually be addressed in proving genocidal intent, the appropriate requirement, if any, for a mental element regarding this circumstance will need to be decided by the Court on a case-by-case basis.

2. Article 11(a)(1)
Genocide by Killing: Elements
a. The perpetrator killed or caused the death of one or more persons;

b. Such person or persons belonged to a particular national, ethnical, racial or religious group;

b. The perpetrator intended to destroy, in whole or in part, that national, ethnical, racial or religious group, as such; and

c. The conduct took place in the context of a manifest pattern of similar conduct directed against that group or was conduct that could itself effect such destruction.

3. Article 11(a)(2)
Genocide by Causing Serious Bodily or Mental Harm: Elements
a. The perpetrator caused serious bodily or mental harm to one or more persons-including, but not limited to, acts of torture, rape, sexual violence or inhuman or degrading treatment;

b. Such person or persons belonged to a particular national, ethnical, racial or religious group;

c. The perpetrator intended to destroy, in whole or in part, that national, ethnical, racial or religious group, as such; and

d. The conduct took place in the context of a manifest pattern of similar conduct directed against that group or was conduct that could itself effect such destruction.

4. Article 11(a)(3)
Genocide by Deliberately Inflicting Conditions of Life Calculated to Bring about Physical Destruction: Elements

a. The perpetrator inflicted certain conditions of life (including but not limited to deliberate deprivation of resources indispensable for survival, such as food or medical services, or systematic expulsion from homes) upon one or more persons;

b. Such person or persons belonged to a particular national, ethnical, racial or religious group;

c. The perpetrator intended to destroy, in whole or in part, that national, ethnical, racial or religious group, as such;

d. The conditions of life were calculated to bring about the physical destruction of that group, in whole or in part; and

e. The conduct took place in the context of a manifest pattern of similar conduct directed against that group or was conduct that could itself effect such destruction.

5. Article 11(a)(4)
Genocide by Imposing Measures Intended to Prevent Births: Elements

a. The perpetrator imposed certain measures upon one or more persons;

b. Such person or persons belonged to a particular national, ethnical, racial or religious group;

c. The perpetrator intended to destroy, in whole or in part, that national, ethnical, racial or religious group, as such;

d. The measures imposed were intended to prevent births within that group; and

e. The conduct took place in the context of a manifest pattern of similar conduct directed against that group or was conduct that could itself effect such destruction.

6. Article 11(a)(5)
Genocide by Forcibly Transferring Children: Elements

a. The perpetrator forcibly* transferred one or more persons;

b. Such person or persons belonged to a particular national, ethnical, racial or religious group;

c. The perpetrator intended to destroy, in whole or in part, that national, ethnical, racial or religious group, as such;

d. The transfer was from that group to another group;

e. The person or persons were under the age of 18 years;

f. The perpetrator knew, or should have known, that the person or persons were under the age of 18 years; and

g. The conduct took place in the context of a manifest pattern of similar conduct directed against that group or was conduct that could itself effect such destruction.

* The term "forcibly" as used throughout these Elements of Crimes is not restricted to physical force, but may include threat of force or coercion, such as that caused by fear of violence, duress, detention, psychological oppression or abuse of power, against such person or persons or another person, or by taking advantage of a coercive environment. However, the last element should not be interpreted as requiring proof that the perpetrator had knowledge of all characteristics of the attack or the precise details of the plan or policy of the State or organization. In the case of an emerging widespread or systematic attack against a civilian population, the intent clause of the last element indicates that this mental element is satisfied if the perpetrator intended to further such an attack

Section 3
Crimes against Humanity: Article 12

1. Introduction

a. The last two elements for each crime against humanity describe the context in which the conduct must take place. These elements clarify the requisite participation in and knowledge of a widespread or systematic attack against a civilian population.

b. "Attack direct against a civilian population" is understood to mean a course of conduct involving the multiple commission of acts referred to in article 12, paragraph 1, of the Statute against any civilian population, pursuant to or in furtherance of a State or organizational policy to commit such attack. The acts need not constitute a military attack. It is understood that "policy to commit such attack" requires that the State or organization actively promote or encourage such an attack against a civilian population.

c. A policy which has a civilian population as the object of the attack would be implemented by State or organizational action. Such a policy may, in exceptional circumstances, be implemented by a deliberate failure to take action, which is consciously aimed at encouraging such attack. The existence of such a policy cannot be inferred solely from the absence of governmental or organizational action.

2. Article 12(a)(1)
Murder: Elements

a. The perpetrator willfully killed one or more persons;

b. The conduct was committed as part of a widespread or systematic attack directed against a civilian population; and

c. The perpetrator knew that the conduct was part of or intended the conduct to be part of a widespread or systematic attack against a civilian population.

3. Article 12(a)(2)

Extermination: Elements

a. The perpetrator willfully killed, either directly or indirectly, one or more persons, including by inflicting conditions of life calculated to bring about the destruction of part of a population including, but not limited to, the deliberate deprivation of resources indispensable for survival, such as food or medical services, or systematic expulsion from homes;

b. The conduct constituted, or took place as part of (including the initial conduct of), a mass killing of members of a civilian population;

c. The coiiduct was committed as part of a widespread or systematic attack directed against a civilian population; and

d. The perpetrator knew that the conduct was part of or intended the conduct to be part of a widespread or systematic attack directed against a civilian population.

4. Article 12(a)(3)

Enslavement: Elements

a. The perpetrator willfully exercised any or all of the powers attaching to the right of ownership over one or more persons, such as by purchasing, selling, lending or bartering such a person or persons, by imposing on them a similar deprivation of liberty, in some circumstances, exacting false labor or otherwise reducing a person to a servile status as defined in the Supplementary Convention on the Abolition of Slavery, the Slave Trade, and Institutions and Practices Similar to Slavery of 1956, or the trafficking in persons, in particular women and children;

b. The conduct was committed as part of a widespread or systematic attack directed against a civilian population; and

c. The perpetrator knew that the conduct was part of or intended the conduct to be part of a widespread or systematic attack directed against a civilian population.

5. Article 12(a)(4)

Deportation or Forcible Transfer of Population: Elements

a. The perpetrator willfully, deported or forcibly transferred, or forcible displaced, without grounds permitted under international law, one or more persons to another State or location, by expulsion or other coercive acts;

b. Such person or persons were lawfully present in the area from which they were so deported or transferred;

c. The perpetrator was aware of the factual circumstances that established the lawfulness of such presence;

d. The conduct was committed as part of a widespread or systematic attack directed against a civilian population; and

e. The perpetrator knew that the conduct was part of or intended the conduct to be part of a widespread or systematic attack directed against a civilian population.

6. Article 12(a)(5)

Imprisonment or Other Severe Deprivation of Physical Liberty: Elements

a. The perpetrator willfully imprisoned one or more persons or otherwise severely deprived one or more persons of physical liberty;

b. The gravity of the conduct was such that it was in violation of fundamental rules of international law;

c. The perpetrator was aware of the factual circumstances that established the gravity of the conduct;

d. The conduct was committed as part of a widespread or systematic attack directed against a civilian population; and

e. The perpetrator knew that the conduct was part of or intended the conduct to be part of a widespread or systematic attack directed against a civilian population.

7. Article 12(a)(6)

Torture: Elements*

a. The perpetrator willfully inflicted severe physical or mental pain or suffering upon one or more persons;

b. Such person or persons were in the custody or under the control of the perpetrator;

c. Such pain or suffering did not arise only from, and was not inherent in or incidental to, lawful sanctions;

d. The conduct was committed as part of a widespread or systematic attack directed against a civilian population; and

e. The perpetrator knew that the conduct was part of or intended the conduct to be part of a widespread or systematic attack directed against a civilian population.

* It is understood that no specific purpose for the torture need be proved for this crime.

8. Article 12(a)(7)

Rape: Elements

a. The perpetrator willfully invaded* the body of a person by conduct resulting in penetration, however slight, of any part of the body of the victim or of the perpetrator with a sexual organ, or of the anal or genital opening of the victim with any object or any other part of the body;

b. The invasion was committed by force, or by threat of force or coercion, such as that caused by fear of violence, duress, detention, psychological oppression or abuse of power, against such person or another person, or by taking advantage of a coercive environment, or the invasion was committed against a person incapable of giving consent**;

c. The conduct was committed as part of a widespread or systematic attack directed against a civilian population; and

d. The perpetrator knew that the conduct was part of or intended the conduct to be part of a widespread or systematic attack directed against a civilian population.

* The concept of "invasion" is intended to be gender-neutral.

** It is understood that a person may be incapable of giving genuine consent if affected by natural, induced or age-related incapacity. This footnote applies to the corresponding elements of enforced prostitution, enforced sterilization, and sexual violence.

9. Article12(a)(7)

Sexual Slavery: Elements*

a. The perpetrator willfully exercised any or all of the powers attaching to the right of ownership over one or more persons, such as by purchasing, selling, lending or bartering such a person or persons, or by imposing on them a similar deprivation of liberty, including, but not limited to, exacting forced labor or otherwise reducing a person to a servile status as defined in the Supplementary Convention on the Abolition of Slavery, the Slave Trade, and Institutions and Practices Similar to Slavery of 1956, or the trafficking in persons, in particular women and children;

b. The perpetrator caused such person or persons to engage in one or more acts of a sexual nature;

c. The conduct was committed as part of a widespread or systematic attack directed against a civilian population; and

d. The perpetrator knew that the conduct was part of or intended the conduct to be part of a widespread or systematic attack directed against a civilian population.

* Given the complex nature of this crime, it is recognized that its commission could involve more than one perpetrator as part of a common criminal purpose.

10. Article 12(a)(7)

Enforced Prostitution: Elements

a. The perpetrator willfully caused one or more persons to engage in one or more acts of a sexual nature by force, or by threat of force or coercion, such as that caused by fear of violence, duress, detention, psychological oppression or abuse of power, against such person or persons or another person, or by taking advantage of a coercive environment or such person's or persons' incapacity to give genuine consent;

b. The perpetrator or another person obtained or expected to obtain pecuniary or other advantage in exchange for or in connection with the acts of a sexual nature;

c. The conduct was committed as part of a widespread or systematic attack directed against a civilian population; and

d. The perpetrator knew that the conduct was part of or intended the conduct to be part of a widespread or systematic attack directed against a civilian population.

11. Article 12(a)(7)

Forced Pregnancy: Elements

a. The perpetrator confined one or more women forcibly made pregnant, with the intent of affecting the ethnic composition of any population or carrying out other grave violations of international law;

b. The conduct was committed as part of a widespread or systematic attack directed against a civilian population; and

c. The perpetrator knew that the conduct was part of or intended the conduct to be part of a widespread or systematic attack directed against a civilian population.

12. Article 12(a)(7)

Sexual Violence: Elements

a. The perpetrator willfully committed an act of a sexual nature against one or more persons or caused such person or persons to engage in an act of a sexual nature by force, or by threat of force or coercion, such as that caused by fear of violence, duress, detention, psychological oppression or abuse of power, against such person or persons or another person, or by taking advantage of a coercive environment or such person's or persons' incapacity to give genuine consent;

b. Such conduct was of a gravity comparable to the offences of rape, sexual slavery, enforced prostitution, and forced pregnancy that are contained in Article 12(a)(7) of the Statute of the Special Tribunal;

c. The perpetrator was aware of the factual circumstances that established the gravity of the conduct;

d. The conduct was committed as part of a widespread or systematic attack directed against a civilian population; and

e. The perpetrator knew that the conduct was part of or intended the conduct to be part of a widespread or systematic attack directed against a civilian population.

13. Article 12(a)(8)

Persecution: Elements

a. The perpetrator severely deprived, contrary to international law, one or more persons of fundamental rights;

b. The perpetrator intentionally targeted such person or persons by reason of the identity of a group or collectivity or targeted the group or collectivity as such;

c. Such targeting was based on political, racial, national, ethnic, cultural, religious, gender, or other grounds that are universally recognized as impermissible under international law;

d. The conduct was committed in connection with any crime within the jurisdiction of the Iraqi Special Tribunal;

e. The conduct was committed as part of a widespread or systematic attack directed against a civilian population; and

f. The perpetrator knew that the conduct was part of or intended the conduct to be part of a widespread or systematic attack directed against a civilian population.

14. Article 12(a)(9)

Enforced Disappearance of Persons: Elements*

a. The perpetrator:

   i. Arrested, detained (even if the arrest or detention was lawful) or abducted one or more persons: or

   ii. Refused to acknowledge the arrest, detention or abduction, or to give information on the fate or whereabouts of such person or persons;

b.

   i. Such arrest, detention or abduction was followed or accompanied by a refusal to acknowledge that deprivation of freedom or to give information on the fate or whereabouts of such person or persons; or

   ii. Such refusal was peceeded or accompanied by that deprivation of freedom.

c. The perpetrator was aware that:

   i. Such arrest, detention or abduction would be followed in the ordinary course of events by a refusal to acknowledge that deprivation of freedom or to give information on the fate or whereabouts of such person or persons; or

   ii. Such refusal was preceded or accompanied by that deprivation of freedom:

d. Such arrest, detention or abduction was carried out by, or with the authorization, support or acquiescence of, a State or a political organization;

e. Such refusal to acknowledge that deprivation of freedom or to give information on the fate or whereabouts of such person or persons was carried out by, or with the authorization or support of, such State or political organization;

f. The perpetrator intended to remove such person or persons from the protection of the law for a prolonged period of time;

g. The conduct was committed as part of a widespread or systematic attack directed against a civilian population; and

h. The perpetrator knew that the conduct was part of or intended the conduct to be part of a widespread or systematic attack directed against a civilian population.

* Given the complex nature of this crime, it is recognized that its commission will normally involve more than one perpetrator as a part of a common criminal purpose.

15. Article 12(a)(10)

Other Inhumane Acts: Elements

a. The perpetrator willfully inflicted great suffering, or serious injury to body or to mental or physical health, by means of an inhumane act;

b. Such act was of a character similar (in terms of the nature and gravity of the act) to the offences that are contained in Article 12(a) of the Statute of the Special Tribunal;

c. The perpetrator was aware of the factual circumstances that established the character of the act;

d. The conduct was committed as part of a widespread or systematic attack directed against a civilian population; and

e. The perpetrator knew that the conduct was part of or intended the conduct to be part of a widespread or systematic attack directed against a civilian population.

Section 4
War Crimes: Article 13

1. Introduction

a. The elements for war crimes under Article 13 shall be interpreted within the established framework of the international law of armed conflict including, as appropriate, the international law of armed conflict applicable to armed conflict at sea.

b. With respect to the last two elements for each crime:

i. There is no requirement for a legal evaluation by the perpetrator as to the existence of an armed conflict or its character as international or non-international;

ii. In that context there is no requirement for awareness by the perpetrator of the facts that established the character of the conflict as international or non-international; and

iii. There is only a requirement for the awareness of the factual circumstances that established the existence of an armed conflict that is implicit in the terms of "took place in the context of and was associated with."

Grave Breaches of the Geneva Convention

2. Article 13(a)(1)

Willful Killing: Elements

a. The perpetrator willfully killed or caused the death of one or more persons;

b. Such person or persons were protected under one or more of the Geneva Conventions of 1949;

c. The perpetrator was aware of the factual circumstances that established that protected status*;

d. The conduct took place in the context of and was associated with an international armed conflict**; and

e. The perpetrator was aware of the factual circumstances that established the existence of an armed conflict.

* With respect to nationality, it is understood that the perpetrator needs only to know that the victim belonged to an adverse party to the conflict.

** The term "international armed conflict" includes military occupation. This footnote also applies to the corresponding elements in each crime under Article 13(a).

3. Article 13(a)(2)

Torture: Elements

a. The perpetrator inflicted severe physical or mental pain or suffering upon one or more persons;

b. The perpetrator intentionally inflicted the pain or suffering for such purposes as: obtaining information or a confession, punishment, intimidation or coercion or for any reason based on discrimination of any kind;

c. Such person or persons were protected under one or more of the Geneva Conventions of 1949*;

f. The perpetrator was aware of the factual circumstances that established that protected status;

g. The conduct took place in the context of and was associated with an international armed conflict; and

h. The perpetrator was aware of the factual circumstances that established the existence of an armed conflict.

*As element 3 requires that all victims must be "protected persons" under one or more of the Geneva Conventions of 1949, these elements do not include the custody or control requirement found in Article l2(a)(6).

4. Article13(a)(2)

Inhuman Treatment: Elements

a. The perpetrator inflicted severe physical or mental pain or suffering upon one or more persons;

b. The perpetrator intended to inflict severe physical or mental pain;

c. Such person or persons were protected under one or more of the Geneva Conventions of 1949;

d. The perpetrator was aware of the factual circumstances that established that protected status;

e. The conduct took place in the context of and was associated with an international armed conflict; and

f. The perpetrator was aware of the factual circumstances that established the existence of an armed conflict.

5. Article 13(a)(2)

Biological Experiments: Elements

a. The perpetrator willfully subjected one or more persons to a particular biological experiment;

b. The experiment seriously endangered the physical or mental health or integrity of such person or persons;

c. The perpetrator knew that intent of the experiment was non-therapeutic and it was neither justified by medical reasons nor carried out in such person's or persons' interest;

d. Such person or persons were protected under one or more of the Geneva Conventions of 1949;

e. The perpetrator was aware of the factual circumstances that established that protected status;

f. The conduct took place in the context of and was associated with an international armed conflict; and

g. The perpetrator was aware of the factual circumstances that established the existence of an armed conflict.

6. Article 13(a)(3)
Willfully Causing Great Suffering: Elements

a. The perpetrator willfully caused great physical or mental pain or suffering to, or serious injury to body or health of, one or more persons;

b. Such person or persons were protected under one or more of the Geneva Conventions of 1949;

c. The perpetrator was aware of the factual circumstances that established that protected status;

d. The conduct took place in the context of and was associated with an international armed conflict; and

e. The perpetrator was aware of the factual circumstances that established the existence of an armed conflict.

7. Article 13(a)(4)
Destruction and Appropriation of Protected Property: Elements

a. The perpetrator willfully destroyed or appropriated certain property;

b. The destruction or appropriation was not justified by military necessity;

c. The destruction or appropriation was extensive and carried out want only;

d. Such property was protected under one or more of the Geneva Conventions of 1949;

e. The perpetrator was aware of the factual circumstances that established that protected status;

f. The conduct took place in the context of and was associated with an international armed conflict; and

g. The perpetrator was aware of the factual circumstances that established the existence of an armed conflict.

8. Article 13(a)(5)
Denying a Fair Trial to Protected Persons: Elements

a. The perpetrator willfully deprived one or more persons of a fair and regular trial by denying judicial guarantees as defined, in particular, in the third and the fourth Geneva Conventions of 1949;

b. Such person or persons were protected under m e or more of the Geneva Conventions of 1949;

c. The perpetrator was aware of the factual circumstances that established that protected status;

d. The conduct took place in the context of and was associated with an international armed conflict; and

e. The perpetrator was aware of the factual circumstances that established the existence of an armed conflict.

9. Article 13(6)
Compelling a Protected Person to Serve in the Forces of a Hostile Force: Elements

a. The perpetrator willfully coerced one or more persons, by act or threat, to take part in military operations against that person's own country or forces or otherwise serve in the forces of a hostile power;

b. Such person or persons were protected under one or more of the Geneva Conventions of 1949;

c. The perpetrator was aware of the factual circumstances that established that protected status;

d. The conduct took place in the context of and was associated with an international armed conflict; and

e. The perpetrator was aware of the factual circumstances that established the existence of an armed conflict.

10. Article 13(a)(7)
Unlawful Confinement: Elements

a. The perpetrator willfully confined or continued to confine one or more persons to a certain location;

b. Such person or persons were protected under one or more of the Geneva Conventions of 1949;

c. The perpetrator was aware of the factual circumstances that established that protected status;

d. The conduct took place in the context of and was associated with an international armed conflict; and

e. The perpetrator was aware of the factual circumstances that established the existence of an armed conflict.

11. Article 13(a)(8)
Unlawful Deportation or Transfer: Elements

a. The perpetrator willfully deported or transferred one or more persons to another State or to another location;

b. Such person or persons were protected under one or more of the Geneva Conventions of 1949;

c. The perpetrator was aware of the factual circumstances that established that protected status;

d. The conduct took place in the context of and was associated with an international armed conflict; and

e. The perpetrator was aware of the factual circumstances that established the existence of an armed conflict.

12. Article 13(a)(9)

Taking Hostages: Elements

    a. The perpetrator seized, detained or otherwise held hostage one or more persons;

    b. The perpetrator threatened to kill, injure or continue to detain such person or persons;

    c. The perpetrator intended to compel a State, an international organization, a natural or legal person or a group of persons to act or refrain from acting as an explicit or implicit condition for the safety or the release of such person or persons;

    d. Such person or persons were protected under one or more of the Geneva Conventions of 1949;

    e. The perpetrator was aware of the factual circumstances that established that protected status;

    f. The conduct took place in the context of and was associated with an international armed conflict; and

    g. The perpetrator was aware of the factual circumstances that established the existence of an armed conflict.

Other Serious Violations of International Law

13. Article 13(b)(l)

Attacking Civilians: Elements

    a. The perpetrator directed an attack;

    b. The object of the attack was a civilian population as such or individual civilians not taking a direct part in hostilities;

    c. The perpetrator intended the civilian population as such or individual civilians not taking direct part in hostilities to be the object of the attack;

    d. The conduct took place in the context of and was associated with an international armed conflict; and

    e. The perpetrator was aware of the factual circumstances that established the existence of an armed conflict.

14. Article 13(b)(2)

Attacking Civilian Objects: Elements

    a. The perpetrator directed an attack;

    b. The object of the attack was civilian objects, that is, objects which are not military objectives;

    c. The perpetrator intended such civilian objects to be the object of the attack;

    d. The conduct took place in the context of and was associated with an international armed conflict; and

e. The perpetrator was aware of the factual circumstances that established the existence of an armed conflict.

15. Article13(b)(3)

Attacking Personnel or Objects Involved in a Peacekeeping or Humanitarian Assistance Mission: Elements

a. The perpetrator directed an attack;

b. The object of the attack was personnel, installations, material, units or vehicles involved in a peacekeeping mission in accordance with the Charter of the United Nations or a humanitarian assistance mission;

c. The perpetrator intended such personnel, installations, material, units or vehicles so involved to be the object of the attack;

d. Such personnel, installations, material, units or vehicles were entitled to that protection given to civilians or civilian objects under the international law of awned conflict;

e. The perpetrator knew or should have known the factual circumstances that established that protected status;

f. The conduct took place in the context of and was associated with an international armed conflict; and

g. The perpetrator was aware of the factual circumstances that established the existence of an armed conflict.

16. Article 13(b)(4)

Excessive Incidental Death, Injury, or Damage to Civilians or Civilian Objects: Elements*

a. The perpetrator launched an attack;

b. The attack was such that it would cause incidental death or injury to civilians or damage to civilian objects and that such death, injury or damage would be of such an extent as to be clearly excessive in relation to the concrete and direct overall military advantage anticipated**;

c. The perpetrator knew that the attack would cause incidental death or injury to civilians or damage to civilian objects and that such death, injury or damage would be of such an extent as to be clearly excessive in relation to the concrete and direct overall military advantage anticipated ***;

d. The conduct took place in the context of and was associated with an international armed conflict; and

e. The perpetrator was aware of the factual circumstances that established the existence of an armed conflict.

* This offense does not address justifications for war or other rules related to *jus ad bellum*. It reflects the proportionality requirement inherent in determining the legality of any military activity undertaken in the context of an armed conflict.

** The expression "concrete and direct overall military advantage" refers to a military advantage that is foreseeable by the perpetrator at the relevant time before the attack. Such advantage may or may not be temporally or geographically related to the object of the attack.

*** As opposed to the general rule set forth in paragraph 4 of the General Introduction, this knowledge element requires that the perpetrator make the value judgment as described therein. Any evaluation of that value judgment made by the perpetrator must be based only on the requisite information available to the perpetrator at the time of the attack.

17. Article 13(b)(5)

Excessive Incidental Damage to the Natural Environment: Elements

a. The perpetrator launched an attack;

b. The attack was such that it would cause incidental damage to the natural environment and that such damage would be of such an extent as to be clearly excessive in relation to the concrete and direct overall military advantage anticipated*;

c. The damage to the natural environment was widespread, long-term and severe;

d. The perpetrator knew that the attack would cause incidental widespread, long-term and severe damage to the natural environment and that such damage would be of such an extent as to be clearly excessive in relation to the concrete and direct overall military advantage anticipated*;

e. The conduct took place in the context of and was associated with an international armed conflict; and

f. The perpetrator was aware of the factual circumstances that established the existence of an armed conflict.

* The expression "concrete and direct overall military advantage" refers to a military advantage that is foreseeable by the perpetrator at the relevant time before the attack. Such advantage may or may not be temporally or geographically related to the object of the attack.

** As opposed to the general rule set forth in paragraph 4 of the General Introduction, this knowledge element requires that the perpetrator make the value judgment as described therein. Any evaluation of that value judgment made by the perpetrator must be based only on the requisite information available to the perpetrator at the time of the attack.

18. Article 13(b)(6)

Attacking Undefended Places: Elernents*

a. The perpetrator willfully attacked one or more towns, villages, dwellings or buildings;

b. The perpetrator was aware that such towns, villages, dwellings or buildings were open for unresisted occupation;

c. Such towns, villages, dwellings or buildings did not constitute military objectives;

d. The conduct took place in the context of and was associated with an international armed conflict; and

e. The perpetrator was aware of the factual circumstances that established the existence of an armed conflict.

* The presence in the locality of persons specially protected under the Geneva Conventions of 1949 or of police forces retained for the sole purpose of maintaining law and order does not by itself render the locality a military objective.

19. Article 13(b)(7)

Killing or Wounding a Person *Hors de Combat:* Elements

a. The perpetrator willfully killed or injured one or more persons;

b. Such person or persons were *hors* de *combat;*

c. The perpetrator was aware of the factual circumstances that established this status;

d. The conduct took place in the context of and was associated with an international armed conflict; and

e. The perpetrator was aware of the factual circumstances that established the existence of an armed conflict.

20. Articlel3(b)(8)

Improper Use of a Flag of Truce: Elements

a. The perpetrator used a flag of truce;

b. The perpetrator made such use in order to feign an intention to negotiate when there was no such intention on the part of the perpetrator;

c. The perpetrator knew or should have known of the prohibited nature or illegality of such use;

d. The perpetrator knew that the conduct could result in death or serious personal injury;

e. The conduct took place in the context of and was associated with an international armed conflict; and

f. The perpetrator was aware of the factual circumstances that established the existence of an armed conflict.

21. Article 13(b)(8)

Improper Use of a Flag, Insignia or Uniform of the Enemy: Elements

a. The perpetrator used a flag, insignia or uniform of the enemy;

b. The perpetrator made such use in a manner prohibited under the international law of armed conflict while engaged in an attack;

c. The perpetrator knew or should have known of the prohibited nature or illegality of such use;

d. The conduct resulted in death or serious personal injury;

e. The perpetrator knew that the conduct could result in death or injury;

f. The conduct took place in the context of and was associated with an international armed conflict; and

g. The perpetrator was aware of the factual circumstances that established the existence of all armed conflict.

22. Article 13(b)(8)

Improper use of a Flag, Insignia or Uniform of the United Nations:
Elements

a. The perpetrator used a flag, insignia or uniform of the United Nations;

b. The perpetrator made such use in a manner prohibited under the international law of armed conflict;

c. The perpetrator h e w of the prohibited nature or illegality of such use;

d. The conduct resulted in death or serious personal injury;

e. The perpetrator knew that the conduct could result in death or serious personal injury;

f. The conduct took place in the context of and was associated with an international armed conflict; and

g. The perpetrator was aware of the factual circumstances that established the existence of an armed conflict.

23. Article 13(b)(8)

Improper use of the Distinctive Emblems of the Geneva Conventions:
Elements

a. The perpetrator used the distinctive emblems of the Geneva Conventions;

b. The perpetrator made such use for combatant purposes (i.e. purposes directly related to hostilities but not including medical, religious, or similar activities) in a manner prohibited under the international law of armed conflict;

c. The perpetrator knew or should have known of the prohibited nature or illegality of such use;

d. The conduct resulted in death or serious personal injury;

e. The perpetrator knew that the conduct could result in death or serious personal injury;

f. The conduct took place in the context of and was associated with an international armed conflict; and

g. The perpetrator was aware of the factual circumstances that established the existence of an armed conflict.

24. Article 13(b)(9)
Transferring Populations Into or Out of Occupied Territory: Elements
   a. The perpetrator:

   i. Willfully transferred, directly or indirectly, parts of its own civilian population into the territory it occupies; or.

   ii. Willfully deported or transferred all or parts of the population of the occupied territory within or outside this territory;

   b. The perpetrator was acting for or on behalf of the Government of Iraq or any of its instrumentalities, including an instrumentality of the Arab Socialist Ba'ath Party;

   c. The conduct took place in the context of and was associated with an international armed conflict; and

   d. The perpetrator was aware of the factual circumstances that established the existence of an armed conflict.

25. Article 13(b)(10)
Attacking Protected Objects: Elements*
   a. The perpetrator directed an attack;

   b. The object of the attack was one or more buildings dedicated to religion, education, art, science or charitable purposes, historic monuments, hospitals or places where the sick and wounded are collected, which were not military objectives;

   c. The perpetrator knew or should have known that the object of the attack were not military objectives;

   d. The perpetrator intended such building or buildings dedicated to religion, education, art, science or charitable purposes, historic monuments, hospitals or places where the sick and wounded are collected, which were not military objectives, to be the object of the attack;

   e. The conduct took place in the context of and was associated with all international armed conflict; and

   f. The perpetrator was aware of the factual circumstances that established the existence of an armed conflict.

* The presence in the locality of persons specially protected under the Geneva Conventions of 1949 or of police forces retained for the sole purpose of maintaining law and order does not by itself render the locality a military objective.

26. Article 13(b)(11)
Mutilation: Elements
   a. The perpetrator intentionally subjected one or more persons to mutilation, in particular by permanently disfiguring the person or persons, or by permanently disabling or removing an organ or appendage;

b. The conduct caused death or seriously endangered the physical or mental health of such person or persons;

c. The conduct was neither justified by the medical, dental or hospital treatment of the person or persons concerned nor carried out in such person's or persons' interest*;

d. Such person or persons were nationals of another State;

e. The conduct took place in the context of and was associated with an international armed conflict; and

f. The perpetrator was aware of the factual circumstances that established the existence of an armed conflict.

* Consent is not a defense to this crime. The crime prohibits any medical procedure which is not indicated by the state of health of the person concerned and which is not consistent with generally accepted medical standards which would be applied under similar medical circumstances to persons who are nationals of the party conducting the procedure and who are in no way deprived of liberty. This footnote also applies to the same element for Article 13(b)(11).

27. Article l3(b)(11)
Medical or Scientific Experiments: Elements

a. The perpetrator intentionally subjected one or more persons to a medical or scientific experiment;

b. The experiment caused death or seriously endangered the physical or mental health or integrity of such person or persons;

c. The perpetrator knew that the conduct was neither justified by the medical, dental or hospital treatment of such person or persons concerned nor carried out in such person's or persons' interest;

d. Such person or persons were nationals of another State;

e. The conduct took place in the context of and was associated with an international armed conflict; and

f. The perpetrator was aware of the factual circumstances that established the existence of an armed conflict.

28. Article 13 (b)(12)
Treacherously Killing or Wounding: Elements

a. The perpetrator invited the confidence or belief of one or more persons that they were entitled to, or were obliged to accord, protection under rules of international law applicable in armed conflict;

b. The perpetrator intended to betray that confidence or belief;

c. The perpetrator killed or injured such person or persons;

d. The perpetrator made use of that confidence or belief in killing or injuring such person or persons;

e. Such person or persons belonged to an adverse party;

f. The conduct took place in the context of and was associated with an international armed conflict; and

g. The perpetrator was aware of the factual circumstances that established the existence of an armed conflict.

29. Article 13(b)(13)

Denying Quarter: Elements

a. The perpetrator declared or ordered that there shall be no survivors or surrender accepted;

b. The perpetrator thereby intended to threaten an adversary or to conduct hostilities such that there would be no survivors or surrender accepted;

c. The perpetrator was in a position of effective command or control over the subordinate forces to which the declaration or order was directed;

d. The conduct took place in the context of and was associated with an international armed conflict; and

e. The perpetrator was aware of the factual circumstances that established the existence of an armed conflict.

30. Article 13(b)(14)

Destroying or Seizing an Adverse Party's Property: Elements

a. The perpetrator willfully destroyed or seized certain property;

b. Such property was property of an adverse party;

c. Such property was protected from that destruction or seizure under the international law of armed conflict;

d. The perpetrator was aware of the factual circumstances that established the status of the property;

e. The destruction or seizure was not justified by military necessity;

f. The conduct took place in the context of and was associated with an international armed conflict; and

g. The perpetrator was aware of the factual circumstances that established the existence of an armed conflict.

31. Article 13(b)(15)

Depriving the Nationals of an Adverse Party of Rights or Actions: Elements

a. The perpetrator effected the abolition, suspension or termination of admissibility in a court of law of certain rights or actions;

b. The abolition, suspension or termination was directed at the nationals of an adverse party;

c. The perpetrator intended the abolition, suspension or termination to be directed at the nationals of the adverse party;

d. The conduct took place in the context of and was associated with an international armed conflict; and

e. The perpetrator was aware of the factual circumstances that established the existence of an armed conflict.

32. Article 13(b)(16)

Compelling Participation in Military Operations: Elements

a. The perpetrator willfully coerced one or more persons by act or threat to take part in military operations against that person's own country or forces;

b. The perpetrator knew that such person or persons were nationals of a hostile party;

c. The conduct took place in the context of and was associated with an international armed conflict; and

d. The perpetrator was aware of the factual circumstances that established the existence of an armed conflict.

33. Article 13(b)(17)

Pillaging: Elements

a. The perpetrator appropriated or seized certain property;

b. The perpetrator intended to appropriate or seize the property for private or personal use*;

c. The appropriation or seizure was without the consent of the owner of the property;

d. The conduct took place in the context of and was associated with an international armed conflict; and

e. The perpetrator was aware of the factual circumstances that established the existence of an armed conflict.

* As indicated by the use of the term "private or personal use", legitimate captures or appropriations or seizures justified by military necessity cannot constitute the crime of pillaging.

34. Article 13(b)(18)

Employing Poison or Poisoned Weapons: Elements

a. The perpetrator willfully employed a substance or a weapon that releases a substance as a result of its employment;

b. The substance was such that it causes death or serious damage to health (not including temporary incapacitation or sensory irritation) in the ordinary course of events, though its toxic properties;

c. The conduct took place in the context of and was associated with an international armed conflict; and

d. The perpetrator was aware of the factual circumstances that established the existence of an armed conflict.

35. Article 13(b)(19)
Employing Prohibited Gases, Liquids, Materials or Devices: Elements
a. The perpetrator willfully employed a gas or other analogous substance or device;

b. The gas, substance or device was such that it causes death or serious damage to health (not including temporary incapacitation or sensory irritation) in the ordinary course of events, through its asphyxiating or toxic properties;

c. The conduct took place in the context of and was associated with an international armed conflict; and

d. The perpetrator was aware of the factual circumstances that established the existence of an armed conflict.

36. Article13(b)(20))
Employing Prohibited Bullets: Elements
a. The perpetrator willfully employed certain bullets;

b. The bullets were such that their use violates the international law of armed conflict because they expand or flatten easily in the human body;

c. The perpetrator was aware that the nature of the bullets was such that their employment would uselessly aggravate suffering or the wounding effect;

d. The conduct took place in the context of and was associated with an international armed conflict; and

e. The perpetrator was aware of the factual circumstances that established the existence of an armed conflict.

37. Article 13(b)(21)
Outrages upon Personal Dignity: Elements
a. The perpetrator willfully humiliated, degraded or otherwise violated the dignity of one or more persons*;

b. The severity of the humiliation, degradation or other violation was of such degree as to be generally recognized as an outrage upon personal dignity;

c. The conduct took place in the context of and was associated with an international armed conflict; and

d. The perpetrator was aware of the factual circumstances that established the existence of an armed conflict.

* For this crime, "persons" can include dead persons. It is understood that the victim need not personally be aware of the existence of the humiliation or degradation or other violation. This element takes into account relevant aspects of the cultural background of the victim.

38. Article 13(b)(22)

Rape: Elements

    a. The perpetrator willfully invaded* the body of a person by conduct resulting in penetration, however slight, of any part of the body of the victim or of the perpetrator with a sexual organ, or of the anal or genital opening of the victim with any object or any other part of the body;

    b. The invasion was committed by force, or by threat of force or coercion, such as that caused by fear of violence, duress, detention, psychological oppression or abuse of power, against such person or another person, or by taking advantage of a coercive environment, or the invasion was committed against a person incapable of giving genuine consent**;

    c. The conduct took place in the context of and was associated with an international armed conflict; and

    d. The perpetrator was aware of the factual circumstances that established the existence of an arrned conflict.

* The concept of "invasions" is intended to be gender-neutral.

** It is understood that a person may be incapable of giving genuine consent if affected by natural, induced or age-related incapacity. This footnote applies to the corresponding elements of enforced prostitution, enforced sterilization, and sexual violence.

39. Article 13(b)(22)

Sexual Slavery: Elements*

    a. The perpetrator willfully exercised any or all of the powers attaching to the right of ownership over one or more persons, such as by purchasing, selling, lending or bartering such a person or persons, or by imposing on them a similar deprivation of liberty, including, but not limited to, exacting forced labor or otherwise reducing a person to a servile status as defined in the Supplementary Convention on the Abolition of Slavery, the Slave Trade, and Institutions and Practices Similar to Slavery of 1956, or the trafficking in persons, in particular women and children;

    b. The perpetrator caused such person or persons to engage in one or more acts of a sexual nature;

    c. The conduct took place in the context of and was associated with an international armed conflict; and

    d. The perpetrator was aware of the factual circumstances that established the existence of an armed conflict.

* Given the complex nature of this crime, it is recognized that its commission could involve more than one perpetrator as part of a common criminal purpose.

40. Article 13(b)(22)
Enforced Prostitution: Elements
 a. The perpetrator willfully caused one or more persons to engage in one or more acts of a sexual nature by force, or by threat of force or coercion, such as that caused by fear of violence, duress, detention, psychological oppression or abuse of power, against such person or persons or another person, or by taking advantage of a coercive environment or such person's or persons' incapacity to give genuine consent;
 b. The perpetrator or another person obtained or expected to obtain pecuniary or other advantage in exchange for or in connection with the acts of a sexual nature;
 c. The conduct took place in the context of and was associated with an international armed conflict; and
 d. The perpetrator was aware of the factual circumstances that established the existence of an armed conflict.

41. Article 13(b)(22)
Forced Pregnancy: Elements
 a. The perpetrator willfully confined one or more women forcibly made pregnant, with the intent of affecting the ethnic composition of any population or carrying out other grave violations of international law;
 b. The conduct took place in the context of and was associated with an international armed conflict; and
 c. The perpetrator was aware of the factual circumstances that established the existence of an armed conflict.

42. Article 13(b)(22)
Sexual Violence: Elements
 a. The perpetrator willfully committed an act of a sexual nature against one or more persons or caused such person or persons to engage in an act of a sexual nature by force, or by threat of force or coercion, such as that caused by fear of violence, duress, detention, psychological oppression or abuse of power, against such person or persons or another person, or by taking advantage of a coercive environment or such person's or persons' incapacity to give genuine consent;
 b. Such conduct was of a gravity comparable to the offences of rape, sexual slavery, enforced prostitution, and forced pregnancy that are contained in Article 13(b)(22) of the Statute of the Special Tribunal;
 c. The perpetrator was aware of the factual circumstances that established the gravity of the conduct;
 d. The conduct took place in the context of and was associated with an international armed conflict; and

e. The perpetrator was aware of the factual circumstances that established the existence of an armed conflict.

43. Article 13(b)(23)

Protected Persons as Shields: Elements

a. The perpetrator moved or otherwise took advantage of the location of one or more civilians or other persons protected under the international law of armed conflict;

b. The perpetrator intended to shield a military objective from attack or shield, favor or impede military operations;

c. The conduct took place in the context of and was associated with an international armed conflict; and

d. The perpetrator was aware of the factual circumstances that established the existence of an armed conflict.

44. Article 13(b)(24)

Attacking Objects or Persons Using the Distinctive Emblems of the Geneva Conventions: Elements

a. The perpetrator attacked one or more persons, buildings, medical units or transports or other objects using, in conformity with international law, a distinctive emblem or other method of identification indicating protection under the Geneva Conventions;

b. The perpetrator intended such persons, buildings, units or transports or other objects so using such identification to be the object of the attack;

c. The perpetrator was aware the factual circumstances that established the protected status;

d. The conduct took place in the context of and was associated with an international armed conflict; and

e. The perpetrator was aware of the factual circumstances that established the existence of an armed conflict.

45. Article 13(b)(25)

Starvation as a Method of Warfare: Elements

a. The perpetrator deprived civilians of objects indispensable to their survival;

b. The perpetrator intended to starve civilians as a method of warfare;

c. The conduct took place in the context of and was associated with an international armed conflict; and

d. The perpetrator was aware of the factual circumstances that established the existence of an armed conflict.

46. Article 13(b)(26)
Using, Conscripting or Enlisting Children: Elements

a. The perpetrator conscripted or enlisted one or more persons into the national armed forces or used one or more persons to participate actively in hostilities;

b. Such person or persons were under the age of 15 years;

c. The perpetrator knew or should have known that such person or persons were under the age of 15 years;

d. The conduct took place in the context of and was associated with an international armed conflict; and

e. The perpetrator was aware of the factual circumstances that established the existence of an armed conflict.

Acts Committed against Persons Taking No Active Art in Hostilities

47. Article 13(c)(l)
Murder: Elements

a. The perpetrator willfully killed one or more persons;

b. Such person or persons were either *hors de combat,* or were civilians, medical personnel, or religious personnel (including those non-confessional non-combatant military personnel carrying out a similar function) taking no active part in the hostilities;

c. The perpetrator was aware of the factual circumstances that established this status;

d. The conduct took place in the context of and was associated with an arrned conflict; and

e. The perpetrator was aware of the factual circumstances that established the existence of an armed conflict.

48. Article 13(c)(1)
Mutilation: Elements

a. The perpetrator intentionally subjected one or more persons to mutilation, in particular by permanently disfiguring the person or persons, or by permanently disabling or removing an organ or appendage;

b. The conduct was neither justified by the medical, dental or hospital treatment of the person or persons concerned nor carried out in such person's or persons' interests;*

c. Such person or persons were either *hors de combat,* or were civilians, medical personnel or religious personnel taking no active part in the hostilities;

d. The perpetrator was aware of the factual circumstances that established this status;

e. The conduct took place in the context of and was associated with an armed conflict; and

f. The perpetrator was aware of the factual circumstances that established the existence of an armed conflict.

* Consent is not a defense to this crime. The crime prohibits any medical procedure which is not indicated by the state of health of the person concerned and which is not consistent with generally accepted medical standards which would be applied under similar medical circumstances to persons who are nationals of the party conducting the procedure and who are in no way deprived of liberty.

49. Article 13(c)(l)

Cruel Treatment: Elements

a. The perpetrator willfully inflicted severe physical or mental pain or suffering upon one or more persons;

b. Such person or persons were either *hors de combat,* or were civilians, medical personnel, or religious personnel taking no active part in the hostilities;

c. The perpetrator was aware of the factual circumstances that established this status;

d. The conduct took place in the context of and was associated with an armed conflict; and

e. The perpetrator was aware of the factual circumstances that established the existence of an armed conflict.

50. Article 13(c)(l)

Torture: Elements

a. The perpetrator inflicted severe physical or mental pain or suffering upon one or more persons;

b. The perpetrator inflicted the pain or suffering for such purposes as: obtaining information or a confession, punishment, intimidation or coercion or for any reason based on discrimination of any kind;

c. Such person or persons were either *hors de combat,* or were civilians, medical personnel or religious personnel taking no active part in the hostilities;

d. The perpetrator was aware of the factual circumstances that established this status;

e. The conduct took place in the context of and was associated with an armed conflict; and

f. The perpetrator was aware of the factual circumstances that established the existence of an armed conflict.

51. Article 13(c)(2)

Outrages Upon Personal Dignity: Elements

a. The perpetrator willfully humiliated, degraded or otherwise violated the dignity of one or more persons;*

b. The severity of the humiliation, degradation or other violation was of such degree as to be generally recognized as an outrage upon personal dignity;

c. Such person or persons were either hors *de* combat, or were civilians, medical personnel or religious personnel taking no active part in the hostilities;

d. The perpetrator was aware of the factual circumstances that established this status;

e. The conduct took place in the context of and was associated with an armed conflict; and

f. The perpetrator was aware of the factual circumstances that established the existence of an armed conflict.

* For this crime, "persons" can include dead persons. It is understood that the victim need not personally be aware of the existence of the humiliation or degradation or other violation. This element takes into account relevant aspects of the cultural background of the victim.

52. Article 13(c)(3)

Taking Hostages: Elements

a. The perpetrator seized, detained or otherwise held hostage one or more persons;

b. The perpetrator threatened to kill, injure or continue to detain such person or persons;

c. The perpetrator intended to compel a State, an international organization, a natural or legal person or a group of persons to act or refrain from acting as an explicit or implicit condition for the safety or the release of such person or persons;

d. Such person or persons were either hors *de* combat, or were civilians, medical personnel or religious personnel taking no active part in the hostilities;

e. The perpetrator was aware of the factual circumstances that established this status;

f. The conduct took place in the context of and was associated with an armed conflict; and

g. The perpetrator was aware of the factual circumstances that established the existence of an armed conflict.

53. Article 13(c)(4)

Sentencing or Execution Without Due Process: Elemeats

a. The perpetrator passed sentence or executed one or more persons*:

b. Such person or persons were either *hors de combat,* or were civilians, medical personnel or religious personnel taking no active part in the hostilities;

c. The perpetrator was aware of the factual circumstances that established this status;

d. There was no previous judgment pronounced by a court, or the court that rendered judgment was not "regularly constituted", that is, it did not afford the essential guarantees of independence and impartiality, or the court that rendered judgment did not afford all other judicial guarantees generally recognized as indispensable under international law**;

e. The perpetrator was aware of the absence of a previous judgment or of the denial of relevant guarantees and the fact that they are essential or indispensable to a fair trial;

f. The conduct took place in the context of and was associated with an armed conflict; and

g. The perpetrator was aware of the factual circumstances that established the existence of an armed conflict.

* The elements laid down in these Elements do not address the different forms of individual criminal responsibility, as enunciated in article 15 of the Statute.

** With respect to elements d and e, the Court should consider whether, in light of all relevant circumstances, the cumulative effect of the factors with respect to guarantees deprived the persons or persons of a fair trial.

War Crimes Committed during Armed Conflict Not of an International Character

54. Article 13(d)(l)
Attacking Civilians: Elements

a. The perpetrator directed an attack;

b. The object of the attack was a civilian population as such or individual civilians not taking direct part in hostilities;

c. The perpetrator intended the civilian population as such or individual civilians not taking direct part in hostilities to be the object of the attack;

d. The conduct took place in the context of and was associated with an armed conflict not of an international character; and

e. The perpetrator was aware of the factual circumstances that established the existence of an armed conflict.

55. Article 13(d)(2)
Attacking Objects or Persons Using the Distinctive Emblems of the Geneva Conventions: Elements

a. The perpetrator attacked one or more persons, buildings, medical units or transports or other objects using, in conformity with international law, a distinctive emblem or other method of identification indicating protection under the Geneva Conventions;

b. The perpetrator intended such persons, buildings, units or transports or other objects so using such identification to be the object of the attack;

c. The perpetrator was aware of the factual circumstances that established the object's protected status;

d. The conduct took place in the context of and was associated with an arrned conflict not of an international character; and

e. The perpetrator was aware of the factual circumstances that established the existence of an armed conflict.

56. Article 13(d)(3)

Attacking Personnel or Objects Involved in a Peacekeeping or Humanitarian Assistance Mission: Elements

a. The perpetrator directed an attack;

b. The object of the attack was personnel, installations, material, units or vehicles involved in a peacekeeping mission in accordance with the Charter of the United Nations or a humanitarian assistance mission;

c. The perpetrator intended such personnel, installations, material, units or vehicles so involved to be the object of the attack;

d. Such personnel, installations, material, units or vehicles were entitled to that protection given to civilians or civilian objects under the international law of armed conflict;

e. The perpetrator was aware of the factual circumstances that established that protection;

f. The conduct took place in the context of and was associated with an armed conflict not of an international character; and

g. The perpetrator was aware of the factual circumstances that established the existence of an armed conflict.

57. Article13(d)(4)

Attacking Protected Objects: Elements*

a. The perpetrator directed an attack;

b. The object of the attack was one or more buildings dedicated to religion, education, art, science or charitable purposes, historic monuments, hospitals or places where the sick and wounded are collected, which were not military objectives;

c. The perpetrator intended such building or buildings dedicated to religion, education, art, science or charitable purposes, historic monuments, hospitals or places where the sick and wounded are collected, which were not military objectives, to be the object of the attack;

d. The perpetrator was aware that the object of the attack was not a military objective;

e. The conduct took place in the context of and was associated with an armed conflict not of an international character; and

f. The perpetrator was aware of the factual circumstances that established the existence of an armed conflict.

* The presence in the locality of persons specially protected under the Geneva Conventions of 1949 or of police forces retained for the sole purpose of maintaining law and order does not by itself render the locality a military objective.

58. Article 13(d)(5)

Pillaging: Elements

a. The perpetrator appropriated or seized certain property;

b. The perpetrator intended to appropriate or seize the property for private or personal use*;

c. The appropriation or seizure was without the consent of the owner of the property;

d. The conduct took place in the context of and was associated with an armed conflict not of an international character; and

e. The perpetrator was aware of the factual circumstances that established the existence of an armed conflict.

* As indicated by the use of the term "private or personal use," appropriations justified by military necessity cannot constitute the crime of pillaging.

59. Article 12(d)(6)

Rape: Elements

a. The perpetrator willfully invaded* the body of a person by conduct resulting in penetration, however slight, of any part of the body of the victim or of the perpetrator with a sexual organ, or of the anal or genital opening of the victim with any object or any
other part of the body;

b. The invasion was committed by force, or by threat of force or coercion, such as that caused by fear of violence, duress, detention, psychological oppression or abuse of power, against such person or another person, or by taking advantage of a coercive environment, or the invasion was committed against a person incapable of giving genuine consent**;

c. The conduct took place in the context of and was associated with an armed conflict not of an international character; and

d. The perpetrator was aware of the factual circumstances that established the existence of an armed conflict.

* The concept of "invasion" is intended to be gender-neutral.

** It is understood that a person may be incapable of giving genuine consent if affected by natural, induced or age-related incapacity. This footnote applies to the corresponding elements of enforced prostitution, enforced sterilization, and sexual violence.

60. Article13(d)(6)

Sexual Slavery: Elements*

a. The perpetrator willfully exercised any or all of the powers attaching to the right of ownership over one or more persons, such as by purchasing, selling, lending or bartering such a person or persons, or by imposing on them a similar deprivation of liberty, including, but not limited to, exacting forced labor or otherwise reducing a person to a servile status as defined in the Supplementary Convention on the Abolition of Slavery, the Slave Trade, and Institutions and Practices Similar to Slavery of 1956, or the trafficking in persons, in particular women and children;

b. The perpetrator caused such person or persons to engage in one or more acts of a sexual nature;

c. The conduct took place in the context of and was associated with an armed conflict not of an international character; and

d. The perpetrator was aware of the factual circumstances that established the existence of an armed conflict.

* Given the complex nature of this crime, it is recognized chat its commission could involve more than one perpetrator as part of a common criminal purpose.

61. Article 13(d)(6)

Enforced Prostitution: Elements

a. The perpetrator willfully caused one or more persons to engage in one or more acts of a sexual nature by force, or by threat of force or coercion, such as that caused by fear of violence, duress, detention, psychological oppression or abuse of power, against such person or persons or another person, or by taking advantage of a coercive environment or such person's or persons' incapacity to give genuine consent;

b. The perpetrator or another person obtained or expected to obtain pecuniary or other advantage in exchange for or in connection with the acts of a sexual nature;

c. The conduct took place in the context of and was associated with an armed conflict not of an international character; and

d. The perpetrator was aware of the factual circumstances that established the existence of an armed conflict.

62. Article13(d)(6)
Forced Pregnancy: Elements

a. The perpetrator willfully confined one or more women forcibly made pregnant, with the intent of affecting the ethnic composition of any population or carrying out other grave violations of international law;

b. The conduct took place in the context of and was associated with an ar191ed conflict not of an international character; and

c. The perpetrator was aware of the factual circumstances that established the existence of an armed conflict.

63. Article 13(d)(6)
Sexual Violence: Elements

a. The perpetrator willfully committed an act of a sexual nature against one or more persons or caused such person or persons to engage in an act of a sexual nature by force, or by threat of force or coercion, such as that caused by fear of violence, duress, detention, psychological oppression or abuse of power, against such person or persons or another person, or by taking advantage of a coercive environment or such person's or persons9 incapacity to give genuine consent;

b. Such conduct was of a gravity comparable to the offences of rape, sexual slavery, enforced prostitution, and forced pregnancy that are contained in Article 13(d)(6) of the Statute of the Special Tribunal;

c. The perpetrator was aware of the factual circumstances that established the gravity of the conduct;

d. The conduct took place in the context of and was associated with an armed conflict not of an international character; and

e. The perpetrator was aware of the factual circumstances that established the existence of an armed conflict.

64. Article 13(d)(7)
Using, Conscripting and Enlisting Children: Elements

a. The perpetrator willfully conscripted or enlisted one or more persons into an armed force or group or used one or more persons to participate actively in hostilities;

b. Such person or persons were under the age of 15 years;

c. The perpetrator knew or should have known that such person or persons were under the age of 15 years;

d. The conduct took place in the context of and was associated with an armed conflict not of an international character; and

e. The perpetrator was aware of the factual circumstances that established the existence of an armed conflict.

65. Article 13(d)(8)
Displacing Civilians: Elements

    a. The perpetrator ordered a displacement of a civilian population;

    b. Such order was not justified by the security of the civilians involved or by military necessity;

    c. The perpetrator was in a position to effect such displacement by giving such order;

    d. The conduct took place in the context of and was associated with an armed conflict not of an international character; and

    e. The perpetrator was aware of the factual circumstances that established the existence of an armed conflict.

66. Article 13(d)(9)
Treacherously Killing or Wounding: Elements

    a. The perpetrator invited the confidence or belief of one or more combatant adversaries that they were entitled to, or were obliged to accord, protection under rules of international law applicable in armed conflict;

    b. The perpetrator intended to betray that confidence or belief;

    c. The perpetrator killed or injured such person or persons;

    d. The perpetrator made use of that confidence or belief in killing or injuring such person or persons;

    e. Such person or persons belonged to an adverse party;

    f. The conduct took place in the context of and was associated with an armed conflict not of an international character; and

    g. The perpetrator was aware of the factual circumstances that established the existence of an armed conflict.

67. Article 13(d)(10)
Denying Quarter: Elements

    a. The perpetrator declared or ordered that there shall be no survivors or surrender accepted;

    b. The perpetrator thereby intended to threaten an adversary or to conduct hostilities such that there would be no survivors or surrender accepted;

    c. The perpetrator was in a position of effective command or control over the subordinate forces to which the declaration or order was directed;

    d. The conduct took place in the context of and was associated with an armed conflict not of an international character; and

    e. The perpetrator was aware of the factual circumstances that established the existence of an armed conflict.

68. Article l3(d)(11)

Mutilation: Elements

a. The perpetrator intentionally subjected one or more persons to mutilation, in particular by permanently disfiguring the person or persons, or by permanently disabling or removing an organ or appendage;

b. The conduct caused death or seriously endangered the physical or mental health of such person or persons;

c. The conduct was neither justified by the medical, dental or hospital treatment of the person or persons concerned nor carried out in such person's or persons' interest*;

d. Such person or persons were in the power of another party to the conflict;

e. The conduct took place in the context of and was associated with an armed conflict not of an international character; and

f. The perpetrator was aware of the factual circumstances that established the existence of an armed conflict.

* Consent is not a defense to this crime. The crime prohibits any medical procedure which is not indicated by the state of health of the person concerned and which is not consistent with generally accepted medical standards which would be applied under similar medical circumstances to persons who are nationals of the party conducting the procedure and who are in no way deprived of liberty. This footnote also applies to the same element for Article 13(d)(11).

69. Article l3(d)(11)

Medical or Scientific Experiments: Elements

a. The perpetrator intentionally subjected one or more persons to a medical or scientific experiment;

b. The experiment caused the death or seriously endangered the physical or mental health or integrity of such person or persons;

c. The perpetrator knew that the conduct was neither justified by the medical, dental or hospital treatment of such person or persons concerned nor carried out in such person's or persons' interest;

d. Such person or persons were in the power of another party to the conflict;

e. The conduct took place in the context of and was associated with an armed conflict not of an international character; and

f. The perpetrator was aware of the factual circumstances that established the existence of an armed conflict.

70. Article 13(d)(12)

Destroying or Seizing the Property of an Adversary: Elements

a. The perpetrator willfully destroyed or seized certain property;

b. Such property was property of an adversary;

c. Such property was protected from that destruction or seizure under the international law of armed conflict;

d. The perpetrator was aware of the factual circumstances that established the status of the property;

e. The destruction or seizure was not required by military necessity;

f. The conduct took place in the context of and was associated with an armed conflict not of an international character; and

g. The perpetrator was aware of the factual circumstances that established the existence of an armed conflict.

Section 5
Violations of Stipulated Iraqi Laws: Article 14

1. Article 14(a)
Unlawful Attempt to Manipulate the Judiciary: Elements

a. The elements of this crime shall be those existing under Iraqi law, but, if necessary, reference can be made to the laws of other jurisdictions, public international law, international law of armed conflict, international human rights law, or international criminal law.

2. Article 14(b)
Wastage of National Resources or Squandering of Public Assets: Elements

a. The elements of this crime shall be those existing under Iraqi law, but, if necessary, reference can be made to the laws of other jurisdictions, public international law, international law of armed conflict, international human rights law, or international criminal law.

3. Article 14(c)
Misuses of Official Office to Wage an Aggressive War against an Arab State: Elements

a. The elements of this crime shall be those existing under Iraqi law, but, if necessary, reference can be made to the laws of other jurisdictions, public international law, international law of armed conflict, international human rights law, or international criminal law.

Summary of 1971 Iraqi Criminal Procedure Law[168]

Numbers relate to paragraphs in the Law on Criminal Proceedings No 23 of 1971. Where these have been amended by Orders and Memoranda of the CPA, this is marked in the summary in italics. The headings are my own, and do not correspond to the headings in the Code.

Initiation of Proceedings

Criminal proceedings are initiated by an oral or written complaint to an examining magistrate, police investigator or official or member of the judicial system (1). Certain complaints (e.g. adultery, slander, and dishonesty s when the aggrieved is a relative or spouse of the perpetrator) can only be set in motion by the aggrieved or someone taking his place in law (3). These complaints are not accepted after three months from when the aggrieved became aware of the (6). If s took place outside Iraq a complaint can only be set in motion with the permission of the Minister of Justice (3). If there are numerous accused, a complaint against one of them is considered against all of them (4). The person who submits a complaint has the right to withdraw from it (9). Investigating officers include police officers, mayors, and public servants where s occur within their area of responsibility (39). They work under the supervision of the Public Prosecutor's Office and are subject to the control of the examining magistrate (40). They can make enquiries, receive statements, question the accused and preserve evidence (41–4). Their task ends when the examining magistrate, investigator or representative of the Public Prosecutor's office arrives (46).

Initial Investigation

The initial investigation is conducted by examining magistrates or investigators acting under their supervision (51). This includes examining the scene, noting evidence of the and injuries sustained (52). If it is not within his geographical area of competence he must submit the matter to the Court of Cassation (53). If 2 or more competent authorities receive complaint about the same, the papers are passed to the authority which received a complaint first (54).

The accused person and his representatives may attend the investigation while it is in progress (57). The magistrate or investigator may prohibit this if the matter in hand so requires.

The investigation commences with the recording of the deposition of the informant, then the testimony of the victim and other prosecution witnesses and anyone else the parties or magistrate wish to be heard (58) Each witness over fifteen years old will give evidence on oath (60). Evidence is given orally, but a witness may refer to written notes if the nature of his evidence so requires. In the case of felonies the magistrate shall record important evidence in writing (61).

Statements shall be entered in the record and read and signed by the witness (63). No question may be put to the witness without the permission of the magistrate or investigator (64). A witness may not be addressed in a declaratory or insinuating manner, and no sign or gesture may be directed at him which would tend to intimidate, confuse or distress him. He may not be interrupted unless his evidence is irrelevant.

One spouse may not give evidence against the other unless he or she is accused of adultery or an against the spouse's person or property (68).

The magistrate or investigator may appoint experts of his own accord or at the request of a party (69). He can compel the complainant or defendant to co-operate in a physical examination, or the taking of photographs or samples (70). Searches should be undertaken by the examining magistrate, investigator, member of police by order of the magistrate, or anyone granted authority by law (72). Further provisions on searches (73–86). Provisions on issuance and serving of summonses (87–91).

Arrest and Detention

Arrest can only be on warrant from a court or judge, or in other cases as stipulated by law (92–108). If the person arrested is accused of an carrying imprisonment, the judge may order him to be held for no more than 15 days on each occasion, or order his release on a pledge with or without bail if he rules that his release will not lead to his escape or prejudice the investigation (109). N.B. CPA Order 31 Section 6 allows a judge to order a person suspected of an punishable by life to be held without bail to trial.

The total period of detention on remand should not exceed one quarter of the maximum sentence for the, and should not in any case exceed 6 months. If a period of more than 6 moths is necessary the judge must seek permission from the criminal court, or order his release with or without bail (i.e. security (114)) (109).

Investigators in locations distant from the office of the judge should hold those accused of felonies (113). They must report the matter to the judge as quickly as possible and carry out whatever order he prescribes.

If an accused person does not give himself up after the issuance and publication of an arrest warrant for a felony, his possessions may be seized (121).

Questioning the Accused

The examining magistrate or investigator may question the accused within 24 hours of his attendance. His statements should be recorded (123). N.B. The right to silence and the right to legal representation are added by CPA Memorandum 3 Section 4c.

The accused has the right to make his statement at any time after listening to the statements of any witness (124. If it becomes clear that the accused is a witness against any other defendant, his testimony is recorded and the 2 cases are separated (125). The accused does not swear an oath unless acting as a witness for other defendants. He does not have to answer any of the questions he is asked.

The use of illegal methods is not permitted to influence the accused or extract a confession. This includes mistreatment, threats, injury, enticement, promises. Psychological influence and the use of drugs or intoxicants (127).

Statements of the accused are recorded and signed. If it includes a confession, the magistrate must record the statement himself, and read it back, and he and the accused must both sign it (128).Testimony which he accused asks to present in his defense, and investigation of any other proof offered by him, should be included in the written report, unless the magistrate decides not to grant the accused's request because he believes it to be an unjustified attempt to impede the investigation or to mislead the judge (129).

The magistrate may offer immunity with the agreement of the criminal court in order to obtain a defendant's testimony against others. The accused loses this immunity if he does not submit a full and true statement. His statements are then used as evidence against him (129).

Transfer for Trial

At the end of the investigation the magistrate decides whether there is an over which he has authority, and whether there is sufficient evidence for a trial. If there is sufficient evidence the case is transferred to the appropriate court (130).

Crimes may be tried together if they result from one action, or actions linked to one another and for a common purpose, or the crimes are of the same type and are committed by the same defendant against the same victim, or the crimes are of the same type and are committed against no more than 3 different victims and occurred within one year of each other (132). Crimes are considered to be of the same type if they are punishable by the same type of penalty as stipulated by the same paragraph of the law.

Transfer of cases is to the Court of Felony or the Court of Misdemeanour as appropriate (134). If the defendant has absconded, he may be transferred for trial in his absence (135). N.B. Paragraph 136, which requires the permission of the Minister of Justice before certain types of case can be transferred, has been suspended by CPA Memorandum 3 Section 4d. Penal Courts consist of the Court of Misdemeanour, the Court of Felony and the Court of Cassation (137).

Trial

The court on receipt of a file must set a date for trial, and inform the prosecution, defense and witnesses (at least 8 days in advance for a felony) (143).

The head of the Court of Felony appoints a lawyer for the defendant if he has not appointed one, and sets remuneration for him (144).

If an accused who has been notified has absconded or is absent without legal excuse, the trial will take place in his absence (147). The trial of an absent defendant is conducted according to the guidelines for the conduct of trials where the defendant is present (149).

Trials must be open unless the court decides that all or part should be held in secret for reasons of security or maintaining decency (152).

The court may prevent the parties and their representatives from speaking at undue length, irrelevance, repetition, or making accusations against a party or person outside the case who is unable to put forward a defense (154).

The court may order that any investigatory procedures be taken, or order a person to hand over information, document or items, if that will assist the investigation (163). The court may appoint experts and may permit the wages of the expert to be borne by the treasury 166).

At trial, the court hears the testimony of the complainant and statements of the civil plaintiff, then sees the evidence and orders the reading of reports, investigations and other documents. The statements of the defendant are then heard, along with the petitions of complainant, civil plaintiff, and civil and public prosecutor (167).

Each witness takes an oath and gives his testimony orally and it is permissible to interrupt him. The court may then ask questions necessary to clarify the facts. The prosecutor, complainant, civil plaintiff, civil official and defendant may discuss the testimony and ask questions and request clarifications to establish the facts (168). N.B. CPA Memorandum 3 Section 4f deletes the requirement that the parties must make such enquiries "via the court".

The testimony should be based on facts that the witness is able to recall via one of his senses (169). The court may order that [a witness's] previous testimony in the initial investigation, or before another criminal court, be heard in front of it is the witness is unable to recall all or some of the facts to which he testified, or if the previous statement clarifies the current statement (170).

If a witness is unable to attend the court may hear his testimony given in the initial investigation. It will be treated as though it were given in front of the court (172). If a witness is excused due to illness or any other reason, a judge may attend at another location to hear the witness and send a written report to the court (173). The parties may attend or be represented and may ask the questions they think appropriate.

The court may ask the defendant any questions considered appropriate to establish the truth (179). N.B. CPA Memorandum 3 Section 4g has deleted the provision that a refusal to answer will be considered as evidence against the defendant.

If it becomes clear that the evidence does not point to the defendant having committed the his release is ordered. If the evidence indicates that the defendant has committed the, he is charged as appropriate, the charge is read to him and clarified and he is asked to enter a plea. If the defendant confesses to the charge, and the court is satisfied of the truth of his confession, then it listens to the defense and issues judgment without the requirement to hear further evidence. If he denies the charge or requests a trial or the court considers his confession is confused or that he does not understand the consequences then the case goes to trial, defense witnesses are heard as well as the remaining evidence for the defense. The commentary of other parties, the prosecutor and the defense are heard. The end of the trial is announced and the court issues its verdict (181).

Verdict

The court issues a verdict of guilty and rules on a penalty if it is satisfied the defendant committed the crime. It issues a verdict of not guilty if it is satisfied the defendant did not commit the crime. If there is insufficient evidence, the charges are dropped and the defendant is released. If it becomes clear the defendant is not legally responsible for his actions, the court issues a judgment of diminished responsibility (182).

Conciliation is acceptable by decision of the examining magistrate or judge if it is requested by the victim or his representative (194). A decision announcing the acceptance of conciliation has the same effect as a verdict of not guilty (198).

The Director of Public Prosecutions may request the Court of Cassation to put an end to a procedure either temporarily or permanently, if there is a reason justifying this action (199). N.B. CPA Memorandum 3 Section 4i dispenses with the need for such a request to be based on the permission of the Minister of Justice. The Court of Cassation accepts the request if it finds that there is justification. The decision to suspend proceedings permanently has the same effect as a not guilty verdict (200).

A court is not permitted in its ruling to rely on evidence which has not been brought up for discussion or referred to before the court (212). The court's verdict is based on the extent to which it is satisfied by the evidence. One testimony is not sufficient for a ruling if it is not corroborated by other convincing evidence or a confession from the accused. The court can accept a confession only if it is satisfied with it (213). N.B. CPA Memorandum 3 Section 4j deletes the words "and if there is no other evidence which proves it to be a lie." The court has absolute authority in evaluating testimony (215).

A confession can only be accepted is it is not given as a result of coercion (218). N.B. CPA Memorandum 3 Section 4k deletes the ensuing qualification. The court retires before giving its ruling. The hearing is resumed and the ruling is read out to the defendant. If the verdict is guilty the court must issue another ruling with the penalty at the same hearing, and explain them both (223). The rulings should contain reasons (224). Rulings may be based on consensus or majority. Any judge dissenting from the majority must explain his views in writing. Any judge dissenting from a guilty ruling must still express his views on penalty for the (224).

Mental Health Issues

If it appears that the accused is not able to conduct his defense through mental illness, proceedings are suspended, and he is placed with a health institution. A specialist government medical committee carries out an examination and presents a report (230). If it appears that the accused is not able to present his own defense, he is placed under the supervision of a government health institution, or handed over to one of his relatives on a surety on condition that he should receive treatment (231). If it appears that the accused was not criminally responsible owing to mental illness at the time of the, the court will issue a judgment of diminished responsibility.

Juveniles

No court action is taken against a child under the age of 7. Juvenile Courts deal with offender between the ages of 7 and 18 (233). If a juvenile is accused with a person over 18, the cases are separated and each tried by the appropriate court (235). It is for the court to ask for help from organisations such as the official health and social services to investigate the situation of the juvenile (236). Proceedings against a juvenile are held in private session (238).

Appeals

If a person tried in absentia does not present himself and object within the relevant period (up to 9 months) the verdict and penalties have the status of a judgment. Any objection is submitted in a petition to the court (243). If it is within the time limit, the court will accept it and examine the case again in the light of the objection and will issue its judgment (245).

The Prosecutor and accused, as well as the complainant and the civil plaintiff, have the right to appeal to the Court of Cassation against provisions, decisions and judgements of the lower courts, based on breach or mistake of law, or fundamental error in the standard procedures or in the assessment of evidence or penalty. A mistake in proceedings cannot be ignored unless it has not been damaging to the defense of the accused (249). Appeals will not be accepted before a final ruling in the case against decisions on matters of jurisdiction, preparatory and administrative decisions, or decisions involving arrest, detention and release with or without bail.

Appeals must be lodged by petition within 30 days of the day of judgment (252). If the sentence is life imprisonment the court which issued it must send a file to the Court of Cassation within 10 days so that it can be reviewed for cassation even if there is no appeal (254). If an appeal is not presented within the time limit it will be formally rejected (258).

The Court of Cassation can summon the relevant parties to hear their statements or for any purpose it requires in order to obtain the truth (258). The Court may confirm or reverse any ruling, or return the documents to the lower court for review or retrial. The Court will explain in its decision the grounds on which it is based (259). It may also change the legal description of the and review the penalty in the light of this (260).

If the case is returned for review, the new ruling is submitted to the Court of Cassation for ratification (263).

The Court may of its own accord or in response to a request from anyone connected with the case ask for the file on any criminal case to check its provisions, rulings, procedures and orders. However, if it does so it may only reverse a not guilty verdict or increase a sentence if it is requested to do so within 30 days of the judgment (264).

Anyone connected with the case may request a correction of a legal error in the decision of the Court of Cassation within 30 days of the decision (266).

The convicted person can request the Public Prosecutor for a retrial if matters or facts are later discovered which prove the innocence of the accused or the falsity of the allegations against him (270). The Public Prosecutor submits the case, together with his assessment, to the Court of Cassation. If the Court finds the request justified it will return the case for a re-trial (275). The court to which the case is returned may decide that there is no just cause to interfere with the original judgment, or may annul the judgment in whole or in part (276).

Penalties

N.B. Provisions concerning the implementation of the death penalty (285–293) are suspended by CPA Memorandum 3 Section 4m.

The period spent in detention is deducted from the final sentence (295).

Conditional discharge of a person given a custodial sentence may be granted if he has served three quarters of his sentence (two thirds in the case of juveniles) and if he has been of good behaviour. This is subject to a number of exceptions (331). The remainder of the sentence of a person released on conditional discharged is suspended (332).

A court may decide to pardon a person in a case in which conciliation is possible (338). The request for pardon is submitted by the victim or his representative. If the victims are numerous, a request for pardon will not be accepted unless it is on behalf of all of them. The request must be unconditional (339).

Legal Assistance and Extradition

Requests by foreign states to pursue an investigation in Iraq must be sent to the Ministry of Justice (353). The Minister of Justice may refer the request to the examining magistrate in whose geographical area it falls in order to achieve the requested measures. The magistrate will submit the documents to the Ministry of Justice for forwarding to the foreign state (354).

BIOGRAPHIES

Michael P. Scharf

Michael Scharf is Professor of Law and Director of the Frederick K. Cox International Law Center at Case Western Reserve University School of Law. From October 2004–March 2005, Professor Scharf served as a member of the elite international team of experts which provided training to the judges and prosecutors of the Iraqi High Tribunal. In February 2005, Professor Scharf and the Public International Law and Policy Group, a Non-Governmental Organization he co-founded, were nominated for the Nobel Peace Prize by six governments and the Prosecutor of an International Criminal Tribunal for the work they have done to help in the prosecution of major war criminals, such as Slobodan Milosevic, Charles Taylor, and Saddam Hussein.

During the first Bush and Clinton Administrations, Professor Scharf served in the Office of the Legal Adviser of the U.S. Department of State, where he held the positions of Counsel to the Counter-Terrorism Bureau, Attorney-Adviser for Law Enforcement and Intelligence, Attorney-Adviser for United Nations Affairs, and delegate to the United Nations General Assembly and to the United Nations Human Rights Commission. In 1993, he was awarded the State Department's Meritorious Honor Award "in recognition of superb performance and exemplary leadership" in relation to his role in the establishment of the International Criminal Tribunal for the former Yugoslavia.

A graduate of Duke University School of Law, and judicial clerk to Judge Gerald Bard Tjoflat on the Eleventh Circuit Federal Court of Appeals, Professor Scharf is the author of over fifty scholarly articles and seven books, including *Balkan Justice*, which was nominated for the Pulitzer Prize in 1998, *The International Criminal Tribunal for Rwanda*, which was awarded the American Society of International Law's Certificate of Merit for the Outstanding book in International Law in 1999, *Peace with Justice*, which won the International Association of Penal Law Book of the Year Award for 2003, and casebooks on *The Law of International Organizations* and *International Criminal Law*.

Professor Scharf has testified as an expert before the U.S. Senate Foreign Relations Committee and the House Armed Services Committee; his Op Eds have been published by the *Washington Post, Los Angeles Times, Boston Globe, Christian Science Monitor,* and *International Herald Tribune*; and he has appeared on ABC World News Tonight with Peter Jennings, Nightline with Ted Koppel, The O-Reilly Factor, The NewsHour with Jim Lehrer, The Charlie Rose Show, the BBC's The World, CNN, and National Public Radio. Professor Scharf also hosts an award-winning Blog on the Saddam Hussein Trial: http://www.law.case.edu/saddamtrial.

Winner of the Case School of Law Alumni Association's 2005 "Distinguished Teacher Award," Professor Scharf teaches International Law, International Criminal Law, Human Rights Law, the Law of International Organizations, and a War Crimes Research Lab. In 2002, Professor Scharf established the War Crimes Research Office at Case Western Reserve University School of Law, which provides research assistance to the Prosecutors of the International Criminal Tribunal for Rwanda, the Special Court for Sierra Leone, the International Criminal Court, and the Iraqi High Tribunal on issues pending before those international tribunals. Copies of over 120 of these research memos are available on the Frederick K. Cox International Law Center War Crimes Research Portal, at: http://www.law.case.edu/war-crimes-research-portal.

Gregory S. McNeal

Gregory S. McNeal is Senior Fellow in Terrorism and Homeland Security and Assistant Director of the Institute for Global Security Law and Policy (http://www.law.case.edu/terrorism) at Case Western Reserve University School of Law.

Mr. McNeal is one of two law professors in the world (along with Institute for Global Security Law and Policy Director Amos N. Guiora) supervising students working on legal assignments used by the Office of the Prosecutor for the Department of Defense *Office of Military Commissions.* The work relates to the Guantanamo detainees through the Institute's exclusive partnership with the U.S. Department of Defense. Mr. McNeal teaches the Case School of Law's Counterterrorism Prosecution Lab, and Advanced Terrorism Prosecution Lab.

A founding Research Fellow of the Institute for Global Security, McNeal assisted in designing and facilitating the Institute's semesterly counterterrorism simulation. He led the development of the Institute's strategic plan and worked to develop its exclusive relationship with the U.S. Coast Guard. He also helped to write legislation for members of the U.S. House of Representatives, including a bill designed to prohibit assistance to foreign entities and governments whose senior leadership includes members of terrorist organizations. Mr. McNeal has advised and consulted with the staff for members of both houses of Congress on issues related to terrorism. He has also worked on international criminal law issues for the trial of Saddam Hussein through the Case School of Law's relationship with the U.S. government's Regime Crimes Liaison Office.

Mr. McNeal was previously a Guest Lecturer and Instructor in the School of Public Affairs at American University where he co-taught a course on just responses to terrorism. He served as an officer in the U.S. Army, earned a JD from the Case School of Law with honors in International Law, earned a Masters in Public Administration with distinction from American University and a degree in International Relations from Lehigh University. A former Federalist Society Chapter President, McNeal served as Executive Editor on *The Harvard Journal of Law and Public Policy* (Volume 29, No. 1). He has appeared on talk radio as an expert commentator, and represents the Institute for Global Security in multiple conferences and tabletop simulations related to terrorism and homeland security. His editorials have appeared in *The New York Times, The Washington Times, National Review Online, The Weekly Standard* and *The Baltimore Sun.*

Contributors' Biographies

M. Cherif Bassiouni

M. Cherif Bassiouni is Distinguished Research Professor of Law at DePaul University College of Law, and President of its International Human Rights Law Institute. He is also President of the International Institute of Higher Studies in Criminal Sciences in Siracusa, Italy, as well as the Honorary President of the International Association of Penal Law (President 1989–2004), based in Paris, France.

He has served the U.N. in a number of capacities, including as: Member and then Chairman of the Security Council's Commission to Investigate War Crimes in the Former Yugoslavia (1992–94); Commission on Human Rights' Independent Expert on The Rights to Restitution, Compensation and Rehabilitation for Victims of Grave Violations of Human Rights and Fundamental Freedoms (1998–2000); Vice-Chairman of the General Assembly's Ad Hoc Committee on the Establishment of an International Criminal Court (1995); and Chairman of the Drafting Committee of the 1998 Diplomatic Conference on the Establishment of an International Criminal Court. In 2004, he was appointed by the United Nations High Commissioner for Human Rights as the Independent Expert on the Situation of Human Rights in Afghanistan.

In 1999, Professor Bassiouni was nominated for the Nobel Peace Prize for his work in the field of international criminal justice and for his contribution to the creation of the International Criminal Court. He has received the following medals: Grand Cross of the Order of Merit (Commander), Federal Republic of Germany (2003); Legion d'Honneur (Officier), Republic of France (2003); Order of Lincoln of Illinois, United States of America (2001); Grand Cross of the Order of Merit, Republic of Austria (1990); Order of Sciences (First Class), Arab Republic of Egypt (1984); Order of Merit (Grand'Ufficiale), Republic of Italy (1977), and Order of Military Valor (First Class), Arab Republic of Egypt (1956). He has also received numerous academic and civic awards, including the Special Award of the Council of Europe (1990); the Defender of Democracy Award, Parliamentarians for Global Action (1998); (The Adlai Stevenson Award of the United Nations Association (1993); and the Saint Vincent DePaul Humanitarian Award (2000).

Professor Bassiouni is the author of 27 and editor of 44 books, and the author of 217 articles on a wide range of legal issues, including international criminal law, comparative criminal law, and international human rights law. His publications have appeared in Arabic, Chinese, Farsi, French, Georgian, German, Hungarian, Italian, and Spanish. Some of these publications have been cited by the International Court of Justice, the International Criminal Tribunal for the Former Yugoslavia (ICTY), The International Criminal Tribunal for Rwanda (ICTR), the United States Supreme Court, as well as by several United States Appellate and Federal District Courts, and also by several State Supreme Courts.

Raymond M. Brown

Raymond M Brown has practiced international humanitarian law, and taught and participated in media coverage of the subject.

Brown served as Co-Counsel to an RUF accused at the Special Court for Sierra Leone (2004) where he defended against allegations of Serious Violations of International Humanitarian Law including Crimes Against Humanity, Violations of Article 3 common to the Geneva Conventions and of Additional Protocol II. He has litigated extradition issues in US Federal and state courts and conducted investigations throughout the US in Kenya, El Salvador, the Cayman Islands, Switzerland, the Bahamas, Colombia, and Sierra Leone. Brown is a Fellow of the American College of Trial Lawyers and of the American Board of Criminal Lawyers.

Brown is a Visiting Professor and Research Scholar at Seton Hall University School of Law. He has taught, inter alia "International Criminal Law," at the school's Newark campus and at the Seton Hall/American University Program at Cairo, Egypt, and at Seton Hall University's John Whitehead School of Diplomacy. Additionally, he has taught "Peacekeeping and Peacemaking" at the School of Diplomacy.

While serving for four years as an anchor at Court TV in the late 90's Brown covered the ICTY, reporting from the Hague and anchoring "War Crimes on Trial" from New York. This program provided daily coverage of the Tribunal's first trial, ICTY v Tadic, and of its first guilty plea, ICTY v Erdemovic. His guests included leading diplomats, policy makers, NGO representatives and international trial experts.

Brown Hosted the syndicated program Inside the Law during the 2000 Season which featured a two part series on each of the following: International

Crimes and International Tribunals; Civil Litigation Arising from the Holocaust; International Intervention in Local Conflicts; Nation Building: Moving Beyond Justice.

Brown also served as Editorial Advisor and guest on numerous programs at Court TV, and on MSNBC-TV, BET-TV, ABC News Radio, NPR, Bloomberg Radio, Radio UNAMSIL (Sierra Leone) dealing with humanitarian and international law issues.

As the Host of the Emmy Award winning New Jersey Network program "Due Process" he has examined international and human rights issues including allegations of Torture at Abu Ghraib, civil rights and immigration issues confronting Muslims after September 11, 2001 with security officials and human rights activists with roles in the "war on terror." Brown was awarded an Emmy as Best Host of a talk program for the 2005 "Due Process" Season.

Since 1999 Brown has been a member of the Board of Human Rights First (formerly the Lawyer's Committee for Human Rights). Brown's writings include articles on the early phases of the Tadic trial, American Responses to Narratives of Violations of Humanitarian Law, the American Role at Nuremberg, and race and media impacts on domestic prosecutions of "terrorists."

David M. Crane

David M. Crane is currently Distinguished Visiting Professor of Law at Syracuse University College of Law. From 2002–2005, he served as the Chief Prosecutor of the Special Court for Sierra. With the rank of Undersecretary General, Mr. Crane's mandate is to prosecute those who bear the greatest responsibility for war crimes, crimes against humanity, and other violations of international human rights committed during the civil war in Sierra Leone during the 1990's. The Office of the Prosecutor is located with the Special Court in Freetown, Sierra Leone.

Prior to his appointment as the Chief Prosecutor, Mr. Crane served over 30 years in the federal government of the United States, mainly with the Department of Defense. Appointed to the Senior Executive Service of the United States in 1997, Mr. Crane has held numerous key positions during his three decades of public service, to include Director of the Office of Intelligence Review, Assistant General Counsel of the Defense Intelligence Agency, and Waldemar A. Solf Professor of International Law at the United States Army Judge Advocate General's School. He has over 20 years of experience as an officer and lawyer in the United States Army.

Mr. Crane holds a Doctorate of Law degree from Syracuse University, a Masters of Arts Degree in African Studies and a Bachelor of General Studies in History, summa cum laude, from Ohio University. Various awards include the Intelligence Community Gold Seal Medallion awarded by the Director of Central Intelligence, the Department of Defense/DoDIG Distinguished Civilian Service Medal, and the Legion of Merit.

Laura Dickinson

Laura A. Dickinson is an Associate Professor at the University of Connecticut School of Law. A graduate of Harvard College and Yale Law School, she subsequently served as a senior policy adviser to Harold Hongju Koh, Assistant Secretary of State for Democracy, Human Rights and Labor at the U.S. Department of State. She also served as a law clerk to Justices Harry A. Blackmun and Stephen G. Breyer on the U.S. Supreme Court, and Judge Dorothy Nelson of the U.S. Court of Appeals for the Ninth Circuit. Professor Dickinson and her students at Connecticut School of Law have been asked to prepare research memoranda for the Iraqi High Tribunal.

Professor Dickinson's publications include *The Promise of Hybrid Courts*, 97 AM. J. INT'L L. 295 (2003), *Using Legal Process to Fight Terrorism: Military Commissions, Detentions, International Tribunals, and the Rule of Law*, 75 S. CAL. L. REV 1407 (2002), and *The Dance of Complementarity: Relationships Among Domestic, International, and Transnational Accountability Mechanisms in East Timor and Indonesia*, in ACCOUNTABILITY FOR ATROCITIES: NATIONAL AND INTERNATIONAL RESPONSES (Jane Stromseth ed., 2003). Her most recent article, *Government for Hire: Privatizing Foreign Affairs and the Problem of Accountability Under International Law*, will be published in the *William and Mary Law Review* this fall.

Mark Drumbl

Mark Drumbl is Associate Professor of Law and Ethan Allen Faculty Fellow at Washington and Lee University School of Law. B.A. 1989, McGill University; M.A. 1991, Institut d'études politiques de Paris/McGill University; J.D. 1994, University of Toronto, summa cum laude; LL.M. 1998, J.S.D. 2002, Columbia University; University of Toronto Fac. Law Review; Associate Editor, Columbia Journal of Transnational Law.

Assistant Professor of Law, Washington and Lee University, 2002–2004; Associate Professor of Law (with tenure), 2004–; Ethan Allen Faculty Fellow, 2003–2004, 2004–2005, 2005–2006; Visiting Fellow, University College, Oxford University (Michaelmas Term 2005); Visiting Associate Professor, Vanderbilt University, School of Law (September 2005); Visiting Scholar, Trinity College, University of Dublin (May 2006). Prior appointments include Adjunct Assistant Professor and Associate-in-Law, Columbia University School of Law; Assistant Professor of Law, University of Arkansas—Little Rock; Visiting Professor of Law, Washington and Lee University (2001).

Research and teaching interests include international law, global environmental governance, contracts, transitional justice, criminal law, comparative law, and law and development; he is currently working on a book that explores punishment for perpetrators of mass atrocity trans-systemically across various international, national, and local legal orders. Professor Drumbl's scholarship has appeared in the NYU, Michigan, Northwestern, Tulane, and North Carolina law reviews, a number of peer-review journals, including Human Rights Quarterly, with shorter review pieces in the American Journal of International Law and Columbia Journal of Transnational Law. He also has authored chapters in edited volumes and participated in numerous symposia. In 2005 his work received the AALS Scholarly Papers Prize and in 2003 the International Association of Penal Law (U.S. Section) Best Article Prize.

Prior to entering law teaching, Professor Drumbl was judicial clerk to Justice Frank Iacobucci of the Supreme Court of Canada. His practice experience includes international arbitration, commercial litigation, and he was appointed co-counsel for the Canadian Chief-of-Defense-Staff before the Royal Commission investigating military wrongdoing in the UN Somalia Mission. Professor Drumbl has served as an expert in litigation in the U.S. federal courts, as defense counsel in the Rwandan genocide trials, and has taught international law in Pakistan.

Mark Ellis

As Executive Director of the International Bar Association (IBA), Mark Ellis leads the foremost international organization of bar associations and individual lawyers in the world. The IBA is comprised of 200 member organizations and 20,000 members from 194 countries.

Prior to joining the IBA, Mr. Ellis spent ten years as the first Executive Director of the Central and East European Law Initiative (CEELI), a project of the American Bar Association (ABA). Providing technical legal assistance to twenty-eight countries in Central Europe and the former Soviet Union, and to the International Criminal Tribunal for the Former Yugoslavia (ICTY) in The Hague, CEELI remains the most extensive technical legal assistance project ever undertaken by the ABA.

In 1999, Mr. Ellis was appointed Legal Advisor to the Independent International Commission on Kosovo, chaired by Justice Richard J. Goldstone. In 2003, he was appointed by OSCE to advise on the creation of Serbia's War

Crimes Tribunal. He is presently a member of the Advisory Panel to the Defense Counsel for the ICTY.

Mr. Ellis was a long-time consultant to The World Bank on investment policies in Central and Eastern Europe and the former Soviet Union, and has been an Adjunct Professor at The Catholic University of America, Columbus School of Law.

Mr. Ellis has degrees in Economics and Law and was twice a Fulbright Scholar at the Economic Institute in Zagreb, Croatia. He is the recipient of two research grants to the European Union and the Institute d'Etudes Europeenes in Brussels, Belgium focusing on the law and institutions of the European Union. Mr. Ellis is currently pursuing a PhD in Law at King's College, University of London.

Mr. Ellis is a frequent speaker and media commentator on international legal issues. He is currently acting as on-air legal analyst for CNN International on the Saddam Hussein trial. Mr Ellis has published extensively in the areas of foreign investment, war crimes tribunals, international humanitarian law, and the development of the rule of law. He is the co-recipient of the American Bar Association's *World Order Under Law Award*, and the recipient of Florida State University's *Distinguished Graduate Award*.

Mr. Ellis is a member of the *Council of Foreign Relations* and serves on a number of boards, including the Central European and Eurasian Law Institute (*CEELI Institute*), the *Institute for Historical Justice and Reconciliation at the Salzburg Seminar* and the DLA Piper Rudnick *'New Perimeter'* probono project. He also serves on the editorial board for the *Journal of National Security Law and Policy*.

Kevin Jon Heller

Kevin Jon Heller is currently a Lecturer on the University of Auckland Faculty of Law in New Zealand. He holds a JD from Stanford Law School (with distinction), an MA in literature from Duke University, and an MA and BA in sociology from the New School for Social Research. After clerking on the Ninth Circuit for Judge William C. Canby, Jr., he practiced criminal defense in Los Angeles for three years, specializing in drug, racketeering, conspiracy, and extradition cases. He also defended Milan Panic, the former Prime Minister of Yugoslavia, against charges that his pharmaceutical company systematically violated the Yugoslavian Asset Control Regulations.

Professor Heller teaches international criminal law, criminal law, and evidence. His publications include: "The Cognitive Psychology of Circumstantial Evidence," 105 Michigan Law Review (2006); "The Rhetoric of Constitutional Necessity—A Response to Sanford Levinson," 40 Georgia Law Review (2006); "Beyond the Reasonable Man? A Sympathetic but Critical Assessment of the Use of Subjective Standards of Reasonableness in Self-Defense and Provocation Cases," 26 *American Journal of Criminal Law* 1 (Fall, 1998); "Whatever Happened to Proof Beyond a Reasonable Doubt? Of Drug Conspiracies, Overt Acts, and *United States v. Shabani*," 49 *Stanford Law Review* 111 (1996); and "Power, Subjectification, and Resistance in Foucault," *SubStance* 79 (April, 1996). He has also edited a collection of essays on the work of Gilles Deleuze and Felix Guattari for the University of Minnesota Press and contributed essays on extradition, the cultural defense, proof beyond a reasonable doubt, and conspiracy to the forthcoming *Encyclopedia of American Civil Liberties*.

He has published a number of articles on US criminal law and social theory, including a comparative analysis of the use of subjective standards of reasonableness in self-defense and provocation cases, and edited a successful collection of essays on the work of Gilles Deleuze for the University of Minnesota Press. He graduated with distinction from Stanford Law School, clerked on the Ninth Circuit, and was a criminal-defense attorney in Los Angeles for three years, specializing in extradition and the defense of transnational crimes.

Contributor, ENCYCLOPEDIA OF AMERICAN CIVIL LIBERTIES (Routledge, 2006). Articles on "Proof Beyond a Reasonable Doubt," "Conspiracy," "Extradition," "Cultural Defense," and "Exemplars."

Book Editor: DELEUZE AND GUATTARI: NEW MAPPINGS IN POLITICS, PHILOSOPHY, AND CULTURE (University of Minnesota Press, 1998) (with Eleanor Kaufman).

Simone Monasebian

Simone Monasebian has extensive experience in prosecuting and defending accused war criminals, as well as providing media commentary on and teaching war crimes related subjects. Ms. Monasebian is currently the Chief of the New York Office of the United Nations Office on Drugs and Crime (UNODC), which is tasked with promoting justice globally. She is also CourtTV's Legal Analyst for the Saddam Hussein Trial, and an Adjunct Professor of International Criminal Law at Seton Hall Law School's Cairo program, at the American University.

Prior to her appointment with the UNODC, Ms. Monasebian served as Principal Defender of the Special Court for Sierra Leone. Pursuant to U.N. Security Council Resolution 1315 (2000), the Special Court, is mandated to try those who bear the greatest responsibility for war crimes committed in Sierra Leone since 30 November 1996. As the Principal Defender at an international war crimes tribunal, Ms. Monasebian was responsible for developing the Defense Office and ensuring the rights of suspects and accused persons by providing an institutional counterbalance to the Prosecution.

Before joining the Special Court, Ms. Monasebian was a Trial Attorney with the United Nations International Criminal Tribunal for Rwanda ("ICTR"), Office of the Prosecutor, where she prosecuted war criminals in complex, multi-defendant cases pursuant to U.N. Security Council Resolution 955 (1994). She was one of the prosecutors responsible for the December 2003 landmark convictions of three media executives who fanned the flames of genocide in their newspaper and radio station. That case raised important principles concerning the role of the media, which had not been addressed at the level of international criminal justice since Nuremberg.

Michael A. Newton

Mike Newton came to Vanderbilt having previously served as an Associate Professor in the Department of Law, United States Military Academy. He is a highly sought after speaker on accountability and conduct of hostilities issues, and is a member of the International Institute of Humanitarian Law. He has made numerous media appearances on CNN, BBC, NPR, and other print and broadcast media. His principal responsibilities at Vanderbilt involve teaching practice-based courses relating to international law and international criminal law as well as developing externships and other educational opportunities for students interested in international legal issues. During his capacity as the Senior Advisor to the United States Ambassador-at-Large for War Crimes Issues, he implemented a wide range of policy positions related to the law of armed conflict, including U.S. support to accountability mechanisms worldwide. After assisting with the establishment of the Iraqi High Tribunal, he has repeatedly taught Iraqi jurists both in Baghdad and other venues and is a member of its academic consortium. He served as the U.S. representative on the U.N. Planning Mission for the Sierra Leone Special Court, and was also a member of the Special Court academic consortium. From January 1999 to August 2000, he served in the Office of War Crimes Issues, U.S. Department of State. He negotiated the Elements of Crimes document for the International Criminal Court, and coordinated the interface between the FBI and the ICTY and deployed into Kosovo to do the forensics fieldwork to support the Milosevic indictment. Over the course of his distinguished military career, Professor Newton practiced international law in a variety of legal and operational environments, including service with the United States Army Special Forces Command (Airborne) in support of units participating in Operation Desert Storm and Operation Provide Comfort in northern Iraq. From 1993 to 1995, he served as the Brigade Judge Advocate for the 194th Armored Brigade (Separate), during which he organized and led the human rights and rules of engagement education for all Multinational Forces and International Police deploying into Haiti. He was a Professor of International and Operational Law at the Judge Advocate General's School, Charlottesville, Virginia from 1996–1999.

Jerrold M. Post

Dr. Jerrold Post is Professor of Psychiatry, Political Psychology and International Affairs and Director of the Political Psychology Program at The George Washington University. Dr. Post has devoted his entire career to the field of political psychology. Dr. Post came to George Washington after a 21 year career with the Central Intelligence Agency where he founded and directed the Center for the Analysis of Personality and Political Behavior, an interdisciplinary behavioral science unit which provided assessments of foreign leadership and decision making for the President and other senior officials to prepare for Summit meetings and other high level negotiations and for use in crisis situations. He played the lead role in developing the "Camp David profiles" of Menachem Begin and Anwar Sadat for President Jimmy Carter and initiated the U.S. government program in understanding the psychology of terrorism. In recognition of his leadership of the Center, Dr. Post was awarded the Intelligence Medal of Merit in 1979, and received the Studies in Intelligence Award in 1980. He received the Nevitt Sanford Award for Distinguished Professional Contributions to Political Psychology in 2002.

A founding member of the International Society of Political Psychology, Dr. Post was elected Vice-President in 1994, and has served on the editorial board of Political Psychology since 1987. A Life Fellow of the American Psychiatric Association, he has been elected to the American College of Psychiatrists and is currently Chair, Task Force for National and International Terrorism and Violence for the APA. Dr. Post received his B.A. magna cum laude and M.D. from Yale. He received his post-graduate training in psychiatry at Harvard Medical School and the National Institute of Mental Health. He has also received graduate training at the Johns Hopkins School of Advanced International Studies. Dr. Post's analysis of Saddam has been featured prominently in the national and international media. He provided his analysis of Saddam's personality and political behavior in testimony at the hearings on the Gulf crisis before the House Armed Services Committee and the House Foreign Affairs Committee. He is a frequent commentator on national and international media on such topics as leadership, leader illness, treason, the psychology of terrorism, Slobodan Milosevic, Yasir Arafat, Osama bin Laden, Saddam Hussein and Kim Jong Il.

Christopher Rassi

Christopher Rassi is an associate with the law firm of Thompson Hine LLP. Mr. Rassi also serves as Adjunct Professor and Deputy Director of the Cox Center War Crimes Research Office at Case Western Reserve University School of Law. In that capacity, he provides research memoranda to the judges of the Iraqi Special Tribunal on issues pending before the Court. In 2004, Mr. Rassi served as Law Clerk to the Honorable Yvonne Mokgoro, Constitutional Court of South Africa, and in 2003 he was a Frederick K. Cox International Law Center Post-Graduate Fellow, clerking for Judge Weinberg de Roca, Appeals Chamber of the International Criminal Tribunal for the former Yugoslavia and Rwanda.

Leila Nadia Sadat

Leila Sadat is the Henry H. Oberschelp Professor of Law at the Washington University School of Law, where she has taught since 1992. A leading authority in international criminal law and human rights, Sadat is particularly well-known for her expertise on the International Criminal Court. Named to chair the International Law Association committee on the Court in 1995, she authored or edited several monographs both in her capacity as chair, and writing individually. In addition, she was an NGO delegate to the U.N. Preparatory Committee and to the 1998 U.N. diplomatic conference in Rome at which the Court was established. In March 2000, her article The New International Criminal Court: An Uneasy Revolution, was published in the Georgetown Law Journal. In 2002 she published a monograph, The International Criminal Court and the Transformation of International Law: Justice for the New Millennium, which was supported by a grant from the United States Institute of Peace and won the "Book of the Year" award from the International Association of Penal Law (American National Section).

More recently she has published several essays on U.S. foreign policy and international criminal law including Terrorism and the Rule of Law, which was published in volume 3 of the Washington University Global Studies Law Review. Her most recent article, Exile, Amnesty and International Law will appear in volume 81 of the Notre Dame Law Review. From May 2001 until September 2003, Professor Sadat served as a Congressional appointee to the nine-member U.S. Commission for International Religious Freedom. More recently, she was tapped to participate in an International Bar Association project to train Iraqi lawyers, judges and prosecutors in human rights. Professor Sadat is often heard on national media, and has an active speaking schedule. She was recently elected Secretary of the American Society of Comparative Law, and Vice-President and Co-Director of Studies of the International Law Association. She is also a member of the American Law Institute and the International Academy of Comparative Law, Vice-President of the International Association of Penal Law (American National Section) and has been a member of the Executive Council and Executive Committee of the American Society of International Law.

Sadat received her J.D. from Tulane Law School, summa cum laude, and holds graduate law degrees from Columbia University School of Law (LLM, summa cum laude) and the University of Paris I—Sorbonne (diplôme d'études approfondies). Sadat practiced international business law for several years in Paris, France, prior to entering law teaching, and is admitted to the bar in Paris and in Louisiana. She clerked for Judge Albert Tate, Jr., on the U.S. Fifth Circuit Court of Appeals, as well as both of France's Supreme Courts, the Cour de Cassation and the Conseil d'Etat.

William A. Schabas

Professor William A. Schabas is director of the Irish Centre for Human Rights at the National University of Ireland, Galway, where he also holds the professorship in human rights law. Before moving to Ireland in 2000, he was professor at the law school of the University of Quebec at Montreal, which he chaired for several years, and a member of the Quebec Human Rights Tribunal. He has also taught as a visiting or adjunct professor at universities in Canada, France and Rwanda, and has lectured at the International Institute for Human Rights (Strasbourg), the Canadian Foreign Service Institute and the Pearson Peacekeeping Centre. He was a senior fellow at the United States Institute of Peace (1998–99). Professor Schabas served as one of three international commissioners of the Sierra Leone Truth and Reconciliation Commission (2002–04).

Professor Schabas holds post-graduate degrees in history and in law from universities in Canada. He is the author of eighteen monographs and more than 170 articles dealing with such subjects as the abolition of capital punishment, international criminal prosecution and issues of transitional justice, in English and French. His writings have been translated into several languages, including Russian, German, Spanish, Portuguese, Chinese, Japanese, Arabic, Frasi and Albanian. He has lectured around the world in the areas of international humanitarian and human rights law, and been a frequent participant in human rights fact-finding missions on behalf of international non-governmental organisations.

David Scheffer

David Scheffer is the Mayer, Brown, Rowe & Maw/Robert B. Helman Professor of Law and Director of the Center for International Human Rights at Northwestern University School of Law in Chicago, Illinois. He recently was a visiting professor at The George Washington University Law School (2004–2005) and a visiting professor at Georgetown University Law Center (2003–2004). He teaches international criminal law, public international law, and international human rights law. Scheffer served as the U.S. Ambassador at Large for War Crimes Issues (1997–2001) and as Senior Adviser and Counsel to the U.S. Permanent Representative to the United Nations, Dr. Madeleine Albright (1993–1996). He led the U.S. negotiating team in the U.N. talks on the International Criminal Court, helped negotiate the creation and support the operations of the International Criminal Tribunals for the former Yugoslavia and Rwanda, and helped negotiate the establishment of the Special Court for Sierra Leone and the Extraordinary Chambers in the courts of Cambodia. He also served on the Deputies Committee of the National Security Council (1993–1996). During his career Scheffer has worked as an attorney with the international law firm of Coudert Brothers (New York and Singapore offices) and in various capacities with the U.S. House of Representatives Committee on Foreign Affairs, the Carnegie Endowment for International Peace, the U.S. Institute of Peace, and (as senior vice president of) the U.N. Association of the U.S.A. He taught previously as an adjunct professor at Columbia, Duke, and Georgetown. Scheffer graduated from Harvard, Oxford (where he was a Knox Fellow) and Georgetown Universities and is a member of the New York and District of Columbia Bars. He has published extensively on international law and politics.

Paul R. Williams

Paul R. Williams holds the Rebecca Grazier Professorship in Law and International Relations at the American University where he teaches in the School of International Service and the Washington College of Law. Professor Williams also directs the Public International Law & Policy Group which provides pro bono legal assistance to developing states and states in transition.

Professor Williams, along with the Public International Law & Policy Group (PILPG) was nominated for the 2005 Nobel Peace Prize by over half a dozen of his pro bono government clients. In the summer of 2005, Professor Williams and a team of PILPG experts were invited to Baghdad to help redraft Previously Professor Williams served in the Department of State's Office of the Legal Advisor for European and Canadian Affairs, as a Senior Associate with the Carnegie Endowment for International Peace, and as a Fulbright Research Scholar at the University of Cambridge.

During the course of his legal practice, Professor Williams has assisted over a dozen states and sub-state entities in major international peace negotiations and in drafting post-conflict constitutions. He has also advised fifteen governments across Europe, Africa and Asia on matters of public international law Professor Williams has authored four books on topics of international human rights, international environmental law and international norms of justice, and over fifteen articles on a wide variety of public international law topics. He regularly publishes op-eds in major newspapers and is frequently interviewed by major print and broadcast media.

Professor Williams earned his Ph.D. from the University of Cambridge, his J.D. from Stanford Law School, and his B.A. from the University of California at Davis.

NOTES

1. President Theodore Roosevelt, *The Man in the Arena: Citizenship in a Republic,* Address at the Sorbonne, Paris (Apr. 23, 1910), *available at* http://theodoreroosevelt.org/research/speeches.htm. The authors thank Michael Newton for bringing this quote to their attention.

2. Reprinted with permission from *Post-Conflict Justice in Iraq: An Appraisal of the Iraq Special Tribunal,* 38 Cornell Journal of International Law 327 (2005).

3. *See* Jean Bottèro, Mesopotamia: Writing, Reasoning, and the Gods 55–200 (Zainab Bahrani & Marc van de Mieroop trans., 1995); George Roux, Ancient Iraq 66–84 (3d ed. 1993). The older civilizations that comprised what is now Iraq are the Sumerians, who go back to 5000 BCE and whose capital Ur was Abraham's place of birth; the Amorites, who founded the cities of Babylon and Akkad and whose empire lasted from 1900 to 1600 BCE; the Hittites, from 1600 to 1100 BCE; the Assyrians, from 1200 to 612 BCE; and the Chaldeans, from 612 to 539 BCE. *Id.* at 66, 104, 179–94, 377–79 tbls. IV–VIII.

4. John Henry Wigmore, A Panorama of the World's Legal Systems 86–93 (1936).

5. David Fromkin, A Peace To End All Peace: The Fall of the Ottoman Empire and the Creation of the Modern Middle East 449–55 (2d ed. 1989). The region, which comprises Iraq and which is generally described in note 4, has also been referred to as "Iraq" throughout history. Some archeological remains going back before the Common Era refer to that region as "Iraq," as do records of the Muslim Abbasid period from approximately 850 to 1250 CE. *See* M. Cherif Bassiouni, Introduction to Islam 18 (1988); *see also* generally Albert Hourani, A History of the Arab Peoples (2d ed. 2003).

6. The area known today as Iraq was ruled by the Persian Empire from 539 to 331 BCE; the Greeks and Macedonians from 331 to 170 BCE; the Parthians from 170 BCE to 224 CE; the Sassanians from 224 to 651 CE; the Arab Muslims from 652 to 1257; the Turkish Ottoman Empire from 1301 to 1918; and the British Empire from 1918 to 1922. Roux, *supra* note 3, at 406–22 tbls. VIII–XI (Persian, Hellenistic, Parthian, Sassanian); Fromkin, *supra* note 5, at 33, 426, 558–67 (Ottoman, British). During World War I, Britain relied on Emir Sherif Hussein of Hejaz to fight against the Turkish Ottoman Empire forces in the Arabian Gulf, Palestine, and what is now Syria, Lebanon, and Iraq. Fromkin, *supra* note 5, at 174, 218–28. Hussein had two sons, Abdullah and Feisal. *Id.* at 113. Feisal became famous for having fought on the British side at the instigation of Thomas Edward Lawrence, popularly known as "Lawrence of Arabia." *Id.* at 497–99. Feisal was made King of Syria in 1920, but due to arrangements between the British and the French, on the French control of these

areas he was made King of the newly constituted Iraq in 1921. *Id.* at 437–40, 442, 446, 499–500, 508. The League of Nations established a protectorate over Iraq in 1922 and gave its administration to the British Empire. *Id.* at 508–10. In 1932, the League of Nations admitted the Kingdom of Iraq into its ranks of independent states. CHARLES TRIPP, A HISTORY OF IRAQ 75 (2000).

7. FROMKIN, *supra* note 5, at 500–64.

8. MICHAEL EPPEL, IRAQ FROM MONARCHY TO TYRANNY: FROM THE HASHEMITES TO THE RISE OF SADDAM 147–52 (2004).

9. *Id.* at 204–08, 241.

10. *Id* at 242, 244.

11. Between 1968 and 1979, Saddam Hussein was Iraq's strongman vice president. For a description of Saddam's criminal activities, see EPPEL, *supra* note 8, at 241–65; CON COUGHLIN, SADDAM: KING OF TERROR 23–175 (2002); and TRIPP, *supra* note 6, at 193–279.

12. TRIPP, *supra* note 6, at 254.

13. *See* EPPEL, *supra* note 8, at 241–65; COUGHLIN, *supra* note 11, 23–275. Human Rights Watch reports on human rights abuses in Iraq are available online at http://hrw.org/doc/?t=mideast_pub&c=iraq&document_limit=20,20 (last visited Mar. 8, 2005).

14. *See generally* STEPHEN C. PELLETIERE, THE IRAN-IRAQ WAR: CHAOS IN A VACUUM (1992) (examining Iraq's objectives and its decision to go to war with Iran); T.M.C. ASSER INSTITUTE, THE GULF WAR OF 1980–88: THE IRAN-IRAQ WAR IN INTERNATIONAL LEGAL PERSPECTIVE (Ige F. Dekker & Harry H.G. Post eds., 1992) (discussing Iran-Iraq border conflicts, the legal implications of the war, criminal responsibility, and the Islamic conception of international law); W. THOM WORKMAN, THE SOCIAL ORIGINS OF THE IRAN-IRAQ WAR (Ige F. Dekker & H.G. Post eds., 1994) (focusing on the social origins and foundations of the war).

15. For a description of the First Gulf War, see generally NORMAN SCHWARZKOPF, IT DOESN'T TAKE A HERO: THE AUTOBIOGRAPHY OF GENERAL H. NORMAN SCHWARZKOPF 291–491 (1992).

16. S.C. Res. 678, U.N. SCOR, 45th Sess., 2963d mtg. at 27–28, U.N. Doc. S/RES/678 (1990).

17. *See* Human Rights Watch, Endless Torment: The 1991 Uprising in Iraq and Its Aftermath, *at* http://hrw.org/reports/1992/Iraq926.htm (June 1, 1992).

18. *See generally* TRIPP, *supra* note 6, at 243–48, 253–59 (discussing Kurdish resistance and suppression).

19. The no-fly zone was imposed in April 1991 with the United States, the UK, and France relying on UN Security Council Resolution 687. S.C. Res. 688, U.N. SCOR, 46th Sess., 2982d mtg. at 31–32, U.N. Doc. S/RES/688 (1991); S.C. Res. 699, U.N. SCOR, 46th Sess., 2994th mtg. at 18–19, U.N. Doc. S/RES/699 (1991). Since Iraq's independence in 1932, the Kurds have called for self-rule in Iraqi Kurdistan. Iraq: Kurdish Autonomy, Library of Congress Country Studies, *at* http://lcweb2.loc.gov/cgi-bin/query/r?frd/cstdy:@field(DOCID+iq0076) (last updated May 1988). The Kurds were first colonized by the Persians, then by the Turkish Ottoman Empire, and when Britain defeated Turkey in World War I, it included what is now Iraqi Kurdistan in that new country. FROMKIN, *supra* note 5, at 503. Kurds in neighboring Turkey constitute almost twenty percent of that country's contemporary population. Turkey: Society, Library of Congress Country Studies, *at* http://lcweb2.loc.gov/cgi-bin/query/r?frd/cstdy:@field(DOCID+tr0006) (last updated Jan.

1995). They are also a minority in Syria. Syria: Kurds, Library of Congress Country Studies, *at* http://lcweb2.loc.gov/cgi-bin/query/r?frd/cstdy:@field(DOCID+sy0036) (Apr. 1987). The Kurds, who are Muslim, have their own language, culture, and traditions. They are not ethnically Arab (of Semitic origin), and have always maintained their claim to nationhood in all three countries, which led to alternating periods of struggle and repression by the governments of Iraq, Turkey, and Syria. Iraq: Kurds, Library of Congress Country Studies, *at* http://lcweb2.loc.gov/cgi-bin/query/r?frd/cstdy:@field(DOCID+iq0032) (last updated May 1988). In 1970, an Autonomy Agreement was negotiated between the Ba'ath regime and Kurdish representatives, establishing an Autonomous Region consisting of the three Kurdish governorates and other adjacent districts determined by census to contain a Kurdish majority. Iraq: Kurdish Autonomy, *supra*. The Autonomous Region was governed by an Executive Council and Legislative Assembly. *Id*. However, genuine self-rule never really existed, and the Ba'ath Party maintained strict control over the Region. *Id*. For example, any local enactments or administrative decisions that were deemed contrary to the "constitution, laws, or regulations" of the central government were countermanded. *Id*.

20. Estimates for the Anfal Campaign alone are 182,000, and estimates of bodies buried in mass graves are between 300,000 and 500,000. See U.S. Department of State, Fact Sheet: Past Repression and Atrocities by Saddam Hussein's Regime, *at* http://www.state.gov/s/wci/fs/19352.htm (Apr. 4, 2003) for compilation of statistics regarding human rights violations of the former Ba'ath regime.

21. *See* Tripp, *supra* note 6, at 194–99.

22. Eppel, *supra* note 8, at 253; Tripp, *supra* note 6, at 202–03.

23. Tripp, *supra* note 6, at 216–23.

24. *Id.*

25. *See supra* notes 19, 20.

26. Tripp, *supra* note 6, at 243. Barzani supported Iran during Iraq's invasion of that country. *Id.* at 229.

27. *See generally* Human Rights Watch & Physicians, Iraqi Kurdistan: The Destruction of Koreme During the Anfal Campaign, *at* http://www.hrw.org/reports/1992/iraqkor/ (Jan. 1993); Human Rights Watch, Genocide in Iraq: The Anfal Campaign Against the Kurds, *at* http://www.hrw.org/reports/1993/iraqanfal/ (July 1993).

28. *See* Human Rights Watch, The Iraqi Government Assault on the Marsh Arabs, *at* http://www.hrw.org/backgrounder/mena/marcharabs1.pdf (Jan. 2003).

29. The tip of the iceberg has been exposed in the ongoing UN investigation of the oil-for-food program from which millions of dollars were illegally siphoned off. *See* Interim Report, Independent Inquiry Committee into the United Nations Oil-for-Food Programme, *at* http://www.iic-offp.org/documents/InterimReportFeb2005.pdf (Feb. 3, 2005); Second Interim Report, Independent Inquiry Committee into the United Nations Oil-for-Food Programme, *at* http://www.iic-offp.org/documents/InterimReportMar2005.pdf (March 29, 2005); *see also* infra note 37; Susan Sachs & Judith Miller, *Saddam's Oil-Food Fraud:* "UN Let Him Do It," Int'l Herald Trib. (Paris), Aug. 13, 2004, at 1. For UN responses to the oil-for-food program criticism, see UN News Centre, Oil for Food Inquiry, *available at* http://www.un.org/apps/news/infocusRel.asp?infocusID=97&Body=Oil-for-Food&Body1=inquiry (last visited Apr. 5, 2005). The program was administered by a committee operating under the Security Council, not under the Secretary General's control. Yet, much of the media's contemporary criticism is unfairly directed against the Secretary

General. *See, e.g.*, Norm Coleman, *Kofi Annan Must Go*, WALL ST. J., Dec. 1, 2004, at A10 (calling for UN Secretary General Kofi Annan's resignation).

30. Although precise numbers are unavailable, the media and other sources, official and unofficial, have reported that one million casualties resulted from the eight-year Iraq-Iran war. *See* Edward T. Pound & Jennifer Jack, *Special Report: The Iraq Connection*, U.S. NEWS & WORLD REP., Nov. 22, 2004, at 46; Death Tolls for Major Wars and Atrocities of the Twentieth Century, *at* http://users.erols.com/mwhite28/warstat2.htm#Iran-Iraq (last updated July 2004) (estimating that approximately 300,000 to 400,000 Iraqis and 600,000 to 700,000 Iranians perished during the Iran-Iraq War). Other estimates place the death toll at 1.5 million. *See* Interview by Dan Rather with Saddam Hussein on CBS News, 60 Minutes (CBS television broadcast, July 1, 2004), *video streaming and transcript available at* http://www.cbsnews.com/stories/2003/02/26/60II/main542151.shtml (last visited Apr. 5, 2005).

After the Gulf War, the U.S. Defense Intelligence Agency's approximated the death toll at around 100,000 Iraqi casualties. Patrick E. Tyler, *Iraq's War Toll Estimated by U.S.*, N.Y. TIMES, June 5, 1991, at A5. However, it is difficult to obtain estimates for this war due to the number of unidentified bodies that were either never recovered or were thrown into mass graves by coalition forces. *Comptons* has stated that 150,000 Iraqi soldiers were killed, and the *World Political Almanac* gives the same figure but includes civilian deaths. *See* Death Tolls for Major Wars and Atrocities of the Twentieth Century, *at* http://users.erols.com/mwhite28/warstat2.htm#Iran-Iraq (citing *Comptons* and *World Political Almanac*) (last updated July 2004).

31. *See* Barbara Crossette, *Iraq Sanctions Kill Children*, N.Y. TIMES, Dec. 1, 1995, at A9. In 1999, the UN estimated that one million Iraqis died due to the UN sanctions pursuant to Security Council Resolution 661. *Id.* The twelve-year embargo was finally lifted on May 22, 2003, when the Security Council adopted Resolution 1483. S.C. Res. 1483, U.N. SCOR, 58th Sess., 4761st mtg., U.N. Doc. S/RES/1483 (2003). The following Security Council Resolutions address the UN-imposed Iraq sanction regime: S.C. Res. 661, U.N. SCOR, 45th Sess., 2933d mtg., U.N. Doc. S/RES/661 (1990); S.C. Res. 665, U.N. SCOR, 45th Sess., 2938th mtg., U.N. Doc. S/RES/665 (1990); S.C. Res. 666, U.N. SCOR, 45th Sess., 2939th mtg., U.N. Doc. S/RES/666 (1990); S.C. Res. 669, U.N. SCOR, 45th Sess., 2942d mtg., U.N. Doc. S/RES/669 (1990); S.C. Res. 670, U.N. SCOR, 45th Sess., 2943d mtg., U.N. Doc. S/RES/670 (1990); S.C. Res. 687, U.N. SCOR, 46th Sess., 2981st mtg., U.N. Doc. S/RES/687 (1991); S.C. Res. 700, U.N. SCOR, 46th Sess., 2994th mtg., U.N. Doc. S/RES/700 (1991); S.C. Res. 706, U.N. SCOR, 46th Sess., 3004th mtg., U.N. Doc. S/RES/706 (1991); S.C. Res. 712, U.N. SCOR, 46th Sess., 3008th mtg., U.N. Doc. S/RES/712 (1991); S.C. Res. 986, U.N. SCOR, 50th Sess., 3519th mtg., U.N. Doc. S/RES/986 (1995); S.C. Res. 1051, U.N. SCOR, 51st Sess., 3644th mtg., U.N. Doc. S/RES/1051 (1996); S.C. Res. 1115 U.N. SCOR, 52d Sess., 3792d mtg., U.N. Doc. S/RES/1115 (1997); S.C. Res. 1129, U.N. SCOR, 52d Sess., 3817th mtg., U.N. Doc. S/RES/1129 (1997); S.C. Res. 1134 U.N. SCOR, 52d Sess., 3826th mtg., U.N. Doc. S/RES/1134 (1997); S.C. Res. 1137 U.N. SCOR, 52d Sess., 3831st mtg., U.N. Doc. S/RES/1137 (1997); S.C. Res. 1143, U.N. SCOR, 52d Sess., 3840th mtg., U.N. Doc. S/RES/1143 (1997); S.C. Res. 1153, U.N. SCOR, 53d Sess., 3855th mtg., U.N. Doc. S/RES/1153 (1998); S.C. Res. 1158, U.N. SCOR, 53d Sess., 3865th mtg., U.N. Doc. S/RES/1158 (1998); S.C. Res. 1175, U.N. SCOR, 53d Sess., 3893d mtg., U.N. Doc.

S/RES/1175 (1998); S.C. Res. 1210, U.N. SCOR, 53d Sess., 3946th mtg., U.N. Doc.
S/RES/1210 (1998); S.C. Res. 1242, U.N. SCOR, 54th Sess., 4008th mtg., U.N. Doc.
S/RES/1242 (1999); S.C. Res. 1266, U.N. SCOR, 54th Sess., 4050th mtg., U.N. Doc.
S/RES/1266 (1999); S.C. Res. 1281, U.N. SCOR 54th Sess., 4079th mtg., U.N. Doc.
S/RES/1281 (1999); S.C. Res. 1284, U.N. SCOR, 54th Sess., 4084th mtg., U.N. Doc.
S/RES/1284 (1999); S.C. Res. 1293, U.N. SCOR, 55th Sess., 4123d mtg., U.N. Doc.
S/RES/1293 (2000); S.C. Res. 1302, U.N. SCOR, 55th Sess., 4152d mtg., U.N. Doc.
S/RES/1302 (2000); S.C. Res. 1330, U.N. SCOR, 55th Sess., 4241st mtg., U.N. Doc.
S/RES/1330 (2000); S.C. Res. 1352, U.N. SCOR, 56th Sess., 4324th mtg., U.N. Doc.
S/RES/1352 (2001); S.C. Res. 1360, U.N. SCOR, 56th Sess., 4344th mtg., U.N. Doc.
S/RES/1360 (2001); S.C. Res. 1382, U.N. SCOR, 56th Sess., 4431st mtg., U.N. Doc.
S/RES/1382 (2001); S.C. Res. 1409, U.N. SCOR, 57th Sess., 4531st mtg., U.N. Doc.
S/RES/1409 (2002); S.C. Res. 1443, U.N. SCOR, 57th Sess., 4650th mtg., U.N. Doc.
S/RES/1443 (2002); S.C. Res. 1447, U.N. SCOR, 57th Sess., 4656th mtg., U.N. Doc.
S/RES/1447 (2002); S.C. Res. 1454, U.N. SCOR, 57th Sess., 4683d mtg., U.N. Doc.
S/RES/1454 (2002); S.C. Res. 1472, U.N. SCOR, 58th Sess., 4732d mtg., U.N. Doc.
S/RES/1472 (2003); S.C. Res. 1483, U.N. SCOR 58th Sess., 4761st mtg., U.N. Doc.
S/RES/1483 (2003).

For a discussion of the legality of these UN sanctions, see W. Michael Reisman & Douglas L. Stevick, *The Applicability of International Law Standards to United Nations Economic Sanctions Programmes*, 9 EUR. J. INT'L L. 86 (1998) (concluding that the Council has failed to give adequate weight to international law and recommending legal principles for mandatory economic sanctions programs); and Paul Conlon, *Legal Problems at the Centre of the United Nations Sanctions*, 65 NORDIC J. INT'L L. 73 (1996) (discussing the legal relationships of the UN Committees and the problems that arise between them). Another estimate that Iraqis and the rest of the Arab world compare to the regime's violations is the estimated 100,000 Iraqis killed by Coalition forces between March 2003 and September 2004. *See* Les Roberts et al., *Mortality Before and After the 2003 Invasion of Iraq: Cluster Sample Survey*, THE LANCET, 364, 1857–64 (2004). The relevance of these comparisons is that opponents of accountability for the Saddam regime raise these estimates to show that the United States is also blameworthy and that it does not come forth with "clean hands" when it condemns this regime.

32. Much of what this Article describes is based on this writer's personal involvement in the process or his direct knowledge of events. Some of these facts, however, are not a matter of public record and cannot be documented. Much more than what is known to this writer is sure to have occurred within the U.S. Government and elsewhere. Consequently, what follows is not presented as a complete description of all endeavors relating to Iraqi post-conflict justice.

33. *See, e.g.*, Human Rights Watch, Justice for Iraq: A Human Rights Watch Policy Paper, *at* http://hrw.org/backgrounder/mena/iraq1217bg.htm (Dec. 2002) (calling for the prosecution of Ba'ath party leadership for human rights violations).

34. In February 1991, a partner of this firm who requested anonymity contacted me to solicit my views on these proposals and my advice on how to advance them.

35. This lack of interest may be due to Arab states' reluctance to establish a precedent of calling Arab leaders to justice or to Arabs' popular resentment of the U.S. military intervention in Iraq and of its support of Israel. Historically, regime change in Arab states

has been accompanied by summary executions or imprisonment of previous regime leaders. Post-conflict justice has not been the practice, although after Gamal Abdel-Nasser's death in Egypt and the assumption of the presidency by Anwar al-Sadat in 1971, a number of former Nasser regime officials were put on trial for various atrocities, including summary executions, torture, and other human rights abuses. Among those defendants was Salah Nasr, a former head of the *Mukhabarat* (Egyptian intelligence), who was convicted and subsequently served a few years in jail. Afterwards, Nasr wrote his memoirs, and blamed Nasser for his actions. *See generally* SALAH NASR, THIKRAYAT: AL-THAWRA, AL NAKSA, AL-MUKHABARAT [REMEMBRANCE: THE REVOLUTION, THE DISASTER AND THE IN-TELLIGENCE] (1999) (Nasr's autobiography).

36. Similar to other Arab countries, Saudi Arabia's reluctance to endorse an Iraqi war crimes tribunal may be explained by a historic lack of interest in international criminal justice. For example, between 1992 and 1994, the Saudis did not contribute to the Voluntary Trust Fund of the UN Security Council Commission of Experts for the Former Yugoslavia. *See Final Report of the U.N. Commission of Experts Pursuant to S.C. Resolution 780* (1992), U.N SCOR, 49th Sess., Annex, at 12, U.N. Doc. S/1994/674 (1994) (enumerating the countries which contributed to the Voluntary Trust Fund).

37. The archives of data related to Iraqi prisoners of war ("POWs") were then called the "Boulder files." Some of that material concerning the Ba'ath regime's Anfal Campaign, *supra* note 20 and accompanying text, and the Marshland people's internal displacement, *supra* note 28 and accompanying text, reportedly was provided to Human Rights Watch, which published reports on these events. Most of these documents came from the Kurdish north after the 1991 uprising. It is estimated that eighteen tons of documents, including prison files, and video and audio recordings documenting individual crimes and widespread abuses of fundamental human rights were collected. Moreover, some documentation was obtained by the coalition forces in Kuwait. Some of these documents have been digitized by the Iraq Foundation, whose President, Rend Rahim, recently served as Iraq's Ambassador to the United States.

38. Such commissions have historically met with a tepid response in the Arab world. *See* discussion *supra* note 36.

39. France, Russia, and the UK had significant economic ties with the Ba'ath regime. In addition, Saddam had bestowed massive financial support on neighboring Arab governments and senior individuals in certain countries including Jordan, Syria, Turkey, Palestine, and Egypt, as well as others, as documentation of Iraqi oil vouchers later indicated. *See* Perry Beacon, Jr., *A Deepening U.N. Scandal*, TIME (London), Nov. 29, 2004, at 16; Bill Gertz, *Saddam Paid Off French Leaders: $1.78 Billion in Oil-Food Funds Went To Buy Influence at the U.N.*, WASH. TIMES, Oct. 7, 2004, at A14. China was also reluctant to see the Security Council become more involved with the business of regime violations investigations.

40. Secretary Albright was, however, interested in pursuing the option of a Security Council Commission. Ambassador David Scheffer, then the Department of State's (DOS) Ambassador-at-large for War Crimes, under the direction of Secretary Albright, was also involved in this process. He had played an important role with the Yugoslavia Commission between 1992 and 1994, which I chaired, and he asked me whether I would chair a similar commission for Iraq.

41. As an expert to the "Working Group on Transitional Justice" under the "Future of Iraq" Project, I prepared a comprehensive post-conflict justice plan in January 2003. *See* M. Cherif

Bassiouni, Iraq Post-Conflict Justice: A Proposed Plan, *available at* http://www. law.depaul.edu/institutes_centers/ihrli/_downloads/Iraq_Proposal_04.pdf (last revised Jan. 2, 2004, based on plan prepared Apr. 28, 2003). The plan was modified in April 2003 after broad governmental and NGO consultations. Among those who worked with me then and who continue to have a leading role in Iraq is Ambassador Feisal Istrabadi, who is Deputy Permanent Representative of Iraq to the UN. Previously, Istrabadi was an aide to General Council ("GC") member Dr. Adnan Pachachi, and, in that capacity, he contributed to the drafting of the Transitional Administrative Law ("TAL"), which is the equivalent of a temporary constitution. For a discussion of the TAL, and accompanying text. Ambassador Istrabadi has been a Senior Fellow at IHRLI since 2002. Another member of the Working Group was Attorney Sermid Al-Sarraf, who has been the IHRLI's Chief of Party in Iraq since October 2003 and who oversees the IHRLI's "Raising the Bar" Project in Iraq (a project designed to restructure legal education in that country. International Human Rights Law Institute, Raising the Bar: Legal Education and Reform in Iraq, *at* http://www.law.depaul.edu/institutes_centers/ihrli/programs/rule_ed-ucation.asp (last visited Apr. 5, 2005). Mr. Al-Sarraf summarized the 700-page report of the "Working Group on Transitional Justice," and the report was publicly released in New York on May 15, 2003. Salem Chalabi was another member of that working group, and he prepared the statute of the Iraqi Special Tribunal ("IHT") on the basis of this writer's proposals. For a description of some details of the "Future of Iraq" Project's, see David Rieff, *Blueprint for a Mess*, N.Y. TIMES, Nov. 2, 2003, at 28; Eric Schmitt & Joel Brinkley, *State Department Study Foresaw Troubles Plaguing Postwar Iraq*, N.Y. TIMES, Oct. 19, 2003, at 1.

42. The coordinator of this project was Thomas Warrick, who was previously Ambassador Scheffer's deputy in the Department of State ("DOS") War Crimes Bureau during the Clinton Administration. Mr. Warrick moved to the Iraq desk to work on Iraqi regime prosecutions shortly before George W. Bush came into office. Mr. Warrick served as my legal counsel when I was the Chairman of the UN Security Commission Established Pursuant to Resolution 780 (1992).

43. As stated above, Salem Chalabi was a member of this working group. He is the nephew of the former GC member Ahmed Chalabi, who was then known for being supported by the DOD's civilian leadership and who later fell out of grace with the U.S. government. Salem relied on this writer's proposed plan to prepare the IHT's Statute. He subsequently became the IHT's Administrator. *See infra* note 63. He was appointed to that post by the GC on May 8, 2004, and was tasked with setting up the organization and structure of the IHT and with working on the selection and vetting of sitting judges, investigative judges, and prosecutors. However, in August 2004, Zuhair Maliky, an investigating judge of Iraq's Central Criminal Court, issued an arrest warrant for Ahmed Chalabi on charges of counterfeiting currency, and an arrest warrant for Salem Chalabi on suspicion of murder. *See* Rajiv Chandrasekaren & Carol D. Leonnig, *Chalabi Back in Iraq, Aide Says: Former US Client Charged with Counterfeiting Currency*, WASH. POST, Aug. 12, 2004, at A19; Jim Krane, *Politics Afoot in a Bid To Rush Saddam Trial, Ousted Tribunal Director Says*, ASSOCIATED PRESS, Sept. 24 2004; Jackie Spinner, *Premier Warns Gunmen in Najaf; Arrest Warrants Issued for Chalabi, Nephew*, WASH. POST, Aug. 9, 2004, at A1. It should be noted that the charges of August 8, 2004, against Ahmed and Salem Chalabi were subsequently reported to have been dropped. Salem Chalabi, who fled to London, resigned his post but is likely to return soon to Iraq. Politics notwithstanding, Salem Chalabi was committed to post-conflict justice in Iraq, and his efforts in that respect should be acknowledged. In Jan-

uary 2005, however, in the latest bizarre twist of events, the Iraqi government made it known that it was going to arrest Ahmed Chalabi and hand him over to Interpol, which has had an outstanding arrest warrant against him since 1992 for an in absentia criminal conviction in Jordan for embezzlement of funds when he was in charge of Petra Bank. *See* Chandrasekaren & Leonnig, *supra*. At the time of his conviction in 1992 by a Jordanian criminal court, Ahmed Chalabi escaped to England. In addition to a twenty-two-year sentence of hard labor, Chalabi's sentence also included an order for restitution of $230 million. Chalabi's status as a wanted criminal in Jordan is well-known, yet he remains a free man and claims that the Jordanian conviction was the product of a political setup. *See* Jane Mayer, *The Manipulator: Ahmed Chalabi Pushed a Tainted Case for War. Can He Survive the Occupation?*, THE NEW YORKER, June 7, 2004, at 58. Most recently, Ahmed Chalabi filed a lawsuit against the Jordanian government in U.S. federal court based on his 1992 conviction for embezzlement and other crimes. *See* Chandrasekaren & Leonnig, *supra*. At the time of this writing, he had just been elected as a member of the new Iraqi legislative body in the January 30, 2005 elections as part of the Shi'? list.

44. *See* Bassiouni, *supra* note 41.

45. This was probably based on a faulty interpretation of a speech made in Arabic by the Ba'athist Minister of Information, Mohammed Saeed Al-Sahhaf, who made public statements days before the attack on Baghdad, some reported on CNN, that Iraqi forces would use "unconventional" means against the United States. What he probably meant by "unconventional" was the guerrilla warfare tactics that some Iraqis employed after the fall of Baghdad. For an in-depth analysis of the war, see JOHN KEEGAN, THE IRAQ WAR (2004).

46. At the time that the ad hoc criminal tribunal was being considered, Congressman Mark Kirk (R., Ill.), the ranking Republican member of the House Appropriations Committee, called this writer and asked him to prepare a statute and a draft Security Council resolution to be forwarded to Secretary of Defense Donald H. Rumsfeld and U.S. Ambassador to Iraq John D. Negroponte.

47. William J. Broad, *A Nation at War: Outlawed Weapons; Some Skeptics Say Arms Hunt Is Fruitless*, N.Y. TIMES, Apr. 18, 2003, at B8; Jodi Wilgoren & Adam Nagourney, *A Nation at War: The Casualties; While Mourning Dead, Many Americans Say Level of Casualties Is Acceptable*, N.Y. TIMES, Apr. 8, 2003, at B1.

48. *See* S.C. Res. 827, U.N. SCOR, 48th Sess., 3217th mtg., U.N. Doc. S/RES/827 (1993); S.C. Res. 955, U.N. SCOR, 49th Sess., 3453d mtg., U.N. Doc. S/RES/955 (1994).

49. *See* S.C. Res 1315, U.N. SCOR, 55th Sess., 4186th mtg., U.N. Doc. S/RES/1315 (2000); Jennifer L. Poole, *Post-Conflict Justice in Sierra Leone, in* POST-CONFLICT JUSTICE.

50. At initial meetings NGOs expressed a preference for an internationally mandated institution. However, a "mixed" international and national tribunal, similar to the Special Court for Sierra Leone, was viewed as the second-best option. *See* Letter from Human Rights Watch to the U.S. Regarding the Creation of a Criminal Tribunal for Iraq (Apr. 15, 2003), *available at* http://www.hrw.org/press/2003/04/iraqtribunal041503ltr.htm (last visited Apr. 5, 2005). For further details of the Sierra Leone Special Tribunal, see Poole, *supra* note 49, and JOHN R.W.D. JONES & STEVEN POWLES, INTERNATIONAL CRIMINAL PRACTICE: THE INTERNATIONAL CRIMINAL TRIBUNAL FOR THE FORMER YUGOSLAVIA, THE INTERNATIONAL CRIMINAL TRIBUNAL FOR RWANDA, THE INTERNATIONAL CRIMINAL COURT, THE SPECIAL COURT FOR SIERRA LEONE, THE EAST TIMOR SPECIAL PANEL FOR SERIOUS CRIMES, WAR CRIMES PROSECUTIONS IN KOSOVO (3d ed. 2003).

51. They were killed by U.S. forces in a raid on their hideout in Mosul on July 22, 2003. *See* Neil MacFarquhar, *Hussein's Two Sons Dead in Shootout, U.S. Says,* N.Y. TIMES, July 23, 2003, at A1.

52. During this time, Rumsfeld indicated that plea bargains with these leaders were possible. *See* Rumsfeld Briefing, *supra* note. Saddam was captured by U.S. forces at Al-Dawr, near Tikrit, on December 13, 2003. *See* Susan Sachs & Kirk Semple, *Ex-Leader, Found Hiding in Hole, Is Detained Without Fight,* N.Y. TIMES, Dec. 14, 2003, at A1.

53. *See* OPEN SOCIETY INSTITUTE & THE UNITED NATIONS FOUNDATION, IRAQ IN TRANSITION, POST-CONFLICT CHALLENGES AND OPPORTUNITIES 85–87 (2004); Bassiouni, *supra* note 41, at 48.

54. *See supra* note 49 and accompanying text.

55. These ideas were discussed on June 11, 2003, at a White House meeting between Kenneth Roth, Executive Director of Human Rights Watch ("HRW"), and Condoleezza Rice, then National Security Adviser to the President. The U.S. Administration argued that Security Council Resolution 1483, operative paragraph 8(i), empowered the CPA to carry out investigations and engage in subsequent prosecutions. *See* S.C. Res. 1483, U.N. SCOR, 58th Sess., 4761st mtg. at 3, U.N. Doc. S/RES/1483 (2003). Paragraph 8(i) is ambiguous in referring to "encouraging international efforts to promote legal and judicial reform." *Id.* Thus, the U.S. Administration employed a great deal of latitude in relying on this paragraph to justify the establishment of an entirely new judicial institution.

56. *See* Bassiouni, *supra* note 41.

57. *See supra* note 41.

58. *See* U.N. General Assembly, General Assembly Adopts $3.16 Billion 2004–2005 Budget as It Concludes Main Part of Fifty-Eighth Session, *at* http://www.un.org/News/Press/docs/2003/ga10225.doc.htm (Dec. 12, 2003). For example, the budgets for the International Criminal Tribunal for the Former Yugoslavia ("ICTY") and the International Criminal Tribunal for Rwanda ("ICTR") in 2004 to 2005 alone were $298.23 million and $235.32 million respectively. Id. Cumulatively the ICTY and ICTR have cost over $1 billion to date. *Id.* Both the ICTY and ICTR have been criticized for their cost and the slow pace of the trials. *See* International Crisis Group, International Criminal Justice for Rwanda: Justice Delayed, *at* http://www.icg.org/home/index.cfm?id=1649&I=1 (June 7, 2001). For a review of the ICTY and ICTR's judicial work and jurisprudence see Megan Kaszubinski, *The International Criminal Tribunal for the Former Yugoslavia, in* POST-CONFLICT JUSTICE, *supra* note at 459–85; Roman Boed, *The International Criminal Tribunal for Rwanda, in* POST-CONFLICT JUSTICE, *supra* note, at 487–98. For an analysis of the ad hoc tribunal's jurisprudence, see generally 1–4 ANNOTATED LEADING CASES OF INTERNATIONAL CRIMINAL TRIBUNALS, INTERNATIONAL CRIMINAL TRIBUNAL FOR THE FORMER YUGOSLAVIA (Andre Klip & Goran Sluiter eds., 1999); JOHN R.W.D. JONES, THE PRACTICE OF THE INTERNATIONAL CRIMINAL TRIBUNALS FOR THE FORMER YUGOSLAVIA AND RWANDA (2d ed. 2000).

59. The death penalty has long been an accepted part of the Iraqi criminal law system. It is a penalty that the majority of Iraqis favor for Saddam and for the senior perpetrators of his regime.

60. *See* authorities cited *supra.*

61. This writer supports this view but differs with the Administration as to the heavy footprints of U.S. government on the process.

62. This was still a period where lack of clarity existed within the Administration as to the channels of authority on this subject. In other words, no one in high authority was leading this project. There was also infighting between the DOS and the DOD, which had ignored the DOS's "Future of Iraq" Project report. The CPA had a human rights office headed by a capable and committed human rights advocate, Sandra Hodgkinson, who is now at the National Security Agency ("NSA"), and her husband, David Hodgkinson, an equally capable and committed CPA official responsible for post-conflict justice, who now serves at the DOS. Their authority, however, was limited, and in fact, even Bremer's authority was limited on this subject. The National Security Council ("NSC") had another capable person responsible for justice issues, Clint Williamson, but his authority was also limited. At the NSC, these issues involved Robert D. Blackwill, then responsible for Iraq and Afghanistan, and Elliot Abrams, who was, and still is, responsible for the Middle East. Neither are lawyers, and they seem to have given justice issues a low priority. The NSC then decided to give the DOJ "lead agency" status over Iraqi justice issues without regard to the fact that the DOJ, a domestic prosecutorial and law enforcement agency, has no experience in such international justice issues and has no expertise on the Iraqi legal system among its personnel. The DOS's Office of War Crimes, headed by Ambassador Pierre-Richard Prosper, was not given the full role that this office was originally set up to play in these matters. Ambassador Prosper was the deputy head of that office under the Clinton Administration. He had previously served in the DOJ and as a prosecutor at the ICTR. It may have been assumed that DOJ would rely on the "Future of Iraq Working Group on Transitional Justice" and its experts, which some in the White House and in the DOD opposed. The DOJ was apparently sensitive to these currents, and it even sent an assessment team to Iraq consisting of distinguished federal judges and prosecutors, none of whom knew the Iraqi legal system, and it excluded U.S. experts of the "Working Group on Transitional Justice."

63. *See* THE STATUTE OF THE IRAQI SPECIAL TRIBUNAL; *Salem Chalabi: Judging Saddam*, 11 MIDDLE E. Q. 325 (2004), *available at* http://www.meforum.org/article/664 (last visited Apr. 5, 2005). While he presided over the GC during September 2003, Salem Chalabi was asked, with the approval of the CPA, by his uncle Ahmed Chalabi, to prepare a draft statute for a special tribunal. Salem Chalabi relied on the draft statute that this author prepared in March 2003, which was intended for a UN Security Council mandated institution. In his attempts to use this draft statute for a national tribunal, Salem Chalabi did not address a number of legal problems, which exacerbated the IHT's legitimacy and credibility problems. Among these legal problems was the fact that the draft statute was modeled on an accusatorial-adversarial model, while Iraqi law is based on an inquisitorial system. As a result of these apparent flaws, a meeting was held at the International Institute of Higher Studies in Criminal Sciences ("ISISC"), Siracusa, Italy, from December 7 to 12, 2003, to review the draft IHT statute with CPA participation, and to address other issues. However, the meeting was called off just days before it was scheduled to commence, because, in the interim, the CPA had decided that the IHT should be promulgated on December 10, given that the capture of Saddam Hussein appeared imminent. For Salem Chalabi's perceptions, see *Salem Chalabi: Judging Saddam, supra*.

64. *See* THE STATUTE OF THE IRAQI SPECIAL TRIBUNAL.

65. For a discussion of the CPA's authority to establish the IST, *see infra* Part IV.B.

66. *See* CPA Transcripts, *Bremer Affirms: Iraq Turns the Page*, Apr. 23, 2004, *available at* http://www.iraqcoalition.org/transcripts/20040423_page_turn.html (last visited Apr. 5, 2005).

67. *See* Neil A. Lewis & David Johnston, *U.S. Team Is Sent To Develop Case in Hussein Trial*, N.Y. TIMES, Mar. 7, 2004, at 1.

68. While all courts have the potential to be undermined or challenged by particularly pugnacious and obstreperous defendants, as is currently the case in the ICTY Milosevic Trial, *see* Keith B. Richburg, *At Tribunal, Milosevic Blames NATO: Yugoslav Ex-Leader Opens Defense, Mostly Ignores Charges*, WASH. POST, Feb. 15, 2002, at A1, a lack of legal clarity existed in Saddam's "arraignment." This disconnect pertained to whether the procedure performed was ad hoc and whether the magistrates were chosen by the United States. The proceedings were choreographed as an American hearing where an investigative judge read an indictment and asked the defendant to plead guilty or not guilty, and was thus more American than Iraqi. There is no such procedure in the Iraqi criminal justice system. The investigative judge, sitting behind a table facing Saddam, was obviously uncomfortable. On the table where he sat facing Saddam Hussein was a copy of the 1971 Iraqi Code of Criminal Procedure, which does not provide for such an American-style arraignment procedure. The investigative judge asked Saddam to enter a plea, something unknown in the Iraqi system, and Saddam, who has a law degree, realized this. Saddam then retorted that he was still a head of state under Iraqi law and that the investigative judge had no legal right or basis to question him. *See* John F. Burns, *Defiant Hussein Rebukes Iraqi Court for Trying Him: Tells Judge He Is Still Lawful President*, N.Y. TIMES, July 2, 2004, at A1.

69. Additional capacity is needed at all levels of the Iraqi judicial system. However, that should not be done in a way that leaves heavy U.S. footprints.

70. Having gotten to know the IST judges, investigative judges, and prosecutors, I can attest to their commitment to justice. Still, they can benefit from more expertise, as they freely acknowledge.

71. G Robertson *The Tyrannicide Brief* (Chatto and Windus 2005) 6.

72. JE Persico *Infamy on Trial* (Penguin 1994) 83.

73. S Milosevic, Statement of Slobodan Milosevic on the Illegitimacy of the Hague Tribunal (Aug. 30, 2001) <http:www.slobodan-milosevic.org/spch-icty.htm>.

74. R McCarthy, 'I Am Saddam Hussein, the President of Iraq', The Guardian, July 2, 2004 75 R Cornwell 'Saddam in the Dock: Listen to His Victims, Not Saddam, Says White House' *The Independent* (2 July 2004) (reporting that Hussein stated, 'This is all theater,' at his first pre-trial hearing) <http://news.independent.co.uk/world/americas/story.jsp?story= 537296>.

76. Defiant Saddam Rejects Court, Charges, CNN.com, July 1, 2004 <http:www.cnn. com/2004/WORLD/meast/07/01iraq.saddam/> Lawyers hired by Saddam Hussein's wife rapidly played the legitimacy card by claiming that the IST could not impose any punishments lawfully because it lacked legitimacy, or lawful creation and accordingly its operation violated core human rights norms. R McCarthy and J Steele '**Saddam** on Trial: **Legitimacy** and Neutrality of Court Will Be *Challenged*' The Guardian (2 July 2004) <http://www.guardian.co.uk/Iraq/Story/0,2763,1252096,00.html>.

77. See generally Regulations annexed to Hague Convention IV Respecting the Laws and Customs of War on Land (1907 Hague Regulations) entered into force 26 Jan 1910, reprinted in A Roberts & R Guelff (eds) *Documentation on the Laws of War* (3rd edn Oxford University Press Oxford 2000) 73; Fourth Geneva Convention (n 14) arts 47–78.

78. 1907 Hague Regulations (n 84) art 42. See also *Department of the Army Field Manual 27–10; The Law of Land Warfare* (Washington 1956) ¶ 351 [FM 27-10]. The whole of

Chapter 6 of the United States Army Field Manual related to the law of armed conflict is devoted to explicating the text of the law related to occupation as well as the United States policy related to occupation.

79. UK Ministry of Defense *The Manual of the Law of Armed Conflict* (Oxford University Press Oxford 2004) 275 ¶ 11.3.

80. FM 27-10 (n 85) ¶ 352.

81. Protocol I (n 15) art 4. The United States policy in this regard is clear that occupation confers only the 'means of exercising control for the period of occupation. It does not transfer the sovereignty to the occupant, but simply the authority or power to exercise some of the rights of sovereignty.' FM 27-10 (n 12) ¶ 358.

82. 1907 Hague Regulations (n 84) art 43.

83. Ibid. The conceptual limitations of foreign occupation also warranted a temporal limitation built into the 1949 Geneva Conventions that the general application of the law of occupation 'shall cease one year after the general close of military operations.' Fourth Geneva Convention (n 14) art 6. Based on pure pragmatism, Article 6 of the IVth Geneva Convention does permit the application of a broader range of specific treaty provisions 'for the duration of the occupation, to the extent that such Power exercises the functions of government in such territory.' ibid. The 1977 Protocols eliminated the patchwork approach to treaty protections with the simple declarative that 'the application of the Conventions and of this Protocol shall cease, in the territory of the Parties to the conflict, on the general close of military operations and, in the case of occupied territories, on the termination of occupation.' Protocol I (n 15) art 3(b).

84. UNSC Res 827 (25 May 1993).

85. UN Charter art 39 (giving the Security Council the power to 'determine the existence of any threat to peace, breach of the peace, or act of aggression' and it 'shall make recommendations, or decide what measures shall be taken in accordance with Articles 41… to maintain or restore international peace and security').

86. *Prosecutor v. Tadic (Decision on the Defense Motion on Jurisdiction)* IT-94-1 (10 August 1995) <http://www.un.org/icty/tadic/trialc2/decision-e/100895.htm> ('This International Tribunal is not a constitutional court set up to scrutinize the actions of organs of the United Nations. It is, on the contrary, a criminal tribunal with clearly defined powers, involving a quite specific and limited criminal jurisdiction. If it is to confine its adjudications to those specific limits, it will have no authority to investigate the legality of its creation by the Security Council.')

87. UN Charter art 24(1).

88. Fourth Geneva Convention (n 14) arts 68 and 78 (permitting detention of civilians for "imperative reasons of security"). See also *Human Rights Watch, A Face and a Name: Civilian Victims of Insurgent Groups in Iraq* Vol 17 No 9(E) (October 2005) (finding that the insurgents in Iraq who are indiscriminately targeting civilians and western contractors are not entitled under the Geneva Conventions to conduct hostilities and are thus committing war crimes).

89. Fourth Geneva Convention (n 14) art 42.

90. *Prosecutor v. Delalic, Mucic, Delic, and Landzo (Celibici) (Judgment)* IT-96-21-T (20 Feb 2001).

91. Fourth Geneva Convention (n 14) art 47.

92. JS Pictet *Principles du droit international humanitaire* (CICR GenÈve 1966) 50.

93. FM 27-10 (n 85) ¶ 370.

94. Fourth Geneva Convention (n 14) art 54 ('the Occupying Power may not alter the status of public officials or judges, or in any way apply sanctions to or take measures of coercion or discrimination against them should they abstain from fulfilling their functions for reasons of conscience.').

95. 1907 Hague Regulations (n 84) art 43.

96. Y Dinstein 'Legislation Under Article 43 of the Hague Regulations: Belligerent Occupation and Peacebuilding' 1 (Fall 2004) Program on Humanitarian Policy and Conflict Research Harvard University Occasional Paper Series 8. See also EH Schwenk 'Legislative Powers of the Military Occupant Under Article 43, Hague Regulations' (1945) 54 Yale LJ 393.

97. L.C. Green, *The Contemporary Law of Armed Conflict* 259 (Juris 1999).

98. Ibid.

99. M Greenspan *The Modern Law of Land Warfare* (University of California Press Berkeley 1959) 223–7.

100. For example, the oath of the Nazi party stated: 'I owe inviolable fidelity to Adolf Hitler; I vow absolute obedience to him and to the leaders he designates for me.' DA Sprecher *Inside the Nuremberg Trial: A Prosecutor's Comprehensive Account* (University Press of America Lanham 1999) 1037–38. Accordingly, power resided in Hitler, from whom subordinates derived absolute authority in hierarchical order. This absolute and unconditional obedience to the superior in all areas of public and private life led in Justice Jackson's famous words to 'a National Socialist despotism equaled only by the dynasties of the ancient East.' Opening Statement to the International Military Tribunal at Nuremberg, II *Trial of the Major War Criminals Before the International Military Tribunal* 100 (1947).

101. G Schwarzenberger *The Law of Armed Conflict* (Stevens London 1968)194.

102. Fourth Geneva Convention (n 14) art 64.

103. Vienna Convention on the Law of Treaties art 31(1) (27 Jan 1980) 1155 UNTS 331, reprinted in 8 ILM (1969).

104. *UK Ministry of Defense, The Manual of the Law of Armed Conflict* (Oxford University Press Oxford 2004) 275 [11.56]. United States doctrine states that the 'occupant may alter, repeal, or suspend laws of the following types:

a. Legislation constituting a threat to its security, such as laws relating to recruitment and the bearing of arms.

b. Legislation dealing with political process, such as laws regarding the rights of suffrage and of assembly.

c. Legislation the enforcement of which would be inconsistent with the duties of the occupant, such as laws establishing racial discrimination.' FM 27-10 (n 85) ¶ 371.

105. Overview of Coalition Provisional Authority <http://www.iraqcoalition.org/bremerbio.html>.

106. Coalition Provisional Authority Regulation 1, http://www.cpa-iraq.org/regulations/20030516_CPAREG_1_The_Coalition_Provisional_Authority_.pdf>.

107. See Letter from the Permanent Representatives of the UK and the US to the UN addressed to the President of the Security Council (8 May 2003) UN Doc S/2003/538 <http://www.globalpolicy.org/security/issues/iraq/document/2003/0608usukletter.htm> (15 April 2005).

108. SC Res 1483 (22 May 2003).

109. General Eisenhower's Proclamation said, 'Supreme legislative, judicial, and executive authority and powers within the occupied territory are vested in me as Supreme Commander of the Allied Forces and as Military Governor, and the Military Government is established to exercise these powers.' Reprinted *in Military Government Gazette, Germany, United States Zone* (Office of Military Government for Germany US 1 June 1946) 1 Issue A (copy on file with author).

110. The Fourth Geneva Convention recognized the importance of individual rights enjoyed by the civilian population and the correlative duties of the occupier to that population. The structure of the Fourth Convention focused on the duties that an Occupying Power has towards the individual civilians and the overall societal structure rather than focusing on the relations between the victorious sovereign and the defeated government. Under the rejected concept of termed 'debellatio,' the enemy was utterly defeated and accordingly the defeated state forfeited its legal personality and was absorbed into the sovereignty of the occupier. Greenspan (n 106) 600–01. The successful negotiation of the Geneva Conventions in the aftermath of World War II marked the definitive rejection of the concept of debellatio, under which the occupier assumed full sovereignty over the civilians in the occupied territory. E Benvenisti *The International Law of Occupation* (Princeton University Press 1993) 92. Debellatio 'refers to a situation in which a party to a conflict has been totally defeated in war, its national institutions have disintegrated, and none of its allies continue militarily to challenge the enemy on its behalf.' ibid 59.

111. SC Res 1483 (22 May 2003) ¶ 5.

112. Ibid.

113. Ibid [4].

114. Coalition Provisional Authority Order Number No 7 (9 June 2003) Doc No CPA/MEM/9 (3 Jun 2003) [2] [3] <http://www.cpa-iraq.org/regulations/index.html#Orders> (copy on file with author).

115. Ibid.

116. Coalition Provisional Authority Memorandum Number 3: Criminal Procedures was revised on 27 June 2004 <http://www.cpa-iraq.org/regulations/20040627_CPAMEMO_3_Criminal_Procedures__Rev_.pdf>.

117. ICCPR (n 12) art 14 (describing analogous provisions derived from international human rights law).

118. UN Charter art 25.

119. Copy on file with author.

120. Fourth Geneva Convention (n 14) art 64 (2).

121. Ibid art 47. See also FM 27-10 (n 85) ¶ 365.

122. Ibid.

123. FM 27-10 (n 85) ¶ 366 (further specifying that 'Acts induced or compelled by the occupant are nonetheless its acts').

124. OM Uhler & H Coursier (eds) *Commentary on the Geneva Convention Relative to the Protection of Civilian Persons in Time of War* (ICRC Geneva 1958) vol IV 274 (explaining the intended implementation of the language of Article 47 Fourth Geneva Convention (n 14) art 47 ('any change introduced to domestic institutions by the occupying power must protect the rights of the civilian population').

125. W M Hudson 'The US Military Government and the Establishment of Democratic Reform, Federalism, and Constitutionalism During the Occupation of Bavaria 1945–47' (Summer 2004) 180 Mil il LR 115, 123.

126. **Editors Note:** This political psychology profile was written prior to the invasion of Iraq. We felt that its inclusion in its entirety provides an outstanding historical background on the evens leading up to the invasion of 2003. Dr. Post has provided a Postcript at the end of the profile, updating his analysis of events through the date of this book's publication.

127. **Editors Note:** Reprinted with permission from 37 Case Western Reserve Journal of International Law 21–40 (2005). This debate was aired nationally on C-SPAN on January 29, 2005. For consistency with the rest of the book, Iraqi Special Tribunal and IST have been changed to Iraqi High Tribunal and IHT respectively.

128. For a fuller treatment of this issue, *See* Michael P. Scharf and Christopher M. Rassi, Do Former Leaders have an International Right to Self-Representation in War Crimes Trials? 20 Ohio State Journal on Dispute Resolution 3–42 (2005).

129. This article is dedicated to Charity Kagwi-Ndungu, for always showing me how "Sisterhood is a powerful thing."

130. UNSCR 13 May 2003.

131. See Iraq: Focus on Women's Needs, posted on the Internet 29 April 2003. Website of InterAction, American Council for Voluntary International Action, Washington, D.C. (http://www.interaction.org/newswire/detail.php?id=1570).

132. See Role of Women in New Iraq of Concern, Posted on Women's E News website 22 April 2003. Article by Gretchen Cook, WeNews Correspondent, New York, New York (http://www.womensenews.org/article.cfm/dyn/aid/1301/context/archive).

133. Interview of Deputy Secretary of State Richard Armitage, BNBC Radio "Today" Transcript 7 May 2003.

134. Although no women prosecutors, judges, or defense attorneys appeared in court during the first 100 days of trial, later in the trial one female defense attorney would be added to the Hussein's defense team. It is interesting to note, however, that after being thrown out of court by the Chief Judge on 5 April 2006, her co-counsel asked that her outburst in court be excused because "women are emotional".

135. See U.S. State Department Country Reports on Human Rights Practices: Iraq 2002, Released by the Bureau of Democracy, Human Rights, and Labor, on March 31, 2003.

136. See Articles 12–14 of the Iraqi Statute.

137. See 6 December 2005 testimony of "Witness A."

138. Summary of Statement by Hon. Elizabeth Odio-Benito, former judge at the ICTY, in Women's Caucus for Gender Justice, "Testimony of Witness A," Victims and Witness in the ICC, Report of Panel Discussions on Appropriate Measures for Victim Participation and Protection in the ICC, July–August 1999 http://www.iccwomen.org/resources/vwicc/.

139. Hon. Navanethem Pillay, cited in Barbara Bedont and Katherine Hall Martinez, "Ending Impunity for Gender Crimes under the International Criminal Court," Brown Journal of World Affairs, vol. 6, Issue 1, pp. 65–85.

140. See Rhonda Copelon, "Gender Crimes As War Crimes: Integrating Crimes Against Women Into International Criminal Law", McGill Law Journal, November 2000.

141. See ICC Statute at Articles 44(2) and 36 (8).

142. Women's Initiative for Gender Justice, "2005 Gender Report Card on the International Criminal Court", at page 4.

143. The Statute of the Iraqi tribunal as well as its Rules of Evidence and Procedure, in many respects amounts to a cut and paste job of the legal documents underlying the Special Court for Sierra Leone, the ICTY and the ICTR. It was thought important enough to require the set up of the Iraqi tribunal to include international advisers. That was because it was felt that they had something to add, and that without an express provision calling for their involvement, they would not be included. The provision in the Iraqi statute, allowing Iraqi lawyers from Iraq and abroad to sit as judges, whether or not they had been judges in the past, could have resulted in a more gender balanced judiciary if this were an encouraged value.

Had the Iraqi tribunal incorporated some of the ICC's provisions regarding the value of women in the selection of judges, prosecutors and other staff, we would have seen a very different Court.

144. *Craig v. Harney*, 331 U.S. 367, 376 (1947).

145. Owen M. Fiss, "The Supreme Court, 1978 Term-Foreword: The Forms of Justice," 93 Harvard Law Review 1, 30 (1979).

146. Paragraph 154 of Law Number 23 of 1971.

147. Paragraph 153 of Law Number 23 of 1971.

148. Rule of Procedure 31.

149. "Contempt Proceedings Against Kosta Bulatovic", Case No. IT-02-54-R77.4, "Decision on Contempt of the Tribunal", 13 May 2005.

150. Prosecutor v. Aleksovski, Case No. IT-95-14/1-AR-R77, "Judgment on Appeal by Anto Nobilo against Finding of Contempt", 30 May 2001 ("Aleksovski Contempt Appeal"), para. 36.

151. *See* In Re Soliman, 134 F. Supp. 2d 1238 (N.D. Ala. 2001); *Grand Jury Subpoena John Doe v. United States*, 150 F.3d 170 (2nd Cir. 1998); *Martinez v. Turner*, 977 F.2d 421 (8th Cir. 1992); *White v. Narick*, 292 S.E. 2d 54 (W.VA. 1982); *Von Holden v. Chapman*, 450 N.Y.S. 2d 623 (N.Y. App. Div. 1982).

152. See Edward Wong, "Hussein Thinks He Will Get Death Penalty but Sees Escape Hatch, His Lawyer Says," New York Times, June 25, 2006, at 6.

153. See Victor v. Nebraska, 511 U.S. 1 (1994).

154. *See*, e.g., ICC Rule 34(1)(a).

155. *See* 32 ILR (1966), 564.

156. *U.S. v. van Leeb*, (1948).

157. *U.S. v. von Weizsacker*, (1949).

158. *See* 8 Trial of the Major War Criminals before the International Military Tribunal (official version, Nuremeberg, 1947), at 549.

159. *See* Jerrold M. Post, MD, *Saddam Hussein: A Political Psychology Profile,*Part I.

160. *See*, e.g., Prosecutor v Simba, ICTR-01-76-T, Judgment and Sentence 13 December 2005, paras. 389–405.

161. See Gustav Becker, Wilhelm Weber, and 18 Others, Vol. VII Law Reports 67.

162. *See* 8 Trial of the Major War Criminals before the International Military Tribunal (official version, Nuremberg, 1947), at 549.

163. *See* Peter Maguire, LAW AND WAR: AN AMERICAN STORY 241 (2000).

164. *See* http://www.rightsmaps.com/html/anfalbeg.html for maps of the sequential campaigns.

165. Report to the President by Mr. Justice Jackson (7 Oct 1946) in American Journal of International Law, No. 49, 1955, pp. 44, 49.

166. Rule of Procedure 59 (Third).

167. Distinguished Research Professor of Law and President, International Human Rights Law Institute, DePaul University College of Law.

168. Prepared by Sylvia de Bertodano for the International Bar Association, reprinted with permission.

Index

DATE DUE